Flutter Engineering

Copyright 2024 Majid Hajian

ISBN: 979-8-88940-557-3

Contents

Contributors and Reviewers

Simon Lightfoot, Mangirdas Kazlauskas, Roman Jaquez, Erick Zanardo, Carlo Lucera, Marco Napoli, Alessio Salvadorini, Pooja Bhaumik, Dominik Roszkowski, Oleksandr Leushchenko, Anna Leushchenko, Tomá Soukal, Danielle Cox, Manuela Sakura Rommel, Verena Zaiser, Cagatay Ulusoy, Mike Rydstrom, Muhammed Salih Guler and Renan Araujo.

Your commitment to detail has ensured the accuracy and clarity of the content.

Cover Design:

The cover art of this book is an outstanding collaboration between human creativity and artificial intelligence. It features an engineered butterfly that represents Flutter Engineering. Thanks to Shirin Sameiee for being a creative artist in bringing this visionary concept to life.

Digital Version:

This book is available in various formats, including PDF, EPUB, and MOBI. Visit Flutterengineering.io for more information and continuous updates.

Preface

My journey in programming has been diverse, from backend and frontend roles to full-stack development, software architecture, and developer relationships. Each step has enriched my insight into exceptional software engineering.

As someone naturally drawn to logic and analysis, I have often considered what makes a great software engineer and how to plan an app and manage its development effectively. "Flutter Engineering" aims to answer these questions and more. This book lays the foundation for a broader understanding of app development, offering knowledge, architectural insights, and advanced Flutter-specific content. This project is your gateway to look at software engineering concepts in Flutter. It is designed to guide, open doors, and help you explore.

During my year-long effort, I approached Flutter from an engineering perspective rather than merely a programming skill. As a Flutter engineer, building an app requires more than just coding skills. The "Flutter Engineering" project (flutterengineering.io) and this book were created to share this knowledge. Welcome to "Flutter Engineering."

0.0.1 Who is this book for?

This book is intended for readers with a basic understanding of Flutter and some experience with Dart programming and Flutter. It is unnecessary to be an expert, but if you have no prior experience with Flutter and want to learn it from scratch, this book may not suit you, as I have this assumption while explaining concepts.

This book is meant to help beginner and professional Flutter developers level up their skills in software engineering.

0.0.2 What you will learn

This book covers various software engineering topics in Flutter and is divided into five parts, each addressing specific areas of interest and expertise.

- Part 1 of this book introduces software engineering concepts specifically relevant to Flutter. It starts by explaining the fundamental principles of Flutter and how they work and then moves on to demonstrate how these concepts can be applied within the Flutter framework. This section also covers coding design patterns that help readers develop a foundational understanding of the subject matter.

- The second part of this material centers on architecture, beginning with basic principles and progressing onto different styles and patterns in architectural design. It covers important concepts such as concurrency, parallelism, dependency injection, and state management. Additionally, this section explores the architectural factors involved in developing offline apps, guiding readers on strategic thinking and decision-making in software architecture.
- Part 3 of this book covers the important software development processes necessary for building a successful app. It covers rules and guidelines, continuous delivery and integration, testing methodologies, and effective documentation practices in a comprehensive manner. This section gives readers the knowledge needed to streamline and efficiently develop apps.
- Part 4 covers important aspects of security and privacy in software development, specifically related to Flutter. It discusses the OWASP Top 10 security risks, privacy standards, and accessibility considerations. The section emphasizes creating inclusive and secure applications that value user privacy.
- Part 5 delves into advanced user interface (UI) concepts, including adaptive and responsive design strategies. It also explores sophisticated topics like custom painting, shaders, internationalization, localization, and effective theming in Flutter. This section enhances the reader's skills in creating visually appealing and user-friendly interfaces.

Whether a beginner or an experienced developer, this book can offer you something to learn. Although the book covers a wide range of topics, discussing each topic in detail could deserve a dedicated book. It is impossible to cover all the details and edge cases in one book, but I have done my best to cover the most important details. I plan to discuss topics I could not detail enough and cover edge cases on flutterengineering.io[1], so subscribe to the newsletter for free access to additional content.

0.0.3   How to use this book

This book has been designed to allow you to read each chapter independently. You are free to start from any part of the book. However, reading an entire part from start to end is always better. Certain fundamental concepts must be understood before proceeding to subsequent chapters. Therefore, I do not recommend starting with chapters that follow the previous chapter. Usually, in the introduction of each chapter, I mention if you should have read another chapter before starting it. Pay attention to this detail to read and understand the book better.

As you progress through this book, you'll encounter various conventions to enhance

---

[1] http://flutterengineering.io/

your reading and learning experience. Knowing these will help you understand and navigate the content more effectively.

1. **Bold Titles and Keywords**: Key concepts, titles, and important keywords are emphasized in **bold** font. This highlights essential information and makes it stand out for easy reference.
2. *Italicized Queries and Comments*: To differentiate, queries or comments within the text are presented in *italic*. This formatting helps distinguish them from the main content, providing additional insights or raising questions for contemplation.
3. Inline `Code`: I have tried to use inline code where it's possible to highlight the difference between regular text and a piece of code within the paragraphs.
4. **Formatted Code Blocks**: The Dart programming language formats the code examples for clarity. The blocks are structured to reflect the appropriate syntax and style of the language.
5. **Pseudo-code Examples**: It's important to note that most code examples are presented as pseudo-code. When integrated into your projects, they are simplified and may require additional coding or imports. This approach aims to focus on the key parts of the code, minimizing distractions and enhancing understanding. In some instances, critical lines within these code blocks are further emphasized in **bold**. Please pay attention to these lines, as they often represent core ideas.
6. **Code Explanations and Comments**: You will find step-by-step explanations following many code blocks. These are intended to clarify the code and guide you through the logic and functionality. While comments are included within the code blocks to aid comprehension, they are kept brief to avoid overloading the code with annotations.
7. **Access to Complete Code Examples**: To view the full working examples, please visit the accompanying website at flutterengineering.io[2]. There, you find where to access and clone the book's example repository, which contains the complete and functional code samples referenced in the book.

By familiarizing yourself with these conventions, you can navigate the book more efficiently and better understand the material. Enjoy your journey into Flutter engineering!

0.0.4   Found a bug?

Every chapter of this book has gone through a complete review process. At least two people have read each chapter, and an editor has also reviewed them. Before publication, the book's examples were tested, and multiple feedbacks were addressed to ensure their accuracy.

---

[2]http://flutterengineering.io/

However, despite all these efforts, some errors may still exist. You may encounter some grammar or spelling mistakes (which I hope you don't), or you may notice technical errors such as code errors or wrong explanations. If you disagree with any part of the book and have a valid reason, please don't hesitate to contact me. Your feedback and review are valuable to me, and I will consider and revise the book to ensure that the next person who reads it experiences different issues.

I appreciate your help in this process.

0.0.5 Contact me

If you would like to contact me, which I highly encourage, especially for sending me feedback and reviews of my book, you can do so in a few different ways. You can subscribe to my website newsletter or email me directly at majid@ flutterengineering.io[3]. Alternatively, you can connect with me directly on social media. I am active on LinkedIn (linkedin.com/in/mhadaily) and Twitter (x.com/mhadaily). You can also find me on YouTube (youtube.com/mhadaily) and GitHub (github.com/mhadaily).

---

[3]mailto:majid@flutterengineering.io

Acknowledgment

I extend my heartfelt gratitude to everyone who has supported and contributed to the creation of this book. First and foremost, I would like to thank my family for their tireless support and patience throughout this journey. Their support and faith in my dreams have been the foundation of my drive.

Thanks to the Flutter Team for doing such amazing work, particularly to Craig Labenz, Leigha Reid, Eric Windmill, Kevin Moore, Kate Lovett, John Ryan, and many more engineers in the Flutter team, whose content inspired me.

I also acknowledge the contribution of the technical reviewers, whose keen eyes and expert knowledge have greatly enhanced the quality of this book. Thank you Simon Lightfoot, Anna Leushchenko, Oleksandr Leushchenko, Mangirdas Kazlauskas, Roman Jaquez, Erick Zanardo, Carlo Lucera, Marco Napoli, Alessio Salvadorini, Pooja Bhaumik, Dominik Roszkowski, Tomá Soukal, Danielle Cox, Manuela Sakura Rommel, Verena Zaiser, Cagatay Ulusoy, Mike Rydstrom, Muhammed Salih Guler and Renan Araujo. Your commitment to detail has ensured the accuracy and clarity of the content.

I am grateful to my friends Taha Tesser, Argel Bejarano, Nilay Coskun, Andrea Bizzotto, Jaime Blasco, Bettina Carrizo, Tomas Piaggio, Enzo Conty, Gonçalo Palma, Chris Swan, Esra Kadah, Randal Schwartz, Frank van Puffelen, Mark O'Sullivan, Anthony Prakash, Lukas Klingsbo, Leo Farias, Abhishek Doshi, Sasha Denisov, Pascal Welsch, Swav Kulinski, Pawan Kumar, Scott Stoll, Remi Rousselet, Filip Hráek, Felix Angelov, Renuka Kelkar, Mais Alheraki, Ahmed Alabd and many more which if I want to name I have to write a book only for that; your passion and dedication to the field have inspired me constantly.

Special thanks to my readers and contributors who send me warm emails and provide lots of valuable feedback. A special mention to Alfred Schilken, whose suggestions have been particularly helpful.

I want to express my gratitude to Codemagic (Martin Jeret) for being the pioneers in supporting this book. I am also grateful to Invertase (Mike Diarmid and Elliot Hesp) for their support in various aspects and Sergiy Yakymchuk from Talsec, who has been an amazing supporter. Thank you all very much.

Lastly, I am thankful to the readers and the Flutter community. Your willingness to learn and grow continually drives me to share my knowledge and experience. This book is for you, and I hope it serves as a useful guide in your Flutter development journey.

Part I

Foundation of Flutter Engineering

CHAPTER 1

Flutter Engineering: Core Concepts

Reviewers: Anna Leushchenko, Oleksandr Leushchenko

Welcome to the exciting world of Flutter engineering! This chapter explores the fundamental principles and concepts that form the basis of successful software development using Flutter. Through this exploration, you will gain valuable insights into the unique perspectives and approaches that distinguish Flutter engineering from conventional programming, equipping you with the knowledge and understanding to craft impactful and enduring applications.

1.1 Engineering Software with Flutter

Throughout my career in software engineering, embracing Flutter has marked a significant evolution in my approach to technology. More than just acquiring a new skill, it has involved adopting a comprehensive strategy that spans the entire software development lifecycle, from design and development to testing and maintenance.

My diverse background in various technologies has helped me gain a better perspective on Flutter, which I see as both a technical tool and a way to promote innovation and creativity in software development. Flutter Engineering takes a holistic approach that carefully balances user experience, efficient time management, scalability considerations, and the trade-offs required to create impactful software.

Flutter's multi-platform architecture enables developers to concentrate on creating an exceptional user experience instead of getting into the nitty-gritty of platform-specific details. Unlike native development, which focuses on adhering to platform guidelines, Flutter prioritizes branding and user experience. This approach encourages developers to prioritize universal usability over platform constraints, leading to a more user-centric mindset.

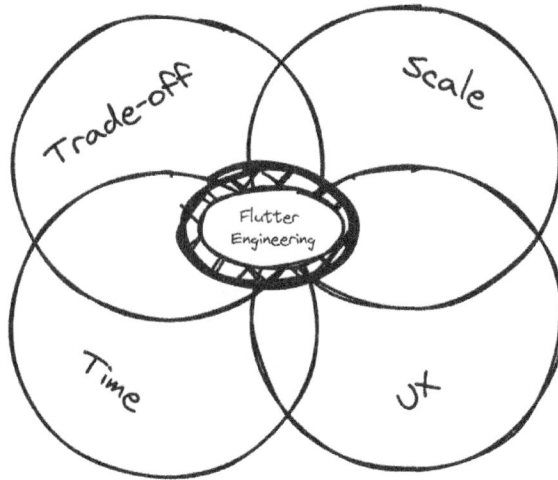

Figure 1.1: Flutter Engineering Pillars

User experience (UX) in Flutter engineering is a critical lens through which every project *must be* analyzed. I constantly ask myself, "*What user will think of this feature? Does it enhance or complicate their experience?*" For example, when creating a Flutter-based educational app, answering these questions helps make the design intuitive and engaging for learners; balancing aesthetics with functionality results in a delightful experience. The challenge is to align this user-centric focus with the technical capabilities of Flutter, ensuring the app is as pleasant to interact with as it is functional.

Time is a vital resource in software development. It is a finite constraint that needs to be managed efficiently to meet project deadlines and deliver value to stakeholders. Time management in software development goes beyond simply hitting milestones. Time is a multifaceted and dynamic element in the realm of Flutter development. It prompts me to frequently ask, "*What is the expected lifespan of my Flutter code? How long this app is going to stay? Year or decade? What is our deadline to deliver?*" These questions go beyond meeting project deadlines and delve into future-proofing the application.

For example, when I work on a Flutter-based smart home app, I focus not only on its immediate launch but also on its adaptability to future IoT trends and technological evolutions. This approach ensures the app remains relevant and functional over time, adapting to user behavior and technology changes. It also reminds me to incorporate the mechanism to upgrade Flutter and other third-party dependencies.

The concept of **scale** in Flutter engineering is complex and thought-provoking. When embarking on a new project, I often consider, "*How many people are involved, and what roles do they play in the development and maintenance of the project? How many end-users will use this application later?*" These questions become particularly relevant in larger-scale projects like a comprehensive logistics application developed with Flutter. Here, the challenge lies in managing a robust codebase and orchestrating a team with diverse expertise, ensuring cohesive and efficient development across different platforms and devices.

Trade-offs in Flutter engineering involve making strategic decisions that balance various aspects of the project. For instance, I often face decisions like, *"Should I implement an advanced, resource-intensive feature that could enhance the user experience but also affect the app's performance on some devices?"* One example is choosing between high-resolution graphics and smooth performance in a gaming app. Another is deciding between implementing an advanced animation that enhances the user experience and maintaining a lean, fast-loading application, which exemplifies the kind of strategic decision-making that defines Flutter engineering. These decisions are not merely technical but also align with the broader objectives of the project and the expectations of its users.

In my experience, engineering software with Flutter is a detailed process of crafting adaptable, scalable solutions that resonate with end-users. It involves a blend of technical skills, strategic planning, and creative problem-solving, all directed toward building functional but also engaging and sustainable applications in the dynamic world of digital technology.

1.2 Unpacking the Core Principles

To fully grasp these concepts, let's explore Flutter app development through the lens of core software engineering principles.

1.2.1 Development Paradigms

In software development, diverse ideologies and methodologies guide the construction of systems. These guiding principles, or development paradigms, offer distinct lenses through which developers approach and shape software.

Different programming languages are often associated with specific paradigms, and the language choice can influence how developers think about and solve problems. Some languages, like Dart, support multiple paradigms.

Across the history of computing, several well-known paradigms have emerged, each leaving a significant imprint on the field. These include Procedural Programming, Object-Oriented Programming (OOP), Functional Programming, Agile Development, Event-Driven programming, Imperative and Declarative programming, etc.

These paradigms, however, seldom exist in isolation. Flutter embraces a **multi-paradigm** programming environment, utilizing various programming techniques where their strengths are most beneficial. Let's explore some of the key threads in this multifaceted approach:

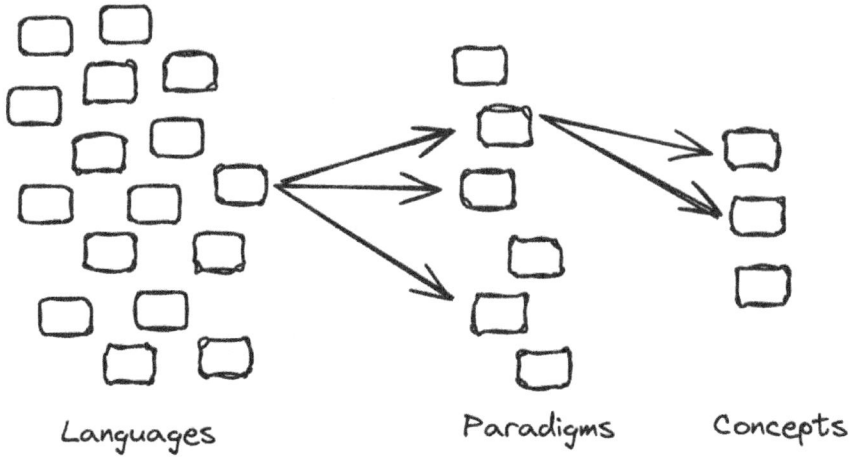

Figure 1.2: Development Paradigms and Concepts

1.2.2 Constraint and Composition Programming

The heart of Flutter's design lies in its use of composition. This approach involves building complex widgets by combining simpler ones. An example is the `TextButton` widget, a composition of other widgets like `Material`, `InkWell`[1], and `Padding`[2].

Imagine your app as a giant Lego masterpiece. Each **widget**, a small, specialized piece (text, buttons, images), snaps together, building complex screens. This method of aggressive composition results in a highly customizable and flexible UI. You will learn more about this in chapter 2.

In Flutter, the layout system employs a form of constraint programming to set the geometry of UI elements. Constraints regarding size, such as minimum and maximum width and height, are passed from parent widgets to their children. The child widgets then adjust their sizes to meet these constraints, allowing Flutter to efficiently lay out the entire UI, often in a single pass. This approach ensures a responsive and consistent layout across different devices.

1.2.3 Imperative and Declarative Programming

In Flutter, imperative programming is applied in scenarios requiring direct, step-by-step operations control. Mobile app business logic frequently involves sequences

---

[1] https://api.flutter.dev/flutter/material/InkWell-class.html
[2] https://api.flutter.dev/flutter/widgets/Padding-class.html

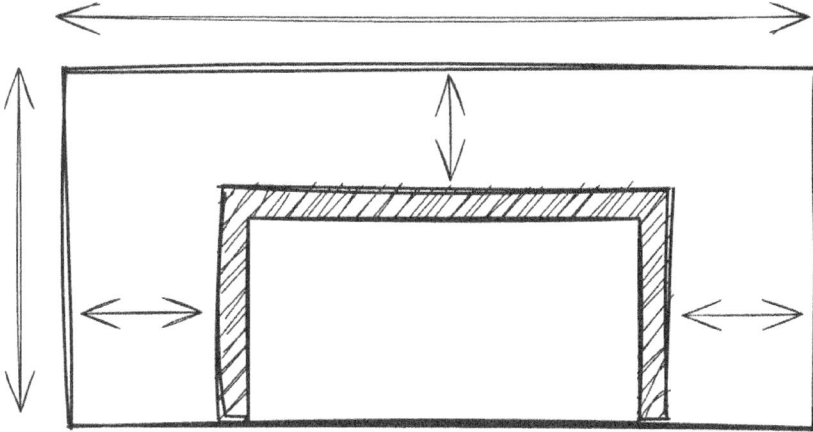

Figure 1.3: Constraints go down. Sizes go up. Parent sets position.

of steps, conditions, and loops. Imperative programming allows developers to express these sequences naturally, making writing and maintaining the logic easier.

Here is a simple example of an imperative-style function with conditional statements:

```
bool isPositive(int x) {
  if (x > 0) {
    print('x is positive');
    return true;
  }
  print('x is negative or zero');
  return false;
}
```

Another common example of imperative programming in Flutter can be seen in unit tests:

```
testWidgets(
  'CustomButton displays a label',
  (WidgetTester tester) async {
    // Describe the situation under test
    await tester.pumpWidget(
        MaterialApp(home: CustomButton(label: 'Test')));

    // List the invariants the test must match
    expect(find.text('Test'), findsOneWidget);
```

```
    // Advance the clock or insert events if necessary
    await tester.tap(find.byType(CustomButton));
    await tester.pump();
  },
);
```

Declarative programming is a key aspect of Flutter's framework, prominently seen in how widgets are constructed. In Flutter, the UI is typically defined using Dart's declarative syntax, where the build methods of widgets consist of single expressions with nested constructors.

Consider the `ListView` widget:

```
ListView(
  children: [
    ListTile(title: Text('Item 1')),
    ListTile(title: Text('Item 2')),
    // Additional list items
  ],
)
```

In this example, `ListView` and its children are defined concisely and expressively.

This approach allows developers to describe what the UI should look like rather than how to construct it step by step, as in imperative programming. The declarative style in Flutter simplifies the process of building complex UIs and enhances the readability and maintainability of the code. Additionally, this method can be seamlessly combined with imperative programming for scenarios where a pure declarative approach might be limited, offering the flexibility to build more dynamic and interactive UIs.

Looking at this code, you may see the application with an AppBar and a centered text. It does not contain the logic that specifies **how** the UI will be constructed, but just the **declaration** of **what** the user will see:

```
class MyApp extends StatelessWidget {
  @override
  Widget build(BuildContext context) {
    return MaterialApp(
      home: Scaffold(
        appBar: AppBar(
          title: Text('Declarative Programming in Flutter'),
        ),
        body: Center(
          child: Text('Hello, Flutter!'),
        ),
      ),
    );
  }
}
```

1.2.4 Functional and Object-Oriented Programming

One of the core concepts of functional programming is called "pure function." Given the same input, it's a function that will always produce the same output and has no observable side effects. The result of a pure function depends only on its input parameters, and it does not modify any external state, which significantly simplifies maintenance and opens doors for many optimizations.

Flutter also embraces functional programming, particularly in `StatelessWidgets`[3] that resemble pure functions. For instance, the `Icon`[4] widget can be viewed as a function mapping its parameters to visual output.

Flutter's emphasis on immutable data structures. The entire `Widget`[5] class hierarchy and supporting classes like `Rect`[6] and `TextStyle`[7] embrace this immutability, keeping your UI stable and reliable.

Dart's `Iterable`[8] API is another example of its functional programming characteristics. Remember those handy functions like `map`, `where`, and `reduce` your use in Dart? These are examples of the functional style frequently used to process lists of values in the framework.

Flutter's framework dances with both class inheritance and dynamic prototypes. Core APIs are built with class hierarchies, where base classes like `RenderObject`[9] define high-level functionalities that subclasses like `RenderBox`[10] specialize, adopting the Cartesian coordinate system for geometry. But it's not just static inheritance – the `ScrollPhysics`[11] class lets you chain instances dynamically at runtime, composing, for example, paging physics with platform-specific quirks, all without needing a pre-chosen platform. This blend of inheritance and dynamic flexibility gives Flutter apps the power to adapt and evolve like never before!

You will learn more about OOP in Dart in Chapter 4.

1.2.5 Abstraction and Encapsulation

Abstraction and encapsulation are fundamental principles in software engineering that Flutter effectively utilizes in its widget-centric architecture.

Abstraction is about simplifying complex systems into more manageable models, and Encapsulation involves grouping data and its associated operations within classes, protecting data integrity, and preventing improper access.

---

[3] https://api.flutter.dev/flutter/widgets/StatelessWidget-class.html
[4] https://api.flutter.dev/flutter/widgets/Icon-class.html
[5] https://api.flutter.dev/flutter/widgets/Widget-class.html
[6] https://api.flutter.dev/flutter/dart-ui/Rect-class.html
[7] https://api.flutter.dev/flutter/painting/TextStyle-class.html
[8] https://api.flutter.dev/flutter/dart-core/Iterable-class.html
[9] https://api.flutter.dev/flutter/rendering/RenderObject-class.html
[10] https://api.flutter.dev/flutter/rendering/RenderBox-class.html
[11] https://api.flutter.dev/flutter/widgets/ScrollPhysics-class.html

Abstraction simplifies complex UI elements into manageable widgets, focusing on essential attributes and functionalities. For example, a `ListView` widget in Flutter abstracts the complex functionalities of a scrollable list into an easy-to-use component.

In the context of Flutter, encapsulation is applied to widget development, and the concept is evident in implementing the `Container` widget. The `Container` widget encapsulates various attributes or properties that define its appearance and behavior. These attributes include width, height, color, padding, margin, and more. Developers interact with the Container using a well-defined set of properties and methods. The encapsulation ensures that the internal details of how the `Container` manages these attributes are hidden from the outside world.

Together, abstraction and encapsulation in Flutter contribute to a framework where complex UI designs are simplified into manageable components, and internal widget states are well-guarded, enhancing usability and maintainability. You'll learn more about these topics in Chapter 4.

1.2.6 Event-Driven Programming

User interactions in Flutter are handled through an event-driven approach.

A prime example of this in Flutter is the use of the `Listenable`[12] class. This class serves as the foundation for the animation system in Flutter, where changes in the animation state are treated as events. `Listenable` provides a subscription model, enabling multiple listeners to register callbacks triggered in response to specific events. This mechanism ensures that various parts of the UI stay updated and in sync with the underlying data or state changes, reflecting the reactive nature of the framework.

In addition, widgets like `GestureDetector`[13] and state management tools utilize events to respond to user inputs, exemplifying event-driven programming in the framework. You will learn more about this in part 2 of this book.

1.2.7 Reactive Programming

In Flutter, reactive programming is a key concept that drives the dynamic nature of UI development. This paradigm is apparent in how widgets react to changes, updating their state and appearance in response to user interactions or internal data changes.

In Flutter's reactive system, any new input provided in a widget's constructor immediately triggers a rebuild of that widget, propagating changes down the widget tree. Conversely, changes in lower-level widgets can propagate up the tree through event handlers and state updates.

---

[12]https://api.flutter.dev/flutter/foundation/Listenable-class.html
[13]https://api.flutter.dev/flutter/widgets/GestureDetector-class.html

---

Flutter leverages Dart's support for streams to provide a reactive programming model, and StreamBuilder is a widget that plays a key role in this paradigm:

```
final StreamController<int> _controller = StreamController<int>();
//
StreamBuilder<int>(
  stream: _controller.stream,
  builder: (context, snapshot) {
    if (snapshot.hasData) {
      return Center(
        child: Text('Data from stream: ${snapshot.data}'),
      );
    } else {
      return Center(
        child: Text('Waiting for data...'),
      );
    }
  },
)
```

Reactive programming is a programming paradigm that revolves around the propagation of changes and handling asynchronous data streams.

1.2.8 Generic Programming

Flutter uses generics to improve type safety and reduce errors. This is visible in widgets like DropdownButton<T> where T represents the type of data source, or classes like State[14]<T> and GlobalKey[15]<T>, where T represents the type of widget or state they are associated with.

1.2.9 Concurrent Programming

Concurrency in Flutter is handled through Dart's async features like Future[16]s[17] and Stream[18]s[19]. This is crucial in scenarios like fetching data from a network or working with long-running tasks.

You will learn more about Concurrency and Parallelism in chapter 9.

---

[14]https://api.flutter.dev/flutter/widgets/State-class.html
[15]https://api.flutter.dev/flutter/widgets/GlobalKey-class.html
[16]https://api.flutter.dev/flutter/dart-async/Future-class.html
[17]https://api.flutter.dev/flutter/dart-async/Future-class.html
[18]https://api.flutter.dev/flutter/dart-async/Stream-class.html
[19]https://api.flutter.dev/flutter/dart-async/Stream-class.html

1.2.10   Cohesion and Coupling

In software engineering, **cohesion** and **coupling** are fundamental principles that can make or break a system's maintainability and efficiency.

Cohesion describes the internal strength of a module and how tightly related its elements are to its core purpose. Ideally, modules exhibit high cohesion, with components that work together towards a single goal. Coupling, however, deals with the degree of interdependence between modules. Striving for low coupling ensures modules interact minimally, minimizing ripple effects when changes are made.

In Flutter's world, two fundamental principles define a maintainable masterpiece: **low coupling and high cohesion**. Let's break down their steps on the Flutter stage:

High Cohesion

Flutter achieves high cohesion by designing widgets that are focused on specific functionalities. For instance, the `Text` widget is solely responsible for displaying a text string with basic styling. Its responsibilities are clear and well-defined, making it highly cohesive. Another example is the `Image` widget, which is dedicated to displaying images and does not intertwine with non-image functionalities.

Low Coupling

Flutter maintains low coupling by allowing widgets to function independently with minimal reliance on each other. For example, the `Scaffold` widget, which provides the basic material design visual layout structure, operates independently of the `FloatingActionButton` widget used for action buttons. Modifications to a `FloatingActionButton`, such as changing its icon or color, do not affect the layout or functioning of the `Scaffold`, demonstrating low coupling between these components.

You may ask about the Theme now. Themes primarily affect visual styling, keeping functionality separate. Customizable themes at different levels reinforce low coupling, ensuring that changes don't tightly bind widgets.

Generally, widgets should rely on established communication channels like callbacks and events, minimizing cascading effects when one changes tune.

When developing with Flutter, it's crucial to integrate the principles of "low coupling, high cohesion" for a robust app architecture. Create widgets that operate independently; for instance, a `PaymentProcessing` widget should not be intricately linked to a `UserDashboard` widget, demonstrating low coupling. Also, design each widget with a focused role, like a `ChatScreen` widget exclusively handling messaging features, ensuring high cohesion.

As you build, regularly ask yourself: "Does changing one widget unnecessarily impact others?" and "Is each widget's purpose and function well-defined and self-contained?" Reflecting on these questions will guide you in creating a more efficient, well-structured Flutter application.

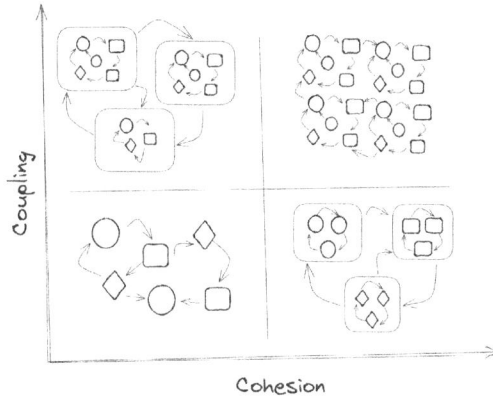

Figure 1.4: Coupling and Cohesion

1.2.11 Separation of Concerns and Modularity

Separation of Concerns (SoC) and Modularity are foundational concepts in software engineering that significantly improve code organization, maintainability, and scalability.

Separation of Concerns is a design principle that involves breaking down a software application into distinct sections, each addressing a specific aspect or concern. This approach helps simplify a program's complexity by allowing developers to focus on one area at a time without being overwhelmed by others. It aids in reducing interdependencies, which in turn makes the application more flexible and easier to maintain. **Modularity**, however, refers to dividing a software system into separate, interchangeable modules, where each module encapsulates a specific functionality. This design approach facilitates easier testing, debugging, and updating of individual components, leading to a more robust and adaptable system.

Flutter's widget-based architecture is inherently modular, each widget encapsulating a specific UI or functional aspect. This aligns with the SoC principle, where concerns like user interface, business logic, and data management are kept distinct.

As a Flutter developer, you can leverage these principles to create robust and efficient applications. For instance, in a Flutter-based to-do application, you can implement SoC by having a separate UI layer with widgets like `TaskListWidget` for displaying tasks. The business logic can be encapsulated in a `TaskManager` class that handles task-related operations. At the same time, data handling can be managed by a `DatabaseService` responsible for storing and retrieving task data. Modularity can be achieved by creating reusable components like a `LoginService` for user authentication. These can be used across different parts of your app or even in other projects, often residing within the `lib` folder or can be extracted and created as individual `pub` packages.

It's also good to know that in Flutter, the concept of Modularity often intersects

---

with "package by feature" architecture, with a unique aspect being that modules can often take the form of widgets. This approach organizes the application into modules based on specific features, where each module, or in many cases, each widget, represents a distinct functionality of the app.

You will learn more about this in Part 2 of this book, where I delve into Architecture.

1.2.12   Design Patterns and Strategies

Design patterns in software engineering are established solutions to common design problems. They act as templates that can be applied to recurring problems in software design, such as managing object creation, facilitating communication between objects, and organizing complex interactions, allowing you to write code that is:

- **Reusable:** The patterns are reusable, saving time and effort while promoting consistency across your app.
- **Maintainable:** Code structured with patterns is easier to understand, modify, and extend in the future.
- **Flexible:** Patterns adapt to different contexts and requirements, making your code more versatile.

Flutter doesn't dictate specific patterns; its core features and architecture naturally lend themselves to various patterns. An excellent example of a design pattern used within the Flutter framework is the **Builder Pattern**. One everyday use of the Builder pattern in Flutter is the `ListView.builder` widget. This pattern is frequently employed in Flutter's widget creation process. The Builder pattern separates the construction of a complex object from its representation, allowing the same construction process to create different representations.

You will learn more about design patterns in Chapter 5.

1.2.13   Efficiency, Scalability, and Trade-offs

In software engineering, particularly in Flutter development, understanding and navigating the complexities of efficiency, scalability, and trade-offs is essential. These concepts focus on how applications utilize resources (efficiency), adapt to growth (scalability), and manage the delicate balance between competing needs (trade-offs). These choices aren't just about financial aspects but encompass various factors like resource allocation, personnel effort, etc.

Moving beyond the mindset of *"because everyone else is doing it"* and towards a consensus-driven approach that prioritizes well-reasoned, context-specific decisions is essential. This mindset is particularly relevant in Flutter when weighing options like state management techniques or integrating external packages.

For instance, choosing `setState` for its simplicity might lead to scalability challenges, whereas advanced methods like BLoC, though initially more complex, offer long-term benefits in scalability and maintainability. Similarly, using `cached_network_image` brings efficiency and enhanced user experience but introduces complexities such as added dependencies, which may affect long-term maintenance and compatibility with Flutter updates.

In my experience, "*It depends*" is particularly significant in software engineering, especially when working with Flutter. This highlights the importance of understanding the specific context of each technology choice. As a developer, I constantly balance factors like ease of use, scalability, and future maintainability. These decisions are more than just about immediate results; they shape the project's long-term health. This requires a deep level of critical analysis and foresight, stressing the need for well-informed and sustainable decisions in the rapidly evolving field of software development.

1.2.14   Verification, Validation, and "Shifting Left"

The Verification and Validation model in software engineering is a process used to ensure that a system meets all its specifications and fulfills its intended purpose. "Verification" involves checking whether the system is built correctly and meets the specified requirements. This is often referred to as "Static Testing." On the other hand, "Validation" checks whether the right system is built and meets the users' needs, known as "Dynamic Testing." This model is crucial for ensuring the quality and reliability of software systems.

In the Flutter context, the Verification and Validation (V&V) model could be tailored to its ecosystem as follows:

1. **Requirement Analysis**: Understanding what the app aims to achieve and the problem it solves for users.
2. **App Architecture**: Defining the overall structure of the app, including state management and navigation strategies.
3. **Feature Design**: Detailing each app feature's implementation plan, encompassing business logic and frontend interface.
4. **Unit Design**: Breaking down features into smaller, testable units, typically individual functions or widgets.

The corresponding testing phases are:

1. **Unit Testing**: Verifying the functionality of individual units or components, especially business logic.
2. **Widget Testing**: Ensuring that Flutter widgets render correctly and interact as expected so the overall widget composition as a feature works.
3. **Integration Testing**: Assessing the interaction between combined units or widgets within the app so the overall architecture works.
4. **User Acceptance Testing**: Validating the app against user requirements, often through manual testing, to ensure it meets their expectations.

The V&V model ensures that the Flutter app is developed correctly and meets its designed needs at each stage, from requirements to acceptance testing.

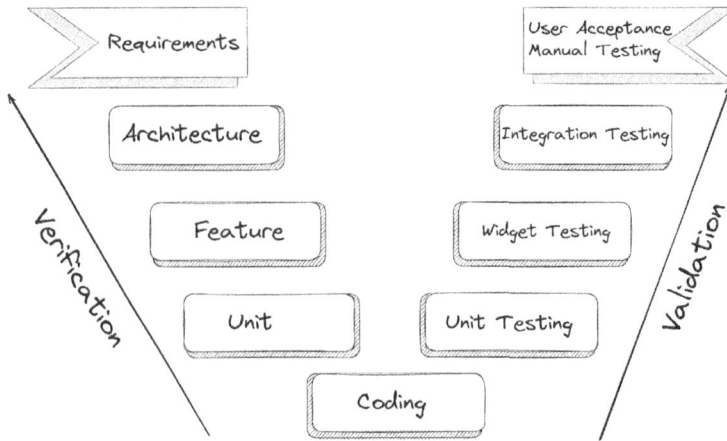

Figure 1.5: Flutter Verification and Validation Model

The "Shifting Left" concept in software development, particularly within Flutter, suggests that investing time in earlier stages of the development lifecycle—such as design, development, and initial testing—is more cost-effective than addressing issues later in the pipeline. The closer an issue is discovered to its introduction (typically on the left side of the development timeline), the less costly it is to fix. This is because issues found during stages like staging or production (on the right side) can be significantly more expensive and time-consuming to resolve due to the complexity of debugging and the potential impact on the user experience.

"Shifting Left" in Flutter effectively means incorporating practices like static code analysis to catch syntactical errors and potential bugs early. Code reviews are essential to ensure quality and catch issues that automated tools might miss. Integrating automation within CI pipelines allows for consistently executing unit, widget, and integration tests, ensuring that new code additions meet quality standards before merging. Additionally, employing feature flags and A/B testing enables developers to test new features selectively in production environments, reducing the risk of widespread issues.

By embedding these practices early and throughout the Flutter development process, teams can mitigate risks, reduce the cost of late-stage defect remediation, and deliver high-quality, robust applications efficiently.

The "Shifting Left" concept emphasizes integrating these processes early in the development cycle. For Flutter developers, it means conducting tests and quality checks right from the initial stages. This early intervention helps detect and fix issues promptly, reducing the cost and time typically associated with later-stage debugging. Implementing these practices in Flutter improves code quality and enhances the application's reliability and user experience.

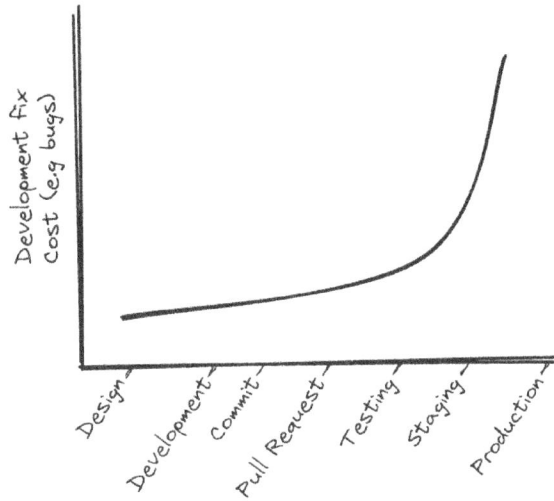

Figure 1.6: Shifting Left Concept in Flutter Development

1.2.15 Informed Decision-Making in Development

In Flutter and software development, informed decision-making often involves weighing quantifiable factors against more nuanced, non-quantifiable aspects. For example, a developer may need to choose between using state management solutions like BLoC, which offers scalability but with added complexity, versus more straightforward options like `setState`, which are easier to implement but may need to scale better for larger apps.

Additionally, decisions in Flutter are sometimes about something other than measurable elements. Consider implementing a custom widget versus using an existing third-party widget. The decision encompasses not just immediate functionality but also factors like long-term maintenance, the reliability of the third-party package, and its alignment with the app's evolving needs.

Balancing these aspects requires careful consideration of both the quantifiable impacts and the less tangible, yet equally important, long-term implications of development choices in Flutter.

1.3 Lifecycle of Flutter Development

Before adapting it for Flutter development, let's understand the Software Development Lifecycle (SDLC). SDLC is a structured framework that defines a series of stages for building and delivering software applications. It provides a roadmap for developers and stakeholders, ensuring quality, efficiency, and predictability throughout development.

There are various SDLC models, each with its specific stages and emphasis. Some popular models include:

- **Waterfall Model:** This linear, sequential model follows a strict stage-gate approach, where each stage must be completed before moving to the next. It is efficient for precise requirements and controlled environments.
- **Agile Model:** This iterative and incremental model emphasizes flexibility and adaptability. It breaks down development into smaller cycles (sprints), enabling continuous feedback and delivery of working software.
- **Spiral Model:** This risk-driven model combines Agile's iterative nature with Waterfall's control. It involves risk assessment throughout the development cycle, making it suited for high-risk projects.

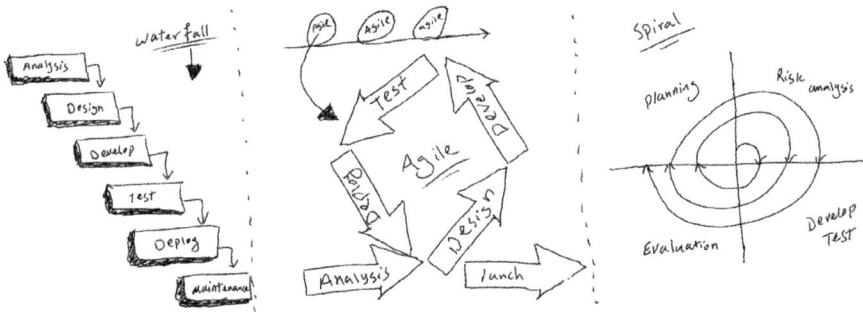

Figure 1.7: Waterfall vs. Agile vs. Spiral Models

Regardless of the chosen model, the core stages of an SDLC typically include:

1. **Analysis**: This phase involves understanding the specific needs and objectives of the Flutter app. It includes gathering detailed requirements from stakeholders and defining the scope of the app.
2. **Design**: Based on the requirements, the overall system architecture for the Flutter app is designed. This includes deciding on the app's navigation flow, state management approach, and overall UI/UX design.
3. **Development**: Here, the actual coding of the Flutter app takes place. Developers write Dart code to implement the defined functionalities, adhering to the design specifications. Developers should write unit and widget tests as part of their best practice in writing code.
4. **Testing**: In this critical phase, the Flutter app undergoes various tests to ensure quality and performance. This includes integration testing and potentially user acceptance testing to validate all aspects of the app.
5. **Deployment**: Once testing is complete and the app is bug-free, it is deployed to the appropriate platforms (e.g., Google Play Store, Apple App Store). This might involve setting up CI/CD pipelines for efficient deployment processes.

6. **Maintenance**: Post-deployment, the app enters the maintenance phase, where it is updated regularly, bugs are fixed, and new features are added as per user feedback or changing requirements. Monitoring the application is another part of this phase. Monitoring is related to crash reporting and bugs, analytics, performance measurement, etc.

In adapting the Software Development Life Cycle (SDLC) for Flutter development, a few specific considerations come into play to leverage the unique features of the framework. During the Requirement Analysis phase, a mobile-first approach is key, but with an eye on potential expansion to web and desktop, thanks to Flutter's versatility. Flutter's hot reload feature facilitates rapid prototyping and iterative feedback, while performance requirements for animations and responsiveness are crucial for diverse device compatibility.

As the process moves into System Design, Development, Testing, and Deployment, selecting appropriate widgets and state management solutions tailored to the application's complexity becomes vital. Dart language features, like null safety and best practices in widget hierarchy and code organization, ensure clarity and efficiency. Testing, a critical phase, encompasses unit, widget, and integration testing to ensure stability and user-friendliness, with performance testing to optimize the app across devices. Finally, the deployment phase benefits from Flutter's ability to share codebases across platforms facilitated through CI/CD pipelines for efficient multi-platform releases.

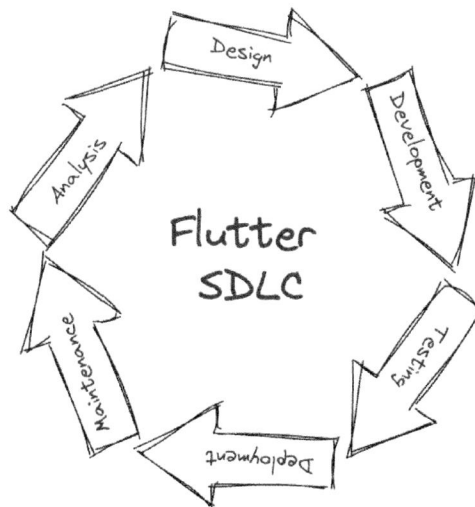

Figure 1.8: Flutter Software Development Life Cycle

Remember, your specific adaptations will depend on the project's size, complexity, and requirements. Choose the tools and practices that best suit your development team and application goals.

1.4   Flutter Engineering vs. Programming

Up to this point, we've explored various facets of software engineering, and at this stage, you should have gained a more comprehensive understanding of this topic. However, I'd like to elaborate further and share my perspective.

In software development, "Flutter engineering" and "programming" represent distinct roles and responsibilities within a project. Programming primarily involves writing code to implement specific functionalities, focusing on code implementation and problem-solving. Programmers are responsible for translating design and requirements into executable code. In contrast, Flutter engineering encompasses a more comprehensive role. Flutter engineers write code, design the system architecture user interface, and make strategic project structure and scalability decisions. They focus on code quality, project management, and innovation, playing a pivotal role in the development process. Understanding these differences is essential for effectively managing a Flutter project and assembling the right team for success.

1.5   Flutter's Position in Tech Evolution

As we conclude this chapter, I'd like to express my perspective on the position of Flutter in the ever-evolving landscape of technology. Flutter occupies a truly unique and exciting position in the tech world.

1.5.1   Multi-platform Approaches

Flutter emerges as a true industry disruptor in an era where multi-platform development has gained paramount importance. Its capability to seamlessly empower developers to craft high-quality, visually captivating applications across diverse platforms represents a paradigm shift. The framework's focus on productivity, creativity, and efficiency has revolutionized our approach to application development, democratizing access for developers and businesses of all scales. The notion that "wherever there's a pixel, Flutter can be found" has fundamentally altered our perceptions of building multi-platform software from a single code base.

In this context, Flutter is a technological enabler and a catalyst for developer growth. It encourages developers to broaden their knowledge and skillsets across various platforms, each with unique attributes. This approach enhances the quality of apps, elevating the user experience and fostering the evolution of developers into seasoned professionals within their field.

1.5.2   Flutter's Role in Broader Tech Ecosystem

Furthermore, Flutter's role in the broader tech ecosystem holds significant importance. It streamlines the complexities of cross-platform development, catalyzing innovation by promoting the creation of visually appealing, responsive, and consistently exceptional user experiences. As we delve deeper into the world of Flutter development in the upcoming chapters, it becomes apparent that Flutter is not merely a tool; it's a driving force that pushes the boundaries of what is achievable in software development.

Flutter's innovative methods for multi-platform development allow developers to focus on creating user experiences rather than on specific technologies or platforms. Additionally, the vibrant Flutter community plays a pivotal role in shaping the technology, fostering greater demand and innovation. Flutter is a remarkable role model to its peers and the broader technology industry as it continues to evolve and leave a lasting mark on the world of software development.

Flutter is relevant in the present and is set to shape the future.

1.6 Conclusion

This chapter has comprehensively explored the fundamental principles and unique philosophy that drive high-quality Flutter development. We've delved into critical paradigms, including abstraction, encapsulation, design patterns, and considerations of efficiency and scalability. The concept of "shifting left" through early verification and validation has been emphasized, setting the stage for informed decision-making throughout the development lifecycle.

Furthermore, we've underlined the distinction between programming and engineering, showcasing how Flutter promotes modularity, separation of concerns, and thoughtful trade-off analysis. We've also situated Flutter within the broader tech landscape, shedding light on its strengths and potential impact compared to other multi-platform approaches.

As we wrap up this chapter, we must ask the following question: How can we harness these foundational insights to create high-performance, maintainable, and aesthetically pleasing Flutter applications? This question will be our guiding star as we embark on the exciting journey of applying these principles in practice and crafting exceptional Flutter experiences in the following chapters.

CHAPTER 2

Unveiling Flutter: Architecture and Engineering Insights

Reviewers: Anna Leushchenko, Oleksandr Leushchenko

In Chapter 1, you learned the basics of Flutter software engineering, explored some challenging concepts, and discovered valuable insights.

Let's dive deeper into the secrets of Flutter and discover what makes it an excellent design. Imagine peeling back the curtain to explore its inner workings and uncovering the cool things that power it. Understanding Flutter is like finding a treasure trove of tips to transform you into a superhero app builder. It's not just about being smart; it's about gaining valuable knowledge to help you create remarkable apps.

Learning how Flutter works is like having a superpower in your app-building toolkit. It's not just about coding; it's about being inspired by Flutter's inner workings, architectural decisions, and the engineering smarts that power it all. Understanding Flutter's ins and outs is essential to unlocking a world of possibilities for your future app-building adventures.

Are you ready to dive right in and get started? Let's not waste any more time - the fun begins now!

2.1 Decoding the Importance of Flutter Internals

Why bother learning how Flutter works when you're focused on building apps? It's a fair question often posed by developers. After all, you're using Flutter, not dissecting it, right? Well, as an experienced software engineer, I understand that knowing the ins and outs of a system is like having a superpower in your toolkit— it empowers you to make informed decisions and tackle problems more effectively. Let's break down why it matters.

Informed Decision-Making: When you grasp Flutter's architecture, you're not just coding but making design choices aligned with core principles. This knowledge empowers you to architect solutions that seamlessly align with Flutter's DNA, leading to more effective and sustainable outcomes.

Efficient Problem-Solving: Picture this—you encounter an unexpected glitch in your app. With knowledge of Flutter internals, you're not fumbling in the dark. Instead, you can trace and resolve the issue back to its roots. This ability to navigate the framework's inner workings streamlines the development process. This also means that you can dive deeper into the framework and contribute to its enhancement, benefiting not only yourself but millions of others who use it. After all, Flutter is open-source, isn't it?

Optimizing App Performance: Exploring Flutter internals isn't just about understanding; it's about optimization. Knowing how Flutter handles rendering, widget lifecycle, and native platform interactions allows you to fine-tune your app for optimal performance. It results in resource-efficient, responsive user experiences that stand out.

Creative Freedom: Have you ever wanted to experiment, innovate, and create something unique? Understanding Flutter internals opens the door to creative freedom. With this knowledge, you can experiment with innovative solutions, pushing the boundaries to craft standout applications.

Imagine you're developing a drawing app in Flutter, and users experience lag when creating detailed illustrations. Understanding Flutter internals, you identify that the app redraws the entire canvas excessively, causing the slowdown. With this insight, you optimize the rendering process by implementing efficient painting techniques. The result? A responsive drawing app with smoother graphics, showcasing the power of delving into Flutter internals for rendering and graphics optimization.

Mastering Flutter internals is more than a theoretical pursuit—it's a practical investment that transforms you from a developer into a problem-solving, decision-making, and innovation-driven app architect.

2.2 The Reactive and Declarative Nature of Flutter

In modern software engineering, two paradigms stand out for their impact on UI development: reactive programming and declarative UIs.

Flutter is a prime example of these concepts in action. Central to Flutter's architecture, these concepts dictate how interfaces are constructed and dynamically respond to data and state changes. This deep dive into Flutter's use of these paradigms reveals the intricacies and sophistication behind its design.

2.2.1 The Essence of Reactive Programming in Flutter

In Flutter, the reactive model interpenetrates its architecture, from how widgets are constructed to how they are rendered on the screen.

1. **Widget Lifecycle:** Widgets in Flutter are the building blocks of the UI and are closely tied to the app's state. When the state changes, the framework triggers a rebuild of the widget tree, starting from the widget corresponding to the changed state. You will learn more about widgets in this chapter.
2. **Rendering Pipeline:** Flutter's rendering engine converts the widget tree into a lower-level tree of render objects. This process, too, is reactive - changes in the widget tree automatically trigger the re-rendering of UI elements. You will learn more about the rendering pipeline in this chapter.

A simple, functional relationship is central to Flutter's reactivity: $UI = f(state)$. This equation signifies that the user interface (UI) is a direct function (f) of the application's state. The `build` method present in Flutter's widgets is the function. When the state of an application changes, the `build()` method is invoked, and the framework takes charge of rendering the UI accordingly. This method is designed to be efficient and free of side effects, which allows it to be called as frequently as needed without performance concerns.

Dart's Contribution to Flutter's Reactivity

Dart's contribution to Flutter's reactivity is multifaceted, extending beyond just being the programming language of choice. It provides a runtime environment and language features well-suited for implementing a reactive UI framework. Let's explore in short:

1. **Efficient Object Handling:** Dart's runtime rapidly creates and destroys objects, which is essential for Flutter's frequent widget rebuilds. Widgets in Flutter are immutable and are often recreated to reflect UI changes. Dart handles this efficiently, ensuring smooth performance.
2. **Garbage Collection:** Dart's generational garbage collection system is finely tuned for object recreation, typically seen in Flutter apps. It efficiently handles the lifecycle of short-lived objects, like widgets, minimizing the impact on app performance.
   1. Generational garbage collection is a memory management technique that improves efficiency by organizing objects by their age into different generations. Most short-lived objects are collected frequently in the 'young' generation. Objects that persist longer are promoted to the 'old' generation, which is collected less often. This strategy speeds up garbage collection by focusing on areas of memory where most objects are likely to be garbage.
3. **Language Features:** Dart's features, like Event Loop, Streams, and Futures, align well with the reactive paradigm, making it easier to handle asynchronous data flows and events in non-blocking I/O operations, which are expected in reactive applications.

Flutter from the lens of "The Reactive Manifesto"

Now, I'd like to delve into the concept of reactive systems, an architectural design approach distinct from the reactive programming paradigm we have explored.

Reactive systems, as conceptualized in "The Reactive Manifesto,[1]" focus on the overarching architecture of distributed, responsive systems. While this approach differs from the specific programming techniques used in reactive programming, observing how its principles align with Flutter's framework is fascinating.

As outlined in the manifesto, reactive systems are characterized by their ability to be Responsive, Resilient, Elastic, and Message-Driven. These characteristics are fundamental to designing systems that are well-equipped to meet the demands of modern applications, which require functionality, robustness, and adaptability to changing conditions and loads.

In contrast, reactive programming, which we have closely associated with Flutter thus far, is more about managing data flows and propagating changes within an application. It involves programming paradigms and techniques that enable applications to react to changes in data or state dynamically and efficiently.

However, when I overlay the principles of reactive systems onto Flutter, I find a striking parallel in its architecture and behavior. While inherently focused on UI development, Flutter's design incorporates aspects of reactivity that resonate with the broader, systemic approach of reactive systems:

- **Responsive:** Flutter's UI updates in real-time in response to state changes, ensuring users receive immediate feedback.
- **Resilient:** Flutter's widget-centric architecture allows individual components to fail without crashing the entire application, showcasing resilience.
- **Elastic:** Flutter adapts to different device capabilities, demonstrating a form of client-side elasticity.
- **Message-Driven:** Flutter employs event loops and streams, emphasizing asynchronous message passing, which is crucial for decoupling components and maintaining a responsive system.

In each of the four pillars outlined above, we can observe a clear reflection of their principles within Flutter's architecture, from rendering pipeline to widget design.

In essence, Flutter, while primarily a tool for UI development, exemplifies the qualities of reactive systems as defined by the manifesto, underscoring its robustness and suitability for building modern applications.

2.2.2 Flutter's Declarative UI Approach

Flutter's declarative approach to UI construction complements its reactive nature; you have learned it briefly in Chapter 1.

In a declarative framework, developers describe *what* the UI should look like at any given moment rather than detailing *how* to transition between different

---

[1] https://reactivemanifesto.org/

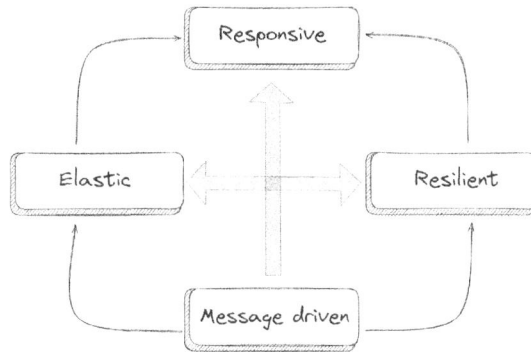

Figure 2.1: The Reactive Manifesto four pillars

UI states. This high-level approach allows for a more intuitive and efficient UI development process.

In Flutter, each widget declares its appearance based on the current state and configuration. The framework, then, takes care of rendering the UI based on these declarations. This separation of concerns simplifies the development process, as developers focus solely on describing the UI while the framework handles the complexities of rendering it.

2.2.3 Connecting Reactive and Declarative Paradigms in Flutter

The real power of Flutter lies in the synergy between its reactive and declarative paradigms. The reactive system ensures that the state is correctly updated, while the declarative nature simplifies describing these UI states.

Consider a simple counter app. The UI consists of a `Text` widget displaying a number and a `FloatingActionButton` to increment that number.

```
class CounterApp extends StatefulWidget {
  const CounterApp({super.key});

  @override
  CounterAppState createState() => CounterAppState();
}

class CounterAppState extends State<CounterApp> {
  int _counter = 0;

  void _incrementCounter() {
    setState(() {
      _counter++;
```

```
    });
  }

  String get _counterText =>
      'time${_counter == 1 ? '' : 's'}.';

  @override
  Widget build(BuildContext context) {
    return Scaffold(
      appBar: AppBar(
        title: const Text('Counter'),
      ),
      body: Center(
        child: Text('Tapped $_counter $_counterText.'),
      ),
      floatingActionButton: FloatingActionButton(
        onPressed: _incrementCounter,
        tooltip: 'Increment',
        child: const Icon(Icons.add),
      ),
    );
  }
}
```

In this example:

- **Reactive:** The `_incrementCounter` method embodies the reactive aspect. The state (`_counter`) changes when the button is pressed, triggering a UI update.
- **Declarative:** The `build` method illustrates the declarative aspect. It describes what the UI should look like based on the `_counter` state. No code specifies how to update the UI when `_counter` changes; Flutter handles this automatically. This is the essence of Flutter's reactive declarative programming: the UI automatically updates in response to state changes.

The process would be more cumbersome if this counter application were built using a non-reactive and imperative approach. After the increment button was pressed, the developer would need to manually fetch the updated counter value, create a new UI element to display the number, and then explicitly instruct the framework to redraw this element on the screen. This not only adds to the complexity of the code but also increases the potential for bugs.

2.3   Flutter's Motto

"Everything is a Widget" is known in the Flutter world. But how and where does this come from? How are widgets immutable, but Flutter is reactively up-

dating UI based on state? How come Flutter is so fast and keeps the refresh rate relatively high?

Let's understand this motto.

In Flutter, composability is central to its design ethos, where the entire user interface is built using widgets, and each widget is an immutable declaration of part of the user interface. Widgets in Flutter serve as the fundamental UI components, and they are nested to create complex interfaces. Every UI element is treated as a widget, from primary elements like text and buttons to more sophisticated components like grids and sliders. This means that UIs created using Flutter can consist of many widgets. This approach allows for high flexibility and reusability, as functionalities like padding are implemented as widgets rather than properties.

Flutter developers are familiar with `StatelessWidget` and `StatefulWidget` as they compose their layout.

However, Flutter provides several additional base widgets. Unique widgets, known as `RenderObjectWidgets`, form the bridge between the high-level widgets and the lower-level rendering layer. These `RenderObjectWidgets` eventually translate into nodes in the underlying render tree, which manages the layout and geometry of the UI. While developers primarily interact with the higher-level widgets, these widgets are intricately linked to the render tree, ensuring that the user interface is flexible in design and efficient in layout and appearance.

I mentioned the render tree, so let me introduce you to the three primary trees in Flutter: the Widget Tree, the Element Tree, and the RenderObject Tree, and understand the purpose of each.

2.3.1 Widget Tree

The Widget Tree is what you, as a Flutter developer, interact with most directly. It's a hierarchy of widgets that defines the structure and properties of the UI. Widgets are made immutable, so whenever their parameters or state change, they are rebuilt with new values.

```
Scaffold(
  appBar: AppBar(
    title: Text('Flutter Trees'),
  ),
  body: Center(
    child: Padding(
      padding: EdgeInsets.all(8.0),
      child: Text('Exploring Flutter Trees'),
    ),
  ),
);
```

When using `StatelessWidget` or `StatefulWidget` classes to create even more widgets, developers implicitly inherit from the `Widget` class:

```
// Flutter source code
// packages/flutter/lib/src/widgets/framework.dart
abstract class StatelessWidget extends Widget {}
abstract class StatefulWidget extends Widget {}
```

And the Widget class is immutable:

```
@immutable
abstract class Widget extends DiagnosticableTree {}
```

There are two questions now: how does a widget recognize where it is in the tree, and how does it even render and react to the state update if the Widget is immutable?

2.3.2 Element Tree

Since widgets do not keep any information about their place in the tree, there is another mechanism in place to provide it. Elements maintain information about the widgets' parents, children, size, RenderObject, etc.

By even looking at the Widget class source code

```
// Flutter source code
// packages/flutter/lib/src/widgets/framework.dart

@immutable
abstract class Widget extends DiagnosticableTree {
  ...
  @protected
  @factory
  Element createElement();
  ...
}
```

It's noticeable that when creating a widget, Flutter calls createElement(), which returns an object of type Element, and Element class implements the BuildContext:

```
abstract class Element
                extends DiagnosticableTree
                implements BuildContext {}
```

The BuildContext should sound familiar, right? It's the parameter of the build() method in widgets! Thus widgets get their elements as parameters of the build method which allows them to know about their place in the UI tree.

```
class CustomWidget extends StatelessWidget {
  const CustomWidget({super.key});

  @override
  Widget build(BuildContext context) {
    return const SizedBox();
  }
}
```

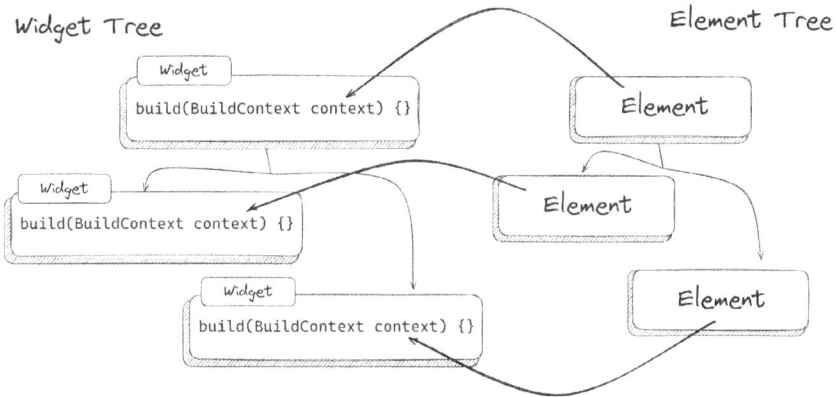

Figure 2.2: Flutter Widget and Element Trees

The elements tree is responsible for maintaining the stability of the widget tree. Elements represent a widget at a particular location in the tree. They are responsible for managing the lifecycle of the widgets and their underlying render objects. Unlike widgets, elements are long-lived and mutable. They persist and manage updates when widgets change.

Diving deeper into Flutter's widget structure, we find intriguing differences in how various widgets are constructed, particularly when examining their elements. Taking `StatelessWidget` and `StatefulWidget` as examples, they extend from `ComponentElement`.

```
// Flutter source code
// packages/flutter/lib/src/widgets/framework.dart
abstract class StatelessWidget extends Widget {
  @override
  StatelessElement createElement() => StatelessElement(this);
}

class StatelessElement extends ComponentElement {}
```

In these cases, the element created is a `StatelessElement`, an extension of `ComponentElement`. However, this differs when looking at other Flutter framework widgets. For instance, `SizedBox`, which extends `SingleChildRenderObjectWidget`, ultimately uses a different kind of element - `RenderObjectElement`.

```
// Flutter source code
// packages/flutter/lib/src/widgets/basic.dart
class SizedBox extends SingleChildRenderObjectWidget {}

// packages/flutter/lib/src/widgets/framework.dart
abstract class SingleChildRenderObjectWidget extends RenderObjectWidget {
  @override
  createElement() => SingleChildRenderObjectElement(this);
}

// packages/flutter/lib/src/widgets/framework.dart
class SingleChildRenderObjectElement extends RenderObjectElement {}
```

ComponentElement acts as a host for other elements, forming the root of its sub-tree. Notably, it doesn't have an associated RenderObject. Instead of directly creating a RenderObject, a ComponentElement indirectly generates RenderObjects by creating other Elements.

On the other hand, RenderObjectElement nodes in the element tree are actively involved in the layout and painting phases of rendering. These elements are linked to corresponding RenderObject nodes in the render tree. The RenderObjects are tasked with more intensive operations like sizing, positioning, hit-testing, and painting, handling the bulk of the work in rendering the UI.

2.3.3 RenderObject Tree

The RenderObject Tree handles the actual layout and rendering of the UI. As a developer, you know that sizing, layout, painting, and schematic are crucial aspects of your application's performance. With RenderObject, you can handle all these tasks seamlessly from one frame to another, saving you time and ensuring your app runs smoothly. This tree is where Flutter performs the layout calculations and paints the UI on the screen. RenderObjects are mutable and responsible for the UI elements' size, position, and rendering.

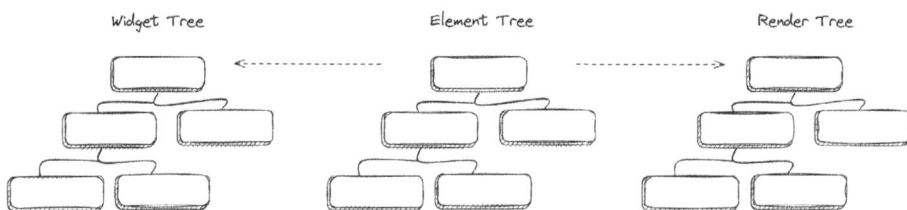

Figure 2.3: Flutter Widget, Element, and Render Object Trees

You've touched on an essential aspect of Flutter's flexibility and power. Beyond just composing widgets, Flutter allows you to delve deeper into the rendering layer. Indeed, you can control the painting and layout aspects by creating your widgets. Let's dive into how you can leverage Flutter's rendering engine to create custom widgets that dictate their layout and painting behavior. This approach opens possibilities for making unique UI elements tailored to your needs. Let's explore this exciting aspect of Flutter development.

2.3.4 Anatomy of a Widget

Exploring the inner workings of a Flutter widget, particularly `SizedBox`, offers a fascinating glimpse into Flutter's architecture. The `SizedBox` widget, a concrete implementation of `SingleChildRenderObjectWidget`, exemplifies the multi-layered approach to widget design in Flutter. Defined in Flutter's source code, `SizedBox` extends from `SingleChildRenderObjectWidget`, an abstract class extending `RenderObjectWidget`.

```
// Flutter Source code
// packages/flutter/lib/src/widgets/basic.dart
class SizedBox extends SingleChildRenderObjectWidget {}
```

But what exactly is `SingleChildRenderObjectWidget`? Unlike the commonly used `StatelessWidget` or `StatefulWidget`, which mainly compose other widgets, `SingleChildRenderObjectWidget` serves a more fundamental purpose in the rendering pipeline.

```
// Flutter Source code
// packages/flutter/lib/src/widgets/framework.dart
abstract class SingleChildRenderObjectWidget
            extends RenderObjectWidget { ... }
```

Delving deeper, you can see that `SingleChildRenderObjectWidget` inherits from `RenderObjectWidget`:

```
// Flutter Source code
// packages/flutter/lib/src/widgets/framework.dart
abstract class RenderObjectWidget extends Widget {}
```

This is where the true power of custom widget creation comes to the forefront. Beyond the capabilities of built-in widgets and the composition-based `StatelessWidget` and `StatefulWidget`, custom widgets like `SizedBox` allow for direct control over layout and painting, tailoring the UI to specific needs.

Examining the `SizedBox` source code reveals its structure and functionality:

```
class SizedBox extends SingleChildRenderObjectWidget {
  const SizedBox({
    super.key,
    this.width,
    this.height,
    super.child,
```

```
  });

  final double? width;
  final double? height;

  @override
  RenderConstrainedBox createRenderObject(
    BuildContext context,
  ) {}

  BoxConstraints get _additionalConstraints {}

  @override
  void updateRenderObject(
    BuildContext context,
    RenderConstrainedBox renderObject,
  ) {}

  @override
  String toStringShort() {}

  @override
  void debugFillProperties(
    DiagnosticPropertiesBuilder properties,
  ) {}
}
```

Key observations include the widget's ability to accept a single child and its implementation of `createRenderObject()` and `updateRenderObject()` methods. The `RenderConstrainedBox` used in these methods is a type of `RenderBox`.

```
class RenderConstrainedBox extends RenderProxyBox {}
class RenderProxyBox extends RenderBox
    with
        RenderObjectWithChildMixin<RenderBox>,
        RenderProxyBoxMixin<RenderBox> {}
```

But what exactly is a `RenderBox`? As you might expect:

```
abstract class RenderBox extends RenderObject {}
```

It is a type of `RenderObject`.

The main tasks of a `RenderObject` in Flutter include:

1. **Perform Layout**: RenderObject provides the fundamental framework for the layout protocol in Flutter. It defines how a widget or a part of the UI should be positioned and sized within the app's UI. `performLayout()` does the work of computing the layout for this render object.

2. **Painting Interface**: It offers a primary painting interface, allowing the rendering of visual elements onto the screen. This includes handling graphics, text, and other visual elements. `paint()` method renders the object into the given context at the given offset.
3. **Lifecycle Management**: `RenderObject` handles the lifecycle of its part in the render tree, including initialization and disposal of resources.

There are three types of RenderObjects.

1. **RenderBox:** Used for widgets that need to define a specific size and position in 2D space
2. **RenderSliver:** Utilized for widgets within scrollable areas, handling how a part of the scrollable area should be rendered.
3. **RenderViewport:** Used for widgets that define a visible window through which users see a part of the content.

But what about widgets without children or with multiple children? Flutter addresses these scenarios with different types of `RenderObjectWidgets`:

LeafRenderObjectWidget

The `LeafRenderObjectWidget` is designed for widgets that are leaf nodes in the widget tree, meaning they do not contain any child widgets. This subclass is typically associated with creating a `RenderBox`, a fundamental render object in Flutter that handles box-model layout, encompassing aspects like width, height, margins, and padding. Widgets best represented as `LeafRenderObjectWidget` include those self-contained and do not need to interact with child widgets, such as a `DecoratedBox` for simple decoration or a `CustomPaint` for custom drawing operations. They are the simplest in terms of layout complexity, focusing on rendering the widget itself without considering child widgets.

SingleChildRenderObjectWidget

Moving up in complexity, the `SingleChildRenderObjectWidget` is tailored for widgets that manage a single child. Like `LeafRenderObjectWidget`, it typically creates a `RenderBox` but with the added responsibility of arranging and positioning one child widget. This subclass is crucial for widgets that apply specific constraints or properties to their child.

MultiChildRenderObjectWidget

For more complex layout scenarios involving multiple child widgets,

`MultiChildRenderObjectWidget` comes into play. This subclass is designed to manage and lay out multiple children, requiring more sophisticated logic to handle the interactions and layout constraints of its children. Examples of widgets in this category include `Row`, `Column`, and `Stack`. Each widget uses `MultiChildRenderObjectWidget` to arrange its children in horizontal, vertical, or overlapping layouts. This subclass is essential for creating customizable widgets that need to manage multiple children in a specific layout.

The RenderObject and Rendering Pipeline in Flutter could fill a book with their complexities. However, the basics covered here should inspire you to create and customize your own render objects. Let's get started.

	Stateless and Stateful Widgets	RenderObjectWidget
build method	yes	no
render objects	no	yes

2.3.5 Build a Widget with a custom RenderObject

Let's aim to build a custom Flutter widget called `LabeledDivider`. This widget will draw a horizontal line across the screen with a label (text) in the middle. It will accept parameters for the label text, the thickness of the line, and the color.

Step 1: Create the `main()` Function

Let's start with a `main()` function to run the app:

```
void main() {
  runApp(MaterialApp(
    home: Scaffold(
      appBar: AppBar(
        title: const Text('Labeled Divider Example'),
      ),
      body: const Column(
        children: [
          Text('Above the divider'),
          LabeledDivider(
            label: 'Divider Label',
            thickness: 2.0,
            color: Colors.blue,
          ),
          Text('Below the divider'),
        ],
      ),
    ),
  ));
}
```

This sets up a basic app with our custom `LabeledDivider` widget.

Step 2: Define `LabeledDivider` Widget

Next, let's define the `LabeledDivider` widget. This widget will accept the following parameters: label, thickness, and color. Since it will not have any child widgets, `LeafRenderObjectWidget` seems to be a good fit for a base class.

```
class LabeledDivider extends LeafRenderObjectWidget {
    const LabeledDivider({
```

```dart
      super.key,
      required this.label,
      this.thickness = 1.0,
      this.color = Colors.black,
    });

  final String label;
  final double thickness;
  final Color color;

  @override
  RenderLabeledDivider createRenderObject(
    BuildContext context,
  ) {
    // This will be completed in a later step
  }

  @override
  void updateRenderObject(
    BuildContext context,
    RenderLabeledDivider renderObject,
  ) {
    // This will be completed in a later step
  }
}
```

Both `createRenderObject()` and `updateRenderObject()` methods are responsible for creating and updating RenderObject, respectively.

Step 3: Create `RenderLabeledDivider`

Now, let's start defining the RenderLabeledDivider class, a RenderBox.

```dart
class RenderLabeledDivider extends RenderBox {
  // Variables and methods will be added in subsequent steps
}
```

Step 4: Define Private Variables and `TextPainter`

We declare private variables and initialize TextPainter in RenderLabeledDivider:

```dart
class RenderLabeledDivider extends RenderBox {
  String _label;
  double _thickness;
  Color _color;
  late TextPainter _textPainter;

  RenderLabeledDivider({
    required String label,
```

```
    required double thickness,
    required Color color,
  })  : _label = label,
        _thickness = thickness,
        _color = color {
    _textPainter = TextPainter(
      textDirection: TextDirection.ltr,
    );
  }
  // Setters and getters will be added next
}
```

Step 5: Create Setters and Getters

The render object receives data all the time, and it needs to set the value to private variables, which can be done via setter and getter.

```
class RenderLabeledDivider extends RenderBox {
  // Existing code...

  set label(String value) {
    if (_label != value) {
      _label = value;
      // Update logic will be added
    }
  }

    String get label => _label;

  // Similar setters for thickness and color
}
```

Step 6: Complete createRenderObject

Back in the LabeledDivider widget, we complete the createRenderObject method:

```
@override
RenderLabeledDivider createRenderObject(
  BuildContext context,
) {
  return RenderLabeledDivider(
    label: label,
    thickness: thickness,
    color: color,
  );
}
```

This method creates an instance of `RenderLabeledDivider` with the provided properties.

Step 7: Complete `updateRenderObject`

In `LabeledDivider`, we also complete the `updateRenderObject` method:

```
@override
void updateRenderObject(
  BuildContext context,
  RenderLabeledDivider renderObject,
) {
  renderObject
    ..label = label
    ..thickness = thickness
    ..color = color;
}
```

This method updates the render object with new properties when the widget rebuilds. So, new variables pass to the setter, and it is up to Render Object to decide what to do with them, if any.

Step 8: Implement `performLayout` in `RenderLabeledDivider`

As mentioned, painting and performing layout are the most important tasks of the RenderObject.

Let's implement `performLayout` in `RenderLabeledDivider`; the method calculates the size of the divider, including the text.

```
@override
void performLayout() {
  _textPainter.text = TextSpan(
    text: _label,
    style: TextStyle(
      color: _color,
    ),
  );
  _textPainter.layout();

  final double textHeight = _textPainter.size.height;
  size = constraints.constrain(
    Size(
      double.infinity,
      _thickness + textHeight,
    ),
  );
}
```

The `paint` method is where we draw the line and text:

```dart
@override
void paint(PaintingContext context, Offset offset) {
  final Paint paint = Paint()..color = _color;
  final double yCenter = offset.dy + size.height / 2;

  // Draw the line
  context.canvas.drawLine(
    offset,
    Offset(offset.dx + size.width, yCenter),
    paint,
  );

  // Draw the text
  final double textStart =
      offset.dx + (size.width - _textPainter.size.width) / 2;
  _textPainter.paint(
    context.canvas,
    Offset(textStart, yCenter - _textPainter.size.height / 2),
  );
}
```

We'll use the `Paint` class and `TextPainter` to draw the line and label.

Step 9: Define `describeSemanticsConfiguration`

Before we start, no worries if you don't know anything about semantics in Flutter. You will learn more about semantics in the Flutter in Accessibility chapter.

The two methods above don't add any value to the semantic system of Flutter; therefore, to update this particularly ensure your app is accessible on this widget, you can call `describeSemanticsConfiguration()`

```dart
import 'package:flutter/semantics.dart';

// ....
@override
void describeSemanticsConfiguration(
  SemanticsConfiguration config,
) {
  super.describeSemanticsConfiguration(config);
  config
    ..isSemanticBoundary = true
    ..label = 'Divider with text: $_label';
}
```

Step 10: Add `markNeedsLayout` and `markNeedsPaint`

Finally, we need to add calls to `markNeedsLayout` and `markNeedsPaint` in the setters of `RenderLabeledDivider`:

```
set label(String value) {
  if (_label != value) {
    _label = value;
    markNeedsLayout();
    // Update semantics when label changes
    markNeedsSemanticsUpdate();
  }
}

set thickness(double value) {
  if (_thickness != value) {
    _thickness = value;
    // Only layout needs to be updated for thickness changes
    markNeedsLayout();
  }
}

set color(Color value) {
  if (_color != value) {
    _color = value;
    // Only painting needs to be updated for color changes
    markNeedsPaint();
  }
}
```

These methods ensure the widget is redrawn or relaid out when its properties change.

- markNeedsPaint is called when the visual appearance needs updating (like color changes).
- markNeedsLayout is when a change affects the layout size (like changing the label or thickness). MarkNeedsPaint is also covered by calling this function, so there is no need to call both simultaneously.
- markNeedsSemanticsUpdate is called to update the semantic information when the label changes.

Labeled Divider Example

Divider Label

Figure 2.4: Creating Customer Widget with RenderObjectWidget

With these implementations, RenderLabeledDivider can layout, paint, and provide semantic information for the LabeledDivider widget and will respond to changes in its properties.

2.3.6 Separation of the Element and RenderObject Trees

Separating the Element and RenderObject trees in Flutter is a critical design decision that enhances the framework's performance, clarity, and type safety.

In Flutter, when a layout change occurs, it's efficient only to update the relevant parts of the layout tree, which is the RenderObject Tree. Because of its compositional nature, the Element Tree typically contains many more nodes. If both trees were combined, updating the layout would involve walking through numerous unnecessary nodes in the Element Tree, leading to performance inefficiencies. By keeping these trees separate, Flutter ensures that layout updates are more focused and efficient, improving overall app performance.

The separation also contributes to a more precise division of responsibilities:

- **Widget Protocol:** The Widget (or Element) Tree focuses on describing the structure and configuration of the UI. It deals with immutable widgets that represent what the UI should look like.
- **Render Object Protocol:** The RenderObject Tree, on the other hand, is concerned with the actual layout and painting. Here, the RenderObjects are mutable and deal with the geometric and visual aspects of the UI.

This clear separation simplifies the API surface for both protocols. Widgets can remain simple and declarative, while RenderObjects can focus on layout and rendering specifics. This reduces the complexity of both systems, lowers the risk of bugs, and eases the testing burden.

Finally, the separation enhances type safety in the layout process. The RenderObject Tree can ensure, at runtime, that its children are of the correct type for their specific coordinate system. For example, a RenderBox expects child RenderObjects that also use box coordinates.

In contrast, the Element Tree, which corresponds to the Widget Tree, is more flexible regarding the types of children it can handle. A single widget can be used in different layout models (like a box or sliver layout) without concern for the coordinate system. If the Element and RenderObject trees were combined, this would necessitate additional type checks and complicate the widget design, as each widget would need to be aware of its children's specific layout constraints and coordinate systems.

This aspect also highlights a fundamental principle of software engineering: the Separation of Concerns. This principle has been thoughtfully implemented in Flutter's architecture, ensuring a clean and efficient design.

2.3.7 Optimization

Flutter's internal optimization strategies and algorithms are fundamental to its ability to handle complex user interfaces efficiently. These optimizations involve careful considerations of computational complexity (often expressed in Big O notation) and specialized algorithms to ensure that performance scales well with increasingly complex UIs.

Big O notation is a mathematical concept used to describe the efficiency of algorithms, particularly in terms of how their performance scales with the size of the input data. In the context of Flutter:

- **O(N) Algorithms:** Many of Flutter's algorithms aim to be linear (O(N)), meaning the time taken grows proportionally with the number of widgets or elements. This is crucial for maintaining responsiveness as the UI complexity increases.
- **Avoiding O(Nš) Scenarios:** Flutter avoids quadratic (O(Nš)) algorithms, where the time taken grows with the square of the number of elements. Such algorithms would lead to significant performance degradations for large UIs.

Flutter's core optimization techniques encompass several key strategies to ensure efficiency, particularly in handling complex UIs.

The layout system is designed for sublinear performance, where layout calculations scale slower than the increase in UI elements, achieved by optimizing layouts of existing elements and minimizing complete tree traversals.

Widget rebuilding is similarly sublinear; widgets are immutable, and only the changed widget and its children are rebuilt, with the framework selectively updating only necessary widgets, reducing superfluous computations.

RenderObjects, crucial for painting and layout, enhance performance through property caching, eliminating the need to recompute or repaint unchanged properties. Tree reconciliation and element updating are streamlined with efficient algorithms that effectively handle scenarios like identical child lists and single modifications, ensuring swift UI updates.

Additionally, Flutter focuses on optimizing memory usage and garbage collection, managing widget lifecycles and related elements, and rendering objects to decrease memory churn and reduce garbage collection frequency, a typical performance hurdle.

These combined optimizations enable Flutter to deliver smooth, responsive interfaces in even the most complex applications.

2.4 Principal Components and Framework Insights

Having delved into the crucial building blocks of Flutter, the Widgets, we're now poised to take a step back and gain a broader understanding of how Flutter functions as an integrated system.

2.4.1 Defining 'Native' in Flutter's Context:

Flutter challenges the conventional definition of 'native' applications. While it doesn't use platform-specific UI libraries, Flutter apps are compiled directly to machine code (ARM or x64 instructions) or JavaScript for web applications. This approach mirrors the native development process in Android and iOS, where code is compiled into machine code executable by the device's runtime environment. However, Flutter's uniqueness lies in its ability to bypass the intermediate byte-code stage (as seen in Android) or the intermediary language stage (as in iOS), leading to efficient and direct execution.

2.4.2 Flutter's Layered Architecture:

Flutter's design is inherently layered and extensible. Each layer in the system depends on the underlying one, yet no layer has privileged access to another. This structure ensures that every part of the framework is optional and replaceable:

Embedder Layer

The Embedder Layer bridges the Flutter engine and the underlying operating system. It's responsible for setting up and managing the application's runtime environment and handling crucial tasks essential for the Flutter application to function correctly on various platforms. Find the source code here: "github.com/flutter/engine/tree/main/shell/platform[2]."

The Embedder is written in languages appropriate for each target platform, such as Java and C++ for Android, Objective-C/Objective-C++ for iOS and macOS, and C++ for Windows and Linux. This allows the Embedder to leverage platform-specific features and optimizations, ensuring that Flutter apps can integrate seamlessly with the native capabilities of the OS.

The design of the Embedder Layer offers the flexibility to embed Flutter code into existing applications as a module or to use Flutter for the entire content of new applications. This versatility makes Flutter suitable for new projects and incremental integration into existing codebases.

The Embedder coordinates with the OS to access rendering surfaces where the Flutter UI can be drawn. This involves managing the graphics context and ensuring Flutter's rendering engine can effectively paint its UI onto the screen.

It handles input events (like touch and keyboard inputs) and integrates with the platform's accessibility features. This ensures Flutter apps provide a responsive and accessible user experience consistent with native applications.

The Embedder manages the application lifecycle, including initialization, execution, and teardown. It also contains the event loop, ensuring user events and system messages are promptly processed and dispatched to the Flutter engine.

The Embedder can expose platform-specific APIs, allowing Flutter applications to utilize native capabilities and functionalities of the operating system, such as GPS, sensors, or local storage.

---

[2]https://github.com/flutter/engine/tree/main/shell/platform

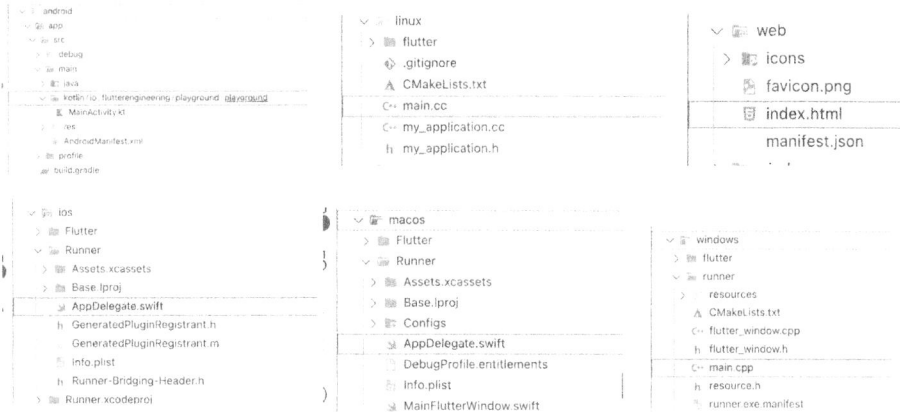

Figure 2.5: Specific platform embedders in Flutter

Part of the app template generated by `flutter create`, the Runner composes the pieces exposed by the platform-specific API of the Embedder into an app package. This package is runnable on the target platform, effectively turning the combination of Flutter and native code into a deployable unit.

Custom Embedders for Extensibility: Beyond the common platforms, Flutter's architecture allows for the creation of custom Embedders. This extensibility enables Flutter to run on various devices and operating systems, even those that are not officially supported, facilitating the deployment of applications across desktops, mobile devices, and embedded systems.

Flutter Engine Layer

The engine is primarily responsible for rasterizing composited scenes. This means it takes the visual elements defined in the Flutter framework and translates them into pixels on the screen, a process essential for rendering the user interface of a Flutter application. You can find the source code here: github.com/flutter/engine/tree/main/shell/common

It provides the low-level implementation of Flutter's core API. This includes handling graphics, text layout, file and network I/O, accessibility support, and plugin architecture. By managing these fundamental aspects, the engine ensures that Flutter apps have a solid base to build.

The engine includes a Dart runtime and a toolchain for compiling Dart code. This is crucial for running Flutter applications primarily written in Dart. The engine handles both ahead-of-time (AOT) compilation for release builds, which results in highly optimized native code, and just-in-time (JIT) compilation for development builds, which allows features like hot reload.

The engine uses Skia on most platforms and Impeller on iOS for graphics rendering. Impeller is also available behind a flag on Android and macOS. You may check the current state of Impeller support by this link

---

docs.flutter.dev/perf/impeller#availability[3]. Skia is an open-source 2D graphics library that provides common APIs that work across various hardware and software platforms. Impeller is a newer graphics renderer optimized for iOS devices, providing direct access to the GPU for enhanced performance.

Text rendering is another critical function of the engine. The text layout engine handles the intricacies of different languages, fonts, and rendering characteristics, ensuring that text in Flutter apps is displayed clearly and correctly across all platforms.

The engine exposes its functionality to the Flutter framework through the `dart:ui` library. This library wraps the underlying C++ code of the engine in Dart classes, making it accessible to the higher-level framework. It includes primitives for graphics, text, and input, among others.

The engine supports a plugin architecture, allowing developers to use or create plugins that extend the capabilities of Flutter apps. These plugins can interface with native platform APIs, providing access to device-specific features.

Platform Adaptability:

The Flutter Engine is designed to be adaptable across different platforms. Whether running on iOS, Android, web, or desktop, the engine interfaces with the platform-specific embedder to ensure seamless integration with the operating system's capabilities and constraints.

Flutter Framework Layer

The Flutter Framework layer is the part of Flutter that most developers interact with directly. Built entirely in Dart, this layer sits atop the Flutter Engine and provides a rich set of tools and APIs for building user interfaces and handling application logic. You can find the source code here: github.com/flutter/flutter/tree/main/packages/flutter/lib[4]

Let's break down its key aspects:

1. Modern, Reactive Framework:

- **Reactive Programming Model:** The Flutter Framework adopts a reactive programming model, which makes it easy to build dynamic user interfaces that respond in real-time to user interactions and state changes.
- **Declarative UI Approach:** Developers declare UIs using widgets, which describe what the UI should look like at any moment. This declarative approach simplifies the process of UI development and enhances the readability and maintainability of code.

2. Widget-Based Architecture:

---

[3]https://docs.flutter.dev/perf/impeller#availability
[4]http://github.com/flutter/flutter/tree/main/packages/flutter/lib

- **Widgets as Building Blocks:** Widgets are the fundamental building blocks of a Flutter app's UI. Everything in a Flutter UI is a widget, from a simple text label to complex layouts.
- **Extensive Widget Library:** Flutter provides a vast library of pre-built widgets, including structural elements (like buttons and menus), stylistic elements (like fonts and colors), and layout aspects (like padding and alignment).

3. **Rich Set of Libraries and APIs:**

- **Foundational Libraries:** These include animation, painting, and gestures, offering commonly used abstractions over the engine's low-level foundation.
- **Rendering Layer:** An abstraction for handling layout, allowing developers to dynamically manipulate a tree of renderable objects.
- **Material and Cupertino Design Libraries:** Comprehensive controls that adhere to Google's Material Design and Apple's Cupertino design standards.

4. **Package Ecosystem:**

- **Rich Ecosystem of Packages:** The Flutter framework is supported by a vast ecosystem of packages, which include platform plugins (like camera and GPS) and platform-agnostic features (like HTTP and animations).
- **Community Contributions:** Many packages are developed by the Flutter community, covering a wide range of functionalities and services.

5. **Integration with the Underlying Engine:**

- **Interaction with Dart:ui:** The framework uses `dart:ui` provided by the engine to interface with lower-level rendering layers, accessing graphics, text, and input primitives.

6. **Emphasis on Customizable UI and High-Level Features:**

- **Customizable and Extensible:** Developers can create bespoke widgets or customize existing ones, tailoring the app's UI to specific design requirements.
- **High-Level Features for App Development:** The framework provides advanced features like navigation and state management, simplifying the development of complex applications.

2.4.3 Composition of a Flutter App

A typical Flutter app created using `flutter create`, relies several interconnected components:

- **Dart App:** The topmost layer, where developers compose widgets into UIs and implement business logic.
- **Framework:** Provides high-level APIs for app development, handling widget tree composition and scene creation.
- **Engine:** Interfaces with the framework and platform-specific components, rasterizing scenes and implementing core APIs.
- **Embedder:** Coordinates with the OS for services like rendering, input management, and event loop management.
- **Runner:** Combines platform-specific APIs into a runnable app package for the target platform.

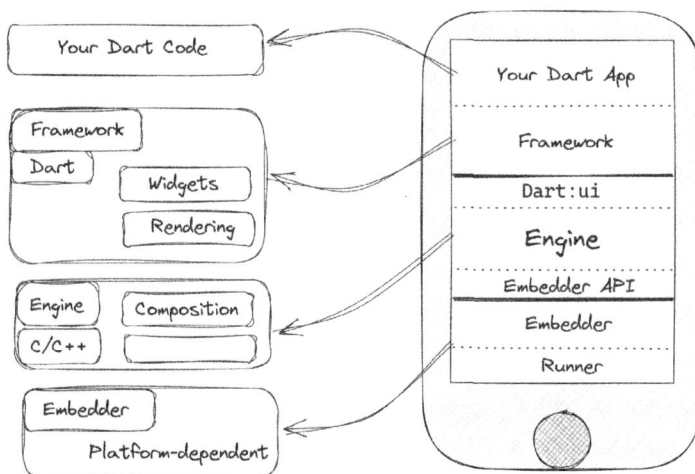

Figure 2.6: Flutter architecture reflected on an app

2.4.4 Flutter's Unique Approach:

Flutter stands apart in its rendering approach. Unlike traditional cross-platform frameworks that use native UI components or web views, Flutter renders UIs using its engine. This method reduces the abstraction layers, leading to better performance and consistency across platforms. Flutter's engine, especially with its graphics capabilities, allows for high-performance rendering, which is essential for smooth and visually appealing applications.

2.5 Graphics, Rendering, and Visualization

Having explored Flutter's architecture and the role of widgets and RenderObjects, it's crucial to understand one of the key pieces of the puzzle: the Renderer. The Renderer in Flutter is the mechanism that translates the UI code, defined by widgets and their associated RenderObjects, into the actual pixels displayed on the screen. It's a bridge between the abstract definitions of the UI and their tangible visual representation.

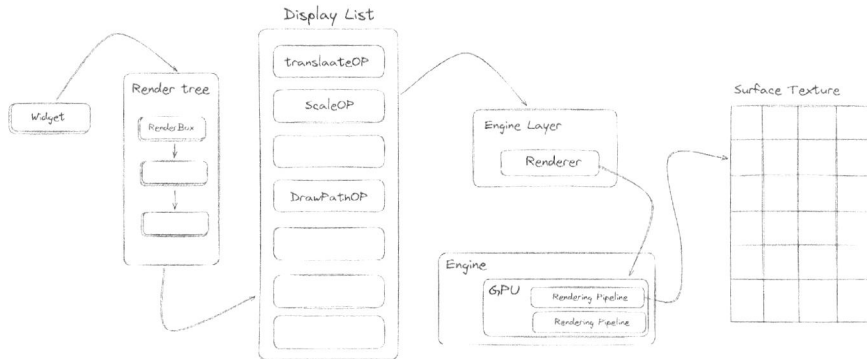

Figure 2.7: How a widget gets rendered on display

The rendering pipeline in Flutter is a multi-step process that transforms the declarative UI components, defined by the developer, into the final visual representation on the user's screen. Let's break down this pipeline to understand how it translates our Flutter code into the vivid interfaces we interact with. The process begins with the widget tree, our UI's blueprint. It's a hierarchical arrangement of widgets, defining the structure and elements of the user interface. Each widget in this tree is linked to a corresponding RenderObject, which holds the key to how these elements are laid out (layout) and how they look (painting).

The Flutter engine takes center stage, receiving instructions from the RenderObjects. These instructions are meticulously compiled into an ordered set of commands known as the display list. The display list is the Renderer's script, detailing what needs to be drawn and where.

With the display list in hand, the Renderer begins its task. It draws the contents of this list onto a surface texture, transforming the UI code into visible pixels on the screen. This step is where the abstract becomes concrete, where our UI design becomes a visual reality.

The Renderer doesn't work alone; it leverages the power of the GPU. By setting up a series of render pipelines, the Renderer ensures that the processing and rendering of the display list are efficient, smooth, and visually appealing.

Let's zoom into Rendering Pipelines.

In Flutter's rendering pipeline, each phase transforms developer-defined UI elements into dynamic and visually appealing interfaces displayed on the screen.

The User Input Phase The rendering process begins with the user input phase. The application responds to user interactions, such as touches, gestures, and keyboard inputs. These interactions often trigger state changes within the application's widgets, setting the stage for updates in the UI. Flutter's handling of these events determines their impact on the widget tree. For example, a button press

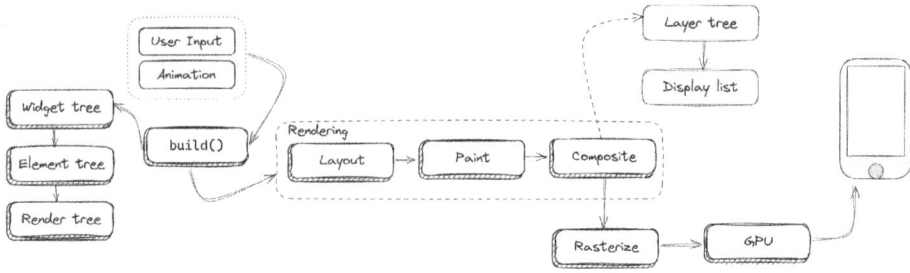

Figure 2.8: Full rendering pipeline in Flutter

might initiate a sequence of widget updates, refreshing the UI to reflect the new state.

The Animation Phase Following user input, the animation phase comes into play. This phase is crucial for adding dynamic effects and smooth transitions to the user interface. Flutter meticulously calculates each frame of an animation, considering factors like time progression and animation curves. The result is a series of frames seamlessly transitioning, enhancing the visual appeal and user experience. This phase ensures that movements and changes in the UI feel fluid and natural.

The Build Phase Next is the build phase, where the widget tree is constructed or reconstructed. Flutter examines widgets' current configuration and state during this phase to determine their organization and structure. This process is not just about creating the widget tree but also updating it. Flutter optimizes performance by rebuilding only the widgets that require updating due to state changes, thus conserving resources.

The Layout Phase In the layout phase, Flutter calculates the size and position of each widget. This phase follows a bottom-up approach, beginning with the leaf nodes (widgets without children) and progressing upwards to the root of the widget tree. The layout process involves each parent widget setting constraints for its children and the children reporting back their sizes. This collaborative process between parent and child widgets is key to determining how each element fits within the overall UI layout.

The Paint Phase The paint phase is where the visual rendering of widgets takes place. In this phase, each render object's `paint()` method is invoked, defining the visual appearance of the widgets. This includes their colors, shapes, textures, and other graphic decorations. For rendering objects with children, the `paint()` method ensures that the children are also painted accordingly. This phase is crucial for establishing the exact look of the UI elements.

```
// Flutter source code
// packages/flutter/lib/src/rendering/proxy_box.dart
class RenderTransform extends RenderProxyBox {
    void paint(context, offset) {
        Layer layer = context.pushTransform(...);
```

```
        }
}
```

The Compositing Phase Following the painting phase is the compositing phase. Here, Flutter organizes the painted widgets into layers. This layering strategy is essential for optimizing the rendering of dynamic content. For example, scrolling interfaces allow the reuse of existing content layers, minimizing the need to repaint the entire interface. Only the new elements entering the viewport are painted, while the rest are efficiently composited from existing layers.

The Rasterization Phase The final stage of the rendering pipeline is rasterization. In this phase, the composited layers are transformed into pixels displayed on the screen. This process is accelerated by the GPU, ensuring fast and smooth rendering. Rasterization is the culminating step where the UI, defined by the widget tree and refined through various phases, becomes visible to the user in its final form.

Each phase of Flutter's rendering pipeline contributes to a seamless transition from code to a visually rich and interactive interface, highlighting the framework's capability to handle complex rendering tasks efficiently and with finesse.

2.6 Navigating Through the Widget and App Lifecycle

Having explored how a widget is rendered on screen, let's dive into the intricate details of the rendering phase.

Initially, it may surprise you to learn that widgets, in the traditional sense, don't have a lifecycle. Widgets are immutable; they cannot be altered once they are created. Thus, when discussing the 'widget lifecycle,' we refer to a broader concept that extends to Elements, State objects, and Render objects. This encompasses tracking the positions of widgets relative to each other and determining when a widget needs to be rebuilt due to state changes or necessary screen updates.

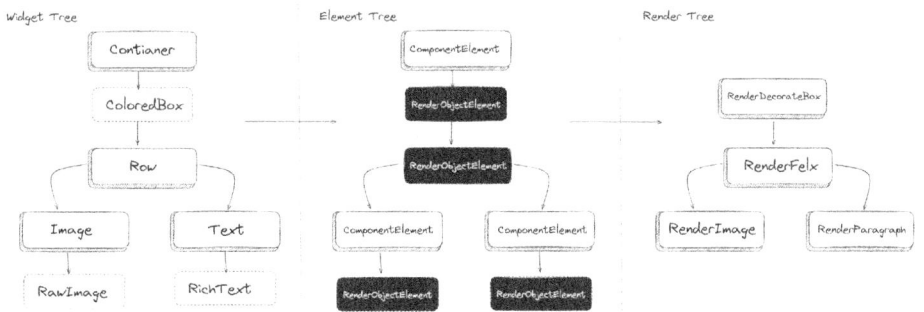

Figure 2.9: The Flutter trees example

Now, let's focus on the class that manages the rendering phase. This class is a crucial part of Flutter's framework, serving as the bridge between the Flutter engine and the framework itself. It plays a pivotal role in scheduling frames, thereby controlling the timing of frame rendering. This functionality is essential for developers to align tasks and callbacks with the app's visual updates, ensuring a smooth and responsive user interface.

```
mixin SchedulerBinding on BindingBase {
    void handleAppLifecycleStateChanged(
    AppLifecycleState state,
  ) {}
    int scheduleFrameCallback(FrameCallback callback, ...) {}
    void addPersistentFrameCallback(FrameCallback callback) {}
    void addPostFrameCallback(FrameCallback callback, ...) {}
    void ensureVisualUpdate() {}
    void scheduleFrame() {}
    void handleDrawFrame() {}
}
```

This initialization is achieved using `WidgetsFlutterBinding.ensureInitialized();`, a method often placed at the beginning of our application before it starts running.

The enum referred to here delineates the different stages of a frame's lifecycle. Grasping these stages is vital for enhancing performance and ensuring tasks are executed effectively within the frame's lifecycle.

```
// binding.dart
enum SchedulerPhase {
  idle,
  transientCallbacks,
  midFrameMicrotasks,
  persistentCallbacks,
  postFrameCallbacks,
}
```

`idle`: This phase occurs when the system is not actively processing a frame. It presents an ideal opportunity to carry out tasks that are not urgent and do not require completion before the next frame. This is also the phase where asynchronous code is typically resolved.

```
void initState() {
    super.initState();
    Future.delayed(
      Duration.zero,
      () => {
        print('${SchedulerBinding.instance.schedulerPhase}'),

          // flutter: SchedulerPhase.idle
      },
    );
  }
```

transientCallbacks: During this phase, the system handles brief callbacks that must be completed before the frame ends. Common tasks in this phase include animations and various visual effects.

```
_controller = AnimationController(
  duration: const Duration(seconds: 1),
  vsync: this,
)
  ..addListener(
    () {
      print(
        '${SchedulerBinding.instance.schedulerPhase}',
      );

      // flutter: SchedulerPhase.transientCallbacks
    },
  )
  ..forward();
```

midFrameMicrotasks: This phase focuses on executing the queued microtasks during the transient callback processing. These microtasks typically emerge from futures resolved in the transient callbacks phase. The mid-frame microtasks phase serves as a crucial juncture, where the framework handles these tasks before proceeding to more sustained phases like persistent callbacks. In Flutter, microtasks can be organized synchronously or asynchronously. This organization is crucial for efficiently managing brief operations that must be completed seamlessly within the ongoing frame processing. By scheduling a microtask, you enable the execution of a specific code segment at the earliest possible moment, just before the commencement of the next event loop cycle.

```
_controller = AnimationController(
  duration: const Duration(seconds: 1),
  vsync: this,
)
  ..addListener(
    () {
      debugPrint(
        '${SchedulerBinding.instance.schedulerPhase}',
      );
      scheduleMicrotask(() async {
        debugPrint(
          '1. ${SchedulerBinding.instance.schedulerPhase}',
        );
        await Future.delayed(Duration.zero);
        debugPrint(
          '2. ${SchedulerBinding.instance.schedulerPhase}',
        );
      });
    });
```

```
    },
  )
  ..forward();

// Print output
// flutter: SchedulerPhase.transientCallbacks
// flutter: 1. SchedulerPhase.midFrameMicrotasks
// flutter: 2. SchedulerPhase.idle
// flutter: SchedulerPhase.transientCallbacks
```

persistentCallbacks: This phase is allocated for more lasting tasks that recur in every frame. Commonly, these tasks involve layout and building operations. Flutter is constructing the widget tree and carrying out layout computations in this phase. This stage is vital for rendering the user interface, ensuring that each frame accurately reflects the desired layout and design.

```
SchedulerBinding.instance.addPersistentFrameCallback(
  (_) {
    // Code here runs during
    // the persistentCallbacks phase of each frame.
    // Typically used for layout and build operations.
    debugPrint(
      '''
      Current phase:
      ${SchedulerBinding.instance.schedulerPhase}
      ''',
    );
    // Layout and state updates can go here.
  },
);
```

postFrameCallbacks: This phase occurs once the current frame has been fully rendered. It is the optimal time for scheduling tasks that need to be executed after the frame is drawn but before the commencement of the next frame. Activities in this phase often involve processing user inputs, refreshing animations by the layout, and preparing data for the upcoming frame. This ensures the application remains responsive and up-to-date with user interactions and visual changes.

```
SchedulerBinding.instance.addPostFrameCallback((_) {
  // Code here is executed after the frame is rendered.
  debugPrint('''
      Current phase:
      ${SchedulerBinding.instance.schedulerPhase}
      ''');
  // Tasks like processing user inputs
  // or preparing for the next frame can be done here.
});
```

Now that you understand how the rendering pipeline schedules frames and its lifecycle, let's focus on the lifecycle of elements and state objects.

To begin, we'll delve into the workings of the StatefulWidget.

```
abstract class StatefulWidget extends Widget {
    const StatefulWidget({ super.key });

    @override
  StatefulElement createElement() => StatefulElement(this);

    @protected
    @factory
    State createState();
}
```

As evident, the StatefulWidget comprises two key methods: `createElement` and `createState`. The `createElement` method is responsible for creating an element and mounting it to the widget tree, while `createState` attaches a state to this element within the tree. Now, let's explore the lifecycle of an Element.

The stages of an Element lifecycle are encapsulated in the `_ElementLifecycle` enum. This enum categorically outlines the distinct phases an Element undergoes during its lifecycle.

```
// widget/framework.dart
enum _ElementLifecycle {
  initial,
  active,
  inactive,
  defunct,
}
```

1. `initial`: In this state, an element has just been created. It must still be fully initialized or part of the active widget tree.
2. `active`: The element transitions to the `active` state once it is fully initialized and integrated into the widget tree. In this phase, the element actively participates in layout and painting processes. Typically, an element spends most of its lifecycle in this state.
3. `inactive`: An element enters the `inactive` state when it is removed from the active widget tree but remains in memory. This situation might arise if a parent widget stops incorporating the child in its build method. Elements in this state have the potential to be reactivated, or they may progress to the `defunct` state.
4. `defunct`: This represents the final phase in the lifecycle of an element. In the `defunct` state, the element is no longer a part of the widget tree and cannot be returned to an active state. Generally, this stage leads to the element's removal from memory (garbage collection).

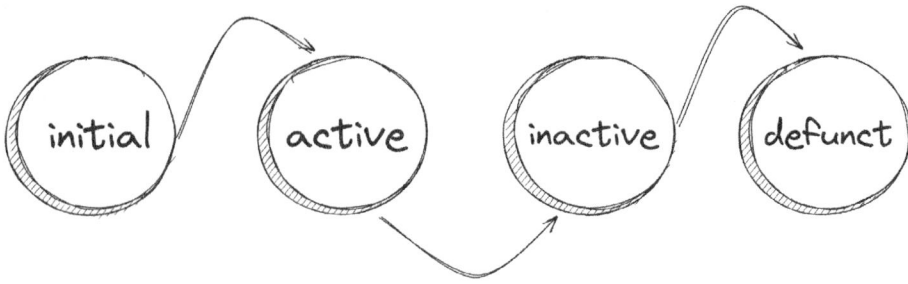

Figure 2.10: Element LifeCycle

Now, let's turn our attention to the lifecycle of the State object. While there is a _StateLifecycle enum that outlines the states of a State object, what's more intriguing is the actual process and changes a State object undergoes during its lifecycle, especially since we, as developers, write and manage State objects directly, unlike Elements which Flutter controls primarily.

To better understand the State object lifecycle, it's essential to consider the flow of the first frame:

1. **Application Start or setState Call**: The application begins, or the setState method is invoked. At this juncture, the Platform Dispatcher schedules a frame for rendering.
2. **Frame Drawing**: This triggers the drawFrame() method on WidgetsBinding. This method is a crucial link between the higher-level application code and the Flutter engine, coordinating the rendering process.

By exploring these methods and the sequence of events, we gain a clearer insight into the lifecycle and functioning of the State object in a Flutter application.

```
WidgetsBinding.instance.drawFrame();
```

Finally, the element and everything beneath it should be carefully managed to avoid unnecessary rebuilds.

However, during the first frame, your widget tree is initially empty. A specific method is invoked to handle this initial state in this scenario.

```
Element inflateWidget(Widget newWidget, Object? newSlot) {}
```

The inflateWidget method is integral to Flutter's framework, operating within the element tree to significantly impact how the UI is rendered. This method is essential in the lifecycle of widgets and their corresponding elements. Here's an overview of its function and significance:

Element Creation: At its core, inflateWidget is responsible for creating an Element for a specific Widget. In Flutter's architecture, a Widget is an immutable configuration, while the `Element` is the dynamic entity that gets mounted in the widget tree and actively engages in the rendering process. This distinction is crucial in understanding the role of `inflateWidget` in the Flutter framework.

```
final Element newChild = newWidget.createElement();
```

Child Addition: The `inflateWidget` method is also responsible for adding the newly created element as a child to the current element, placing it in a specific 'slot.' In Flutter, the concept of 'slots' is instrumental in managing the positioning of elements within the tree. This is particularly important for elements with multiple children, ensuring they are organized and displayed correctly in the UI hierarchy.

```
newChild.mount(this, newSlot); // `this` is child's parent
```

Control Over Element Creation: Although the `inflateWidget` function is commonly invoked by the `updateChild` method, it can also be directly utilized by subclasses requiring a finer degree of control over element creation. This capability is beneficial for crafting more complex widgets, allowing for tailored behavior and specific configurations in the element creation process.

```
final Element? updatedChild = updateChild(
  newChild,
  newWidget,
  newSlot,
);
```

Handling Global Keys: In instances where the widget being processed possesses a global key, and there is an existing element in the tree with the same global key, the `inflateWidget` method will repurpose that element. This process may involve relocating the element from a different part of the tree or reactivating it from a pool of inactive elements. Such reuse of elements is pivotal for preserving state and identity consistency throughout the widget tree, ensuring a stable and efficient UI behavior.

```
final Key? key = newWidget.key;
if (key is GlobalKey) { ... }
```

Element Lifecycle State: Once an element is generated by the `inflateWidget` method, it is already mounted and in its lifecycle's "active" state. This status indicates that the element is primed and ready to engage in the rendering process.

This sequence is particularly noteworthy because activating the mounting process in this method eventually invokes `initState`.

```
state.initState()
```

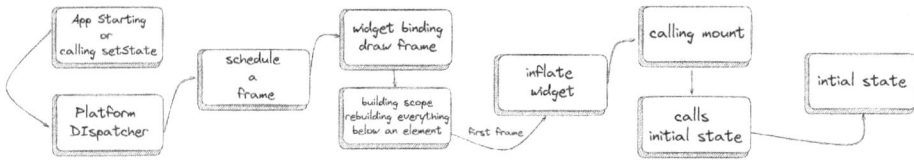

Figure 2.11: First frame path to initState()

This marks the beginning of the State lifecycle. After completing the first frame, Flutter enters the `idle` state, awaiting further frames. This is typically the point where `setState` is called.

Having established the state object and the Element, Flutter maintains a list of 'Dirty Elements.' In this context, calling `setState` triggers a specific method, `markNeedsBuild`, which signals the need to rebuild the affected elements. This process is a key part of how Flutter manages state changes and updates the UI accordingly.

```
// Flutter Source code
// packages/flutter/lib/src/widgets/framework.dart
void setState(VoidCallback fn) {
    ...
    _element!.markNeedsBuild();
}
```

At this stage, Flutter resumes its cycle of scheduling another frame. Once it completes the tasks for the current frame, it moves on to the next. This cycle results in the rebuilding of elements, ultimately invoking the `performRebuild()` method. This method is crucial as it prompts the state to execute the `didChangeDependencies()` function before the `build` method. This sequence is integral to Flutter's process for updating and rendering elements in response to state changes.

```
// Flutter Source code
// packages/flutter/lib/src/widgets/framework.dart
class StatefulElement extends ComponentElement {

    @override
  void performRebuild() {
    if (_didChangeDependencies) {
      state.didChangeDependencies();
      _didChangeDependencies = false;
    }
        // ultimately here build() and updateChild() is called
        // built = build();
        // _child = updateChild(_child, built, slot);
    super.performRebuild();
  }
}
```

The `updateChild` method plays a vital role in Flutter's widget framework, particularly in managing the update cycle of elements. Here is a simplified version of this method, as derived from the framework:

```
// Flutter Source code
// packages/flutter/lib/src/widgets/framework.dart
Element? updateChild(
  Element? child,
  Widget? newWidget,
  Object? newSlot,
) {
  if (newWidget == null) {
    if (child != null) {
      deactivateChild(child);
    }
    return null;
  }

  Element newChild;

  if (child != null) {
    if (child.widget == newWidget) {
      // If the widget is the same,
      // update the slot if necessary.
      if (child.slot != newSlot) {
        updateSlotForChild(child, newSlot);
      }
      newChild = child;
    } else if (Widget.canUpdate(child.widget, newWidget)) {
      // If the widget types are compatible,
      // update the widget.
      if (child.slot != newSlot) {
        updateSlotForChild(child, newSlot);
      }
      child.update(newWidget);
      newChild = child;
    } else {
      // If the widgets are incompatible,
      // deactivate the old child
      // and create a new element.
      deactivateChild(child);
      newChild = inflateWidget(newWidget, newSlot);
    }
  } else {
    // If there's no existing child,
    // create a new element.
    newChild = inflateWidget(newWidget, newSlot);
  }
```

```
    return newChild;
}
```

The initial state change triggered by this method occurs when it switches the state to 'inactive', achieved through the invocation of the `deactivateChild` method.

```
  if (newWidget == null) {
    if (child != null) {
      deactivateChild(child);
    }
    return null;
  }
```

At this juncture, if the frame is completed and the state remains deactivated, the widget transitions to the 'dispose' state, leading to its disposal. Significantly, this method facilitates subsequent steps to reactivate a child, returning it to the 'active' state in the lifecycle. Interestingly, if the method identifies a new element's presence, it invokes the `inflateWidget` function, as previously discussed. This process underscores the dynamic and responsive nature of Flutter's element and state management.

```
else {
    // If there's no existing child, create a new element.
    newChild = inflateWidget(newWidget, newSlot);
}
```

Additionally, this call performs another crucial action: it updates the child element with the `newWidget`.

```
// If the widget types are compatible, update the widget.
if (child.slot != newSlot) {
  updateSlotForChild(child, newSlot);
}
child.update(newWidget);
newChild = child;
```

Examining the `update` method reveals that it plays a key role in this phase of the lifecycle, specifically in updating the state and properties of the widget.

```
class StatefulElement extends ComponentElement {
    ...
    void update(StatefulWidget newWidget) {
    ...
        state.didUpdateWidget(oldWidget);
    }
}
```

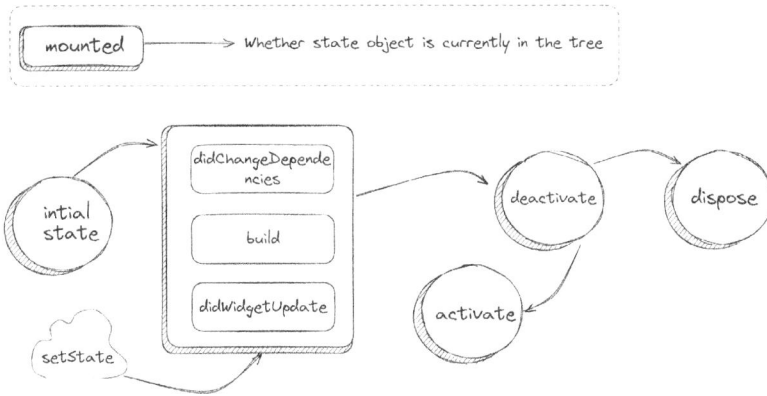

Figure 2.12: The StatefulWidget lifeCycle

Indeed, the steps involved in understanding Flutter's workings are extensive. Let's briefly recap the lifecycle of a StatefulWidget:

1. **createState()**: Activated upon the creation of the StatefulWidget. This method is responsible for creating the state object.
2. **initState**: This is called once the state object is integrated into the widget tree, primarily for initial data setup based on the context or the widget itself.
3. **didChangeDependencies**: Triggered right after **initState** and whenever there's a change in the widget's dependencies. It's beneficial for widgets that depend on inherited widgets.
4. **build**: This method is responsible for making the widget's UI. It is called following **initState**, **didChangeDependencies**, and whenever there is a need to update the UI due to state changes.
5. **setState**: While not a lifecycle method in the traditional sense, **setState** is a vital function that initiates the widget's rebuild when its state changes.
6. **didUpdateWidget**: Executed when there's a change in the widget's configuration, aiding in responding to alterations in widget properties.
7. **deactivate**: This method is called when the widget is removed from the tree, with the possibility of being reinserted later.
8. **dispose**: Invoked when the widget is permanently removed from the tree; this method is used for resource release.
9. **reassemble**: Activated during hot reloads, **reassemble** allows the widget to adapt to code changes.

This summary provides a comprehensive overview of the various stages and functions integral to the lifecycle of a StatefulWidget in Flutter.

```
class LifecycleWidget extends StatefulWidget {
  const LifecycleWidget({Key? key}) : super(key: key);
```

```dart
  @override
  LifecycleState createState() => LifecycleState();
}

class LifecycleState extends State<LifecycleWidget> {
  int _counter = 0;

  LifecycleState() {
    print('Constructor, mounted: $mounted');
  }

  @override
  void initState() {
    super.initState();
    print('initState, mounted: $mounted');
  }

  @override
  void didChangeDependencies() {
    super.didChangeDependencies();
    print('didChangeDependencies, mounted: $mounted');
  }

  @override
  Widget build(BuildContext context) {
    print('Build method');
    return Column(
      children: [
        Text('Counter: $_counter'),
        ElevatedButton(
          onPressed: _incrementCounter,
          child: const Text('Increment'),
        ),
      ],
    );
  }

  void _incrementCounter() {
    setState(() {
      _counter++;
      print('setState, new counter value: $_counter');
    });
  }

  @override
  void didUpdateWidget(covariant LifecycleWidget oldWidget) {
    super.didUpdateWidget(oldWidget);
    print('didUpdateWidget, mounted: $mounted');
```

```
  }

  @override
  void deactivate() {
    super.deactivate();
    print('deactivate, mounted: $mounted');
  }

  @override
  void dispose() {
    super.dispose();
    print('dispose, mounted: $mounted');
  }

  @override
  void reassemble() {
    super.reassemble();
    print('reassemble, mounted: $mounted');
  }
}
```

In this example, each lifecycle method includes a `print` statement for demonstration purposes, which logs the method name and whether the widget is mounted. The `_incrementCounter` method demonstrates the use of `setState` to trigger a rebuild.

2.6.1 Lifecycle of a RenderObject

In Section 2.3.5, we delved into the construction of a `RenderObject` and familiarized ourselves with its three key functionalities: Layout, Size, and Semantics. This understanding is a foundation for comprehending how `RenderObjects` integrate into the broader context of a Flutter application's lifecycle, managing layout, visual appearance, and accessibility features.

The `RenderObject` class in Flutter's rendering library is a fundamental building block of the framework's rendering layer. It is an abstract class that adds `DiagnosticableTreeMixin` and implements the `HitTestTarget` interface. This class plays a crucial role in defining the layout and painting protocols for the rendering tree, which is the structure Flutter uses to compose and display the UI. Here's the basic structure of the `RenderObject` class:

```
// Flutter source code
// packages/flutter/lib/src/rendering/object.dart
abstract class RenderObject
    with DiagnosticableTreeMixin
    implements HitTestTarget {
  // ...
  PipelineOwner? get owner => _owner;
```

```
  // ...
}
```

The `owner` property in `RenderObject` is of type `PipelineOwner`. This is a pivotal component in the rendering pipeline of Flutter. The `PipelineOwner` manages the rendering pipeline, coordinating the phases of layout, painting, compositing, and semantics processing for `RenderObjects`.

- **Managing the Rendering Pipeline**: `PipelineOwner` is responsible for driving the rendering pipeline. It maintains the state of render objects that have requested updates at each stage of the pipeline, such as layout changes or painting requests.
- **Importance in the Render Tree**: Every `RenderObject` in the render tree is associated with a `PipelineOwner`. This association allows the `PipelineOwner` to manage the lifecycle and updates of each `RenderObject` efficiently, ensuring that the UI is rendered correctly and efficiently.
- **Handling Layout and Paint Updates**: `PipelineOwner` triggers and manages updates for layout and paint. When a `RenderObject` needs to update its layout or visual representation, it notifies the `PipelineOwner`, orchestrating the necessary updates in the rendering pipeline.

`RenderObject` also implements the `HitTestTarget` interface, which is crucial for handling events in the Flutter UI.

```
/// An object that can handle events.
abstract interface class HitTestTarget {
  /// Override this method to receive events.
  void handleEvent(
    PointerEvent event,
    HitTestEntry<HitTestTarget> entry,
  );
}
```

- **Event Handling**: As a `HitTestTarget`, a `RenderObject` can respond to various events, particularly pointer events such as taps, drags, and gestures. This is essential for user interaction within the app.
- **Hit Testing Mechanism**: The `handleEvent` method is overridden by concrete subclasses of `RenderObject` to provide specific behaviors when an event occurs. Hit testing determines which `RenderObject` in the render tree should receive an event based on the event's location and the geometry of the `RenderObjects`.

Let's explore this lifecycle, focusing on the key functions and concepts.

Initialization

The journey begins with creating a RenderObject, usually invoked via the `createRenderObject` method of a widget. This phase sets up the initial state and properties of the RenderObject, as well as its relationships with other objects in the rendering tree.

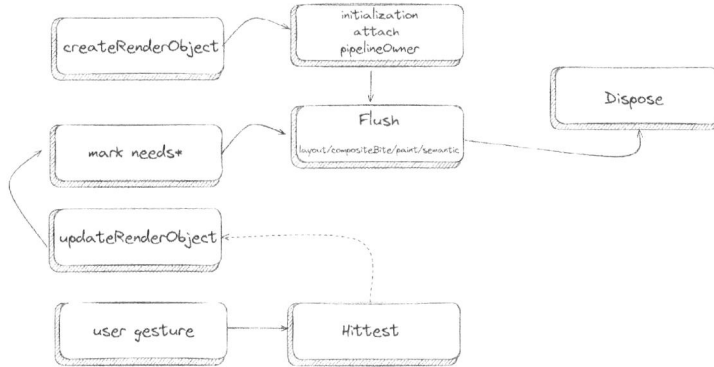

Figure 2.13: Lifecycle of a RenderObject

```
@override
RenderObject createRenderObject(BuildContext context) {
  return MyRenderObject();
}
```

In this phase, the RenderObject is instantiated with its essential properties, attached to the owner (`PipelineOwner`), preparing it to be laid out and rendered on the screen.

Layout (flushLayout Phase)

Managed by the `PipelineOwner`, the layout phase involves calculating the size and position of the RenderObject in the UI. The `performLayout` method is overridden to define the specific layout logic. The two relevant functions you are familiar with `performLayout`, `markNeedsLayout` indicate this phase. This phase is critical for determining how a RenderObject fits within the UI, influencing its visual and functional behavior.

Compositing Bits Update (flushCompositingBits Phase)

During this phase, RenderObjects update their compositing bits. It's a process to determine whether the RenderObject or its children require compositing layers for effects like clipping or transformations. This happens after the Layout but before the Painting.

Painting (flushPaint Phase)

In the painting phase, the RenderObject translates its layout information into a visual representation. It's responsible for defining the actual appearance of UI elements. Relevant methods that you worked with `paint`, `markNeedsPaint` represents this phase.

This phase brings the UI to life by visually rendering the RenderObject based on its layout calculations.

Semantics (flushSemantics Phase)

If semantics are enabled, this stage compiles the semantic information for the RenderObject. This data is crucial for accessibility, enabling assistive technologies to interpret and interact with the UI. The two methods `describeSemanticsConfiguration` and `markNeedsSemanticsUpdate`, marking this phase.

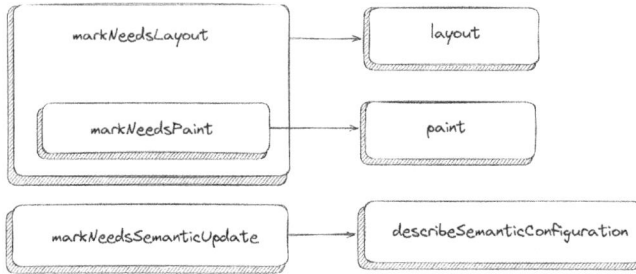

Figure 2.14: The MarkNeeds* methods relationship with each phase

Event Handling and Hit Testing

RenderObjects respond to user interactions through the process of hit testing. The `hitTest` method is implemented to determine if the RenderObject or any of its children have been interacted with. This step ensures that user interactions are accurately detected and responded to.

To implement the `hitTest` method for your `RenderLabeledDivider`, you need to determine whether a given point, typically from a user's touch interaction, intersects with the area occupied by the divider. Since the divider is a line with text, the hit test can be more complex than a simple geometric shape. However, for simplicity, let's assume that any touch within the bounds of the RenderBox is considered a hit. Here's an example of how you might implement this:

```
class RenderLabeledDivider extends RenderBox {
  // ...
  @override
  bool hitTest(
    HitTestResult result, {
    required Offset position,
  }) {
    // Check if the incoming position
      // is within the bounds of this render box
    final BoxHitTestEntry entry = BoxHitTestEntry(
      this,
      position,
    );
    if (size.contains(position)) {
      result.add(entry);
```

```
      return true;
    }
    return false;
  }
// ...
}
```

In this implementation, the `hitTest` method checks if the `position` (the point of interaction) is within the `size` of the `RenderLabeledDivider`. If it is, the method adds an entry to the `HitTestResult` and returns `true`, indicating a hit. If not, it returns `false`, indicating no hit.

This is a basic implementation. Depending on your specific use case, you should refine this to consider more complex shapes or areas, especially if the divider or text has unique interactive behaviors.

Update Triggered by Events

User interactions or state changes can trigger updates in the RenderObject. This is managed by calling the appropriate `markNeeds*` function, initiating a new cycle of layout, painting, or semantics as needed.

```
class RenderLabeledDivider extends RenderBox {
// ...
  set label(String value) {
    if (_label != value) {
      _label = value;
      markNeedsSemanticsUpdate();
      markNeedsLayout();
    }
  }
// ...
}
```

This mechanism allows the RenderObject to react dynamically to changes and user interactions.

Disposal

The final stage in a RenderObject's lifecycle involves disposing of resources and performing necessary cleanup. This step is crucial for resource management and maintaining application performance.

```
class RenderLabeledDivider extends RenderBox {
// ...
  @override
  void dispose() {
    layer?.dispose();
    _textPainter.dispose();
    super.dispose();
```

```
  }
  // ...
}
```

Throughout these stages, the `PipelineOwner` is pivotal in ensuring that each RenderObject is processed at the right time. This lifecycle, from initialization to disposal, is foundational to how Flutter renders widgets, handles user interactions, and maintains a smooth, responsive UI.

2.6.2   App LifeCycle in Flutter

In Flutter, managing app lifecycle events can be done using two approaches: The `WidgetsBindingObserver` mixin and `AppLifecycleListener` class.

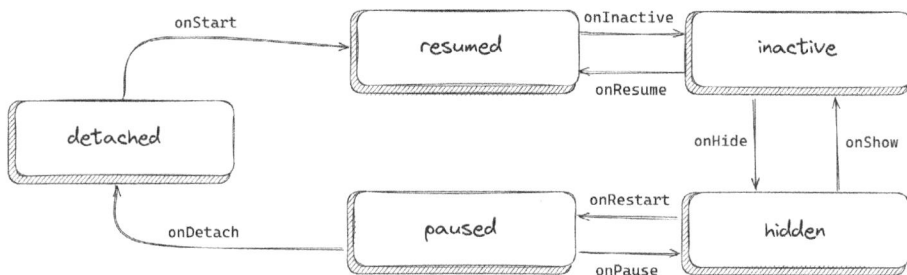

Figure 2.15: Flutter app lifecycle diagram

The `AppLifecycleListener` class leverages the `WidgetsBindingObserver` mixin under the hood but adds several benefits, like structured callbacks for different lifecycle events.

```
// Flutter source code
// packages/flutter/lib/src/widgets/app_lifecycle_listener
class AppLifecycleListener
    with WidgetsBindingObserver, Diagnosticable {}
```

Using `WidgetsBindingObserver` Mixin

This approach involves implementing the `WidgetsBindingObserver` mixin in your widget's state class and overriding the `didChangeAppLifecycleState` method.

```
import 'package:flutter/material.dart';

class MyLifecycleWatcher extends StatefulWidget {
  const MyLifecycleWatcher({super.key});

  @override
  createState() => MyLifecycleWatcherState();
```

```
}

class MyLifecycleWatcherState extends State<MyLifecycleWatcher>
    with WidgetsBindingObserver {
  @override
  void initState() {
    super.initState();
    WidgetsBinding.instance.addObserver(this);
  }

  @override
  void dispose() {
    WidgetsBinding.instance.removeObserver(this);
    super.dispose();
  }

  @override
  void didChangeAppLifecycleState(AppLifecycleState state) {
    if (state == AppLifecycleState.paused) {
      // Handle app going into the background
    } else if (state == AppLifecycleState.resumed) {
      // Handle app coming to the foreground
    }
  }

  @override
  Widget build(BuildContext context) {
    return Container(); // Your widget structure
  }
}
```

Using `AppLifecycleListener` Class

The `AppLifecycleListener` class offers a more structured and comprehensive approach to lifecycle management. This class provides specific callbacks for various lifecycle events, allowing for more targeted responses.

```
class MyLCListener extends StatefulWidget {
  @override
  createState() => MyLifecycleListenerState();
}

class MyLifecycleListenerState extends State<MyLCListener> {
  late final AppLifecycleListener _listener;

  @override
  void initState() {
    super.initState();
    _listener = AppLifecycleListener(
```

```
      onStateChange: _onStateChange,
      onResume: _onResume,
      onInactive: _onInactive,
      onHide: _onHide,
      onShow: _onShow,
      onPause: _onPause,
      onRestart: _onRestart,
      onExitRequested: _onExitRequested,
      onDetach: _onDetach,
    );
  }

  void _onStateChange(AppLifecycleState state) {}
  void _onResume() {}
  void _onInactive() {}
  void _onHide() {}
  void _onShow() {}
  void _onPause() {}
  void _onRestart() {}
  void _onExitRequested() async {}
  void _onDetach() {}

  @override
  void dispose() {
    _listener.dispose();
    super.dispose();
  }

  @override
  Widget build(BuildContext context) {
    return Scaffold(
      appBar: AppBar(title: Text('App Lifecycle Demo')),
      body: Center(child: Text('Lifecycle Listener')),
    );
  }
}
```

In Flutter, the onResume event is triggered when your application becomes active and visible to the user. This is the ideal time to restart any paused animations or refresh user data. It ensures that everything is up-to-date and running smoothly when the user returns to the app.

The onInactive event occurs when the app enters an inactive state. This doesn't mean the app is closed; instead, it might be transitioning to a background state. During this phase, you should pause ongoing tasks or animations that don't need to run when the app isn't directly interacting with the user.

When the onHide event is called, your app is not visible anymore, but it's still running in the background. This is a crucial time to reduce memory usage and save the app's current state. Such optimizations ensure that your app remains efficient and doesn't consume unnecessary resources when not in use.

The `onShow` event is the opposite of `onHide`. It's invoked when your app is coming back from a hidden state. You might re-establish connections or resources released or reduced when the app was hidden.

During the `onPause` phase, the app is not currently visible to the user and is running in the background. This is the moment to pause activities that shouldn't continue while the app is not in the foreground, such as heavy data usage tasks or a running game.

The `onRestart` event signifies that the app is resuming from a paused state. It's an opportunity to renew tasks or refresh the app content paused or stopped during the `onPause` state.

The `onExitRequested` callback is different for cases where the exit is cancelable. This is the right place to implement logic like prompting users to save changes before the app closes, ensuring a smooth user experience and data integrity.

Lastly, the `onDetach` event happens when your app is detached from any host views. This typically occurs when the app is entirely shutting down. In this phase, releasing resources tied to the app is essential to avoid memory leaks and ensure a clean app shutdown.

Both methods provide practical ways to handle app lifecycle events in Flutter. While `WidgetsBindingObserver` offers a more direct approach, `AppLifecycleListener` enhances this by providing a structured and robust framework for managing these events, making it easier to write clean, maintainable code that responds appropriately to various lifecycle states.

2.7   Managing Constraints in Flutter UI

Flutter's UI framework represents a paradigm shift from traditional layout systems. Understanding how Flutter manages constraints is essential for creating fluid, adaptable UIs. This chapter goes into deeps of Flutter's layout mechanics, primarily focusing on the core principle: "**Constraints go down. Sizes go up. Parent sets position.**"

2.7.1   The Core Principle of Flutter Layout

At the heart of Flutter's layout system is a simple yet profound rule: "Constraints go down. Sizes go up. Parent sets position." This principle is crucial for comprehending how widgets are sized and positioned in Flutter.

1. **Constraints Go Down:** In Flutter, every widget receives a set of constraints from its parent. These constraints define the widget's minimum and maximum allowable sizes (width and height). Flutter widgets are more disciplined, strictly adhering to the constraints provided by their parent.

2. **Sizes Go Up:** Once a widget receives its constraints, it determines its size within these limits. This size is then communicated upwards to the parent. The child widget has the freedom to choose any size that fits within the constraints, but it cannot exceed them.
3. **Parent Sets Position:** After determining the sizes of its children, the parent widget is responsible for positioning them. This involves specifying the exact location of each child on the screen, both horizontally and vertically.

Understanding Flutter's One-Pass Layout

Flutter's efficiency in rendering comes from its one-pass layout process. Each widget is laid out only once, and the process cannot be reversed or iterated. This approach leads to high-performance layouts but also introduces certain limitations:

- Widgets are constrained to the sizes dictated by their parent, limiting the freedom to select any arbitrary size.
- A widget's position on the screen is determined by its parent, not the widget itself.
- The layout of a single widget can only be fully understood by considering the entire widget tree.

2.7.2 Practical Examples of Flutter Layout with Code

Container within a Screen:

In this example, a `Container` without explicit dimensions is placed directly under the screen, represented by the central widget in a Flutter app. The screen's constraints force the `Container` to fill the entire screen.

```
import 'package:flutter/material.dart';

void main() {
  runApp(MaterialApp(
    home: Scaffold(
      body: Container(
        // To visualize the container,
        // we give it a color (blue)
        color: Colors.blue,
      ),
    ),
  ));
}
```

Here, the `Container` will expand to fill the entire screen because the screen's dimensions constrain it.

Centered Container with Specific Size:

This example shows a `Container` with a specified width and height centered within its parent using the `Center` widget.

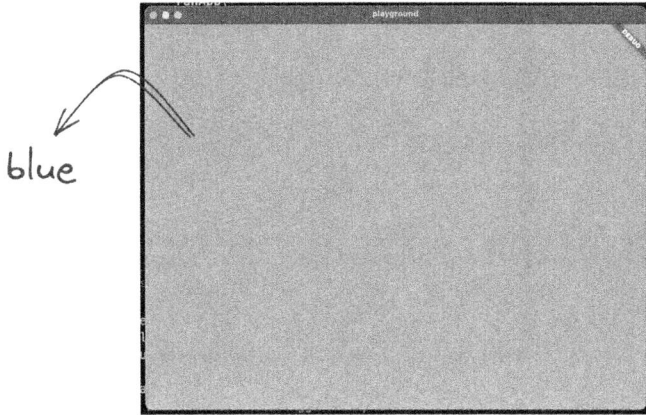

Figure 2.16: Container Without Explicit Dimensions (entire screen is blue)

```
void main() {
  runApp(MaterialApp(
    home: Scaffold(
      body: Center(
        child: Container(
          width: 100.0,
          height: 100.0,
          color: Colors.blue,
        ),
      ),
    ),
  ));
}
```

The Center widget allows the Container to be as big as its dimensions (100x100 in this case) and centers it within the available space.

ConstrainedBox Usage:

Here, a ConstrainedBox applies specific constraints to a Container within it.

```
import 'package:flutter/material.dart';

void main() {
  runApp(MaterialApp(
    home: Scaffold(
      body: ConstrainedBox(
        constraints: const BoxConstraints(
          minWidth: 50.0,
          maxWidth: 150.0,
          minHeight: 50.0,
```

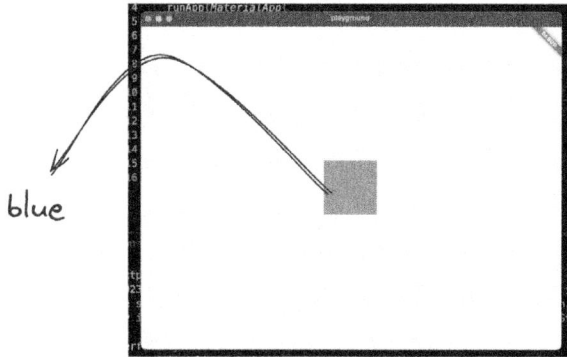

Figure 2.17: Container and Center Widgets

```
      maxHeight: 150.0,
    ),
    child: Container(
      color: Colors.green,
    ),
    ),
   ),
  ));
}
```

The Container inside the ConstrainedBox will adjust its size to fit the specified constraints (between 50x50 and 150x150).

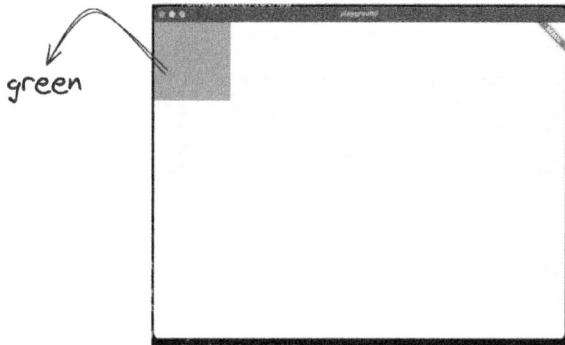

Figure 2.18: Demo of ConstrainedBox

Row and Expanded Widgets:

This example demonstrates how a Row widget with children wrapped in Expanded widgets distributes space.

```
void main() {
  runApp(MaterialApp(
    home: Scaffold(
      body: Row(
        children: <Widget>[
          Expanded(
            flex: 2,
            child: Container(
              color: Colors.amber,
            ),
          ),
          Expanded(
            flex: 1,
            child: Container(
              color: Colors.blue,
            ),
          ),
        ],
      ),
    ),
  ));
}
```

In the Row, there are two Container widgets wrapped in Expanded widgets. The first Container (amber-colored) is given twice the space of the second one (blue-colored) due to their flex properties (2 and 1, respectively).

The Row distributes space among its children based on these flex values, disregarding their preferred sizes.

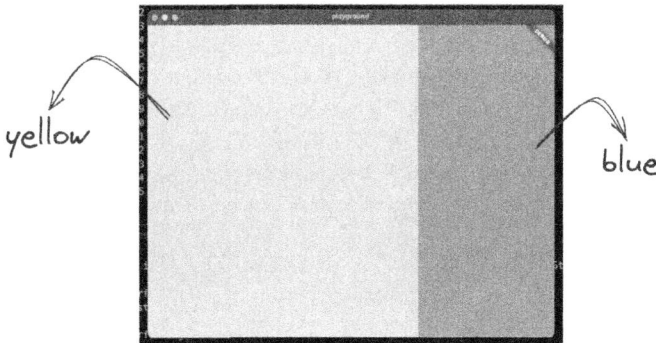

Figure 2.19: A demonstration of Expanded

These code examples illustrate how different widgets in Flutter behave under various constraints and in different parent-child relationships. Understanding these interactions is key to mastering Flutter's layout system.

2.7.3   Tight vs. Loose Constraints in Flutter

Understanding the distinction between tight and loose constraints in Flutter is critical for mastering its layout system. This distinction affects how widgets behave and size themselves.

Tight Constraints

Tight constraints are precise and non-flexible, offering a single size for the widget to adopt. They occur when the minimum and maximum dimensions (width and height) are the same. In such a scenario, a widget has no choice but to take the exact size specified by these constraints.

- **Example of Tight Constraints:**
  - Imagine a `Container` widget within a `Scaffold`. The `Scaffold` might provide tight constraints to the `Container`, specifying the exact dimensions it must adhere to. The `Container` will then occupy that much space, no more and no less.
  - Another instance is the top-level widget in a Flutter application, often constrained by the device's screen size, resulting in a tight constraint.

Tight constraints are like a direct order: "You must be exactly this size, no negotiation."

Loose Constraints

Loose constraints are more flexible, providing a range within which a widget can decide its size. These constraints specify a minimum and a maximum size, and the widget can choose any size within this range.

- **Example of Loose Constraints:**
  - Consider a `Container` wrapped within a `Center` widget. The `Center` widget tells the `Container` that it can be any size it wants as long as it's within the screen's bounds. If the `Container` doesn't have a fixed size or sufficient content to dictate its size, it can decide to be any size up to the maximum the `Center` allows.
  - A `Column` with unconstrained height behaves similarly, allowing its children to choose their heights within the given range.

Loose constraints are more of a guideline: "You can be any size within this range."

Practical Implications

Understanding tight versus loose constraints is crucial when designing a responsive Flutter UI. This knowledge helps in predicting how widgets will behave in different scenarios:

- Widgets with tight constraints are predictable in size but offer less flexibility.
- Widgets with loose constraints provide more dynamic layouts but require careful management to avoid layout issues like overflow.

Consider a common mistake: placing a `ListView` (which prefers to be as big as possible) inside a `Column` without wrapping it in an `Expanded` widget. The `Column` provides unbounded height to its children, which can confuse the `ListView`. Understanding that the `Column` provides loose constraints helps diagnose and fix such layout issues.

Grasping Flutter's layout system's nuances, mainly how constraints and sizes are managed, is fundamental for building responsive and aesthetically pleasing applications. This system's uniqueness lies in its structured approach, where the constraints flow downward, sizes bubble upward, and parents determine the positioning. With practice and attention to these principles, developers can harness the full potential of Flutter's robust UI framework.

2.8 Significance and Usage of Keys in Flutter

In Flutter, the `Widget` class includes a constructor that can take a `Key` as an optional parameter. This is a scenario that Flutter developers are likely to have encountered in their development experiences.

```
// Flutter source code
// packages/flutter/lib/src/widgets/framework.dart
abstract class Widget extends DiagnosticableTree {
  const Widget({ this.key });

  final Key? key;

  // Other properties and methods...
}
```

A `Key` in Flutter is a distinctive identifier for `Widgets`, `Elements`, and `SemanticsNodes`. It plays a crucial role in the framework's widget lifecycle management. When a widget is rebuilt, its key determines whether the new widget should be used to update an existing element in the widget tree. This means that if the key of the new widget matches the key of the current widget associated with an element, Flutter will update that element with the new widget. Otherwise, it will create a new element for the new widget.

This mechanism is vital for maintaining the state and identity of widgets, especially in dynamic lists or complex interfaces where the structure of the widget tree changes frequently. Using keys, developers can ensure that the framework accurately tracks and updates widgets, leading to more predictable and efficient UI behavior.

Let's start learning different types of keys in Flutter and when to use them.

UniqueKey

This key is used when a widget needs a unique identity every time it's built, ensuring it's always considered distinct. For instance, in a dynamic list where

you want each item to maintain its identity during updates, you would use a
UniqueKey. A practical example is a chat application where each message is
unique and needs to be individually identifiable even after updates.

```
ListView.builder(
  itemBuilder: (BuildContext context, int index) {
    return ListTile(key: UniqueKey(), title: Text('Message $index'));
  },
);
```

ValueKey: When a widget needs to be identified by a specific value, ValueKey
is the go-to. It's perfect for cases where a unique value, like an ID, distinguishes
widgets. For example, in a to-do list app, each to-do item might have a unique
ID, and using ValueKey helps Flutter identify and manage these items effectively.

```
ListView.builder(
  itemBuilder: (BuildContext context, int index) {
    return ListTile(
      key: ValueKey(todoItems[index].id),
      title: Text(todoItems[index].title),
    );
  },
);
```

ObjectKey: Similar to ValueKey, it uses the identity of an entire object. This
key suits complex data structures where the widget's identity is tied to the object's identity. For instance, in an e-commerce app, each product in a list can be
uniquely identified using ObjectKey, allowing Flutter to correctly manage widgets
representing different products.

```
ListView.builder(
  itemBuilder: (BuildContext context, int index) {
    return ListTile(
      key: ObjectKey(products[index]),
      title: Text(products[index].name),
    );
  },
);
```

GlobalKey: This is a globally unique key used across the entire app. It's commonly employed for accessing widgets from different app parts, like managing
form states. A practical use case is a form widget where you want to access its
state from a different part of your app to perform actions like validation or data
submission.

```
final GlobalKey<FormState> formKey = GlobalKey<FormState>();
```

```
// In the Form widget
Form(
  key: formKey,
  child: TextFormField(),
);

// Elsewhere in the app
if (formKey.currentState.validate()) {
  // Process data
}
```

PageStorageKey: This key saves a widget's state when it's not in view, specifically in scrollable lists. For example, in a news app with a long list of articles, you can use `PageStorageKey` to maintain the scroll position, ensuring that when a user returns to the list after reading an article, they are returned to the same position.

```
ListView.builder(
  key: PageStorageKey<String>('news-list'),
  itemBuilder: (BuildContext context, int index) {
    return ListTile(title: Text('Article $index'));
  },
);
```

Choosing the right type of key in Flutter is essential for effective widget management, especially in dynamic and complex interfaces.

Using Keys in Flutter Testing

Keys can also be highly beneficial in widget testing. For instance, you can use a ValueKey or Key to find a specific widget. Here's an example:

```
void main() {
  testWidgets(
    'Example Widget Test',
    (WidgetTester tester) async {
      await tester.pumpWidget(
        const MaterialApp(
          home: Column(
            children: [
              Text(
                'Flutter',
                key: Key('specific_widget'),
              ),
              Text('Flutter'),
            ],
          ),
        ),
      );
```

```
    // There are two Flutter text widgets
    // expect(find.text('Flutter'), findsExactly(2));

    // So you may use a Key to find a specific widget.
    const specificWidgetKey = Key('specific_widget');
    expect(
      find.byKey(specificWidgetKey),
      findsOneWidget,
    );
  },
 );
}
```

In this test, while we have two widgets by adding a key, we can differentiate them by a specific key. This approach is beneficial for ensuring that your app's forms and other interactive elements behave as expected.

2.9   Conclusion

In this chapter, we have delved into the depths of Flutter's architecture, unraveling its reactive and declarative nature and its emphasis on reduced coupling and increased cohesion. By exploring its principal components, graphics rendering, and the widget lifecycle, we've understood how Flutter's design optimizes performance and developer experience.

In conclusion, these architectural insights enable us to build robust and scalable Flutter applications. The theoretical knowledge gained here forms the foundation for practical development, guiding us to create high-performance, user-centric Flutter experiences. This exploration prepares us to apply these principles in practice, expanding the potential of multi-platform app development with Flutter.

CHAPTER 3

Flutter's Integration with Native Platforms

Reviewers: Anna Leushchenko, Oleksandr Leushchenko

In the previous chapter, we covered many of Flutter's internals. In this chapter, we will see how Flutter allows you to integrate with Native Platforms.

Flutter's ability to integrate with native platforms is one of its most powerful features, allowing developers to leverage platform-specific functionalities alongside Flutter's cross-platform capabilities. This integration is primarily achieved through Platform Channels and Dart FFI (Foreign Function Interface).

3.1 Platform Channel

Platform Channels are a critical feature of Flutter that bridges the gap between Dart and native platform code. They provide a way for Flutter apps to communicate with the underlying platform, whether it's Android, iOS, macOS, Linux, or Windows. This communication is vital for accessing native functionalities like cameras, GPS, sensors, and other platform-specific features not exposed directly by the Flutter framework, including 3rd-party SDKs not created for Flutter.

Platform Channels mainly offer three types of communication methods:

- **MethodChannel**: This is used for asynchronous method invocations. A Flutter app can send a method call to the native side, which performs a specific function and returns a result. It's ideal for tasks like fetching sensor data, battery status, or processing data using native capabilities.

  Use Case: Fetching the current battery level or accessing device information.

- **EventChannel**: Used for creating a data stream from native code to Dart. It is useful when listening to continuous or periodic native events, like sensor readings or location updates.

  Use Case: Subscribing to sensor data updates or GPS location changes.

- **BasicMessageChannel**: Flutter is a communication channel that sends and receives messages between Dart and platform-specific code on Android and iOS. Unlike `MethodChannel`, which is used for method calls, `BasicMessageChannel` is suited for simple, asynchronous message exchanges. It supports various data serialization formats and codecs, such as JSON, binary, or custom-defined formats.

  Use Case: Sending and receiving custom data structures.

Let's create a step-by-step example using `MethodChannel` in Flutter. We'll build a simple application where the Flutter part (Dart code) communicates with the native platform (Android) to retrieve the device's battery level.

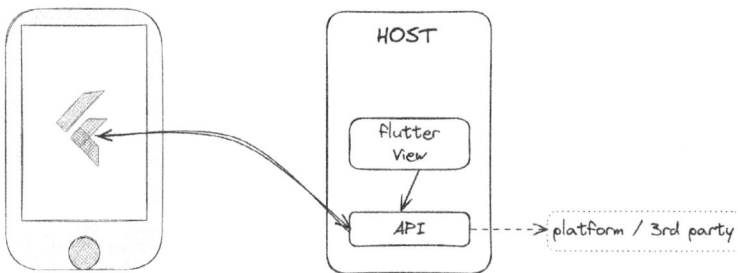

Figure 3.1: Method channel in Flutter

Step 1: Define the MethodChannel in Flutter (Dart)

In your Flutter app, you need to import `package:flutter/services.dart` and define a `MethodChannel`.

```dart
import 'package:flutter/material.dart';
import 'package:flutter/services.dart';

class BatteryLevel {
  static const methodChannel = MethodChannel(
// A name must be the same as
// the name in the native implementation.
    'io.flutterengineering.battery/methods',
  );

  static Future<int?> getBatteryLevel() async {
    try {
      final batteryLevel =
          await methodChannel.invokeMethod<int>(
        'getBatteryLevel',
      );
      return batteryLevel;
```

```
    } catch (e) {
      debugPrint(e.toString());
      return null;
    }
  }
}
```

Step 2: Handle the Method Call in Native Android Code (Kotlin)

In your Android project, you must override the `configureFlutterEngine` method in your `MainActivity` or the respective activity.

```kotlin
import io.flutter.embedding.android.FlutterActivity
import io.flutter.embedding.engine.FlutterEngine
import io.flutter.plugin.common.MethodChannel
import android.os.BatteryManager
import android.content.Context

class MainActivity : FlutterActivity() {
private val CHANNEL = "io.flutterengineering.battery/methods"

    override fun configureFlutterEngine(
            flutterEngine: FlutterEngine
        ) {
        MethodChannel(
            flutterEngine.dartExecutor.binaryMessenger,
            CHANNEL
        )
        .setMethodCallHandler { call, result ->
            if (call.method == "getBatteryLevel") {
                val batteryLevel = getBatteryLevel()
                if (batteryLevel != null) {
                    result.success(batteryLevel)
                } else {
                    result.error(
                        "UNAVAILABLE",
                        "Battery level not available.",
                        null
                    )
                }
            } else {
                result.notImplemented()
            }
        }
    }

    private fun getBatteryLevel(): Int? {
        val batteryManager =
        getSystemService(
```

```
        Context.BATTERY_SERVICE
    ) as BatteryManager
    return batteryManager
    .getIntProperty(
        BatteryManager.BATTERY_PROPERTY_CAPACITY
    )
  }
}
```

Step 3: Call the Method from Flutter

Now, you can call getBatteryLevel from your Flutter code to retrieve the battery level from the native platform.

```
void main() async {
  WidgetsFlutterBinding.ensureInitialized();
  final batteryLevel = await BatteryLevel.getBatteryLevel();
  print("Battery Level: $batteryLevel%");
}
```

Step 4: Run Your App

Run your Flutter app. The method getBatteryLevel will invoke the native platform code, and the battery level will be fetched and printed in the console.

There are a few notes that you should keep in mind.

- The above example is for Android using Kotlin. For iOS, you need to implement similar logic in Swift or Objective-C in your iOS project, and the same is true for macOS, Windows, and Linux. The native part requires you to know about the platform and the language you have to write the logic.
- Always ensure that the channel name matches between Dart and native code.
- You need to handle permissions and platform-specific configurations as needed. For example, accessing certain hardware features on Android might require specific permissions in your AndroidManifest.xml.

3.1.1   Introduction to Pigeon in Flutter

Pigeon[1] is a tool developed for Flutter applications to facilitate seamless and type-safe communication between Dart and native code (Java/Kotlin for Android, Objective-C/Swift for iOS). It addresses the complexity and boilerplate code often associated with platform channels by providing a more straightforward, robust way to call native platform functions from Dart code. Pigeon generates code that

---

[1] https://pub.dev/packages/pigeon

sets up these communication channels, ensuring that the data types and method signatures are consistent and correctly implemented on both the Dart and native sides of an application.

Pigeon[2] operates by defining clear interfaces in Dart, which describe the methods that can be invoked across the platform barrier. After defining these interfaces, Pigeon generates corresponding Dart and native code. This auto-generated code includes the logic for marshaling data across the platform channel and handling method calls. The primary use of Pigeon is in scenarios where complex data needs to be shared between Flutter and native modules or when there's a need for frequent and consistent method calls across platforms. It is beneficial in large-scale projects where maintaining type safety and reducing boilerplate code is crucial for efficiency and maintainability. Pigeon supports communication with Android and iOS platforms, leveraging Java, Kotlin, Objective-C, and Swift for the respective native implementations.

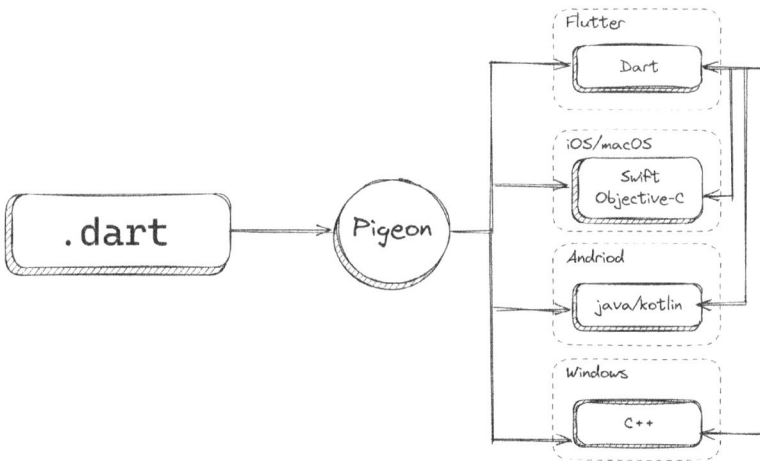

Figure 3.2: Pigeon in Flutter

3.2 Dart FFI

Dart's `dart:ffi` library enables mobile, command-line, and server applications running on Dart Native to interact with native C APIs, providing a critical link for accessing and executing system-level code. The Foreign Function Interface (FFI) feature allows Dart code to perform native operations like reading, writing, and managing memory directly. FFI can support programming languages compiled into C, such as C++, Objective-C, Go, and Rust.

---

[2]https://pub.dev/packages/pigeon

Let's create a basic example of using Dart's Foreign Function Interface (FFI) in a Flutter application to see how many steps you need to take.

Creating a "Hello World" example using Dart FFI in a Flutter application involves several steps. This example will demonstrate calling a simple C function that returns a "Hello, World!" string from Dart. We'll go through the process step by step.

Step 1: Write the C Function

First, you must create a C file containing the function you want to call from Flutter.

```c
// **hello_world.c**
const char* hello_world() {
    return "Hello, World!";
}
```

Step 2: Compile the C Code to a Shared Library

Next, compile this C file into a shared library. The command varies based on your operating system. For instance, on Linux or macOS, you can use:

```
// Mac
clang -dynamiclib -o libhello_world.dylib hello_world.c
// Linux
gcc -shared -fPIC -o libhello_world.so hello_world.c
// Windows
gcc -shared -o hello_world.dll hello_world.c
```

This command will generate a shared library file named `libhello_world.dylib` on Mac, `libhello_world.so` on Linux, or `hello_world.dll` on Windows.

At this point, you must add this library to the platform, which varies from platform to platform. Always consult with Flutter documentation for proper steps. I am going to write steps for macOS

1- Open the `yourapp/macos/Runner.xcworkspace` in Xcode.

2- Drag your precompiled library (`libhello_world.dylib`) into `Runner/Frameworks`.

3- Click `Runner` and go to the `Build Phases` tab.

- Drag `libhello_world.dylib` into the `Copy Bundle Resources` list.
- Under `Embed Libraries`, check `Code Sign on Copy`.
- Under `Link Binary With Libraries`, set the status to `Optional`. (We use dynamic linking, no need to statically link.)

4- Click `Runner` and go to the `General` tab.

- Drag `libhello_world.dylib` into the **Frameworks, Libraries, and Embedded Content** list.

- Select **Embed and Sign**.

5- Click **Runner** and go to the **Build Settings** tab.

- In the **Search Paths** section, configure the **Library Search Paths** to include the path where `libhello_world.dylib` is located.

You can check docs.flutter.dev/platform-integration for other platforms.

Step 3: Create Dart FFI Bindings

In your Flutter project, create a Dart file to set up the FFI bindings to your C function. You also need to add `ffi` package to your Flutter project.

```dart
// **lib/hello_world_bindings.dart**
import 'dart:ffi';
import 'package:ffi/ffi.dart';

typedef HelloWorldFunc = Pointer<Utf8> Function();
typedef HelloWorld = Pointer<Utf8> Function();

class HelloWorldBindings {
  HelloWorldBindings()
      : _lib = DynamicLibrary.open('libhello_world.dylib');
  final DynamicLibrary _lib;

  String helloWorld() {
    final HelloWorld helloWorld = _lib
        .lookup<NativeFunction<HelloWorldFunc>>(
            'hello_world')
        .asFunction();
    return helloWorld().toDartString();
  }
}
```

Step 4: Use the FFI Function in Your Flutter App

Now, you can use the FFI binding in your Flutter app.

```dart
// lib/main.dart
import 'package:flutter/material.dart';
import 'hello_world_bindings.dart';

void main() {
  final helloWorldBindings = HelloWorldBindings();
  runApp(
    const MyApp(
      helloWorldBindings: helloWorldBindings,
    ),
```

```
    );
}

class MyApp extends StatelessWidget {
  const MyApp({super.key, this.helloWorldBindings});

  final HelloWorldBindings helloWorldBindings;

  @override
  Widget build(BuildContext context) {
    final message = helloWorldBindings.helloWorld();
    return MaterialApp(
      home: Scaffold(
        body: Center(
          child: Text(message),
        ),
      ),
    );
  }
}
```

Step 5: Run Your Flutter App

Run your Flutter application. The app will use Dart FFI to call the native
`hello_world` function, and you should see "Hello, World!" displayed on the
screen.

There are a few things you need to keep in mind.

- Ensure the shared library (`libhello_world.dylib` or its equivalent on your
  OS) is placed correctly where Dart FFI can access it.
- Integrating the shared library might differ slightly depending on your target
  platform (iOS, Android, macOS, Windows, Linux).
- Always follow the steps to add correctly to each platform by consulting
  docs.flutter.dev/platform-integration
- For iOS and Android, specific configurations are needed to include the native
  library in the build process.

Indeed, using Dart FFI in Flutter to interface with native C functions, as demonstrated in the "Hello World" example, can be intricate and laborious. It involves
multiple steps, like writing native code, compiling it into a shared library, and manually writing the bindings in Dart. While powerful, this process can be daunting
and error-prone, especially for developers unfamiliar with native development or
the nuances of inter-language communication.

The Flutter team has developed two significant tools to simplify and streamline
this process: FFIgen and JNIgen.

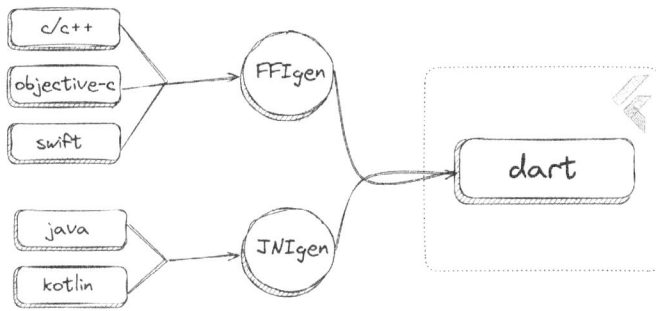

Figure 3.3: FFigen and JNIgen for easier Dart interoperability

3.3 FFIgen

FFIgen[3] automates the creation of Dart FFI bindings. By parsing C header files, it generates Dart code to interface with the C functions directly, dramatically reducing the manual effort and potential for errors. This tool is handy for more extensive C libraries or when you need to update bindings frequently.

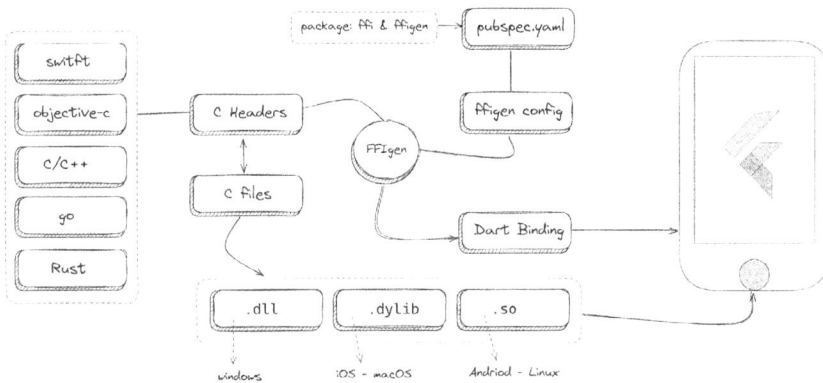

Figure 3.4: FFIgen in nutshell

As for the hello work example above, rewrite it with FFIgen.

Step 1: Write the C Function and Header

First, write your C function along with a header file.

---

[3]https://pub.dev/packages/ffigen

```
// **hello_world.c**
#include "hello_world.h"

const char* hello_world() {
    return "Hello, World!";
}
```

hello_world.h

```
#ifndef HELLO_WORLD_H
#define HELLO_WORLD_H

const char* hello_world();

#endif // HELLO_WORLD_H
```

Step 2: Compile the C Code to a Shared Library

Next, compile this C file into a shared library. The command varies based on your operating system. After that, add the library to the platform. This step is the same as before, as mentioned in the previous example.

Step 3: Add dependencies and configuration

Add `ffigen` package to your Flutter project's dev dependencies and `ffi` to your dependencies `pubspec.yaml`then add configurations to Pubspec File:

```
ffigen:
  output: 'lib/FFIgen/hello_world_bindings.dart'
  headers:
    entry-points:
      - 'hello_world.h'
```

This configuration tells FFIgen to generate Dart bindings from `hello_world.h` and put them in `lib/FFIgen/hello_world_bindings.dart`.

Step 3: Run FFIgen

Execute FFIgen to generate the bindings:

```
flutter pub run ffigen
```

This will create `hello_world_bindings.dart` with the necessary Dart code to call your C function.

```
// hello_world_bindings.dart
// AUTO GENERATED FILE, DO NOT EDIT.
//
// Generated by `package:ffigen`.
```

```
// ignore_for_file: type=lint
import 'dart:ffi' as ffi;

class NativeLibrary {
  /// Holds the symbol lookup function.
  final ffi.Pointer<T> Function<T extends ffi.NativeType>(
    String symbolName,
  ) _lookup;

  /// The symbols are looked up in [dynamicLibrary].
  NativeLibrary(ffi.DynamicLibrary dynamicLibrary)
      : _lookup = dynamicLibrary.lookup;

  /// The symbols are looked up with [lookup].
  NativeLibrary.fromLookup(
      ffi.Pointer<T> Function<T extends ffi.NativeType>(
        String symbolName,
      ) lookup)
      : _lookup = lookup;

  ffi.Pointer<ffi.Char> hello_world() {
    return _hello_world();
  }

  late final _hello_worldPtr = _lookup<
      ffi.NativeFunction<ffi.Pointer<ffi.Char> Function()>>(
    'hello_world',
  );
  late final _hello_world = _hello_worldPtr
      .asFunction<ffi.Pointer<ffi.Char> Function()>();
}
```

Step 4: Use the FFI Function in Your Flutter App and run the app

Now, you can use the generated bindings in your app.

```
// lib/main.dart
import 'dart:ffi';
import 'dart:io';

import 'package:ffi/ffi.dart';
import 'package:flutter/material.dart';
import 'FFIgen/hello_world_bindings.dart';

void main() {
  runApp(MyApp());
}

class MyApp extends StatelessWidget {
```

```
MyApp({super.key});

final nativeLibrary = NativeLibrary(
  DynamicLibrary.open(
    Platform.isMacOS ? 'libhello_world.dylib' : '',
  ),
);

@override
Widget build(BuildContext context) {
  final helloWorld = nativeLibrary.hello_world();
  // Convert the Pointer<Char> to a Dart String
  final String stringHelloWorld =
      helloWorld.cast<Utf8>().toDartString();

  return MaterialApp(
    home: Scaffold(
      body: Center(
        child: Text(
          'lib.hello_world(): $stringHelloWorld',
        ),
      ),
    ),
  );
}
}
```

There's an important point to note, which is relevant when writing this book. Certain conversions, such as transforming a Pointer<Char> into a Dart string, must be done manually.

```
final helloWorld = nativeLibrary.hello_world();
final String stringHelloWorld =
    helloWorld.cast<Utf8>().toDartString();
```

This may change later as the FFIgen is under active development.

Overall, consider the scenario where you're dealing with a substantial library. In such a case, the role of FFIgen in streamlining your work could be immensely beneficial.

lib.hello_world(): Hello, World!

Figure 3.5: Output of FFIgen

3.4 JNIgen (Java Native Interface Generator)

JNIgen[4] serves a similar purpose to Java. It facilitates Dart and Java code communication, allowing Flutter apps to access Java libraries and Android-specific functionalities more efficiently. JNIgen automates the generation of Dart-JNI bindings, making it more straightforward to leverage Java code within Flutter apps.

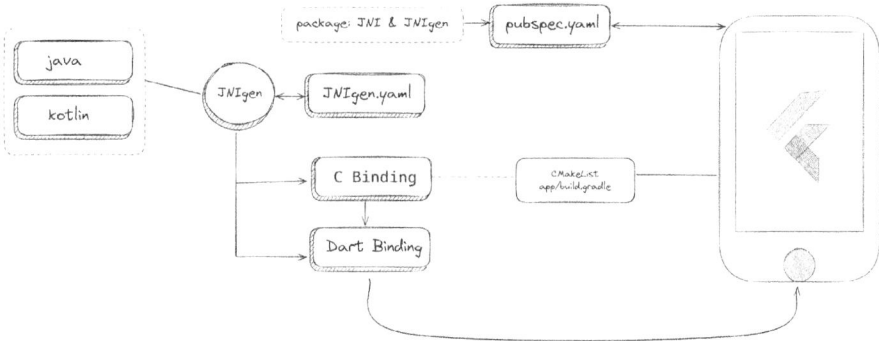

Figure 3.6: JNIgen in nutshell

3.5 Conclusion

Flutter's integration with native platforms is achieved primarily through Platform Channels and Dart FFI. Platform Channels bridge the gap between Dart and native platform code, allowing Flutter apps to communicate with the underlying platform. Dart FFI enables applications to interact with native C APIs. Tools

---

[4]https://pub.dev/packages/jnigen

like Pigeon, FFIgen, and JNIgen simplify the process of creating bindings and facilitating communication between Dart and native code.

CHAPTER 4

Applying Engineering Principles in Flutter

Reviewers: Anna Leushchenko, Oleksandr Leushchenko

The foundation of many robust software developments, including frameworks like Flutter, is deeply rooted in Object-Oriented Programming (OOP) and general software engineering principles. Understanding these core concepts is important for creating resilient and efficient applications.

Through my years of assisting developers in learning various aspects of software development, I've observed a recurring theme: many questions and challenges arise from a need for more solid grounding in foundational principles. Therefore, it's essential to invest time in mastering these fundamental concepts. Doing so makes it easier to tackle more complex topics in the future and enhances your understanding of the frameworks you use, like Flutter.

Building on the insights from Chapter 1, this chapter delves into how the concept of 'shifting left' applies to software development and your learning and life journey. Embracing this approach means investing more time upfront in understanding and (re)learning foundational principles. This early investment in mastering core concepts like Object-Oriented Programming and software engineering, especially in frameworks like Flutter, sets the stage for a smoother journey. By solidifying your grasp on these basics, you'll be better equipped to comprehend more complex topics, making future learning and development endeavors significantly more manageable and efficient.

Let's explore how Flutter utilizes these foundational principles and how they contribute to more effective application development.

4.1 OOP Analysis

Flutter's design is inherently synergistic with OOP principles. This analysis aims to showcase how Flutter leverages the power of Dart's OOP features to offer a more structured, modular, and scalable approach to app development. We'll examine the intricacies of defining classes, objects, and their interactions, which are foundational for building Flutter applications that are aesthetically pleasing and functionally robust.

Before we start, let's answer this question: **What is OOP?**

OOP is a method of structuring and designing flexible, natural, well-crafted, and testable applications. It's centered around objects that interact cleanly with each other. The process begins with identifying classes based on application requirements. These classes represent the entities and concepts of the application, each with distinct responsibilities. OOP emphasizes the logical separation of these responsibilities to minimize overlap, adhering to the principle of separation of concerns.

In OOP, no class exists in isolation; understanding how classes relate to one another is crucial. These relationships determine how objects derived from the classes collaborate to fulfill the application's functionalities. A key aim of OOP is to enhance code reusability by extracting common features among classes into separate, reusable classes. This approach not only shortens development time but also contributes to creating more robust applications.

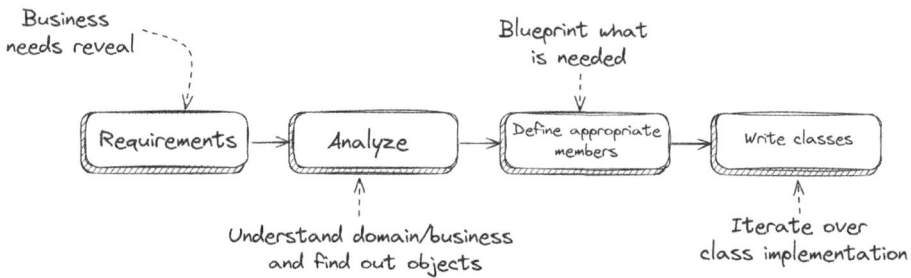

Figure 4.1: The process to define a class members

Developing in the OOP style is an iterative process. It often involves identifying classes, assigning and re-evaluating their responsibilities, and refining their inter-relationships. This cyclical nature allows continuous improvement and adaptation of the application's structure to new requirements and challenges.

4.1.1 Objects, Classes, and Inheritance

In OOP, the terms "object" and "class" are fundamental but distinct. A class is a blueprint or code that defines properties (like `emailAddress` and `firstName`) and methods (like `validate`). These elements collectively define what members a class has and provide a structure for a specific type of object. For instance, a Customer class might be designed to handle customer-related data and operations.

In Dart, the concept of classes is central to its design. Classes are essentially user-defined data types encapsulating data and behavior, serving as templates for creating objects. Every class in Dart, except the `Null` class, inherits from the `Object` class. This inheritance pattern reinforces that almost everything in Dart can be treated as an `Object`.

When discussing objects in Dart, they refer to specific instances of classes, embodying the unique state and behavior defined in their class blueprint. Creating an object in Dart means bringing a class to life, together with its properties (state) and methods (behavior).

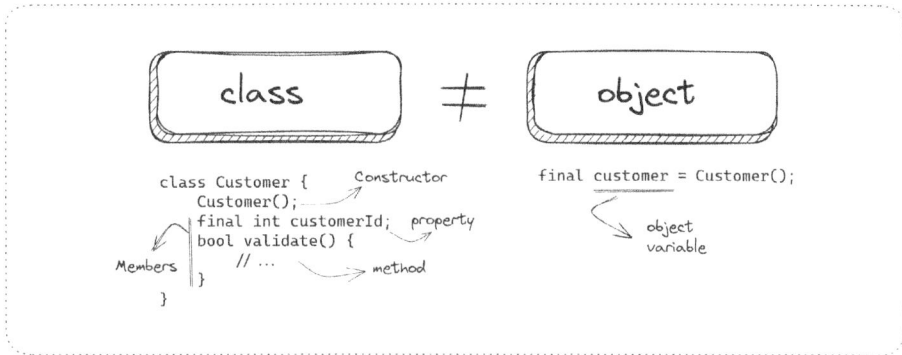

Figure 4.2: class vs object

A common question in Dart relates to using functions and how they fit into the OOP framework. In Dart, functions themselves are objects and belong to the `Function` type. This characteristic allows functions to be treated like any other object: they can be assigned to variables, passed as arguments, or even have their own methods.

Furthermore, Dart supports "callable" classes. By implementing a `call()` method in a class, you enable instances of that class to be invoked as if they were functions.

Consider the following example:

```dart
class WannabeFunction {
  String call(String a, String b, String c) => '$a $b $c!';
}

void main() {
  final wf = WannabeFunction();
  final output = wf('Hello', 'there,', 'world');

  print(output); // Output: 'Hello there, world!'
}
```

In this example, `WannabeFunction` class defines a `call()` method. When an instance of this class (`wf`) is called with arguments, it behaves like a function, concatenating the provided strings with spaces and an exclamation mark.

This functionality illustrates the flexibility of Dart's approach to OOP, where the lines between objects and functions blur, offering a more dynamic and fluid programming experience. To explore these concepts, one can look into the Dart

SDK's `sdk/lib/core`[1] repository.

Inheritance

Inheritance is a fundamental concept in object-oriented programming, allowing subclasses to derive properties and methods from superclasses. This approach enhances code reuse, improves readability, and establishes a hierarchical structure for managing complex software systems.

In Dart, inheritance is facilitated using the `extends` keyword. Through this, a subclass can extend a superclass, thereby inheriting its properties and methods. Dart's model supports single inheritance, meaning a class can inherit from only one superclass at a time.

However, Dart also allows for multilevel inheritance, where a class can inherit from a superclass that itself is a subclass of another class. This creates a chain of inheritance extending to the `Object` class, the root of all Dart classes. All classes inherit from the `Object` **implicitly** even if there is no `extends Object` code written.

A subclass in Dart can access and utilize the methods and properties of its superclass through the `super` keyword. Additionally, subclasses can override inherited methods to provide specialized behavior. This is typically indicated with the `@override` annotation, signifying that the subclass method intentionally replaces a method from its superclass. This mechanism is key for extending and customizing functionality in a controlled and readable manner.

Flutter extensively utilizes Dart's inheritance model. For instance, the `RenderObject` class hierarchy in Flutter is a prime example of inheritance.

```
abstract class RenderObject {...}

abstract class RenderBox extends RenderObject {...}

class RenderFlex extends RenderBox {...} //<---
```

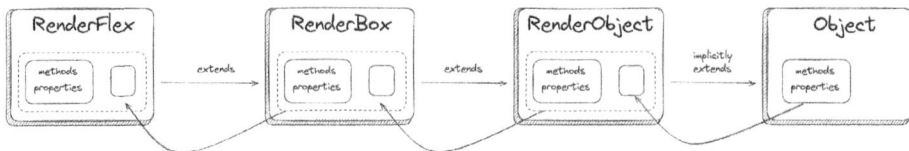

Figure 4.3: RenderFlex inheritance

In the upcoming section, we'll delve into using the `abstract` keyword. But first, let's examine an intriguing aspect of how Flutter utilizes inheritance, particularly in the `Flex` widget, creating a `RenderObject` from `RenderFlex`.

---

[1] https://github.com/dart-lang/sdk/tree/main/sdk/lib/core

```dart
class Flex extends MultiChildRenderObjectWidget {
// Rest of the code
  @override
  RenderFlex createRenderObject(BuildContext context) {
    return RenderFlex(...) //<---
    }

  @override
    void updateRenderObject(
        BuildContext context,
        covariant RenderFlex renderObject, //<---
    ) {}
// Rest of the code
}
```

An interesting detail to note is the use of the covariant keyword in the updateRenderObject method:

```dart
abstract class RenderObjectWidget extends Widget {
  void updateRenderObject(
    BuildContext context,
    covariant RenderObject renderObject,//<---
  ) {}

  //
}

abstract class MultiChildRenderObjectWidget
    extends RenderObjectWidget {
  //
}

class Flex extends MultiChildRenderObjectWidget {
  @override
  void updateRenderObject(
    BuildContext context,
    covariant RenderFlex renderObject,//<---
  ) {
    //
  }

  //
}
```

Here, the covariant keyword is used to refine the parameter type in the overridden method. In Dart, covariant allows a subclass to specify a parameter type that is more specific than the one in its superclass. This feature enhances type safety and precision in methods that are overridden.

To illustrate how this might be applied in your Flutter app, let's explore Flutter's implementation of inheritance and the `covariant` keyword in widget gesture handling. We'll focus on two widgets as examples: `DraggableWidget` and `TapWidget`.

```dart
abstract class Gesture {}

class DragGesture extends Gesture {}

class TapGesture extends Gesture {}

abstract class CustomGestureWidget {
  void handleGesture(covariant Gesture gesture);
}

class DraggableWidget extends StatelessWidget
    implements CustomGestureWidget {
  const DraggableWidget({
    super.key,
    required DragGesture gesture,
  });
  @override
  void handleGesture(covariant DragGesture gesture) {
    // ...
  }
  // ...
}

class TapWidget extends StatelessWidget
    implements CustomGestureWidget {
  const TapWidget({
    super.key,
    required TapGesture gesture,
  });
  @override
  void handleGesture(covariant TapGesture gesture) {
    // ...
  }

  // ...
}
```

In this example, `DraggableWidget` and `TapWidget` implement `CustomGestureWidget` and override the `handleGesture` method to handle specific gestures, utilizing the `covariant` keyword for precise type specification.

4.1.2 Polymorphism via Widgets

Polymorphism in object-oriented programming allows objects from different classes to be treated under a standard interface. It enables methods to perform differently based on the object's class. In Dart, polymorphism is achieved by declaring subclass methods with the same name and signature as in the base class but with different implementations. They should be annotated with @override annotation for better readability.

```dart
abstract class Animal {
  void makeSound();
}

class Dog extends Animal {
  @override
  void makeSound() {
    print('Bark!');
  }
}

class Cat extends Animal {
  @override
  void makeSound() {
    print('Meow!');
  }
}

void main() {
  final List<Animal> animals = [Dog(), Cat()];

  for (final animal in animals) {
    animal.makeSound();  // Polymorphism in action
  }
}
```

There are many examples in Flutter for polymorphism such as:

```dart
class ScrollPhysics {
//...
  ScrollPhysics applyTo(
    ScrollPhysics? ancestor,
  ) {
    return ScrollPhysics(
      parent: buildParent(ancestor),
    );
  }
//...
}
```

```
class BouncingScrollPhysics extends ScrollPhysics {
//...
  @override
  BouncingScrollPhysics applyTo(
    ScrollPhysics? ancestor,
  ) {
    return BouncingScrollPhysics(
      parent: buildParent(ancestor),
      decelerationRate: decelerationRate,
    );
  }
//...
}

class ClampingScrollPhysics extends ScrollPhysics {
//..
  @override
  ClampingScrollPhysics applyTo(
    ScrollPhysics? ancestor,
  ) {
    return ClampingScrollPhysics(
      parent: buildParent(ancestor),
    );
  }
//...
}
```

In the context of Flutter, all widgets are classes that inherit from the `Widget` class. The `Widget` class itself has a `build` method, and this method is meant to be overridden by subclasses, i.e., concrete widgets you use, to define the specific UI elements that the widget represents.

4.1.3   Encapsulation in Dart

Encapsulation is a fundamental concept in object-oriented programming, including in Dart, the language commonly used with Flutter. Encapsulation bundles the data (variables) and the methods (functions) that manipulate the data into a single unit or class.

It also involves restricting access to the inner workings of that class, which is a key aspect of achieving data hiding and abstraction. Here's how encapsulation works in Dart:

Defining Class and Members

In Dart OOP, you encapsulate by creating a class. This class includes fields (data) and methods (functions operating on the data).

Access Modifiers

Dart uses implicit access modifiers to control visibility. By default, all members of a class in Dart are **public**. If you want to make a member private, you prefix it with an underscore (_). Private makes it hidden from access.

```dart
class Person {
  String? _firstName;
  String? _lastName;
  String get name => '$_firstName $_lastName';
}
```

It's interesting to know that class can also be made private using underscore symbol as a name prefix (_); consider a common scenario where you have a state object like _MyHomePageState:

```dart
class MyHomePage extends StatefulWidget {
  @override
  State<MyHomePage> createState() => _MyHomePageState();
}

class _MyHomePageState extends State<MyHomePage> {
  ...
}
```

Private members in a library (file) are only accessible within the same library (file).

Getters and Setters

Dart offers getters and setters to control access to the properties of a class. Getters and setters are particular methods that provide read and write access to an object's properties. This way, you can implement data validation, logging, and other logic inside these methods.

```dart
class User {
    String? _email;

    String get email => _email ?? ''; // Getter

    set email(String value) { // Setter
        if (value.contains('@')) {
            _email = value;
        }
    }
}
```

Constructor

Constructors in Dart initialize the class's properties when an object is created. They can also enforce specific rules or conditions upon object creation, contributing to encapsulation.

Private Constructors

In Dart, a private constructor is created by prefixing the constructor's name with an underscore (_). It's a technique used to restrict the instantiation of a class to within the class itself or the same library. This is particularly useful in scenarios like implementing the Singleton pattern (don't stress if you don't understand what singleton is. We will talk about patterns in Chapter 5), where control over instance creation is crucial.

```
class Singleton {
  // Private constructor with a specific name
  Singleton._internal();

  static final Singleton instance = Singleton._internal();
}
```

In this example, `Singleton._internal()` is a private named constructor. The underscore before `internal` indicates that it's private, and the specific name (`_internal`) is just a convention and can be any name you choose. Even `_` is a valid name: you can omit the name and do `Singleton._()`.

To access the singleton instance, you can use `Singleton.instance`. To ensure that every instance creation returns the same object instance, you can add a factory constructor:

```
class Singleton {
  Singleton._internal(); // Private constructor

  static final Singleton instance = Singleton._internal();

  factory Singleton() => instance; // Factory constructor
}
```

The `Singleton()` factory constructor returns the same class `instance` with this setup. This pattern is ideal in Dart for maintaining a single class instance across the entire application, ensuring consistency and controlling resource usage.

4.1.4   Abstraction In Dart

Abstraction in OOP is a key concept that simplifies complex systems by modeling classes based on real-world entities. Abstraction enables cleaner, more understandable, and maintainable code by separating the 'what' from the 'how.'

One primary way to achieve abstraction in OOP is through interfaces. Interfaces serve as contracts or blueprints for a class, defining a set of methods the class must implement. They enable different classes to have different implementations of the same set of behaviors, promoting flexibility and scalability in software design.

```
abstract class Clickable {
  void onClick();
}


class CustomIconButton extends Clickable {
  @override
  void onClick() {
    // Specific implementation for CustomIconButton
  }
}
```

To delve further into this concept, it's important to note that in Dart, any class can inherently act as an interface. This capability guarantees that various widgets conform to a predetermined structure or agreement.

```
class Clickable {
  void onClick() {} // with concrete implementation
}

class CustomIconButton implements Clickable {
  @override
  void onClick() {
    // Specific implementation for CustomIconButton
  }
}

// Inherit OnClick from parent
class CustomIconButton2 extends Clickable {}
```

In Dart and Flutter, the concepts of extends and implements are fundamental to understanding object-oriented programming and design patterns.

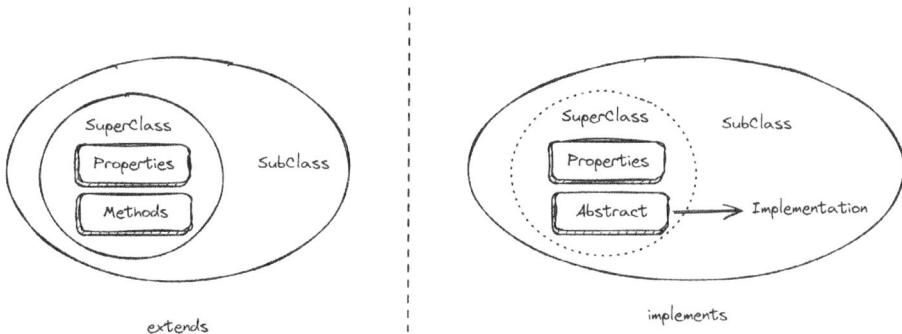

Figure 4.4: Class Inheritance vs Class Implementation Relationship

Let's explore the differences:

- **Extends**: The `extends` keyword is used when a class derives from another class, known as the parent or superclass. By using `extends`, the child class inherits all the properties, methods, and behaviors of the parent class. It's a code reuse mechanism and builds a hierarchical relationship between classes. In Flutter, this is commonly observed when custom widgets extend foundational widgets like `StatelessWidget` or `StatefulWidget`, thereby inheriting their functionalities and features.
- **Implements**: Conversely, `implements` is used when a class declares that it will adopt the contract (i.e., all the methods and properties) defined by another class or interface. However, unlike `extends`, `implements` don't inherit the implementation of the methods. Instead, it mandates that the implementing class provide its version of those methods. This approach is crucial for enforcing consistency and adherence to a defined contract or API, which is particularly useful in creating custom components that must follow a specific interface, as demonstrated in the `Clickable` example.

Additionally, Dart allows for abstraction by using the `abstract` class modifier. An `abstract` class is a class that can't be instantiated directly and often includes abstract methods (without implementation). It serves as a template for other classes, compelling them to implement the abstract methods and adhere to a specific design structure. This is another way to enforce a contract among different classes, ensuring they provide specific functionalities as defined by the abstract class.

```
abstract class Drawable {
  // abstract method without concrete implementation
  void draw();
}


class Circle implements Drawable {
  @override
  void draw() {
    // Implementation of draw method
  }
}
```

In the example mentioned, we establish a contract using abstract methods without implementation (no method body). When employing the `implements` keyword, it becomes necessary to provide a concrete implementation for each of these methods, tailored to the specific requirements of the use case.

This practice exemplifies an effective strategy for scaling and is extensively utilized in Flutter development. Let's explore an example that might be more relatable or familiar in this context.

```
abstract class ThemeStrategy {
  ThemeData getTheme();
}
```

```
class LightThemeStrategy implements ThemeStrategy {
  @override
  ThemeData getTheme() => ThemeData.light();
}

class DarkThemeStrategy implements ThemeStrategy {
  @override
  ThemeData getTheme() => ThemeData.dark();
}
```

In the earlier example, we introduced an abstract method with a concrete implementation, representing another design pattern using abstract classes. Here, using the `implements` keyword, a child class inherits the concrete implementation from the parent class. This allows the child to focus solely on implementing the abstract methods without providing full implementations for all inherited methods. This technique helps modify or extend the behavior in the child's class.

Abstract classes cannot be instantiated from their library or external libraries. One may question if there's an alternative approach to this.

New Interface Modifier vs. Abstract Keyword in Dart

In Dart 3.0, several new class modifiers have been introduced, including the notable `interface` class modifier. Let's explore this in detail:

- **Interface Modifier**: Dart's recent update includes the `interface` modifier, providing a more apparent distinction between the definition of an interface and its implementation. When you declare a class with the `interface` keyword, it is meant to be implemented rather than extended. This ensures that when an instance method of such a class calls another instance method on `this`, it consistently invokes a known implementation from the same library. In Dart programming language, a "library" refers to a collection of code that provides reusable and modular functionality. Dart libraries organize and package code into logical units, making managing and maintaining large-scale applications easier. Inside the library, classes declared with the "interface" keyword behave the same as plain old classes; however, outside the library, they can not be extended. This is extremely useful when working on SDKs or other utility codes. This approach effectively mitigates the fragile base class problem[2] by preventing other libraries from overriding methods in ways that could lead to unexpected behaviors.

```
interface class Thinker {
  int answer() => 42;
}
```

---

[2]https://en.wikipedia.org/wiki/Fragile_base_class

```
// this line will not compile outside
// of the library where Thinker is declared
class MyThinker extends Thinker {}

// always valid
class WrongThinker implements Thinker {
  @override
  int answer() => 5;
}
```

- **Abstract Keyword**: The `abstract` keyword is still used to define abstract classes that combine implemented and non-implemented methods. Abstract classes can be extended or implemented but cannot be instantiated. They are ideal for scenarios where a class only requires a partial, concrete implementation of its entire interface. Remember, abstract classes cannot be instantiated from their library or an external library. They often include abstract methods that lack implementation.
- **Combining Both**: An interesting approach is to combine the `abstract` and `interface` keywords to define an abstract interface. This class type can only be implemented (not extended) and includes abstract members, such as methods or properties, without implementation. This makes it particularly suitable for creating contract interfaces. The interface modifier's most common application is defining a pure interface. When you combine the `interface` and `abstract` modifiers, you get an abstract interface class from which other libraries can implement but not inherit. Like an abstract class, a pure interface can contain abstract members.

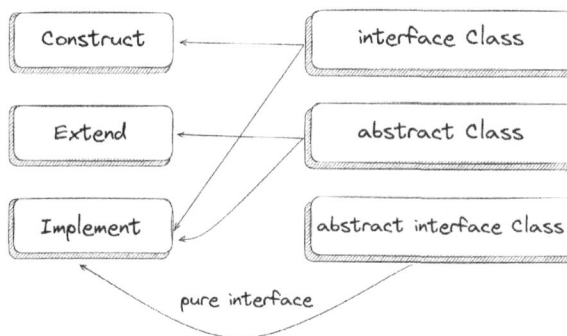

Figure 4.5: Pure interface via abstract interface class modifiers

Let's delve into an example of a pure interface within the Flutter framework, a context that should be familiar to many.

```
// Pure interface for a data fetching service
abstract interface class DataService {
```

```
  Future<String> fetchData();
}

// Implementation of DataService for
// fetching data from a network API
class NetworkDataService implements DataService {
  @override
  Future<String> fetchData() async {
    // Implement network request logic here
    return 'Data from network';
  }
}

// Implementation of DataService
// for fetching mock data (useful for testing)
class MockDataService implements DataService {
  @override
  Future<String> fetchData() async {
    return 'Mock data';
  }
}
```

In a typical Flutter application, you might inject the appropriate `DataService` implementation depending on your needs. For example, you might use `NetworkDataService` in production and `MockDataService` during testing.

This approach offers several benefits:

1. **Flexibility**: You can easily switch between different data sources without changing the consuming code.
2. **Testability**: It's more accessible to test components using a mock data service implementation.
3. **Maintainability**: The application's data fetching logic is more organized and easier to maintain.

This pattern of using an abstract class as a pure interface is one aspect of scalable and maintainable app development in Flutter.

4.1.5   The Power of Mixins in Flutter

Mixins in Dart offer a robust feature set frequently utilized by Flutter developers, particularly in animation contexts. A prime example is the `SingleTickerProviderStateMixin`, commonly used in Flutter projects. Here's an elementary demonstration of its usage:

```
// ...
class ExampleState extends State<Example>
```

```
  with SingleTickerProviderStateMixin {
  late AnimationController controller;
  @override
  void initState() {
    super.initState();
    controller = AnimationController(
      duration: Duration(),
// Adding SingleTickerProviderStateMixin mixin to
// the ExampleState enabled us to pass `this` as
// a vsync parameter of AnimationController
// constructor, which expects an instance
// of TickerProvider class.
      vsync: this,
    );
  }
  // ...
}
```

The `SingleTickerProviderStateMixin` is notable for its utilization of the `with` keyword, along with the incorporation of `on` and `implements`:

```
// packages/flutter/lib/src/widgets/ticker_provider.dart
mixin SingleTickerProviderStateMixin<
       T extends StatefulWidget> on State<T>
   implements TickerProvider {
// ...
}
```

```
// packages/flutter/lib/src/scheduler/ticker.dart
abstract class TickerProvider {
  const TickerProvider();
  @factory
  Ticker createTicker(TickerCallback onTick);
}
```

In Dart, mixins serve as a mechanism for code reuse, offering more flexibility than traditional inheritance. They enable adding functionalities to a class without necessitating inheritance, a significant advantage in Dart's single inheritance model.

Principal Concepts of Mixins in Dart

1. **Mixin Creation**: Mixins are crafted using the `mixin` keyword, akin to class creation but specifically for integration into other classes.
2. **Utilization of Mixins with `with`**: The `with` keyword facilitates the horizontal addition of a mixin's features to a class, contrasting with vertical extension in traditional inheritance.

3. **Mixin Usage Restriction with** on: The on keyword defines the classes into which a mixin can be integrated, allowing for controlled application and prevention of misuse.

4. **Interface Implementation**: Mixins can implement interfaces (remember, in Dart, every class is an implicit interface), ensuring interface requirements are met.

Consider the following example, which introduces two mixins, ServiceLoggerMixin and WidgetLoggerMixin, both implementing a Logger interface:

```
abstract class Logger {
  void log(String message);
}

mixin ServiceLoggerMixin implements Logger {
  @override
  void log(String message) {
    debugPrint('Service: $message');
  }
}

mixin WidgetLoggerMixin on Widget implements Logger {
  @override
  void log(String message) {
    debugPrint('Widget: $message');
  }
}
```

These mixins can be applied in Flutter as follows:

```
class MyWidget extends StatefulWidget with WidgetLogger {}

class _MyWidgetState extends State<MyWidget>
with SingleTickerProviderStateMixin, ServiceLoggerMixin {
  // ...
  @override
  void initState() {
    log('initState'); // provided by ServiceLogger mixin
    // Output: flutter: Service: initState
  }
  // ...
}
```

Dart 3.0 introduces specific mixin constraints to foster cleaner, more predictable code:

- Mixins are prohibited from having constructor, simplifying object creation.

- They are disallowed from including an extends clause, underscoring their role as feature additions rather than base classes.

Introducing the `mixin` class modifier in Dart 3.0 introduces a new approach to defining and using mixins. This modifier explicitly designates a mixin, distinguishing it from regular classes and interfaces, thereby clarifying code intentions and appropriate usage.

Expanding on the `ServiceLoggerMixin` example demonstrates the `mixin` class modifier's application:

```
mixin class ServiceLoggerMixinClass implements Logger {
  @override
  void log(String message) {
    debugPrint('ServiceClass: $message');
  }
}
```

Mixin classes are subject to the same restrictions as mixins and classes:

- Neither mixins nor mixin classes can contain `extends` or `with` clauses.
- Classes and mixin classes cannot include an `on` clause.

The `mixin` class modifier, combined with other modifiers like `abstract`, offers enhanced flexibility. For instance, an abstract mixin class can mimic the `on` directive:

```
abstract mixin class ServiceLoggerAbstractMixinClass {
  void log(String message);

  void toPrint() {
    if (kDebugMode) { // only in debug mode.
      print('ClassName: ${objectRuntimeType(this, '')}');
    }
  }
}
```

Application examples include:

```
class CustomWidget extends StatelessWidget
    with ServiceLoggerAbstractMixinClass {
  CustomWidget({super.key}) {
    toPrint(); // from abstract mixin class
  }

  @override
  Widget build(BuildContext context) {
```

```
    log('build');

    return Container();
  }

  @override
  void log(String message) {
    debugPrint('CustomWidget: $message');
  }
}
```

Moreover, it can be used with the `extends` method:

```
class CustomServiceLoggerAbstractMixinClass
    extends ServiceLoggerAbstractMixinClass {
  @override
  void log(String message) {
    // Implementation details
  }
}
```

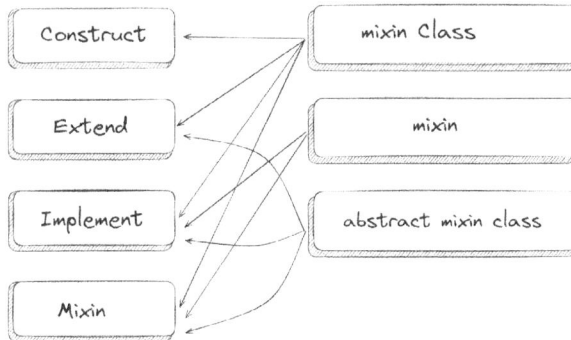

Figure 4.6: abstract mixin class

In summary, integrating modifiers and mixins in Dart significantly enhances the flexibility and power of adding functionalities to Flutter in a streamlined manner.

4.2 Implementing Classic Software Principles

As you may have realized, OOP plays a crucial role in software development, particularly with Dart and Flutter. However, the journey doesn't end there. In software engineering, there are additional principles that you might or might not have applied in your daily practice. Drawing inspiration from the framework,

Flutter engineers should leverage these principles to create more robust applications. These applications will perform better and be more accessible to maintain over time. Let's dive in.

4.2.1 KISS (Keep It Simple, Stupid)

In software engineering, the KISS principle, "Keep It Simple, Stupid," is a fundamental design guideline emphasizing the value of simplicity. This principle has been widely adopted in programming, advocating for straightforward, uncomplicated solutions over complex ones. In software development, complexity often introduces a higher risk of errors, makes code more difficult to understand and maintain, and can lead to greater resource consumption. Therefore, applying KISS means creating efficient, easy-to-understand, and managed solutions.

To effectively apply KISS in Flutter development, it's advisable to focus on reusing widgets and writing clear, concise code. Avoid premature optimization, as it often leads to unnecessary complexities. Code should be readable and easily understood, with short and specific methods. Regular refactoring is also important to identify and eliminate any creeping complexities. Utilize Flutter's extensive range of built-in widgets and functionalities to avoid reinventing the wheel. Lastly, seeking peer feedback can be invaluable in spotting and simplifying overly complex code segments.

The key takeaway is that simpler solutions are often more effective, especially in a framework like Flutter, where readability and maintainability are crucial for long-term project health. Over-engineering often manifests through unnecessarily complex solutions for simple tasks, adding speculative features not needed in the current stage, or implementing excessive abstraction. Other indicators include constant refactoring without substantial benefits and declining code readability and maintainability. Refrain from over-engineering.

4.2.2 SOLID Principles in Flutter

The SOLID principles are guidelines for object-oriented programming that aim to make software designs more understandable, flexible, and maintainable. Let's explore how these principles can be applied in the context of Flutter development.

1. Single Responsibility Principle (SRP)

This principle states that a class should have only one reason to change. Applying SRP often involves separating the responsibilities of UI widgets from business logic in the context of Flutter. Widgets should be responsible for displaying data and handling user interactions but should not contain extensive business logic or data fetching code. By separating UI widgets from the business logic class, each component has a single responsibility. Changes to the UI presentation do not impact the logic for fetching or processing data. Changes to the data-fetching logic do not affect how the UI is presented.

2. Open/Closed Principle (OCP)

Classes should be open for extension but closed for modification. This way, when the time comes to update the class behavior, it can be done without changes in the base class code, but in its descendants. This is especially important when developing distributable or utility libraries. Consider this example:

```
abstract class Shape {
  double area();
}

class Rectangle implements Shape {
  Rectangle(this.width, this.height);

  final double width;
  final double height;

  @override
  double area() { //<---
    return width * height; //<---
  }//<---
}

class Circle implements Shape {
  Circle(this.radius);

  final double radius;

  @override
  double area() { //<---
    return 3.14 * radius * radius; //<---
  } //<---
}

// usage
class AreaCalculator {
  double totalArea(List<Shape> shapes) {
    double area = 0;
    for (final shape in shapes) {
      // without knowing each shape, you can get area
      area += shape.area(); //<---
    }
    return area;
  }
}
```

3. Liskov Substitution Principle (LSP)

Objects should be replaceable with instances of their subtypes without altering the correctness of the program. In Flutter, ensure that your subclass widgets can be used wherever their parent class is expected. Flutter's StatelessWidget and `StatefulWidget` are examples of how the Liskov Substitution Principle is applied. Developers can seamlessly switch between these two types of widgets based on whether the state is needed for a particular part of the UI without affecting the overall structure of the application.

4. Interface Segregation Principle (ISP)

Clients should not be forced to depend on interfaces they do not use. In Flutter, this means designing lean and focused interfaces (or abstract classes). For instance, If you have an interface for widget interaction, don't lump unrelated methods into it. Instead, create separate interfaces for different functionalities, like `TapHandler` and `LongPressHandler`.

5. Dependency Inversion Principle (DIP)

High-level modules should be **independent** of low-level modules. Both should **depend** on **abstractions**. In Flutter, this principle guides the structuring of dependencies for more reusable and testable code. For a widget that requires a data source, depend on an abstract `DataSource` interface rather than a concrete `DatabaseDataSource`. This makes switching out data sources or mock data for testing possible.

I avoided repeating the examples as we have explored many of them in the OOP section.

Applying SOLID principles encourages the development of modular widgets, promotes reusability, and facilitates testing. While it may require more effort and forethought during the design phase, adhering to these principles ultimately leads to a more efficient and scalable development process.

4.2.3 Embracing DRY (Don't Repeat Yourself)

In software engineering, the DRY (Don't Repeat Yourself) principle is a crucial concept aimed at reducing redundancy in code. Coined by Andy Hunt and Dave Thomas in "The Pragmatic Programmer," DRY emphasizes having a single, unambiguous representation for every piece of knowledge and logic in a system. Its primary goal is to make software more maintainable, understandable, and extensible. When DRY is applied effectively, changes must be made in one place, significantly reducing the chance of typical inconsistencies and errors in redundant code.

Flutter's capability to develop multi-platform applications from a single codebase aligns with the DRY principle, enhancing efficiency and consistency across various platforms. For instance, the `Theme` class and its associated themes, like `ThemeData`, help adhere to the DRY principle by centralizing the styling information for widgets like `ElevatedButton`. Developers can define a theme once and apply it across multiple application parts, ensuring a consistent look and feel. The `ElevatedButtonTheme` widget supports the DRY principle by preventing the need to set button styles across multiple instances of `ElevatedButton` redundantly.

The key is to identify repetitive code patterns and encapsulate them into reusable widgets while also being mindful of not over-complicating the system with unnecessary abstractions.

4.2.4   YAGNI (You Aren't Gonna Need It)

YAGNI, which stands for "You Aren't Gonna Need It," is a principle that encourages developers to implement things only when they are necessary. Originating from Extreme Programming, this concept advises against adding functionality until required. The YAGNI principle is fundamental in an age where over-engineering is a common pitfall, leading to bloated, complex, and difficult-to-maintain codebases.

The core message of YAGNI is to only work on features or aspects of the project that are currently out of stock. This approach saves time and effort and keeps the focus on delivering what is essential for the project's current stage. It's about maximizing productivity and efficiency by not getting sidetracked by features or functionalities that may seem helpful in the future but have no immediate application.

Applying YAGNI in Flutter development, which involves building applications for multiple platforms from a single codebase, can be particularly impactful. Flutter's rich set of features and widgets can tempt developers to add numerous functionalities and complex UI elements that may not be immediately required.

For example, consider a Flutter app for displaying user profiles. A YAGNI-compliant approach would implement the essential features, such as displaying the user's name and contact information. On the other hand, a non-YAGNI approach might involve preemptively adding features like profile customization options or advanced analytics, even if they aren't part of the initial requirements.

Another example is implementing complex caching mechanisms or performance optimizations in parts of the application that do not experience performance issues. Engineers enjoy solving puzzles, but introducing unnecessary complexity could complicate maintenance. Remember, no code means no bugs! Having extra features requires developers to maintain them, making the app more difficult to use. Keep it simple – less is more.

By focusing only on necessities, developers can create more streamlined, efficient, and manageable applications. This approach reduces the risk of project bloat and keeps the development process focused and agile. It reminds developers to build what's needed now and not what might be required.

4.2.5   The "Tell, Don't Ask" Principle

The "Tell, Don't Ask" principle in software engineering advocates for object-oriented programming that emphasizes the importance of telling objects what to do rather than asking them for data and acting upon that data. This principle aims to enhance the encapsulation and coherence of objects by reducing the amount of information they expose about their internal states.

In practice, "Tell, Don't Ask" involves shifting from an approach where you re-trieve data from an object to make decisions (thus exposing the object's internal structure) to delegating the decision-making process to the object itself. This principle helps to maintain a clear separation of concerns, making the code more modular, easier to maintain, and less prone to errors due to incorrect manipulation of internal states.

In Flutter, which is predominantly used for UI development, "Tell, Don't Ask" can be particularly relevant when managing the state and behavior of widgets. Imagine a Flutter application widget displaying different content based on a toggle state. The widget should manage this toggle state internally rather than relying on external components to dictate its behavior.

In this non-compliant version, the widget exposes its state, and external logic is used to determine what to display:

```
class AskToggleWidget extends StatelessWidget {
  final bool isExpanded;

  AskToggleWidget({
    super.key,
    required this.isExpanded,
  });

  @override
  Widget build(BuildContext context) {
    return isExpanded
        ? Text('Expanded View')
        : Text('Collapsed View');
  }
}
```

Usage:

```
bool toggleState = false; // External state management
AskToggleWidget(toggleState: toggleState);
// External logic needed to change `toggleState`
```

In the compliant version, the widget manages its toggle state and decides internally what to display:

```
class TellToggleWidget extends StatefulWidget {
  @override
  _TellToggleWidgetState createState() =>
      _TellToggleWidgetState();
}

class _TellToggleWidgetState
```

```
    extends State<TellToggleWidget> {
  bool _isExpanded = false;

  void _toggle() {
    setState(() {
      _isExpanded = !_isExpanded;
    });
  }

  @override
  Widget build(BuildContext context) {
    return Column(
      children: [
        ElevatedButton(
          onPressed: _toggle,
          child: Text('Toggle View'),
        ),
        _isExpanded
            ? Text('Expanded View')
            : Text('Collapsed View'),
      ],
    );
  }
}
```

Usage:

```
// The widget handles its state internally.
TellToggleWidget();
```

In the "Tell, Don't Ask" compliant version, `TellToggleWidget` encapsulates the logic for toggling its view. This approach promotes better encapsulation and state management within the widget itself. The widget handles its state changes, aligning with sound object-oriented design principles and making the codebase more robust and maintainable.

Let me give you another example, which is common in Flutter apps that interact with a remote service or API. Suppose a Flutter app needs to operate a remote service, such as fetching data or triggering an action on a server. In this approach, the Flutter app makes an extra call to check if an operation is available before actually performing it:

```
class DataService {
  bool isDataAvailable() {
    // Logic to check if the operation is available
    return true; // Simulated response
  }
```

```
  Future<String?> fetchData() async {
    // Perform the operation
  }
}

class AskDataServiceWidget extends StatefulWidget {
  const AskDataServiceWidget({super.key});

  @override
  AskDataServiceWidgetState createState() =>
      AskDataServiceWidgetState();
}

class AskDataServiceWidgetState
    extends State<AskDataServiceWidget> {
  final DataService service = DataService();
  String data = 'No data yet';

  @override
  void initState() {
    super.initState();
    _fetchData();
  }

  Future<void> _fetchData() async {
    if (service.isDataAvailable()) {
      final String? fetchedData = await service.fetchData();
      if (fetchedData != null) {
        setState(() {
          data = fetchedData;
        });
      }
    }
  }

  @override
  Widget build(BuildContext context) {
    return Center(
      child: Text(data),
    );
  }
}
```

AskDataServiceWidget checks if the data is available before fetching it in this
version. This results in two separate calls: one to check availability and another
to fetch the data.

In the "Tell" approach, the Flutter app tells the service to operate. The service
internally decides whether the operation is available:

```
class DataService {
  Future<String?> fetchData() async {
    if (_isDataAvailable()) {//<---
      // Fetch and return data
      return "Fetched Data";
    }
    return null;
  }

  bool _isDataAvailable() {
    // Logic to check data availability
    return true;
  }
}
```

In the TellDataServiceWidget, the widget tells the service to fetch the data. The decision to check data availability is encapsulated within the DataService:

```
class TellDataServiceWidget extends StatefulWidget {
  const TellDataServiceWidget({super.key});

  @override
  TellDataServiceWidgetState createState() =>
      TellDataServiceWidgetState();
}

class TellDataServiceWidgetState
    extends State<TellDataServiceWidget> {
  final DataService service = DataService();
  String data = 'No data yet';

  @override
  void initState() {
    super.initState();
    _fetchData();
  }

  Future<void> _fetchData() async {
    final String? fetchedData = await service.fetchData();
    setState(() {
      data = fetchedData ?? 'No data available';
    });
  }

  @override
  Widget build(BuildContext context) {
    return Center(
      child: Text(data),
```

```
    );
  }
}
```

This makes the widget's code more focused on its primary function of displaying data. At the same time, the service handles the decision-making about data fetching, resulting in a cleaner and more maintainable code structure.

This also follows the principle of taking out the business logic from widgets responsible solely for rendering the UI. You will learn more about this concept in the Architecture part of this book.

4.3   Conclusion

This chapter has covered applying and integrating engineering principles in Flutter. We explored using OOP in Dart. We also delved into classic software principles and their relevance in Flutter development. These principles, such as DRY, SOLID, KISS, YAGNI, and "Tell, Don't Ask," guide developers toward creating more robust, efficient, and maintainable applications. Each principle offers unique insights and benefits, contributing to a more streamlined and effective development process.

Finally, the chapter highlighted the importance of these principles in the context of Flutter's multi-platform development capabilities. By embracing these principles, developers can maximize the efficiency and consistency of their Flutter applications across various platforms. As we progress, these foundational concepts will continue to play a crucial role in shaping practical and scalable Flutter applications.

CHAPTER 5

Design Patterns in Flutter

Reviewer: Mangirdas Kazlauskas

This chapter focuses on design patterns in Flutter, which are essential for efficient and scalable app development. The chapter aims to provide developers with a comprehensive understanding of various design patterns designed specifically for Flutter. Developers can write cleaner, more maintainable, reusable code using these patterns.

Initially inspired by architectural patterns, these strategies have been adapted to the software domain and gained significant attention with the influential work of the "Gang of Four" in their seminal book "Design Patterns: Elements of Reusable Object-Oriented Software." These evolving patterns have become an integral part of modern software engineering.

From exploring fundamental concepts to examining patterns like Singleton, Factory, and Observer, I provide practical insights and examples to demonstrate how these patterns can be effectively implemented in Flutter projects. Whether a beginner or an experienced Flutter developer, this chapter is a valuable guide to enhancing your app architecture and facilitating your development process.

5.1   Decoding the Role of Design Patterns

Design patterns are standardized, reusable solutions to common coding problems. They emerged due to recognizing that many problems developers face are not unique and can be solved using proven methodologies.

Patterns are broadly classified into three categories: **Creational**, dealing with object creation; **Structural**, focusing on class or object composition; and **Behavioral**, which is about object interaction and responsibility. Each category addresses specific aspects of software design and aids in organizing code in a robust and scalable manner.

Let's look at some of the most commonly used design patterns I have encountered in Flutter applications. Please note that these are not all the design patterns;

there are plenty more out there, but I have found the following patterns to be the most useful.

5.2 Creational Patterns

Creational design patterns are a set of design patterns that focus on creating objects in a manner that is appropriate for the given situation. The act of creating objects can sometimes lead to design problems or add unnecessary complexity to the overall design. Let's explore some of them.

5.2.1 Singleton

The Singleton Design Pattern is a fundamental concept in software architecture that ensures a class has only one instance and provides a global point of access to it. This pattern is crucial for controlling resources and actions that logically require a single point of operation within an application.

When to Use

Singletons are often used when controlled access to a single resource is necessary. Some common examples include:

- **Configuration Management**: Managing settings and configurations that are global to the entire application.
- **Database Connection Pools**: Ensuring there is a single point of managing database connections.
- **Logging**: Implementing a logging service that is accessible across the application.
- **State Management**: Holding application-wide state, like user sessions.

Here's a basic example of implementing a Singleton in Flutter and Dart:

```
class AppConfig {
  static final AppConfig _instance = AppConfig._internal();

  AppConfig._internal();

  factory AppConfig() => _instance;

  String appName = 'My Flutter App';
  String appVersion = '1.0.0';

  // Additional configuration settings...
}
```

In this example, `_instance` is a private static member that holds the singleton instance, and the constructor is private to prevent external instantiation.

Pitfalls

- **Overuse**: Singleton pattern can lead to overuse, as it's tempting to make many components singletons unnecessarily.
- **Unit Testing Challenges**: Due to their nature, singletons can be difficult to mock during unit tests, leading to challenges in testing components that depend on them.
- **Misinterpretation**: It's easy to mistakenly evolve a singleton into a factory pattern, especially when modifications are made to accept parameters in the `getInstance` method.

Figure 5.1: Singleton Design Pattern

Example from Flutter Framework

You may have seen `WidgetsBinding.instance`. This is one of the examples of Singleton used in the Flutter framework.

Testing Singleton in Flutter/Dart

Testing a Singleton in Flutter can be challenging due to its global state and the fact that it's often impossible to reset it between tests. However, you can make the Singleton pattern more testable by designing the singleton with testing in mind, such as allowing the injection of dependencies or using a resettable singleton for testing purposes. Here's an example:

```
class AppConfig {
  static AppConfig _instance = AppConfig._internal();

  AppConfig._internal();

  factory AppConfig() => _instance;

  // Reset the singleton, useful in tests
  @visibleForTesting
```

```
  static void reset() => _instance = AppConfig._internal();

  // Configuration settings...
}
```

With the **reset** method, you can reset the state of the Singleton in your tests, ensuring that each test starts with a clean slate.

```
void main() {
  // This setup runs
  // before each test to reset the singleton
  setUp(() {
    AppConfig.reset();
  });

  test('Singleton instance should be the same', () {
    final instance1 = AppConfig._instance;
    final instance2 = AppConfig._instance;

    // Test whether both instances are the same instance
    expect(identical(instance1, instance2), isTrue);
  });

  test('Singleton should retain its state', () {
    final instance = AppConfig.instance;
    instance.appName = 'Test App';

    // Create another reference to the singleton
    final instance2 = AppConfig.instance;

    // Test whether the second reference
    // sees the updated state
    expect(instance2.appName, 'Test App');
  });

  // Add more tests as needed
  // for different aspects of the singleton
}
```

This approach helps mitigate one of the key challenges of testing singletons in an application.

5.2.2   Factory Method

The Factory Method Design Pattern in Flutter is an excellent approach to creating objects where the exact type of object to be instantiated is determined at runtime, or the subclass needs to decide. It is beneficial in scenarios where you must create different objects based on specific conditions, such as the platform on which the app is running.

When to Use

The Factory Method pattern is ideal in scenarios like:

- **Platform-Specific Implementation**: Creating different objects based on the platform (iOS, Android, Web, etc.).
- **Dynamic Creation**: When the object type needs to be decided at runtime based on specific conditions.
- **Decoupling Object Creation**: Separating the creation logic from the usage, promoting modular and maintainable code.

Here's an example in Flutter where the Factory Method is used to create platform-specific widgets:

```
abstract class PlatformWidgetFactory {
  Widget createWidget();
}

class IOSWidgetFactory extends PlatformWidgetFactory {
  @override
  Widget createWidget() {
    return CupertinoButton(
      child: Text('iOS Button'),
      onPressed: () {},
    );
  }
}

class AndroidWidgetFactory extends PlatformWidgetFactory {
  @override
  Widget createWidget() {
    return ElevatedButton(
      child: Text('Android Button'),
      onPressed: () {},
    );
  }
}

class WebWidgetFactory extends PlatformWidgetFactory {
  @override
  Widget createWidget() {
    return TextButton(
      child: Text('Web Button'),
      onPressed: () {},
    );
  }
```

```
}

// Usage in the app
void main() {
  PlatformWidgetFactory widgetFactory;

  if (Platform.isIOS) {
    widgetFactory = IOSWidgetFactory();
  } else if (Platform.isAndroid) {
    widgetFactory = AndroidWidgetFactory();
  } else {
    widgetFactory = WebWidgetFactory();
  }

  Widget myWidget = widgetFactory.createWidget();

  runApp(
      MyApp(home: Scaffold(body: Center(child: myWidget))));
}
```

In this example, `PlatformWidgetFactory` is an abstract class with a `createWidget` method. The `IOSWidgetFactory`, `AndroidWidgetFactory`, and `WebWidgetFactory` are concrete implementations creating platform-specific widgets.

Pitfalls

- **Complexity**: Implementing a Factory Method can unnecessarily complicate the codebase for straightforward scenarios.
- **Misuse**: It's easy to incorrectly implement this pattern, especially if the creation logic needs to be correctly placed in subclasses.
- **Design Rigidity**: Requires thoughtful design upfront and needs to be easily refactored into an existing codebase.

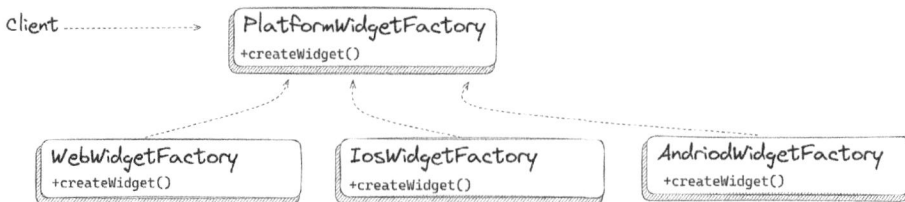

Figure 5.2: Factory Design Pattern

Testing Factory Method in Flutter/Dart

Testing involves verifying that the correct widget types are created for each platform:

```
void main() {
  test('IOSWidgetFactory should create a CupertinoButton',
      () {
    PlatformWidgetFactory factory = IOSWidgetFactory();
    final widget = factory.createWidget();

    expect(widget, isA<CupertinoButton>());
  });

  test(
      'AndroidWidgetFactory should create an ElevatedButton',
      () {
    PlatformWidgetFactory factory = AndroidWidgetFactory();
    final widget = factory.createWidget();

    expect(widget, isA<ElevatedButton>());
  });

  test('WebWidgetFactory should create a TextButton', () {
    PlatformWidgetFactory factory = WebWidgetFactory();
    final widget = factory.createWidget();

    expect(widget, isA<TextButton>());
  });
}
```

In these tests, the Factory Method's ability to create the appropriate widget type for each platform is verified, ensuring the pattern is correctly implemented in your Flutter application.

5.3   Structural Patterns

Structural patterns are essential in software design, aiming to simplify the design by identifying a simple way to realize relationships between entities. These patterns focus on how classes and objects are composed to form larger structures. The primary goal is to ensure that changes in one part of a system require minimal alterations in other parts, thus promoting reusability and flexibility.

When to use structural patterns often depends on the need to form large object structures from individual parts. These patterns are beneficial when a system requires an interface that differs from the interfaces of individual components or when integrating different systems with incompatible interfaces.

Key structural patterns include Adapter, Bridge, Composite, Decorator, Facade, Flyweight, and Proxy; however, in this section, I am going over Adapter, Composite, Decorator, Facade, and Proxy.

5.3.1 Adapter

The Adapter Design Pattern is valuable for reconciling interface incompatibilities. In Flutter, it is a pivotal tool for integrating widgets with varying interfaces, ensuring they fit seamlessly within an application's design and functionality. This pattern is particularly beneficial when you have widgets with different interfaces or behaviors that must be harmonized to work together.

Concepts and Design Considerations

- **Harmonizing Widget Interfaces**: The Adapter pattern in Flutter is predominantly used to reconcile differences between widget interfaces, making them compatible.
- **Enhancing Flexibility**: This pattern allows for greater flexibility in UI design, enabling the integration of diverse widgets without modifying their core functionalities.
- **Client-Centric Design**: The adapter focuses on the needs of the component (client) that integrates the adapted widget, ensuring that the final UI is cohesive and functions as intended.

Implementation in Flutter

An example scenario in Flutter might involve adapting a custom widget to fit into a layout or design scheme it wasn't initially designed for. For example, widgets need a child of type `RenderSilver`, which, in this case, using `SliverToBoxAdapter` could do the adaption.

```
CustomScrollView(
  slivers: [
    const SliverPadding(
      padding: EdgeInsets.all(5.0),
      sliver: SliverToBoxAdapter( //<---
        child: Text('Test'), //<---
      ), //<---
    ),
  ],
);
```

Another example is where you have different media players. This example acts like the plug types in different countries.

```
abstract interface class MediaPlayer {
  void play(String audioType, String fileName);
}

// Adaptee Class
class MyAppMediaPlayer {
  void playMp3(String fileName) {}
```

```dart
  void playMp4(String fileName) {}
}

// Adapter class
class MediaAdapter implements MediaPlayer {
  MediaAdapter(this.myAppMediaPlayer);

  final MyAppMediaPlayer myAppMediaPlayer;

  @override
  void play(String audioType, String fileName) {
    if (audioType.toLowerCase() == 'mp3') {
      myAppMediaPlayer.playMp3(fileName);
    } else if (audioType.toLowerCase() == 'mp4') {
      myAppMediaPlayer.playMp4(fileName);
    }
  }
}

class AppMediaPlayer implements MediaPlayer {
  @override
  void play(String audioType, String fileName) {
    final mediaAdapter = MediaAdapter(MyAppMediaPlayer());
    mediaAdapter.play(audioType, fileName);
  }
}

class CustomWidgetMediaPlayer extends StatelessWidget {
  const CustomWidgetMediaPlayer({
    super.key,
    required this.type,
    required this.fileName,
    required this.adapter,
  });

  final String type;
  final String fileName;
  final MediaPlayer adapter;

  @override
  Widget build(BuildContext context) {
    return TextButton(
      onPressed: () {
        adapter.play(type, fileName);
      },
      child: const Text('Play'),
    );
  }
```

```
}

class MyApp extends StatelessWidget {
  const MyApp({super.key});

  @override
  Widget build(BuildContext context) {
    return MaterialApp(
      home: Scaffold(
        body: Center(
          child: Column(
            children: [
              CustomWidgetMediaPlayer(
                type: 'mp3',
                fileName: 'file.mp3',
                adapter: AppMediaPlayer(),
              ),
              CustomWidgetMediaPlayer(
                type: 'mp4',
                fileName: 'file.mp4',
                adapter: AppMediaPlayer(),
              ),
            ],
          ),
        ),
      ),
    );
  }
}
```

You can have a media player that either adapts to audio or video or even more. The `CustomWidgetMediaPlayer` only accepts the adapter, which is typed `MediaPlayer`

Pitfalls

- **Unnecessary Complexity**: Using adapters for simple UI changes can lead to an unnecessarily complex widget tree.
- **Performance Impact**: While generally minimal, adding layers through adapters can impact performance in more complex UIs.
- **Misuse as a Design Shortcut**: Adapters should not be used to circumvent proper widget design and layout planning. Their primary role is integration, not fixing fundamental design flaws.

Testing Adapter Pattern in Flutter/Dart

Testing involves ensuring that the adapter correctly modifies or integrates the target widget as required:

```
class MockMyAppMediaPlayer extends Mock
    implements MyAppMediaPlayer {}
```

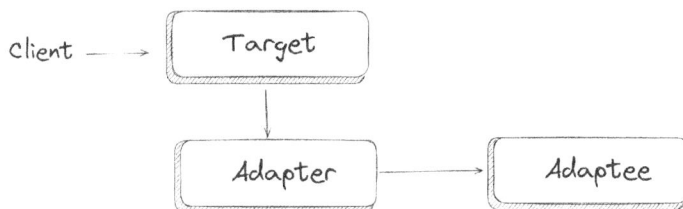

Figure 5.3: Adapter Design Pattern

```dart
void main() {
  group('MediaAdapter Tests', () {
    test('Should call playMp3 when MP3 is played', () {
      final mediaPlayer = MockMyAppMediaPlayer();
      final mediaAdapter = MediaAdapter(mediaPlayer);

      mediaAdapter.play('mp3', 'song.mp3');

      verify(mediaPlayer.playMp3('song.mp3')).called(1);
    });

    test('Should call playMp4 when MP4 is played', () {
      final mediaPlayer = MockMyAppMediaPlayer();
      final mediaAdapter = MediaAdapter(mediaPlayer);

      mediaAdapter.play('mp4', 'video.mp4');

      verify(mediaPlayer.playMp4('video.mp4')).called(1);
    });
  });
  group('AppMediaPlayer Tests', () {
    testWidgets(
        'Should display two buttons and react to taps',
        (WidgetTester tester) async {
      await tester.pumpWidget(const MyApp());

      expect(find.byType(CustomWidgetMediaPlayer),
          findsNWidgets(2));

      await tester.tap(
          find.widgetWithText(TextButton, 'Play').first);
      await tester.pump();
    });
  });
}
```

You will learn more about testing in chapter 15.

5.3.2 Decorator

The Decorator Design Pattern in Flutter is a structural pattern that dynamically adds new functionality to objects without altering their structure. This pattern is handy when you want to enhance the behavior of widgets in a flexible and scalable way, following the principle of single responsibility.

Concepts and Design Considerations

- **Enhancing Functionality**: The Decorator pattern is chosen when there's a need to add behavior or functionality to individual objects without affecting others in the same hierarchy.
- **Beyond Simple Inheritance**: Unlike simple inheritance, the Decorator pattern uses composition alongside inheritance to add new functionalities. It's not about overriding but complementing existing behavior.
- **Single Responsibility Principle**: Each class in the Decorator pattern focuses on one aspect of functionality, adhering to the principle that a class should do one thing and do it well.
- **Combining Inheritance and Composition**: The pattern often involves a common component with added functionalities in the subcomponents, achieved through a combination of inheritance for type compatibility and composition for dynamic behavior enhancement.

Implementation in Flutter

In Flutter, the Decorator pattern can be beneficial for adding new behaviors to widgets. For example, consider a scenario where you need to add border and padding decoration to a `Text` widget without altering its core functionality:

```
// Base Component
abstract class TextComponent {
  Widget build(BuildContext context);
}

// Concrete Component
class SimpleText extends TextComponent {
  final String text;

  SimpleText(this.text);

  @override
  Widget build(BuildContext context) {
    return Text(text);
  }
}
```

```dart
// Decorator
abstract class TextDecorator extends TextComponent {
  final TextComponent decoratedText;

  TextDecorator(this.decoratedText);
}

// Concrete Decorators
class BorderText extends TextDecorator {
  BorderText(super.decoratedText);

  @override
  Widget build(BuildContext context) {
    return Container(
      decoration: BoxDecoration(
        border: Border.all(color: Colors.black),
      ),
      child: decoratedText.build(context),
    );
  }
}

class PaddingText extends TextDecorator {
  PaddingText(super.decoratedText);

  @override
  Widget build(BuildContext context) {
    return Padding(
      padding: const EdgeInsets.all(8.0),
      child: decoratedText.build(context),
    );
  }
}

class MyApp extends StatelessWidget {
  const MyApp({super.key});

  @override
  Widget build(BuildContext context) {
    TextComponent text = SimpleText('Hello, World!');
    TextComponent borderedText = BorderText(text);
    TextComponent paddedText = PaddingText(borderedText);

    return MaterialApp(
      home: Scaffold(
        body: Center(
          child: paddedText.build(context),
        ),
```

```
      ),
    );
  }
}
```

In this example, `SimpleText` is the base component, and `BorderText` and `PaddingText` are decorators that add border and padding functionalities, respectively, without modifying the underlying `SimpleText`.

Pitfalls

- **Class Proliferation**: One potential drawback is the creation of numerous small classes for each new feature, leading to a more extensive class hierarchy.
- **Complexity**: Overusing the Decorator pattern can lead to a complex codebase that may be difficult to maintain.
- **Confusion with Inheritance**: It's crucial to distinguish between using decorators to enhance functionality and simple inheritance. Decorators should add functionality dynamically without altering the concrete class itself.

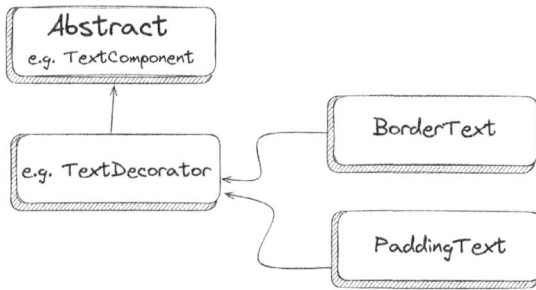

Figure 5.4: Decorator Design Pattern

Testing Decorator Pattern in Flutter/Dart

Testing involves verifying that each decorator adds its intended functionality without altering the base component:

```
void main() {
  testWidgets('BorderText adds a border',
      (WidgetTester tester) async {
    TextComponent text = SimpleText('Test');
    TextComponent borderedText = BorderText(text);

    // Wrap the component in a
    // MaterialApp and Scaffold to provide context
    await tester.pumpWidget(MaterialApp(
```

```
    home: Scaffold(
      body: Center(
        child: Builder(
          builder: (BuildContext context) {
            return borderedText.build(context);
          },
        ),
      ),
    ),
  ));

  final borderedTextFinder = find.byType(Container);
  expect(borderedTextFinder, findsOneWidget);

  final Container container =
      tester.firstWidget(borderedTextFinder);
  expect(container.decoration, isA<BoxDecoration>());

  BoxDecoration decoration =
      container.decoration as BoxDecoration;
  expect(decoration.border, isNotNull);
  });

  // ... other test cases ...
}
```

This test ensures that the `BorderText` decorator correctly adds a border to the `SimpleText` widget, confirming the functionality and effectiveness of the Decorator pattern within the Flutter application.

5.3.3   Composite

The Composite Design Pattern in Flutter is a structural pattern that organizes objects into tree structures to represent part-whole hierarchies. This pattern makes it possible to treat individual objects and compositions of objects uniformly, which is particularly useful in Flutter's widget-centric design.

Concepts and Design Considerations

- **Uniform Treatment of Components**: The core idea of the Composite pattern is to handle individual objects and their compositions in the same manner. This is achieved by representing them in a tree structure.
- **Tree-Structured Design**: The pattern organizes components into a tree hierarchy where each node is either a 'Leaf' (individual object) or a 'Composite' (a group of objects).
- **Simplification with Flexibility**: While the Composite pattern simplifies the structure by treating all objects uniformly, it can sometimes oversimplify, leading to reliance on runtime checks for object compatibility.

- **Component Interface**: Both leaf and composite objects adhere to a common component interface, allowing operations to be applied consistently to individual elements or their groups.

Implementation in Flutter

In Flutter, the Composite pattern can build complex UI structures where individual widgets and groups are treated similarly. For example, creating a menu with a sub-menu can be a typical use case for the composite pattern.

```
// Abstract class for all menu items (leaf and composite)
abstract interface class MenuItem implements Widget {
  // All submenu should open onTap
  void expand(bool expanded);
}

// Leaf node
class SimpleMenuItem extends StatelessWidget
    implements MenuItem {
  const SimpleMenuItem({
    super.key,
    required this.title,
    required this.action,
  });

  final Function() action;
  final String title;

  @override
  void expand(_) {
    // Leaf node, do nothing
  }

  @override
  Widget build(context) {
    return ListTile(title: Text(title), onTap: action);
  }
}

// Composite node that can contain other menu items
class Submenu extends StatefulWidget implements MenuItem {
  Submenu({
    super.key,
    required this.title,
    required this.children,
    this.expandAll = false,
  });

  final String title;
```

```
  final bool expandAll;
  final List<MenuItem> children;

  bool childrenExpanded = false;

  @override
  void expand(expanded) {
    childrenExpanded = expanded;
    for (final child in children) {
      child.expand(expanded);
    }
  }

  @override
  SubmenuState createState() => SubmenuState();
}

class SubmenuState extends State<Submenu> {
  @override
  Widget build(context) {
    return ExpansionTile(
      title: Text(widget.title),
      initiallyExpanded: widget.childrenExpanded,
      onExpansionChanged:
          widget.expandAll ? widget.expand : null,
      children: widget.children,
    );
  }
}

// Usage example
class MenuApp extends StatelessWidget {
  const MenuApp({super.key});

  @override
  Widget build(BuildContext context) {
    return ListView(
      children: [
        SimpleMenuItem(
          title: 'Edit',
          action: () => debugPrint('Edit'),
        ),
        Submenu(
          title: 'File',
          children: [
            SimpleMenuItem(
              title: 'New',
              action: () => debugPrint('New file'),
```

```
          ),
          Submenu(
            // Tap on this would open all submenu
            expandAll: true,
            title: 'Recent Files',
            children: [
              SimpleMenuItem(
                title: 'File1.txt',
                action: () =>
                    debugPrint('Open File1.txt'),
              ),
              Submenu(
                title: 'Submenu in submenu',
                children: [
                  SimpleMenuItem(
                    title: 'New',
                    action: () => debugPrint('New file'),
                  ),
                  Submenu(
                    title: 'Archive',
                    children: [
                      SimpleMenuItem(
                        title: 'file.zip',
                        action: () =>
                            debugPrint('file.zip'),
                      ),
                    ],
                  ),
                ],
              ),
            ],
          ),
        ],
      ),
    ],
  );
}
}
```

In this example, SimpleMenuItem represents a leaf, and SubMenu is a composite that groups multiple MenuItem objects.

Remember that in Flutter, composition with StatelessWidget and StatefullWidget is preferred over inheritance.

Pitfalls

- **Over-Simplification**: Composite can sometimes simplify structures to the point where it's challenging to enforce constraints on what can be added to the composition.

- **Potential for Large Hierarchies**: If not managed carefully, the composite structure can grow large and unwieldy, mainly if each object contains its collection of child objects.

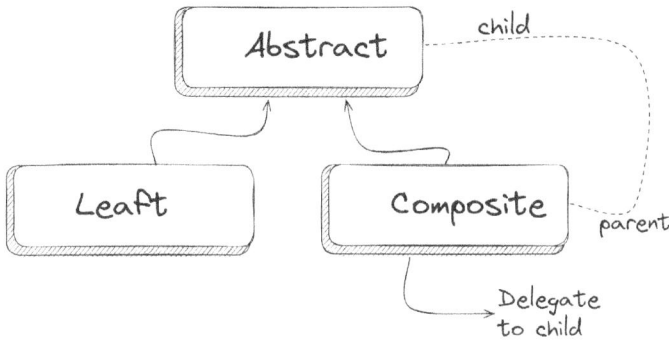

Figure 5.5: Composite Design Pattern

Testing Composite Pattern in Flutter/Dart

Testing involves ensuring that both individual components and their compositions function as expected:

```
void main() {
  testWidgets(
    'Submenu should display its title and child items',
    (WidgetTester tester) async {
      await tester.pumpWidget(
        MaterialApp(
          home: Scaffold(
            body: Submenu(
              title: 'Test Submenu',
              children: [
                SimpleMenuItem(
                    title: 'Child Item', action: () {}),
              ],
            ),
          ),
        ),
      );

      // Verify the submenu title is displayed
      expect(find.text('Test Submenu'), findsOneWidget);

      // Expand the submenu to see child items
      await tester.tap(find.text('Test Submenu'));
      await tester.pumpAndSettle();
```

```
    // Verify the child item is displayed
    expect(find.text('Child Item'), findsOneWidget);
  },
);

  // Additional tests for Submenu and other components
}
```

This test confirms that `SubMenu` successfully renders a composition of `SimpleMenuItem` widgets, verifying the effectiveness of the Composite pattern in the Flutter application.

5.3.4 Proxy

The Proxy Design Pattern in Flutter is a structural pattern that provides a surrogate or placeholder for another object to control access to it. This pattern is beneficial for managing resource-intensive operations, adding security layers, or handling remote service calls in a Flutter application.

Concepts and Design Considerations

- **Intermediary Object**: The Proxy pattern introduces an intermediary (the proxy) to interact with the real object. This intermediary can control access, manage the lifecycle, or add additional functionalities.
- **Remote, Virtual, and Protection Proxies**: Proxies can serve various purposes, like handling remote service calls (Remote Proxy), controlling resource-intensive objects (Virtual Proxy), or adding security measures (Protection Proxy).
- **Interface-Based Design**: The proxy is typically implemented based on an interface, with the actual object and its proxy sharing the same interface, ensuring seamless interaction.
- **Simplification and Control**: While the proxy simplifies access to complex or remote objects, it also controls how and when the underlying object is accessed or modified.

Implementation in Flutter

In Flutter, a common use case for the Proxy pattern is to control the rendering of widgets, particularly when dealing with resource-intensive operations or conditional rendering based on user permissions.

For example, consider a scenario where you have a widget that should only be accessible to certain users:

```
abstract class AccessibleWidget {
  Widget build(BuildContext context);
}
```

```dart
// Real Widget
class RestrictedContentWidget implements AccessibleWidget {
  @override
  Widget build(BuildContext context) {
    return const Text(
      'Restricted Content',
      key: Key('restrictedContentKey'),
    );
  }
}

// Proxy
class AccessControlProxyWidget extends AccessibleWidget {
  final AccessibleWidget protectedWidget;
  final bool hasAccess;

  const AccessControlProxyWidget({
    super.key,
    required this.protectedWidget,
    required this.hasAccess,
  });

  @override
  Widget build(BuildContext context) {
    return hasAccess
        ? protectedWidget.build(context)
        : const Text('Access Denied');
  }
}

bool checkUserAccess() {
  return true;
}

// Usage in the app
void main() {
  runApp(MaterialApp(
    home: Scaffold(
      body: AccessControlProxyWidget(
        protectedWidget: RestrictedContentWidget(),
        hasAccess:
            // A function to check user access
            checkUserAccess(),
      ),
    ),
  ));
}
```

In this implementation:

- `RestrictedContentWidget` is the real widget that contains sensitive or re-stricted content.
- `AccessControlProxyWidget` acts as a proxy, controlling access to `RestrictedContentWidget` based on the `hasAccess` flag.
- When the variable `hasAccess` is `true`, the `RestrictedContentWidget` is accessible; otherwise, an "Access Denied" message is displayed.

Pitfalls

- **Single Proxy Limitation**: The Proxy pattern typically involves using a single proxy for a given object, which can be limiting when multiple func-tionalities like security and auditing are needed.
- **Overhead**: Introducing a proxy adds another layer of abstraction, which can complicate the code and may lead to unexpected behaviors, especially with remote proxies.
- **Confusion with Similar Patterns**: The Proxy pattern can be easily confused with patterns like Decorator or Adapter, especially when the dis-tinction is unclear.

Contrast to Other Patterns

- **Proxy vs. Decorator**: Unlike a decorator, whose primary purpose is dy-namically adding functionality, a proxy is set at compile time and is more about controlling access to an object.
- **Runtime vs. Compile-Time Behavior**: While the behavior of a decora-tor is usually determined at runtime through chaining, the functionality of a proxy is determined at compile time.

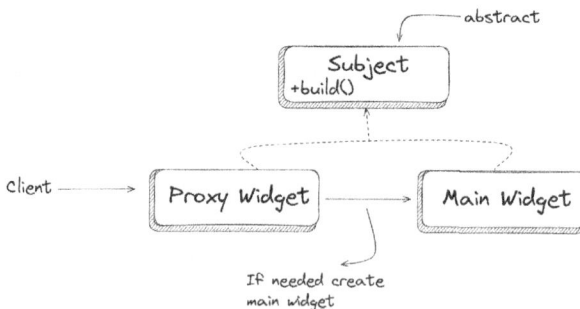

Figure 5.6: Proxy Design Pattern

Testing Proxy Pattern in Flutter/Dart

Testing a proxy involves verifying both the proxy's control mechanism and the interaction with the real object:

Design Patterns in Flutter

```
void main() {
  group(
    'AccessControlProxyWidget',
    () {
      // Test when access is granted
      testWidgets(
        ' displays content when access is granted',
        (WidgetTester tester) async {
          // Build the widget with access granted
          await tester.pumpWidget(
            MaterialApp(
              home: AccessControlProxyWidget(
                protectedWidget: RestrictedContentWidget(),
                hasAccess: true,
              ),
            ),
          );

          // Verify that the restricted content is displayed
          expect(
            find.byKey(const Key('restrictedContentKey')),
            findsOneWidget,
          );
          expect(
            find.text('Restricted Content'),
            findsOneWidget,
          );
        },
      );

      // Test when access is denied
      testWidgets(
        'displays "Access Denied" when access is denied',
        (WidgetTester tester) async {
          // Build the widget with access denied
          await tester.pumpWidget(
            MaterialApp(
              home: AccessControlProxyWidget(
                protectedWidget: RestrictedContentWidget(),
                hasAccess: false,
              ),
            ),
          );

          // Verify that the "Access Denied" message
          // is displayed instead of the restricted content
          expect(
            find.byType(RestrictedContentWidget),
```

```
                findsNothing,
            );
            expect(
                find.text('Access Denied'), findsOneWidget);
        },
    );
    },
);
}
```

These tests collectively validate that the `AccessControlProxyWidget` functions as intended, controlling access to the protected widget based on the specified conditions.

5.3.5 Facade

The Facade Design Pattern in Flutter is a structural approach that provides a simplified interface to a more complex underlying system, such as a set of libraries, a framework, or a complex group of interrelated classes. This pattern is key in reducing complexity and improving the usability of such systems.

Concepts and Design Considerations

- **Simplification of Complex Interactions**: The Facade pattern creates a simple interface to a complex subsystem. It's advantageous in scenarios where the client code needs to interact with a complex library or a system of classes.
- **Refactoring Tool**: Often used in refactoring, the Facade pattern helps wrap a poorly designed or overly complex API to make it more accessible and easier to understand.
- **Composition Over Inheritance**: Facades usually employ composition rather than inheritance, meaning they contain instances of different classes in the subsystem rather than extending them.
- **Lifecycle Management**: While the facade can manage the lifecycle of the objects it interacts with, it mainly focuses on streamlining the interface.

Implementation in Flutter

In Flutter, a Facade could simplify complex operations like network requests, data parsing, and UI rendering. For example, consider a scenario with several steps to fetch, process, and display data:

```
// Complex subsystem classes
class NetworkManager {
  Future<String> fetchData() async {
    // Implementation...
    return 'Data';
  }
```

```dart
}

// Complex subsystem classes
class DataProcessor {
  String processData(String data) {
    // Implementation...
    return 'Processed Data';
  }
}

// Facade
class DataFacade {
  final NetworkManager _networkManager = NetworkManager();
  final DataProcessor _dataProcessor = DataProcessor();

  Future<String> fetchDataAndProcess() async {
    String data = await _networkManager.fetchData();
    return _dataProcessor.processData(data);
  }
}

// Usage in a Flutter app
void main() {
  runApp(MaterialApp(
    home: Scaffold(
      body: FutureBuilder<String>(
        future: DataFacade().fetchDataAndProcess(),
        builder: (context, snapshot) {
          if (snapshot.connectionState ==
              ConnectionState.done) {
            return Text(
              snapshot.data ?? 'No data',
            );
          } else {
            return const CircularProgressIndicator();
          }
        },
      ),
    ),
  ));
}
```

In this example:

- NetworkManager and DataProcessor are part of a complex subsystem.
- DataFacade acts as a facade, providing fetchDataAndProcess to handle the fetching and processing of data.
- The primary function uses DataFacade to retrieve and display data, abstracting away the complexities of the underlying operations.

Pitfalls

- **Over-Simplification**: A facade can sometimes oversimplify a system, which may be problematic for clients who need more control or access to the underlying complexity.
- **Incorrect Usage**: Using a facade in a new system might indicate underlying design issues. It's often more suitable as a refactoring tool for existing complex systems.
- **Single Responsibility**: As a facade tends to aggregate functionalities, ensuring it doesn't become a "god object" that violates the Single Responsibility Principle is essential.

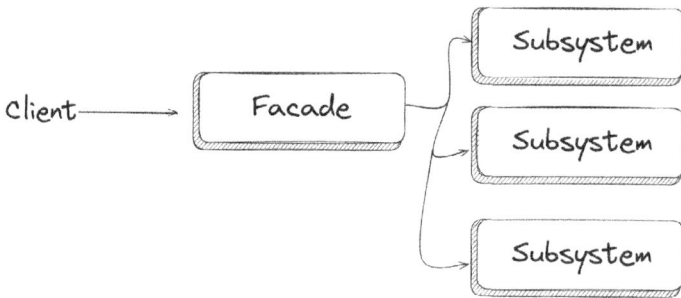

Figure 5.7: Facade Design Pattern

Testing Facade Pattern in Flutter/Dart

Testing a facade involves ensuring that it correctly integrates and simplifies the operations of the underlying subsystem:

```dart
void main() {
  testWidgets(
    'DataFacade should fetch and process data',
    (WidgetTester tester) async {
      await tester.pumpWidget(
        MaterialApp(
          home: Scaffold(
            body: FutureBuilder<String>(
              future: DataFacade().fetchDataAndProcess(),
              builder: (context, snapshot) {
                if (snapshot.connectionState ==
                    ConnectionState.done) {
                  return Text(snapshot.data ?? 'No data');
                } else {
                  return const CircularProgressIndicator();
                }
              },
```

```
            ),
          ),
        ),
      );

      // Verify the Facade's functionality
      // Additional assertions
      // depending on the expected behavior
    },
  );
}
```

In this test, we verify that the `DataFacade` correctly fetches and processes the data, and the result is appropriately displayed in the UI. This ensures that the facade effectively simplifies and manages the operations of the underlying complex subsystem.

5.4 Behavioral Patterns

Behavioral patterns are a cornerstone in software design, focusing primarily on communication and interaction between objects. In contrast to structural patterns, which concentrate on object composition, behavioral patterns are all about effective communication and the delegation of responsibilities among objects. They help define how various objects and classes interact and manage control flow across them.

The use of behavioral patterns is appropriate when there is a need to manage algorithms, relationships, and responsibilities between objects and when the behavior of a set of objects depends on their state. These patterns are essential in scenarios where it becomes necessary to encapsulate complex control logic in a manner that is easy to understand, maintain, and extend.

Some well-known behavioral patterns include the Observer, Strategy, Interpreter, Command, Iterator, State, Visitor, Memento, Mediator, and Chain of Responsibility.

I will review Command, Observer, Strategy, and Template Methods in this chapter.

5.4.1 Command

The Command Design Pattern in Flutter encapsulates actions or requests as objects, particularly with undo functionality. This pattern allows for flexible operations like executing and undoing commands, making it highly suitable for applications with complex user interactions.

Concepts and Design Considerations

- **Action Encapsulation**: Encapsulates each action or request as an object, allowing for dynamic operation handling.
- **Decoupling**: Separates the objects issuing commands from the objects executing them, enhancing modularity.
- **Undo and Redo**: Supports undoing and redoing actions, a key feature in many user interfaces, by keeping a history of executed commands.
- **Flexibility and Scalability**: Offers the flexibility to extend and add new commands without altering existing code.

Implementation in Flutter

A typical implementation in Flutter could involve a drawing application where user actions like drawing lines can be undone:

```
// Command Interface
abstract class Command {
  String get name;
  void execute();
  void undo();
}

// Concrete Command for Drawing
class DrawCommand implements Command {
  DrawCommand();

  @override
  String get name => 'DrawCommand';

  @override
  void execute() {}

  @override
  void undo() {}
}

// Concrete Command for ChangeColor
class ChangeColorCommand implements Command {
  ChangeColorCommand();

  @override
  String get name => 'ChangeColorCommand';

  @override
  void execute() {}

  @override
  void undo() {}
}
```

```dart
// Command Manager to handle execution and undoing
class CommandManager {
  final _commandList = ListQueue<Command>();

  bool get hasHistory => commandHistoryList.isNotEmpty;

  List<String> get commandHistoryList =>
      _commandList.map((c) => c.name).toList();

  void executeCommand(Command command) =>
      _commandList.add(command);

  void undo() {
    if (_commandList.isEmpty) return;
    _commandList.removeLast().undo();
  }
}

class MyApp extends StatefulWidget {
  final CommandManager commandManager;

  const MyApp({
    super.key,
    required this.commandManager,
  });

  @override
  State<MyApp> createState() => _MyAppState();
}

class _MyAppState extends State<MyApp> {
  @override
  Widget build(BuildContext context) {
    return MaterialApp(
      home: Scaffold(
        appBar: AppBar(
          title: const Text('Command Pattern Example'),
        ),
        body: Column(
          key: const Key('drawButtonKey'),
          mainAxisAlignment: MainAxisAlignment.center,
          children: [
            TextButton(
              onPressed: () {
                widget.commandManager.executeCommand(
                  DrawCommand(),
                );
                setState(() {});
```

```
        },
        child: const Text('Tap to draw'),
      ),
      TextButton(
        onPressed: () {
          widget.commandManager.executeCommand(
            ChangeColorCommand(),
          );
          setState(() {});
        },
        child: const Text('Tap to Change Color'),
      ),
      if (widget.commandManager.hasHistory)
        TextButton(
          onPressed: () {
            widget.commandManager.undo();
            setState(() {});
          },
          child: const Text('Press to undo'),
        ),
      Expanded(
        child: ListView.builder(
          itemCount: widget.commandManager
              .commandHistoryList.length,
          itemBuilder: (context, index) {
            return Text(
              widget.commandManager
                  .commandHistoryList[index],
            );
          },
        ),
      )
    ],
  ),
),
);
}
}
```

In this example:

- `DrawCommand` is a concrete implementation of `Command` that handles drawing actions.
- `ChangeColorCommand` is a concrete implementation of `Command` that handles changing color actions.
- `CommandManager` manages the execution and undoing of commands.

Pitfalls

- **Complexity**: Managing a history of commands can become complex, especially in large applications with many actions.
- **Resource Management**: Storing a history of commands might consume significant memory, depending on the nature of the commands.
- **State Consistency**: Ensuring consistent application state across undo and redo operations can be challenging.

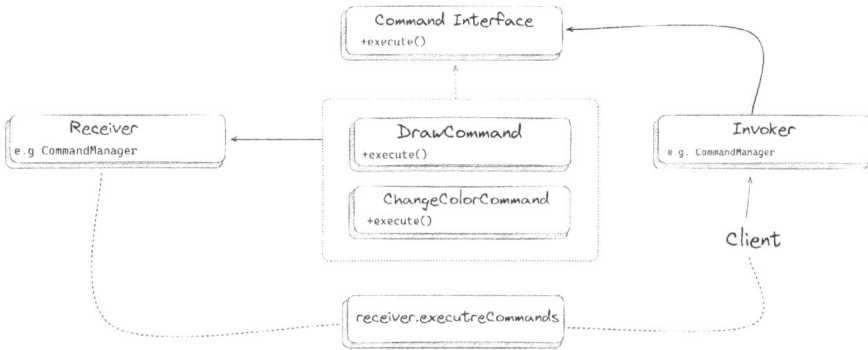

Figure 5.8: Command Design Pattern

Testing Command Pattern in Flutter/Dart

Testing involves verifying both the execution and the undoing of commands:

```dart
void main() {
  testWidgets(
      'MyApp should execute and undo commands correctly',
      (WidgetTester tester) async {
    // Create a CommandManager
    // and build the MyApp widget
    CommandManager commandManager = CommandManager();
    await tester.pumpWidget(
      MyApp(commandManager: commandManager),
    );

    // Find the buttons
    Finder drawButton = find.text('Tap to draw');
    Finder changeColorButton =
        find.text('Tap to Change Color');
    Finder undoButton = find.text('Press to undo');

    // Execute the DrawCommand
    await tester.tap(drawButton);
    await tester.pump();

    // Verify that the DrawCommand
    // is added to the history
```

```
    expect(find.text('DrawCommand'), findsOneWidget);

    // Execute the ChangeColorCommand
    await tester.tap(changeColorButton);
    await tester.pump();

    // Verify that the ChangeColorCommand
    // is added to the history
    expect(find.text('ChangeColorCommand'), findsOneWidget);

    // Undo the last command (ChangeColorCommand)
    await tester.tap(undoButton);
    await tester.pump();

    // Verify that the ChangeColorCommand
    // is removed from the history
    expect(find.text('ChangeColorCommand'), findsNothing);
    // Verify that the DrawCommand
    // is still in the history
    expect(find.text('DrawCommand'), findsOneWidget);

    // Undo the DrawCommand
    await tester.tap(undoButton);
    await tester.pump();

    // Verify that the DrawCommand
    // is removed from the history
    expect(find.text('DrawCommand'), findsNothing);
  });
}
```

This test checks whether the `DrawCommand` is executed on tap and correctly undone when the undo button is pressed. Depending on the drawing logic, you might need to adjust the verification steps to match the implementation.

5.4.2 Observer

The Observer Design Pattern establishes a one-to-many relationship between objects. This pattern allows an object, known as the subject, to notify an array of other objects, known as observers, about its state changes. The Observer pattern is particularly prevalent in reactive programming in Flutter, especially when dealing with streams and dynamic data updates.

Concepts and Design Considerations

- **Reactive Programming**: Central to reactive programming, this pattern enables systems to react dynamically to changes in their environment or state.

- **Decoupling of Subject and Observers**: The pattern promotes a modular and flexible architecture by separating the subject from its observers.
- **Dynamic Subscriptions**: Observers can dynamically subscribe or unsubscribe from the subject, allowing for flexible interaction models.
- **Broadcast Communication**: When the subject changes its state, it broadcasts this change to all its observers, ensuring synchronized updates.

Implementation in Dart

Here's a simple Dart implementation:

```dart
abstract class Observer {
  void update();
}

class Subject {
  List<Observer> _observers = [];

  void attach(Observer observer) {
    _observers.add(observer);
  }

  void detach(Observer observer) {
    _observers.remove(observer);
  }

  void notifyObservers() {
    for (final observer in _observers) {
      observer.update();
    }
  }
}

class ConcreteObserver implements Observer {
  @override
  void update() {
    print("Observer updated.");
  }
}

void main() {
  final subject = Subject();
  final observer = ConcreteObserver();
  final observer2 = ConcreteObserver();
  subject.attach(observer);
  subject.attach(observer2);

  subject.notifyObservers(); // Notifies the observer
}
```

```
// Observer updated.
// Observer updated.
```

Implementation in Flutter

In Flutter, `ChangeNotifier` is commonly used for the subject, providing a straightforward way to implement the Observer pattern:

```dart
class CounterObserver with ChangeNotifier { //<---
  int _count = 0;

  int get count => _count;

  void increment() {
    _count++;
    notifyListeners(); //<---
  }
}

class CounterConcreteObserver extends StatelessWidget {
  const CounterConcreteObserver({
    super.key,
    required this.counterNotifier,
  });

  final CounterObserver counterNotifier;

  @override
  Widget build(BuildContext context) {
    return Center(
      child: Column(
        mainAxisAlignment: MainAxisAlignment.center,
        children: <Widget>[
          const Text(
            'Current counter value:',
          ),
          ListenableBuilder( //<---
            listenable: counterNotifier, //<---
            builder: (
              BuildContext context,
              Widget? child,
            ) {
              return Text(
                '${counterNotifier.count}',
              );
            },
          ),
        ],
      ),
```

```dart
      );
    }
}

class MyApp extends StatefulWidget {
  const MyApp({super.key});

  @override
  State<MyApp> createState() => _MyAppState();
}

class _MyAppState extends State<MyApp> {
  final _counter = CounterObserver();

  @override
  Widget build(BuildContext context) {
    return MaterialApp(
      home: Scaffold(
        appBar: AppBar(
          title: const Text(
            'ListenableBuilder Example',
          ),
        ),
        body: Column(
          children: [
            CounterConcreteObserver(
              counterNotifier: _counter,
            ),
            CounterConcreteObserver(
              counterNotifier: _counter,
            ),
          ],
        ),
        floatingActionButton: FloatingActionButton(
          onPressed: _counter.increment,
          child: const Icon(Icons.add),
        ),
      ),
    );
  }
}
```

This pattern's implementation using streams or `ChangeNotifier` makes it an essential tool for creating dynamic and responsive user interfaces.

Pitfalls

- **Over-Notification**: The subject might notify observers more often than necessary, which can lead to performance issues.

- **Complexity**: Managing many observers or intricate update logic can become complex.
- **Debugging Challenges**: Due to the indirect nature of communication, debugging issues related to notifications can be tricky.

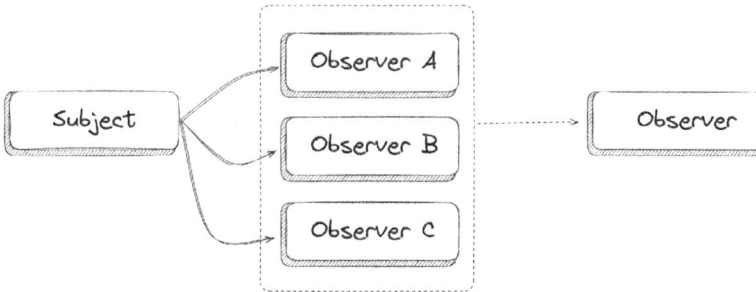

Figure 5.9: Observer Design Pattern

Testing Observer Pattern

To test the given Flutter application, which uses the `CounterObserver` class with `ChangeNotifier` and `CounterConcreteObserver` widget, we need to verify that when the counter is incremented, all instances of `CounterConcreteObserver` in the UI reflect the updated count.

Here's how you can write the test:

```
void main() {
  testWidgets(
    'Counter value should update on increment',
    (WidgetTester tester) async {
      // Build our app and trigger a frame
      await tester.pumpWidget(const MyApp());

      // Verify initial state of counter
      expect(find.text('Current counter value:'),
          findsNWidgets(2));
      expect(find.text('0'), findsNWidgets(2));

      // Find and tap the FloatingActionButton
      await tester.tap(find.byIcon(Icons.add));
      await tester.pump();

      // Verify that the counter has incremented
      expect(find.text('1'), findsNWidgets(2));
    },
  );
}
```

This test ensures that the `CounterObserver` correctly notifies its listeners (in this case, the `CounterConcreteObserver` widgets) about changes in its state and that these changes are reflected in the UI.

5.4.3 Strategy

The Strategy Design Pattern is useful when dynamically selecting algorithms or processes during runtime. It eliminates conditional statements and encapsulates algorithm strategies in separate classes, leading to more flexible and maintainable code.

Concepts and Design Considerations

- **Flexibility in Algorithm Selection**: Strategy pattern allows different algorithms or strategies to be selected at runtime based on the context, reducing reliance on conditional logic.
- **Decoupling of Strategy and Context**: The pattern decouples the implementation details of an algorithm from the code that uses it, making the system easier to extend and maintain.
- **Interface or Abstract Class-Based Design**: Strategies typically adhere to a common interface or an abstract class, ensuring that all concrete strategy implementations have a uniform structure.
- **Client Awareness**: Clients are aware of the available strategies and choose the appropriate one, allowing dynamic strategy switching.

Implementation in Flutter

In Flutter, the strategy pattern can dynamically change the behavior of widgets or other components based on user interaction or other runtime conditions.

```
abstract class SortingStrategy {
  List<int> sort(List<int> dataset);
}

class AscendingSort implements SortingStrategy {
  @override
  List<int> sort(List<int> dataset) {
    dataset.sort((a, b) => a.compareTo(b));
    debugPrint(dataset.toString());
    return dataset;
  }
}

class DescendingSort implements SortingStrategy {
  @override
  List<int> sort(List<int> dataset) {
    dataset.sort((b, a) => a.compareTo(b));
    debugPrint(dataset.toString());
```

```dart
    return dataset;
  }
}

class ContextStrategy {
  final SortingStrategy strategy;
  ContextStrategy(this.strategy);

  List<int> executeStrategy(List<int> dataset) {
    return strategy.sort(dataset);
  }
}

class SortingWidget extends StatelessWidget {
  final List<int> dataset;
  final ContextStrategy contextStrategy;

  const SortingWidget({
    super.key,
    required this.dataset,
    required this.contextStrategy,
  });

  @override
  Widget build(BuildContext context) {
    final sortedData =
        contextStrategy.executeStrategy(dataset);
    return ListView.builder(
      itemCount: sortedData.length,
      itemBuilder: (_, index) => ListTile(
        title: Text(
          sortedData[index].toString(),
        ),
      ),
    );
  }
}

class SortingHome extends StatefulWidget {
  const SortingHome({super.key});

  @override
  _SortingHomeState createState() => _SortingHomeState();
}

class _SortingHomeState extends State<SortingHome> {
  List<int> dataset = [3, 1, 4, 1, 5, 9];
  SortingStrategy currentStrategy = AscendingSort();
```

```dart
  void toggleSortingStrategy() {
    setState(() {
      currentStrategy = currentStrategy is AscendingSort
          ? DescendingSort()
          : AscendingSort();
    });
  }

  @override
  Widget build(BuildContext context) {
    return Scaffold(
      appBar: AppBar(
        title: const Text('Sorting Example'),
      ),
      body: SortingWidget(
        dataset: dataset,
        contextStrategy: ContextStrategy(
          currentStrategy,
        ),
      ),
      floatingActionButton: FloatingActionButton(
        onPressed: toggleSortingStrategy,
        child: const Icon(Icons.sort),
      ),
    );
  }
}

void main() {
  runApp(
    const MaterialApp(
      home: Scaffold(
        body: SortingHome(),
      ),
    ),
  );
}
```

In this Flutter example:

- SortingStrategy is an interface for different sorting algorithms.
- AscendingSort and DescendingSort are concrete implementations of SortingStrategy.
- Context uses a SortingStrategy to sort a dataset.
- SortingWidget uses Context to display sorted data.

Pitfalls

- **Increased Number of Classes**: Each strategy requires its class, which can lead to more classes in the application.
- **Client Awareness**: Clients must know the different strategies to select the appropriate one.
- **Complexity in Management**: Managing multiple strategies and their interactions can become complex in larger applications.

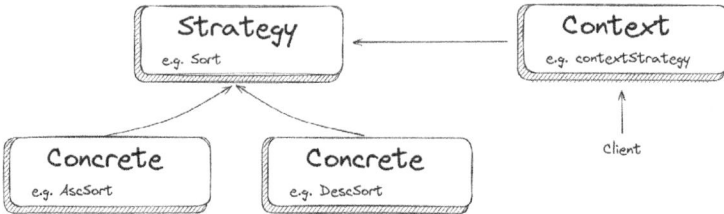

Figure 5.10: Strategy Design Pattern

Testing Strategy Pattern

To test the `SortingWidget` in Flutter, you can simulate rendering the widget with different sorting strategies and then verify the order of items in the list. The key here is to ensure that the `SortingWidget` correctly displays data sorted according to the selected sorting strategy.

Here's how you can write a test for this scenario:

```
void main() {
  List<int> testData = [3, 1, 4, 5, 9];

  testWidgets(
    'SortingWidget displays data sorted by AscendingSort',
    (WidgetTester tester) async {
      ContextStrategy sortingContext = ContextStrategy(
        AscendingSort(),
      );

      await tester.pumpWidget(
        MaterialApp(
          home: Scaffold(
            body: SortingWidget(
              dataset: testData,
              contextStrategy: sortingContext,
            ),
          ),
        ),
      );
```

```dart
      List<int> expectedSortedData =
          sortingContext.executeStrategy(testData);
      for (int i = 0; i < expectedSortedData.length; i++) {
        expect(
          find.widgetWithText(
            ListTile,
            expectedSortedData[i].toString(),
          ),
          findsOneWidget,
        );
      }
    },
  );

  testWidgets(
    'SortingWidget displays data sorted by DescendingSort',
    (WidgetTester tester) async {
      ContextStrategy sortingContext = ContextStrategy(
        DescendingSort(),
      );

      await tester.pumpWidget(
        MaterialApp(
          home: Scaffold(
            body: SortingWidget(
              dataset: testData,
              contextStrategy: sortingContext,
            ),
          ),
        ),
      );

      List<int> expectedSortedData =
          sortingContext.executeStrategy(testData);
      for (int i = 0; i < expectedSortedData.length; i++) {
        expect(
          find.widgetWithText(
            ListTile,
            expectedSortedData[i].toString(),
          ),
          findsOneWidget,
        );
      }
    },
  );
}
```

These tests ensure that the SortingWidget appropriately interacts with different sorting strategies and accurately reflects their sorted output in the UI.

5.4.4 Template Method

The Template Method Design Pattern is particularly effective for promoting code reuse in framework and library design. It's an essential technique in object-oriented programming, especially within Inversion of Control (IoC) frameworks. The pattern focuses on defining an algorithm's skeleton in an abstract class method while allowing subclasses to redefine specific steps of this algorithm without changing its structure.

Concepts and Design Considerations

- **Algorithm Structure**: The template method pattern is built around an abstract base class that outlines the steps of an algorithm. Subclasses then customize these steps.
- **Hooks and Operations**: Hooks are optional steps that may be overridden, while operations are essential steps that subclasses must implement.
- **Class-Based Approach**: The pattern operates on a class hierarchy, where the base class controls the flow of the algorithm, and concrete classes implement specific parts of it.
- **Compile-Time Algorithm Selection**: The template method defines the algorithm at compile time, making it suitable for situations where the algorithm's structure is fixed and only parts of its execution vary.

Implementation in Flutter

In Flutter, the Template Method pattern can define a common workflow or behavior for a set of widgets, with specific parts of the workflow being customizable.

```
abstract class BaseWidget extends StatelessWidget {
  const BaseWidget({super.key});

  @override
  Widget build(BuildContext context) {
    return Scaffold(
      appBar: AppBar(title: Text(appBarTitle())),
      body: buildBody(context),
    );
  }

  String appBarTitle();
  Widget buildBody(BuildContext context);
}

class ConcreteWidget extends BaseWidget {
  const ConcreteWidget({super.key});

  @override
  String appBarTitle() => 'Concrete Widget';
```

```
  @override
  Widget buildBody(BuildContext context) {
    return const Center(
      child: Text('Concrete implementation of buildBody.'),
    );
  }
}

void main() {
  runApp(const MaterialApp(home: ConcreteWidget()));
}
```

In this Flutter example:

- BaseWidget is an abstract class defining the template (build method).
- appBarTitle (hook) and buildBody (operation) are parts of the algorithm that subclasses can customize.
- ConcreteWidget is a subclass that provides specific implementations for the customizable parts of the BaseWidget.

Pitfalls

- **Class Hierarchy Complexity**: The template method can lead to a complex class hierarchy and may confuse.
- **Restricted Flexibility**: The algorithm's structure is fixed in the base class, which may sometimes limit flexibility.
- **Design Overhead**: Implementing the template method requires careful planning to identify the parts of the algorithm that should be customizable.

Template Method vs. Strategy

- The Template Method pattern is class-based and extends a base class, focusing on the same algorithm with different implementations of its parts. It's chosen at compile time.
- The Strategy pattern, conversely, encapsulates the entire algorithm per strategy based on a contract or interface. It's used when there's a need to pick an algorithm at runtime, allowing the client to select an algorithm while using the application.

Template Method vs. Factory Method

- The Factory Method pattern uses a method in a base class to create objects, but the actual creation is deferred to subclasses. This pattern is about creating objects without specifying the exact class of object that will be created. The focus is on object creation with flexibility in what is being created, and the decision about which class to instantiate is made at runtime.

- On the other hand, the Template Method pattern defines the skeleton of an algorithm in an operation, deferring some steps to subclasses. The Template Method lets subclasses redefine specific steps of an algorithm without changing the algorithm's structure.

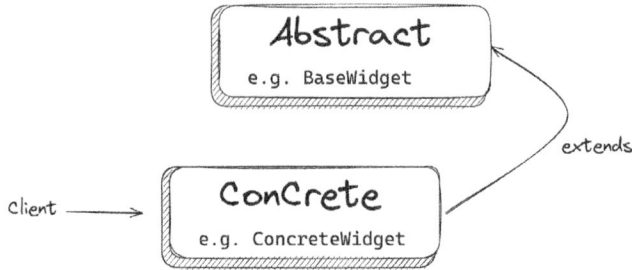

Figure 5.11: Template Method Design Pattern

Testing Template Method Pattern

To effectively test the implementation of the Template Method pattern in the provided Flutter example, we need to verify that `ConcreteWidget` correctly overrides and implements the abstract methods defined in `BaseWidget`. The test will ensure that the `ConcreteWidget` displays the expected AppBar title and body content as defined in its implementations of `appBarTitle` and `buildBody`.

```dart
void main() {
  group(
    'ConcreteWidget',
    () {
      testWidgets(
        'Display the correct AppBar title and body content',
        (WidgetTester tester) async {
          // Build the ConcreteWidget
          await tester.pumpWidget(
            const MaterialApp(
              home: ConcreteWidget(),
            ),
          );

          // Verify that the AppBar title is correct
          // as per ConcreteWidget's implementation
          expect(
              find.text('Concrete Widget'), findsOneWidget);

          // Verify that the body content is correct
          // as per ConcreteWidget's implementation
          expect(
```

```
        find.text(
          'Concrete implementation of buildBody.',
        ),
        findsOneWidget,
      );
    },
  );
},
);
}
```

This test ensures that the `ConcreteWidget` correctly overrides the abstract methods from `BaseWidget` and that these overridden methods are being adequately executed, reflecting the intended behavior of the Template Method pattern.

5.5   Conclusion

In this chapter, together, we've explored a diverse range of design patterns in the context of Flutter, each serving a unique purpose in software architecture. As we've seen, understanding and applying these patterns can significantly enhance the quality, maintainability, and scalability of your Flutter applications.

I have yet to cover all the design patterns in this chapter, so it's insufficient to understand them fully. There are still many corner cases, examples in different contexts, pure Dart implementations, and more complex scenarios in Flutter that we still need to discuss. This topic alone can be a book of more than 500 pages. Therefore, I only touched the surface to give you an idea of how an engineer should apply these principles in a Flutter app.

For those looking to deepen their understanding of design patterns, two seminal works stand out: "Design Patterns: Elements of Reusable Object-Oriented Software" by the "Gang of Four" and "Head First Design Patterns" by O'Reilly. The former offers a foundational exploration of classic design patterns, laying the groundwork for understanding their principles and applications. The latter provides a more approachable and practical perspective, making complex concepts accessible and engaging.

For those seeking a comprehensive resource tailored to Flutter, Flutter Design Patterns (flutterdesignpatterns.com[1]) emerges as the go-to destination. This invaluable resource by Mangirdas Kazlauskas, a GDE for Flutter and Dart, thoroughly examines all 23 design patterns from the seminal "Gang of Four" book. Each pattern is meticulously dissected in separate articles, offering in-depth explanations, real-world challenges solved using Dart and Flutter, and interactive

---

[1] https://flutterdesignpatterns.com/

code examples for hands-on learning. This comprehensive resource empowers developers of all skill levels to master design patterns and build robust, maintainable Flutter applications.

Part II

Architecture

CHAPTER 6

Architectural Foundations

Reviewer: Roman Jaquez

When I was first introduced to software architecture a few years ago, I thought my extensive experience in developing and engineering software might seamlessly transition into a role as an architect. However, I soon realized this wasn't the case. A software architect requires a deep understanding of constructing various systems at different scales and a solid grasp of foundational principles.

The diversity in its definitions intrigued me during my early days of exploring software architecture as I sought to integrate this knowledge into my work. Some describe software architecture as the blueprint of a system, while others view it as a roadmap guiding the development process. Martin Fowler's well-known whitepaper, 'Who Needs an Architect?', ultimately resonates with Ralph Johnson's definition: '**Architecture is about the important stuff. Whatever that is**.' This statement might seem simplistic initially, but I find it profoundly insightful. The essence of software architecture lies in identifying what is crucial (i.e., what is architectural) and then focusing efforts on maintaining the integrity of those key elements.

I also recommend 'Fundamentals of Software Architecture,' a book published by O'Reilly and authored by Mark Richards and Neal Ford. They describe software architecture as multidimensional, comprising the system's structure, architectural characteristics ("-ilities"), architectural decisions, and design principles. This definition resonates deeply with me and has been a guiding principle in various career stages.

In this chapter, I will briefly explore these dimensions, offering insights into how Flutter engineers can conceptualize software architecture and apply this knowledge to the Flutter apps they build.

6.1 The Critical Role of Architectural Decisions

In software architecture, the role of a software architect encompasses a wide range of responsibilities, extending from expert programming to establishing strategic

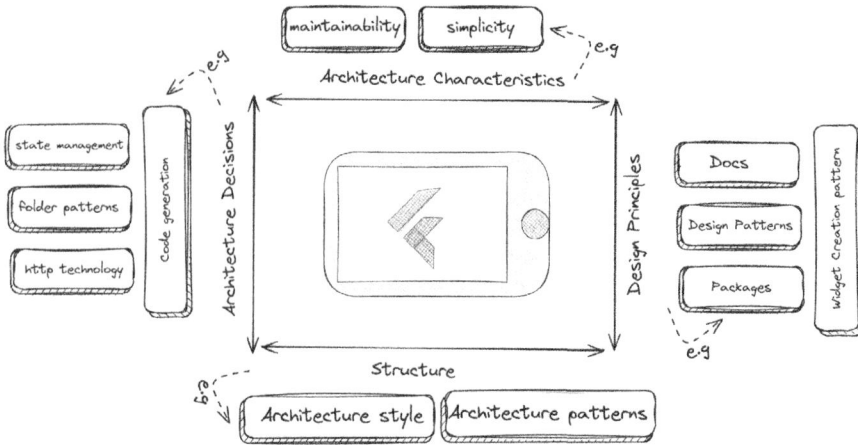

Figure 6.1: Four Dimensions of Architecture in Flutter Context

technical direction. Central to this role are the expectations placed on architects, which emphasize guiding technology decisions through architecture decisions and design principles. This approach enables teams to make informed choices, ensuring architectural decisions facilitate the right technical solutions while maintaining necessary flexibility. Architecture Decision Records (ADRs) documents often capture these decisions, which detail each architectural choice's context, rationale, and implications. ADRs are a valuable tool for documenting why specific decisions were made, helping maintain a clear and accessible record of the project's architectural evolution.

It is a good practice to document the system's architecture along with ADRs for reference by the development team.

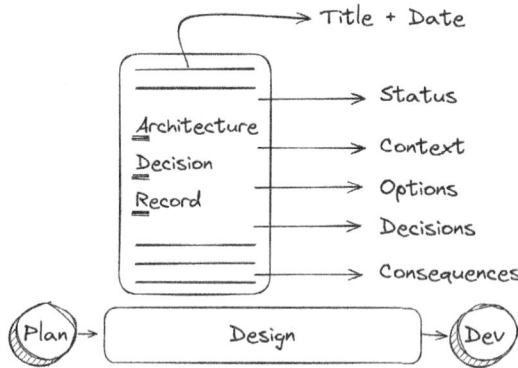

Figure 6.2: Architecture Decision Records Content

A practical software architect must have exceptional interpersonal skills, including leadership, facilitation, and cultivating a team culture of trust, openness, and transparency to ensure that every member feels heard and valued, not just the architect, as these are crucial for leading development teams and differentiating themselves in the industry. Involving the team in architectural decisions creates a sense of investment and collective ownership.

Leadership and communication are as important as technical expertise, playing a key role in an architect's ability to coach teams, convey architectural decisions, and maintain their position in a competitive field.

In the context of Flutter development, these architectural expectations translate into decisions that shape the entire framework of a Flutter application. For example, a Flutter architect might guide the team towards using a specific architectural pattern, like MVVM or Bloc, to ensure an organized and maintainable codebase. However, the architect would typically not mandate the exact state management tool based on their suitability for the project. Not all projects are created equal, and approaching architecture as a "cookie-cutter" may harm the project's long-term success.

While the architect in a Flutter project typically doesn't mandate a specific state management tool, their role is crucial in influencing this decision. The architect guides the engineering team in choosing the most suitable tool by providing comprehensive reasoning and evaluating the system's needs, along with their extensive knowledge of the available options. Their broad understanding of various state management solutions like Provider, Riverpod, or Bloc helps present the pros and cons of each, thereby aiding the team in making an informed decision. Sometimes, the architect may also directly select a tool if it aligns closely with the project's architectural needs. The architect's influence is key in ensuring that the team's choice supports the overall architectural strategy of the Flutter application.

Moreover, continuous analysis and adaptation of the architecture are also critical in Flutter, given the platform's evolving nature. This might involve re-evaluating the use of certain packages or integrations as newer, more efficient options become available. Ensuring compliance with these architectural decisions, like adhering to a chosen folder structure, naming convention, or widget composition practices, is critical to maintaining a consistent and efficient development process.

Additionally, understanding the specific business domain, whether e-commerce, healthcare, or finance, enables a Flutter architect to tailor the app architecture to effectively meet technical and business needs.

6.2   Variables Influencing Architectural Choices

When considering **software architecture**, various factors significantly influence architectural decisions. **Business requirements** are paramount, setting the overall objectives and functionalities of the project. Whether it involves specific performance targets or compliance with industry regulations, these requirements critically shape the architectural approach. The **existing technology infrastructure** also plays a crucial role, especially when integrating with legacy systems or adopting new technologies.

Budget and resource constraints are key determinants, shaping the scope and scale of the project and influencing the selection of cost-effective or more resource-intensive solutions. **Performance needs** like speed, reliability, and up-time are central to the architectural strategy, dictating the necessary technology and structure.

The **expertise of the development team** is another vital factor. Having teams with diverse disciplines and experience levels can promote a learning-friendly environment and supportive atmosphere, which architects can leverage to identify opportunities for interaction and enhance problem-solving and productivity.

The team's familiarity with specific languages and frameworks can significantly guide architectural choices, balancing the ideal architectural vision with practical capabilities. **Future scalability and maintainability** considerations ensure the architecture adapts and evolves as the project grows.

Additionally, the **organizational structure** plays a subtle yet significant role in shaping software architecture. This is encapsulated in **Conway's Law**, which states: "**Any organization that designs a system (defined broadly) will produce a design whose structure is a copy of the organization's communication structure.**" This principle suggests that the architecture of a system often mirrors the hierarchical and communication patterns of the organization that develops it. The impact of this is seen in how components and teams are organized and how they interact within the project.

Regarding **security and compliance**, particularly in sensitive sectors, these requirements can impose specific architectural constraints to ensure data integrity and adherence to regulations. Keeping abreast of **market trends** and **industry standards** provides valuable insights, aligning the architecture with current best practices. This keeps the core architecture design flexible as well as future-proof.

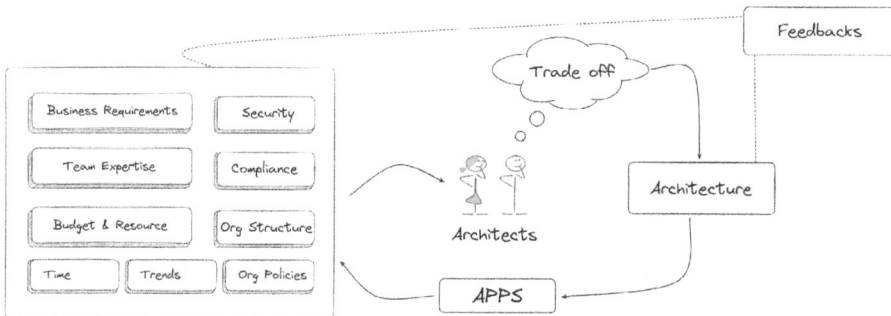

Figure 6.3: Variables Influencing Software Architectural Choices

In the Flutter context, these variables are just as critical. Business requirements favor Flutter for its multi-platform capabilities. The team's proficiency with Dart and Flutter influences architectural choices, while budget considerations may impact the decision to use open-source packages. Performance needs are especially crucial in Flutter, focusing on UI responsiveness and smooth animations. Selecting an appropriate state management solution is key for scalability. Security

---

Architectural Foundations

considerations guide the architecture around data handling and network communications. Lastly, staying updated with the evolving Flutter ecosystem allows for leveraging new features and best practices, ensuring the app remains contemporary and efficient. Balancing these variables effectively is essential for developing a robust, scalable, and successful Flutter application.

6.3   Navigating the Architectural Landscape

Software architecture requires understanding the broad spectrum of architectural styles, patterns, and frameworks available in software design. This process requires architects to assess these options against their specific project's unique requirements, constraints, and goals. The focus is on making informed decisions that effectively marry the project's needs with the most suitable architectural approach, ensuring a robust, adaptable, and innovative solution. This careful navigation is key to developing a cohesive and efficient architecture that aligns with the software project's current and future demands.

But the scope is so broad. How can I find the best for my app? Mainly if I have limited knowledge.

6.3.1   Finding the Right Fit

The key lies in a structured approach to decision-making, which involves thoroughly understanding your app's specific requirements, constraints, and goals. It's crucial to start by identifying your app's core functionalities and performance expectations. This understanding helps narrow the architectural options that align with your app's needs.

Remember, there's often no **one-size-fits-all** solution; the "**right fit**" is finding an architecture that effectively addresses your app's unique challenges and objectives. In my journey as an architect, two fundamental laws from the book "Fundamentals of Software Architecture" have profoundly influenced my approach to software development and real life.

First Law: "*Everything in software architecture is a trade-off.*" This principle extends beyond software architecture to all aspects of decision-making. It implies that there are always compromises and consequences in every choice. The key is recognizing that if something lacks a trade-off, it's likely that the trade-off still needs to be identified. This law teaches the importance of thorough analysis and consideration of all potential impacts before deciding.

Second Law: "Why is more important than how." This law shifts the focus from the methods and techniques used in architecture to the underlying reasons and objectives behind each decision. It emphasizes the need to deeply understand the 'why' behind our choices, ensuring that every architectural decision aligns with the broader goals and requirements of the project.

Reflecting on these laws reinforces the significance of careful deliberation and a purpose-driven mindset. Whether in software architecture or life, understanding the trade-offs and focusing on the rationale behind decisions is crucial to making an informed, practical "**right fit.**"

6.4   Cultivating an Architectural Mindset

In software engineering, cultivating an architectural mindset is essential for designing technically robust systems strategically aligned with broader business objectives. This mindset, often called Architectural Thinking, extends beyond technical proficiency, encompassing a comprehensive understanding of the technological landscape and its implications on software design. It involves a holistic view that considers the entire lifecycle of a system, from inception to deployment and beyond. This broad perspective is crucial in making informed decisions that balance technical capabilities with strategic goals.

For software architects, the **Breadth of Knowledge** is a fundamental aspect of this mindset. It involves staying current with technological advancements, understanding different programming paradigms, and being adept in various architectural patterns. In Flutter development, this means mastering the Flutter framework and understanding how it integrates with other technologies and fits into the broader software development ecosystem. In short, the more you know about stuff you don't know, the better.

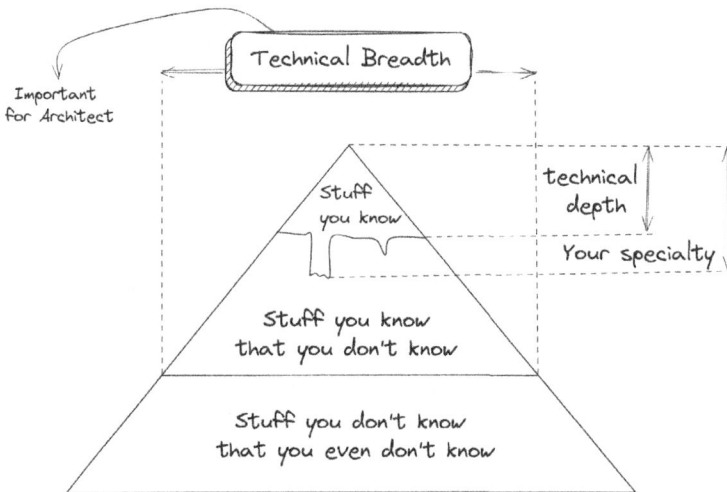

Figure 6.4: Technical Breadth Pyramid

Analyzing **Trade-offs** is another critical component of Architectural Thinking. Every decision in software architecture involves a balance of performance, scalability, maintainability, and cost. For a Flutter architect, this translates into making choices that impact the application's performance, user experience, and long-term viability. For example, selecting a state management solution in Flutter or opting for native widgets versus custom solutions has significant implications on these aspects.

Moreover, aligning these technical decisions with **Business Drive** is vital. Understanding the business context and objectives ensures that technical solutions are feasible and add value to the business. In Flutter development, this could mean leveraging the framework's cross-platform capabilities to meet business goals of broader reach and faster feature development.

Ultimately, architectural thinking in software engineering, particularly in Flutter development, is about making technically sound and strategically aligned choices, ensuring the software's success in both technical and business realms.

6.5 Iterative Architecture

In an environment where business requirements are constantly shifting and technology is rapidly evolving, the approach to software architecture must be agile and adaptable. This necessitates an iterative process of architectural development, where the design and structure of software are continuously refined to align with the changing landscape. The iterative approach recognizes that the perfect architecture at the outset is less crucial than the ability to evolve and adapt over time. As business needs shift and technological advancements emerge, the architecture must be flexible enough to accommodate these changes, ensuring that the software remains relevant, efficient, and effective.

Central to the concept of iterative software architecture is the notion that it is driven by the collective needs of the team rather than being dictated by a selected group of experts. Architects in this framework play a role that is less about authoritarian decision-making and more about aligning, guiding, and supporting the team. Their role is to facilitate decision-making, making crucial decisions only when necessary. In this sense, architecture is treated similarly to code: it is expected to be revisited, reviewed, analyzed, and revised regularly.

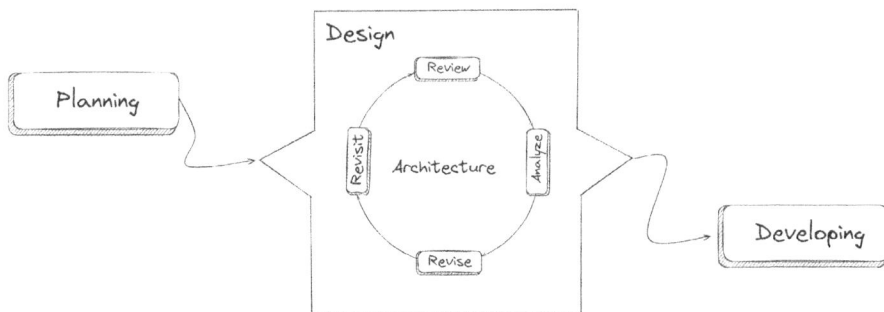

Figure 6.5: Iterative Architecture Mindset

This approach ensures that architectural decisions align with the current business, technical, and organizational requirements, allowing for a more responsive and effective software development process.

6.5.1 Evolving Through Feedback and Mistakes

In software development, particularly with adaptive frameworks like Flutter, the importance of evolving architecture through feedback and learning from mistakes cannot be overstated. This approach requires a willingness to revise and improve architectural decisions as project requirements and technologies evolve. An iterative process, where user and team feedback is continually integrated, ensures the architecture remains relevant and efficient.

For example, in Flutter, an initial state management choice might later be found inadequate. Adapting to this realization, perhaps by adopting a more advanced state management solution, enhances the app's scalability and maintainability.

This cycle of adaptation and learning is crucial for maintaining a robust and effective architecture in the fast-changing software development landscape.

6.6 Striking a Balance: Simplicity vs. Complexity

A common challenge in software architecting is the tendency towards over-engineering, adding multiple layers and abstractions to manage complexity, which is sometimes associated with the software's robustness, sophistication, or maturity. However, it's critical to recognize the costs associated with complexity. Additional layers often mean higher maintenance needs, a steeper learning curve for new team members, and potential limitations on the system's flexibility and adaptability. Conversely, simplicity in architecture is about more than being rudimentary but about being efficient and straightforward, facilitating easier maintenance, quicker onboarding, and greater adaptability.

The value of simplicity in software architecture lies in its power to minimize maintenance costs, enhance system robustness, and facilitate easier understanding and modification. Simple designs, by having fewer components, are less prone to failure and more manageable for new developers to grasp, reducing the onboarding time. They also offer more flexibility, allowing the system to evolve with changing requirements. However, achieving simplicity means maintaining functionality. It's about finding that sweet spot where the system fulfills its requirements without unnecessary layers of complexity. The key is allowing the architecture to evolve iteratively, letting more complex structures develop organically as needed rather than forcing them prematurely. This approach ensures that simplicity is maintained as long as possible and complexity is introduced only when justified and manageable.

Consider how often small-scale apps could efficiently function with a basic three-layer architecture and simple state management like `setState` and opt for elaborate solutions like Clean Architecture with multiple data layers instead. This unnecessary complexity can significantly slow down a development team, hindering their ability to ship quickly and bringing maintainability issues in the long run, often with the prize of shipping slower features for the business.

It's crucial to remember that simplicity in architecture isn't about being basic or underdeveloped; it's about being effective, efficient, and facilitating faster delivery.

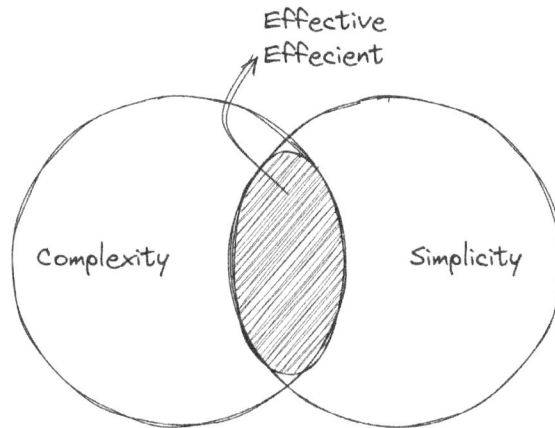

Figure 6.6: Balancing Complexity and Simplicity for Effectiveness and Efficiency

The goal is to choose an architecture that is as simple as possible to meet the app's needs, thereby streamlining development and avoiding over-complication.

When deciding on architectural change, ask yourself: Is this solution simple enough – meaning effective and efficient – to solve the current problem while being maintainable for the foreseeable future?

6.7 Conclusion

The journey through software architecture is a delicate balance between simplicity and complexity, driven by the evolving needs of both the project and the business. The key takeaway is maintaining a flexible, iterative approach to architecture, where simplicity is valued to achieve efficiency, maintainability, and adaptability. This approach involves continuously evaluating and refining decisions based on feedback and changing requirements, ensuring the architecture remains aligned with the project's goals.

In this chapter, we've focused on specific aspects of software architecture. Still, it's important to note that we have yet to delve into architectural characteristics like Scalability, Reliability, Availability, Maintainability, Security, Usability, Modularity, Flexibility, Portability, Testability, and Interoperability. Additionally, the intricacies of measuring these characteristics and using them to make informed decisions should have been covered, as well as component-based thinking or modularity, as they are beyond the scope of this book.

Two highly recommended resources for those looking to delve deeper into these concepts are "Fundamentals of Software Architecture" and "Software Architecture, The hard part." Both books offer invaluable insights into the principles and practices of effective software architecture.

CHAPTER 7

Introducing Architecture Styles

Reviewer: Roman Jaquez

In this book, we've explored various principles and core concepts of software engineering, some clear and others more complex. When stepping into software architecture, you often come across two terms: 'Architectural Styles' and 'Architectural Patterns.'

These terms are sometimes used interchangeably, and there are official resources such as Microsoft MSDN[1] that consider them to be the same thing. However, some experts in the field, such as software architects George Fairbanks and Michael Keeling[2], who differentiate between these terms, or the authors of "Fundamentals of Software Architecture," clearly advocate for different terms to be used in software architecture.

I prefer to distinguish between them, so let me define each.

Architectural Patterns, often called "Software Design Patterns," address recurring architectural problems. For example, the Model-View-Controller (MVC) pattern helps to separate the user interface from the model. In other words, it resolves a specific issue. I want to emphasize that the "Design Patterns" we learned in the previous chapters differ from Architectural Patterns in scope. They are more localized and have less impact on the code base. These patterns are specific to a particular section of the code base, for example, how to instantiate an object when we only know what type needs to be instantiated at runtime (maybe a Factory Class?).

On the other hand, Architectural Style is a broader design approach that provides a high-level organizational blueprint rather than direct solutions to problems. Styles like Client/Server or MicroKernel deal with structure and design philosophy, including guidelines, principles, and standards.

---

[1] https://learn.microsoft.com/en-us/previous-versions/msp-n-p/ee658117(v=pandp.10)
[2] http://georgefairbanks.com/blog/architecture-patterns-vs-architectural-styles/

In this chapter, we will not delve into the typical architecture and details of each aspect, as it would require several books, which I have mentioned before. The purpose is to share some key beneficial concepts to consider while building Flutter applications. Therefore, this chapter is a partial foundation for architecting an entire system.

Understanding the differences between these concepts is critical in software architecture, particularly in versatile frameworks like Flutter. It allows for a deeper comprehension and more effective application of architectural principles in software development.

7.1 Architectural Styles Knowledge

Besides widening your knowledge breadth, understanding architectural styles has three key benefits.

1. **Common Language**: They establish a universal vocabulary for developers, enabling clear and concise communication.
2. **Technology Agnostic Conversations**: Architectural Styles facilitate discussions that exceed specific technologies or patterns, focusing instead on broader design considerations.
3. **Focus Area Organization**: They allow the categorization of architecture based on key focus areas, aiding in selecting appropriate styles for different project needs.

This knowledge is integral for Flutter developers to create scalable, maintainable, and efficient applications, ensuring that the architectural foundation aligns with the project's goals and capabilities.

7.2 Layered (n-tier) Style

The Layered (n-tier) architectural style is a cornerstone in software architecture, which essentially comes from the Monolith architecture style, offering a systematic and modular approach to application design. This style inspires Flutter architecture.

This style is characterized by organizing functionality into distinct layers, each with a defined role and responsibility. These layers are stacked vertically, each serving a specific function related to the system's operation.

This layer perfectly fits into Conway's law. The law is probably best stated, by its author, as:

> Any organization that designs a system (defined broadly) will produce a design whose structure is a copy of the organization's communication structure. — Melvin Conway —

This is one of the main reasons this architecture is widely used in many companies.

Typically, software architecture consists of four layers: Presentation, Business, Persistence, and Database. These layers are often in UI segments named as presentation, Application, Business, and Data layers. The components of each layer are organized horizontally within that layer.

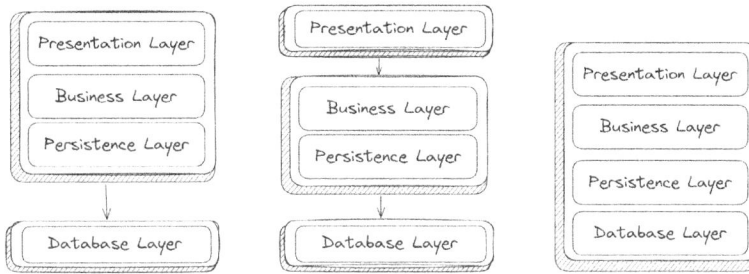

Figure 7.1: Different Deployment Variants of Layered Architecture Style

There are several benefits to this architecture.

- **Clear Functional Separation**: Each layer in the architecture is designated with a specific function. The upper layers, such as the User Interface (UI), interact with the lower layers, including the business logic and data. This structure enables a two-way flow of information. Data is transmitted downwards following a unidirectional data flow principle, while events and user interactions propagate upwards (known as bubbling up).
- **"High Cohesion' and "Loose Coupling"**: Ensuring that each layer contains functionalities closely related to its defined role, enhancing maintainability. Layers interact through well-defined interfaces, minimizing dependencies and allowing flexibility in modifying or replacing components.
- **Abstraction and Isolation**: Facilitates handling changes and technology upgrades at specific layers without affecting others.

Architects define how each layer should communicate or be isolated in a particular style. For instance, each layer can either be open or closed. If a layer is closed, a request must not pass through that layer and should go to the lower layer by skipping the higher one. Layer isolation is particularly important for changes that need to be made. Consider a scenario where you have three layers in your architecture (one of the well-known architecture patterns widely used in Flutter, which you will learn about in the next chapter), and you decide to open access from the presentation layer to the data layer directly. In such a situation, changing components in the data layer will affect the business and presentation layers, making the architecture tightly coupled. Therefore, whether a layer should be open depends on your software requirements, but it's nice to know that these are usually defined in the architecture style of layers.

Although this style is usually considered high-level architecture by the entire organization, the layered (n-tier) style is particularly beneficial in Flutter development.

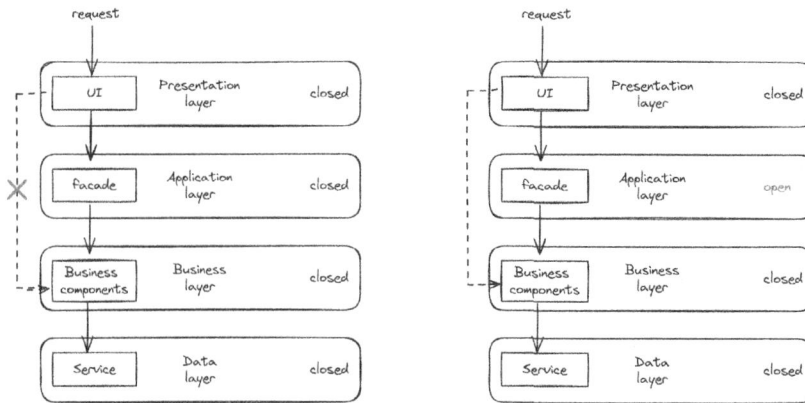

Figure 7.2: Layers of Isolation in UI Segments

Flutter apps can leverage this architectural style to separate UI (presentation layer) from business logic and data handling (business and data layers). Multiple architectural patterns fit this style. You will learn more about popular layered patterns in the next chapter.

7.3 Event-Driven Architecture (EDA)

Event-driven architecture (EDA) is a distributed and asynchronous architectural style well-known for being scalable and high-performing. This type of architecture is based on the interaction between event producers and consumers. Producers are responsible for generating events that reflect a change in state or occurrence, while consumers listen to these events and respond to them in almost real-time. Have you heard of Kafka or RabbitMQ? If so, that is where EDA architecture is involved.

The benefits of Event-Driven Architecture (EDA) are numerous, particularly in building responsive, scalable, and flexible applications:

- **Decoupling of Components**: EDA promotes loose coupling between event producers and consumers, enhancing flexibility and making the system easier to maintain and extend.
- **Scalability**: EDA can handle high volumes of events due to its asynchronous nature, making it ideal for scaling applications to meet varying demand levels.
- **Improved Fault Tolerance**: The decoupled nature of EDA means that a failure in one component doesn't necessarily bring down the entire system, improving overall fault tolerance.

There are usually two topologies of this style: "Broker" and "Mediator". I believe going into depth about these is outside the scope of this book. There are books about EDA with many more details. Two known EDA implementations are the **publish/subscribe (pub/sub)** model and the **event stream** model. Here is a brief overview of both.

- **Pub/Sub Model**: The infrastructure tracks subscriptions and dispatches events to each subscriber. Once an event is received, it can't be replayed, and new subscribers won't see past events. A broker facilitates the processing and passing of events from publishers to subscribers.
- **Event Streaming Model**: Events are recorded in a log with strict ordering and durability. Clients read from any part of the stream and are responsible for tracking their position, allowing them to join anytime and replay events.

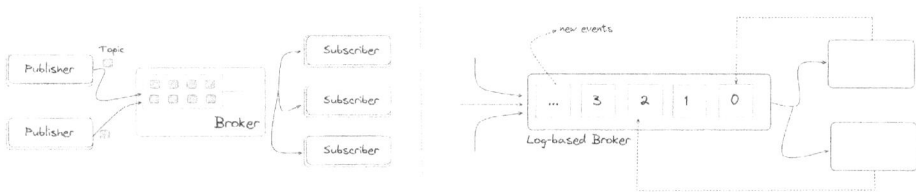

Figure 7.3: Pub/Sub Model vs. Event Streaming

This may remind you of a part of your app that you have already implemented and could leverage in your Flutter app. Let me give you an example. In this case, you can leverage the pub/sub model.

Implementing analytics metrics in a Flutter app using an Event-Driven Architecture (EDA) can effectively decouple the tracking logic from the rest of your app. You can create an event management system (acting as Broker or Event Bus[3]) using Dart's native capabilities, such as Stream and StreamController. Here's how you can do it:

Define Event Classes: Create classes for the analytics events you want to track.

```
class PageViewEvent {
  String pageName;
  PageViewEvent(this.pageName);
}

class UserActionEvent {
  String actionName;
  Map<String, dynamic> parameters;
  UserActionEvent(this.actionName, this.parameters);
}
```

---

[3]https://docs.aws.amazon.com/eventbridge/latest/userguide/eb-event-bus.html

---

Create a Custom Event Manager: Implement a custom event manager using `StreamController` that will manage the broadcasting of events.

```
class EventManager {
  final _controller = StreamController.broadcast();

  void dispose() {
    _controller.close();
  }

  void fire(dynamic event) {
    _controller.add(event);
  }

  Stream get stream => _controller.stream;
}
```

Set Up Analytics Service: Create an analytics service that listens to the stream of events and processes them accordingly.

```
class AnalyticsService {
  final FirebaseAnalytics _analytics = FirebaseAnalytics();

  void listenToEvents(Stream eventStream) {
    eventStream.listen(
      (event) {
        if (event is PageViewEvent) {
          _analytics.setCurrentScreen(
              screenName: event.pageName);
        } else if (event is UserActionEvent) {
          _analytics.logEvent(
            name: event.actionName,
            parameters: event.parameters,
          );
        }
      },
    );
  }
}
```

Initialize and Listen to Events: In your main app file or function, initialize the AnalyticsService and listen to events.

```
// global variable now
// Better to use a dependency injection
// you will learn about this later in this part of the book
final eventManager = EventManager();
```

```
main() {
  // You will learn in this part of the book how
  // to use Dependency Injection to inject this
  // where needed rather than using a Global variable.
  // but for now we keep it simple.
  final analyticsService = AnalyticsService();

  analyticsService.listenToEvents(
    eventManager.stream,
  );

  runApp(const MyApp());
}
```

Publish Events: You can now publish events from anywhere in your app by using the eventManager.

```
eventManager.fire(
  UserActionEvent(
    'AppStarted',
    {'appVersion': '1.0.0'},
  ),
);
```

This approach provides a custom solution for handling events in your Flutter app, facilitating a decoupled architecture for analytics tracking. To expand further on this implementation, if you use Navigator 1 or 2, you can use NavigatorObserver, create your own, and fire. Here is the code to demonstrate the idea.

```
class AnalyticsNavigatorObserver extends NavigatorObserver {
  @override
  void didPush(
    Route<dynamic> route,
    Route<dynamic>? previousRoute,
  ) {
    super.didPush(route, previousRoute);
    eventManager.fire(
      PageViewEvent(
        route.settings.name ?? 'unknown',
      ),
    );
  }
}
```

Then you can use it in MaterialApp:

```
class MyApp extends StatelessWidget {
  const MyApp({super.key});
```

```dart
  @override
  Widget build(BuildContext context) {
    return MaterialApp(
      title: 'Analytics',
      home: MyHomePage(title: 'Analytics'),
      //<--- --->//
      navigatorObservers: [AnalyticsNavigatorObserver()],
    );
  }
}
```

or essentially firing an event anywhere in the component directly

```dart
class ExamplePage extends StatelessWidget {
  const ExamplePage({super.key});

  @override
  Widget build(BuildContext context) {
    return Scaffold(
      appBar: AppBar(
        title: const Text('Analytics'),
      ),
      body: Center(
        child: Column(
          mainAxisAlignment: MainAxisAlignment.center,
          children: <Widget>[
            ElevatedButton(
              onPressed: () {
                eventManager.fire( //<---
                  UserActionEvent(
                    'ButtonClicked',
                    {'buttonId': 'startButton'},
                  ),
                );
              },
              child: const Text('Start'),
            ),
          ],
        ),
      ),
    );
  }
}
```

Dart's Stream and StreamController allows full control over the event system, making it flexible and tailored to your specific requirements.

Implementing the EDA, particularly the event bus pattern, can be made simpler with packages available on pub.dev.

7.4 Microkernel (Plug-in) Architecture

The Microkernel Architecture, also known as a plug-in architecture, is a style that separates a minimal functional core system (the microkernel) from extended functionalities and features that are implemented as plug-ins. This architecture is characterized by its flexibility and extensibility, allowing applications to easily adapt and scale by adding or removing plug-ins without altering the core system.

This architecture has two main components: a core system known as microkernel and plug-in components.

- **Microkernel**: The heart of the architecture, responsible for basic operations and managing plug-ins. It handles core processes and offers common services to the plug-ins.
- **Plug-ins**: Modules or components can be added to the microkernel to extend its capabilities. These are typically developed independently and can be dynamically loaded or unloaded during runtime.

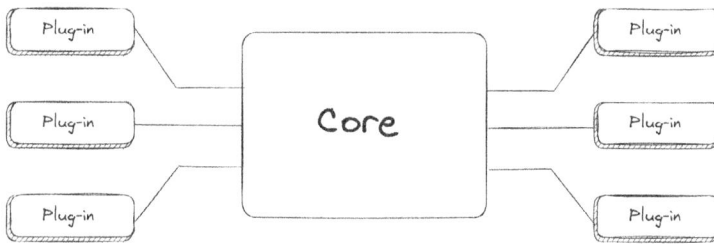

Figure 7.4: Microkernel core components

You may have seen this architecture style in many products, including your browser or IDEs. There are several advantages to using this style, including:

- **Flexibility and Scalability**: New features can be added as plug-ins without modifying the core system, making the system highly adaptable.
- **Maintainability**: Separation of core functionality and extended features simplifies maintenance and upgrades.
- **Customization**: Allows for tailored solutions where users can choose which plug-ins to install based on their needs.

In the Microkernel (Plug-in) Architecture, the Registry and Contracts are two common parts. These parts facilitate the interaction between the microkernel and its plug-ins, ensuring seamless integration and functioning of the entire system.

Registry:

- The Registry acts as a central directory in the architecture. It keeps track of the available plug-ins and their capabilities. When plug-ins are loaded into

---

the system, they register themselves with the Registry, providing information about their functions, interfaces, or services they offer.

- It serves as a lookup service where the microkernel and other plug-ins can discover and access the functionalities provided by different plug-ins. This setup allows for the dynamic addition or removal of plug-ins without disrupting the core system.

Contracts:

- Contracts, often defined as interfaces or abstract classes, specify a set of methods and properties that plug-ins must implement. They establish a formal agreement between the microkernel and plug-ins, detailing how they should interact with the core system and each other.
- By adhering to these contracts, plug-ins ensure compatibility with the microkernel, allowing them to communicate and operate cohesively. Contracts provide a way to enforce consistency and standardization, making sure that plug-ins adhere to the expected protocols and data formats.

Together, they allow for a flexible and well-organized system where new functionalities can be integrated smoothly without compromising the integrity or stability of the core system. This setup is particularly beneficial in environments where modularity, extensibility, and maintainability are key requirements.

Although this style may have a higher level of complexity than directly using it in Flutter, certain concepts can be taken from its architecture and applied in Flutter. Let me explain how it can be used in a particular scenario. Suppose you create an app with multiple teams working on different views as value streams (owning the entire feature). Each team should have complete control over the module they are designing and developing from start to finish. Here's a simplified illustration using Flutter's dynamic capabilities, focusing on a hypothetical e-commerce app:

Defining the Microkernel: The microkernel is the base of your app. It handles core functionalities like network requests, user authentication, and basic UI elements.

```
class Microkernel {
  void authenticateUser() {
    // Handle user authentication
  }

  void initializeCoreUI() {
    // Initialize core UI components
  }

  // Other core functionalities...
}
```

Creating Plug-in Contracts: Define an interface that all plug-ins must implement. This ensures that the microkernel can interact with them uniformly.

```
abstract class PluginInterface {
  void load();
  Widget buildWidget();
  // Other necessary methods...
}
```

Implementing Plug-ins: Develop plug-ins as separate classes that implement the PluginInterface. Each plug-in can represent a feature like a product category.

```
class ElectronicsPlugin implements PluginInterface {
  @override
  void load() {
    // Load resources, data, etc.
  }

  @override
  Widget buildWidget() {
    return ElectronicsWidget();
  }
}

class ClothingPlugin implements PluginInterface {
  @override
  void load() {
    // Load resources, data, etc.
  }

  @override
  Widget buildWidget() {
    return ClothingWidget();
  }
}

// ... other plugin implementations
```

Registry and Dynamic Loading: The Registry keeps track of available and active plug-ins. It can load or unload plug-ins based on user actions or app state.

```
class PluginRegistry {
  List<PluginInterface> _availablePlugins = [
    ElectronicsPlugin(),
    ClothingPlugin()
  ];
  List<PluginInterface> _activePlugins = [];

  void activatePlugin(PluginInterface plugin) {
    plugin.load();
```

```
    _activePlugins.add(plugin);
  }

  void deactivatePlugin(PluginInterface plugin) {
    _activePlugins.remove(plugin);
  }

  List<Widget> getActivePluginWidgets() {
    return _activePlugins
        .map((p) => p.buildWidget())
        .toList();
  }
}
```

Integrating with the Flutter App: You can use the Registry to manage plugins in your main app based on user interactions or choices.

```
class MyApp extends StatelessWidget {
  final PluginRegistry _registry = PluginRegistry();

  @override
  Widget build(BuildContext context) {
    // Example: Activate 'ElectronicsPlugin'
    // based on user choice
    _registry.activatePlugin(ElectronicsPlugin());

    return MaterialApp(
      home: Scaffold(
        body: Column(
          children: _registry.getActivePluginWidgets(),
        ),
      ),
    );
  }
}
```

This example provides a basic structure for a Microkernel (Plug-in) Architecture in Flutter. The `Microkernel` class handles core app functionalities, `PluginInterface` defines a contract for plug-ins, and `PluginRegistry` manages the plug-ins. Each plug-in can be activated or deactivated, reflecting in the UI as needed.

Using the router as a registry part in your Flutter app is a much more flexible way. Let me write another example here.

Core Application: The main application initializes and decides which plugins to load based on the app configuration. It also sets up the routing for the entire application.

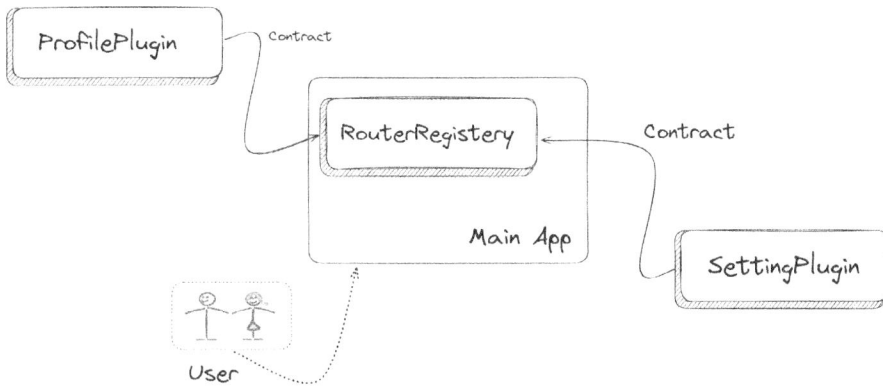

Figure 7.5: Microkernel via Router Registry in Flutter

```dart
// Imagine ProfilePlugin and SettingsPlugin
// either added as an independent
// package or it's an internal package
// in the same repository
void main() {
  final appConfig = { //<---
    'loadProfile': true,
    'loadSettings': true
  };

  if (appConfig['loadProfile']!) { //<---
    ProfilePlugin().register();
  }
  if (appConfig['loadSettings']!) { //<---
    SettingsPlugin().register();
  }

  runApp(const MyApp());
}

class MyApp extends StatelessWidget {
  const MyApp({super.key});

  @override
  Widget build(BuildContext context) {
    return MaterialApp(
      title: 'Plugin Demo',
      theme: ThemeData(primarySwatch: Colors.blue),
      home: const HomePage(),
      onGenerateRoute: RouterRegistry.generateRoute,
    );
  }
```

```
}

class HomePage extends StatelessWidget {
  const HomePage({super.key});

  @override
  Widget build(BuildContext context) {
    return Scaffold(
      appBar: AppBar(title: const Text('Plugin Demo Home')),
      body: Center(
        child: Column(
          mainAxisSize: MainAxisSize.min,
          children: <Widget>[
            ElevatedButton(
              onPressed: () => Navigator.pushNamed(
                context,
                '/profile',
              ),
              child: const Text('Go to Profile'),
            ),
            ElevatedButton(
              onPressed: () => Navigator.pushNamed(
                context,
                '/settings',
              ),
              child: const Text('Go to Settings'),
            ),
          ],
        ),
      ),
    );
  }
}
```

As you can see here, even based on **appConfig,** I can detach or attach a plugin to the core. Indeed, an example is simple and requires restarting the app, but it can be much smarter.

Create Registry: The RouterRegistry class is the central point for managing routes registered by different plugins.

```
class RouterRegistry {
  static final Map<String, WidgetBuilder> _routes = {};

  static void registerRoute(
      String routeName, WidgetBuilder builder) {
    _routes[routeName] = builder;
  }
```

```
  static Route<dynamic> generateRoute(
      RouteSettings settings) {
    if (_routes.containsKey(settings.name)) {
      return MaterialPageRoute(
        builder: _routes[settings.name]!,
      );
    } else {
      return MaterialPageRoute(
        builder: (_) => Scaffold(
          body: Center(
            child: Text(
                'No route defined for ${settings.name}'),
          ),
        ),
      );
    }
  }
}
```

Define the Abstract Contract (Plugin Interface): Create an abstract class that declares the methods that all plugins must implement. This class acts as a contract that plugin classes must fulfill.

```
abstract class PluginContract {
  void register();
  // Other common methods can be added here
}
```

Implement the Contract in Plugins: Modify the ProfilePlugin and SettingsPlugin to implement the newly created abstract class, PluginContract.

```
class ProfilePlugin implements PluginContract {
  @override
  void register() {
    RouterRegistry.registerRoute(
      '/profile',
      (context) => const ProfilePage(),
    );
  }
}

class ProfilePage extends StatelessWidget {
  const ProfilePage({super.key});

  @override
  Widget build(BuildContext context) {
    return Scaffold(
      appBar: AppBar(
```

```
        title: const Text('Profile'),
      ),
      body: const Center(
        child: Text('This is the profile page!'),
      ),
    );
  }
}

class SettingsPlugin implements PluginContract {
  @override
  void register() {
    RouterRegistry.registerRoute(
      '/settings',
      (context) => const SettingsPage(),
    );
  }
}

class SettingsPage extends StatelessWidget {
  const SettingsPage({super.key});

  @override
  Widget build(BuildContext context) {
    return Scaffold(
      appBar: AppBar(title: const Text('Settings')),
      body: const Center(
        child: Text('This is the settings page!'),
      ),
    );
  }
}
```

Remember, this conceptual framework can be expanded and refined based on the specific requirements of your Flutter application.

Let me show you how to expand this contract between Core and Plug-ins. Imagine we want to have a common analytics service. Update the `PluginContract` to include a reference to the `AnalyticsService`.

```
abstract class PluginContract {
  late final AnalyticsService analyticsService;

  void register();

  void setAnalyticsService(AnalyticsService service) {
    analyticsService = service;
  }
```

```
    // Other common methods and properties...
}
```

Now, all Plug-ins must register and have access to the `AnalyticsService` provided by the core system.

```
class ProfilePlugin implements PluginContract {
  @override
  late final AnalyticsService analyticsService;

  @override
  void register() {
    RouterRegistry.registerRoute(
      '/profile',
      (context) => const ProfilePage(),
    );
    analyticsService.trackEvent('ProfilePluginLoaded', {});
  }

  @override
  void setAnalyticsService(AnalyticsService service) {
    analyticsService = service;
  }
}
```

When initializing plugins, the core system should provide them with the analytics service.

```
void main() {
  final appConfig = {
    'loadProfile': true,
    'loadSettings': true
  };

  final analyticsService = AnalyticsService();

  if (appConfig['loadProfile']!) {
    final profilePlugin = ProfilePlugin();

    profilePlugin.setAnalyticsService(analyticsService);

    profilePlugin.register();
  }

  if (appConfig['loadSettings']!) {
    SettingsPlugin().register();
  }
```

```
  runApp(const MyApp());
}
```

In this setup, the core system is responsible for instantiating and providing the AnalyticsService to each plugin. Plugins can then track events or perform other analytics-related tasks using this service.

A common question is how to enforce an architecture pattern to the plugin. There are several aspects to consider while answering this question. For example, all teams can agree to follow the same architectural pattern principles and common best practices across all plugins. However, as long as plugins are using contracts that are built up, they can handle their internal private implementation as they want.

Handling many different patterns in one application across different plugins is not optimal. Therefore, all teams developing plugins should follow a common pattern, best practices, set of rules, and guidelines agreed upon between them. Usually, in a larger company, there is an infrastructure or enabler team, which works on tools and guidelines that every other team would use, making it easier to be consistent.

7.5   Other Architectures and Paradigms

Architectural styles continue after the ones covered so far in this book. There are several other architectures and paradigms that, although beyond the scope of this text, are valuable for developers to explore. These include:

- **Microservices Architecture**: A style where an application is structured as a collection of loosely coupled services, each implementing a specific business capability. This approach offers high scalability and flexibility, making it suitable for complex applications with rapidly evolving business requirements.
- **Service-based Architecture**: Similar to microservices but often with larger service scopes, this architecture emphasizes using services as the main component for building applications. It's particularly useful for integrating diverse systems or building applications that require a high degree of interoperability.
- **Space-based Architecture**: Designed to address scalability issues in traditional database-driven applications, this architecture utilizes a "space" that acts as both memory and data storage, supporting large, distributed data sets.
- **Pipeline Architecture**: In this style, data processing happens in stages (much like an assembly line), and it's particularly useful for streamlining complex transformations and workflows.

Beyond architectural styles, there are also important conceptual frameworks that can greatly influence app development in Flutter. One such concept is **Domain-Driven Design (DDD)**. DDD introduces patterns and principles that are highly applicable to Flutter development, such as:

- **Modularization**: Breaking down the app into smaller, manageable packages. This can be done internally within the app and externally through separate libraries or services.
- **Ubiquitous Language**: Establishing a common language across the organization to ensure a shared understanding of the domain among all team members. This approach fosters clear communication and consistency in the codebase.
- **Bounded Contexts**: Defining clear boundaries for these modules or packages. In Flutter, this could mean separating different functionalities of the app into distinct Dart packages or using Flutter's modularization capabilities like creating packages to maintain clear boundaries.

These advanced concepts and architectural styles provide a broader perspective on building sophisticated and scalable applications. While not all may directly apply to every Flutter project, understanding these varied paradigms can enhance a developer's ability to design and implement robust, efficient, and maintainable applications.

7.6   Conclusion

Understanding these architectural styles is not just about technical architecture; it's about adopting a mindset prioritizing maintainability, scalability, and efficient problem-solving. As technology continues to evolve, these architectural styles are also rapidly evolving and changing, and reading again here, there is no one-size-fits-all design and architecture.

The key takeaway is the importance of selecting the right architecture that aligns with your application's project requirements, team dynamics, and long-term vision. This knowledge forms a strong foundation for building high-quality, robust Flutter applications that stand the test of time and changing technological landscapes.

CHAPTER 8

UI Architecture Patterns

Reviewer: Roman Jaquez

The previous chapter discussed the difference between architectural styles and patterns. As mentioned, "Architectural Patterns," often called "Software Design Patterns," address recurring architectural problems and solve specific issues. They usually come by defining practices and implementation.

Architecture patterns have been created to solve presentation layer challenges in high-level architecture styles, specifically with UI challenges. The present chapter focuses on patterns that are particularly relevant to UI development in Flutter. Some of these patterns are more well-known in the industry, such as BLoC or MVVM.

Understanding different patterns, strengths, and limitations is important when choosing an approach that aligns with the project's objectives. However, it's essential to acknowledge that becoming an expert in any technical area takes much time and practice. Just like any other field, proficiency in these patterns is developed over years of hands-on experience in their implementation. In the upcoming two chapters, we will take an architectural perspective to examine the broader aspects of applying patterns. We won't delve into implementation details or rare scenarios but instead aim to establish a foundational understanding of pattern selection in Flutter UI development. This will set the stage for more advanced study in the future.

8.1 The Landscape of UI Architectures

The landscape of UI architecture in software development, particularly for frameworks like Flutter, is diverse and evolving. In Flutter development, choosing the right UI architecture involves weighing these factors against the specific needs and goals of the project. It's about balancing technical requirements, the application's complexity, and the development team's dynamics.

As we explore various architectural patterns, we must consider how they align with key factors that significantly impact application design, development, and maintenance. Factors such as:

- **Data Binding**: Architectures vary in synchronizing the UI and underlying data models. Effective data binding ensures UI updates are responsive and consistent with the application's state. In Flutter, this is especially important given its reactive framework.
- **Separation of Concerns**: A fundamental principle in many UI architectures is the clear separation between the user interface, business logic, and data handling layers. This separation enhances the maintainability and scalability of the application, allowing developers to focus on one aspect of the application at a time.
- **Managing Complexity**: As applications grow in features and user interfaces become more intricate, the chosen architecture must handle this increasing complexity without becoming overly convoluted. This often involves modularizing the application into smaller, manageable components.
- **Scalability and Team Efficiency**: The architecture should support scaling the application and the development team. It should facilitate adding new features and handle increasing users, all while enabling the team to maintain or improve development speed.

Although it's helpful to be familiar with various UI architecture patterns, it's important to remember that there's no such thing as the "best" pattern. An appropriate pattern relies on several factors; what works for one project may not necessarily work for another.

8.2 Prominent Flutter Architectures

In the Flutter ecosystem, several prominent architectures stand out for their effectiveness in building robust and scalable applications. Interestingly, many of these patterns can be traced back to the layered architectural styles we explored in the previous chapter. Let's get started.

8.2.1 Three-layer

The Three-Layer Architecture is a fundamental pattern in Flutter app development, providing a structured approach to organizing code and functionality. This architecture is divided into three main layers:

1. **Presentation (UI) Layer**: This is the topmost layer, primarily dealing with the user interface. Flutter consists of widgets and screens defining visual elements and user interactions. The Presentation Layer is responsible for displaying information to the user and capturing user inputs, which are then passed down to the business logic layer.

2. **Business Logic Layer**: Often referred to as the domain layer, it contains the application's core business logic. This layer processes the data received from the presentation layer, applies business rules and validations, and then communicates with the data layer for data persistence or further processing. It bridges the presentation and data layers, decoupling the user interface from the data handling logic.

3. **Data Layer**: The bottom layer is where data management occurs. It involves data persistence, retrieval, and data sources such as databases, network calls, and APIs. The data layer abstracts the origin of the data so that the business logic layer and presentation layer do not need to know where and how the data is stored or fetched.

Generally speaking, all layers are closed off, meaning no high-level layer can directly access more than one layer below it.

Implementing the Three-Layer Architecture in Flutter offers several benefits:

- **Separation of Concerns**: Each layer has a distinct responsibility, making the codebase more organized, maintainable, and scalable.
- **Easier Testing and Debugging**: Since the concerns are separated, testing and debugging individual application parts is easier.
- **Flexibility**: Changing the UI or modifying data sources has minimal impact on the rest of the application, provided the interfaces between layers remain consistent.

Although separating presentation, domain, and data is a standard approach in application architecture, it's most effective at a smaller scale. As an application grows and each layer becomes more complex, further modularization becomes necessary. Instead of strictly adhering to presentation-domain data, especially for larger systems, you may need to introduce other modules and layers. This pattern is great because of this flexibility.

The *repository* pattern, also known in the Android and Flutter communities, is inspired by this pattern. This is one of the simplest patterns that can be easily implemented, understood, and scaled to fit many Flutter applications of different sizes.

When architecting a layered structure for a Flutter application, several key principles should guide your design to ensure effectiveness and maintainability:

Clearly Defined Data Layer: Establish a well-structured data layer responsible for managing data sources and persistent storage. This layer interacts with databases, network services, and other data providers.

Clearly Defined UI Layer: Develop a distinct UI layer focused on presentation and user interactions. It should display information and respond to user inputs, leveraging Flutter's powerful widget system.

Access Rules Between Layers: Define explicit access protocols for how different layers interact. It's crucial to refer back to fundamental concepts of layer

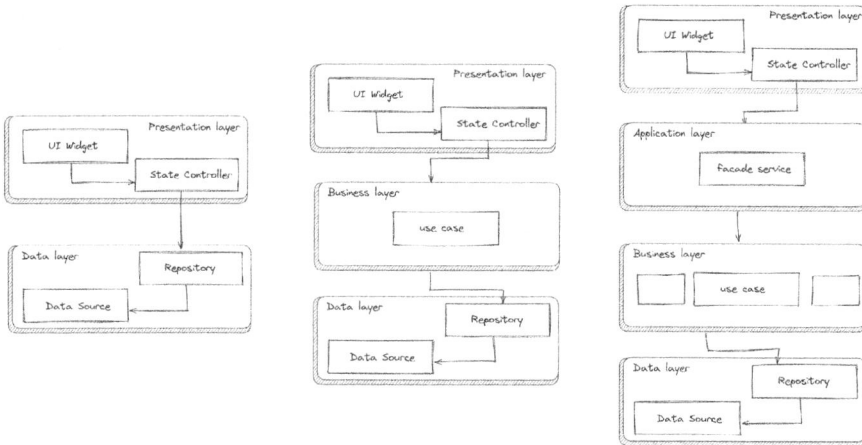

Figure 8.1: Layer Architecture Patterns Variations Promoting Repository Pattern

interaction, ensuring that the communication is organized and follows predefined pathways.

Immutability and Single Source of Truth: By having a single source of truth and an immutable data store, unexpected side effects can be prevented. This ensures that the data store is modified only by the corresponding layer, making it thread-safe and performant.

Understanding Component Purposes: Define clear roles for each component in your architecture. For instance, a repository should manage data operations, a service should handle business logic, and state managers should coordinate state and data retrieval for UI components. Ensure that UI widgets primarily interact with the state manager for data.

Avoid Over-engineering: Embrace simplicity in your architectural design. Start with a straightforward structure and only introduce additional layers or complexity when necessary. Premature complexity can lead to technical debt, making the application harder to maintain and evolve.

Folder Structure: Typically, layers will show them in the context of folder organization. The folders can be either Feature or Function first.

```
// Feature first folders
lib
|--common
|     |--widgets
|     |--themes
|     |--settings
|     |--utils
|--constants
|--localization
|--features
|     |--profile
```

UI Architecture Patterns

```
|          |--presentation
|              |--widgets
|              |--state
|          |--business
|              |--usecase
|          |--data
|              |--repository
|              |--data
|     |--setting
|     |--cart
|--routing
```

The Function or Layer's first example is as follows:

```
// Function or Layer first
lib
|--common
|     |--widgets
|     |--themes
|     |--settings
|     |--utils
|--constants
|--localization
|--presentation
|   |--widgets
|     |--profile
|     |--setting
|   |--state
|     |--profile
|     |--setting
|--business
|   |--usecase
|--data
|   |--repository
|   |--data
|--routing
```

Consider the application, team, and architecture pattern when choosing between folder options. Providing a definitive answer for many software engineering aspects is difficult since everything depends on specific circumstances and variables. **It Depends**. These are principles that I learned over time.

One of the best practices in feature-based architecture for larger applications is introducing an API interface for each feature. This way, all the implementation details are hidden behind the API. If you need access from one feature to another, you can call via the API interface and not directly access the implementation. This makes your features loosely coupled and helps to avoid unnecessary dependencies between them. Although it introduces a lot of overhead, leveraging this approach when your application becomes big enough is highly recommended.

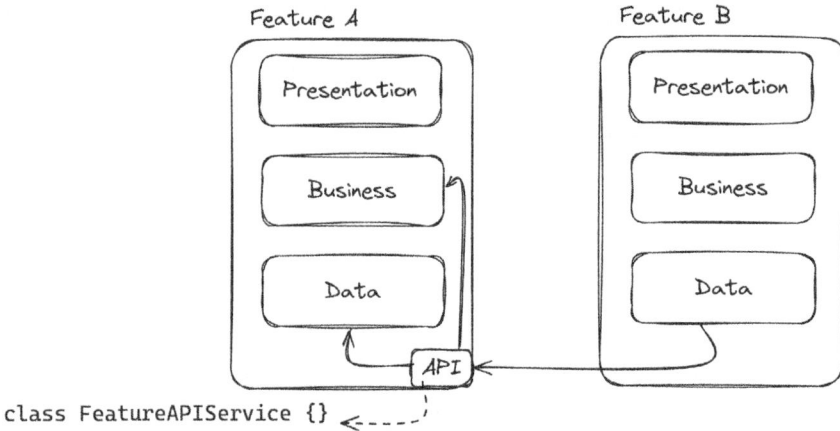

Figure 8.2: Feature API to Hide Feature Layers Details Implementation

Let's implement a three-layer repository architecture pattern without any dependencies or packages.

Let's walk through the updated implementation of your Flutter Todo app, explaining each layer and their interactions in detail.

Domain Layer

Data Sources: `LocalTodoDataSource` and `RemoteTodoDataSource` are implementations of the `TodoRepository` interface. They handle data-related operations like fetching, adding, updating, and deleting todos. The Interface could be optional depending on the size of your application, but this is a good practice.

```
// local_datasource.dart
class LocalTodoDataSource implements TodoRepository {
  @override
  Future<void> addTodo(TodoDataModel todo) {
    throw UnimplementedError();
  }

  @override
  Future<void> deleteTodo(String id) {
    throw UnimplementedError();
  }

  @override
  Future<List<TodoDataModel>> fetchTodos() {
    return Future.delayed(
      const Duration(seconds: 5),
      () => List<TodoDataModel>.generate(
        10,
        (index) => TodoDataModel(
```

```
        id: '$index',
        title: 'Todo $index',
        isCompleted: false,
        createdAt: DateTime.now().toLocal().toString(),
        updatedAt: DateTime.now().toLocal().toString(),
      ),
    ),
  );
}


  @override
  Future<void> updateTodo(TodoDataModel todo) {
    throw UnimplementedError();
  }
}

// remote_datasource.dart
class RemoteTodoDataSource implements TodoRepository { ... }
```

Data Model: TodoDataModel represents the data structure of a to-do item, including serialization methods for converting to and from JSON. This data model stays within the data layer.

```
// todo_data_model.dart
class TodoDataModel {
  TodoDataModel({
    required this.id,
    required this.title,
    this.createdAt,
    this.updatedAt,
    this.isCompleted = false,
  });

  final String id;
  final String title;
  final bool isCompleted;
  final String? createdAt;
  final String? updatedAt;

  factory TodoDataModel.fromJson(Map<String, dynamic> json) {
    return TodoDataModel(
      id: json['id'],
      title: json['title'],
      isCompleted: json['isCompleted'],
      createdAt: json['createdAt'],
      updatedAt: json['updatedAt'],
    );
  }
```

```
  toJson() {
    return {
      'id': id,
      'title': title,
      'isCompleted': isCompleted,
      'createdAt': createdAt,
      'updatedAt': updatedAt,
    };
  }
}
```

Repository: `_TodoRepositoryImpl` is a concrete implementation of the `TodoRepository` interface. It decides whether to fetch data from the local or remote data source. In this file, I have created a global variable called `todoRepositoryInstance` for dependency injection. It is important to note that using global variables for dependency injection is not considered a good practice. However, I have implemented it this way to keep the code simple without external packages. This way, you can better understand the implementation of the different layers without any extra noise. As you can see, this has been purely done using Flutter's built-in features.

```
// Abstract Interface to ensure all repositories
// and data sources are sharing common interface
abstract interface class TodoRepository {
  Future<List<TodoDataModel>> fetchTodos();
  Future<void> addTodo(TodoDataModel todo);
  Future<void> updateTodo(TodoDataModel todo);
  Future<void> deleteTodo(String id);
}

// I intentionally used a private class
// for this example, I do not want to expose this class
class _TodoRepositoryImpl implements TodoRepository {
  final LocalTodoDataSource localDataSource;
  final RemoteTodoDataSource remoteDataSource;

  const _TodoRepositoryImpl(
    this.localDataSource,
    this.remoteDataSource,
  );

  @override
  Future<List<TodoDataModel>> fetchTodos() async {
    try {
      return await remoteDataSource.fetchTodos();
    } catch (e) {
      return localDataSource.fetchTodos();
```

```
    }
  }

  @override
  Future<void> addTodo(TodoDataModel todo) async {
    // Implement logic combining local and remote data sources
  }

  @override
  Future<void> deleteTodo(String id) async {
    // Implement logic combining local and remote data sources
  }

  @override
  Future<void> updateTodo(TodoDataModel todo) async {
    // Implement logic combining local and remote data sources
  }
}

// Typically, this would be a singleton
// or you must use a dependency injection framework
final todoRepositoryInstance = _TodoRepositoryImpl(
  LocalTodoDataSource(),
  RemoteTodoDataSource(),
);
```

Domain Layer - Business Logic

Todo Domain Model: Todo extends `TodoDataModel`, adding domain-specific logic, such as generating a slug from the title. This is the main model that the presentation layer uses. It's generally better to keep these separated. However, since this app's data model shares every property with the domain model, I've extended it to inherit and add my domain logic.

```
// Domain Model with Business Logic
// Model (entity) class
class Todo extends TodoDataModel {
  Todo({
    required super.id,
    required super.title,
    super.isCompleted,
    // create URL from title a domain logic
    required this.slug,
  });

  final String slug;

  // business logic here for the domain
  factory Todo.fromDataModel(TodoDataModel dataModel) {
```

```
    return Todo(
      id: dataModel.id,
      // You can manipulate the data from the data layer here
      // before it is passed to the presentation layer
      title: ValidatorUseCases.text(dataModel.title),
          //For example, we call here slufigy to create a new value
      slug: ValidatorUseCases.slugify(dataModel.title),
      isCompleted: dataModel.isCompleted,
    );
  }

  toDataModel() {
    return TodoDataModel(
      id: id,
      title: title,
      isCompleted: isCompleted,
    );
  }
}
```

Use Cases: TodoUseCases defines the business operations related to todos, like getting todos. _TodoUseCases implements these operations using the TodoRepository. Here is where you get access to the data layer. I created a global variable called 'todosUseCasesInstance'. This variable ensures that an instance of use cases is available in the presentation layer. Although this may not be considered a best practice, it demonstrates the correct relationship between layers and components.

```
// This seems redundant here
// But since I am creating
// a global variable of instance from
// the concrete implementation
// I wanted to expose an interface
// to the presentation layer instead
abstract interface class TodoUseCases {
  Future<List<Todo>> getTodos();
  Future<void> addTodo(Todo todo);
}

// concrete implementation
class _TodoUseCases implements TodoUseCases {
  // dependency to the repository from the data layer
  _TodoUseCases(this.repository);

  final TodoRepository repository;

  Future<List<Todo>> getTodos() async {
    // call data layer methods
```

```dart
    final todos = await repository.fetchTodos();
    // add business-related logic here
    // For example, "fromDataModel" contains domain logic
    return todos
        .map(
          (todo) => Todo.fromDataModel(todo),
        )
        .toList();
  }

  Future<void> addTodo(Todo todo) {
    // add business-related logic here
    final todoDataModel = todo.toDataModel();
    return repository.addTodo(todoDataModel);
  }
}

// Typically this would be a singleton
// or you must use a dependency injection framework
final todosUseCasesInstance = _TodoUseCases(
  todoRepositoryInstance,
);
```

Other Use Cases: ValidatorUseCases provides static data validation and transformation methods, such as sanitizing text input and generating slugs. This is for demonstration purposes. However, it is recommended to separate use cases into their relevant files and classes.

```dart
// Additional Utility Use Cases If related to Todos
class ValidatorUseCases {
  static String text(String text) {
    return text.trim();
  }

  // This is just an example of a business logic method
  static String slugify(String input) {
    // Lowercase and replace
    // non-alphanumeric characters with hyphens
    final nonAlphanumeric = RegExp(r'[^a-z0-9\s-]');
    final normalized = input
        .toLowerCase()
        .replaceAll(nonAlphanumeric, '-');

    // Trim whitespace and hyphens,
    // then replace multiple consecutive hyphens
    final trimmed = normalized.trim().replaceAll(
          RegExp(r'-{2,}'),
          '-',
```

```
    );

    // Optionally convert remaining spaces
    //to hyphens (depending on your needs)
    final hyphenatedSpaces = trimmed.replaceAll(
      ' ',
      '-',
    );

    return hyphenatedSpaces;
  }
}
```

Presentation Layer

State: TodoState is an abstract class that defines the structure of the UI state.
_TodoState is a concrete implementation that manages the UI state and communicates with the domain layer to fetch todos. I am creating a global variable todoStateInstance to send it to the screen implementation for the same reason as I mentioned earlier. As you can see here I am just using changeNotifier a built-in feature in Flutter and this still works in my architecture pattern.

```
abstract class TodoState extends ChangeNotifier {
  List<Todo> get todos;
  Future<void> getTodos();
}

class _TodoState extends TodoState {
  _TodoState(this.todoUseCases);

  TodoUseCases todoUseCases;

  List<Todo> _todos = [];

  @override
  List<Todo> get todos => _todos;

  @override
  Future<void> getTodos() async {
    _todos = await todoUseCases.getTodos();
    notifyListeners();
  }
}

// typically this would be a singleton
// or you must use a dependency injection framework
final TodoState todoStateInstance = _TodoState(
  todosUseCasesInstance,
);
```

UI Widgets: `TodoListScreen` is a stateless widget that interacts with `TodoState` to display a list of todos. It triggers data fetching on initialization and rebuilds the UI when the state changes. I'm utilizing the `ListenableBuilder` to keep track of changes in the todo state notifier and rebuild the UI.

```
class TodoListScreen extends StatelessWidget {
  TodoListScreen({
    super.key,
    required this.todoState,
  }) {
    todoState.getTodos(); //<---
  }

  final TodoState todoState;

  @override
  Widget build(BuildContext context) {
    return Scaffold(
      appBar: AppBar(title: const Text('Todo List')),
      body: ListenableBuilder( //<---
        listenable: todoState,
        builder: (BuildContext context, Widget? child) {
          return ListView.builder(
            itemCount: todoState.todos.length,
            itemBuilder: (context, index) {
              return Text(todoState.todos[index].title);
            },
          );
        },
      ),
    );
  }
}
```

The main purpose of this example is to understand how different layers interact with each other. You can utilize a package to manage dependency injection or opt for a smarter UI state management. The best part is that if you desire to replace state management with a different approach, you won't have to make any modifications except in the UI section where the state is built and in the state implementation, where it uses a change notifier. I have emphasized this all along - state management is just a single component of your architecture. If you have planned your architecture well, you can easily substitute it with something else.

This architecture provides a clear separation of concerns, ensuring each layer focuses on its specific responsibilities. The domain layer handles business logic and data transformations, the data layer manages data fetching and persistence, and the presentation layer deals with rendering the UI and responding to user interactions. This setup facilitates the maintainability, testability, and scalability of the application.

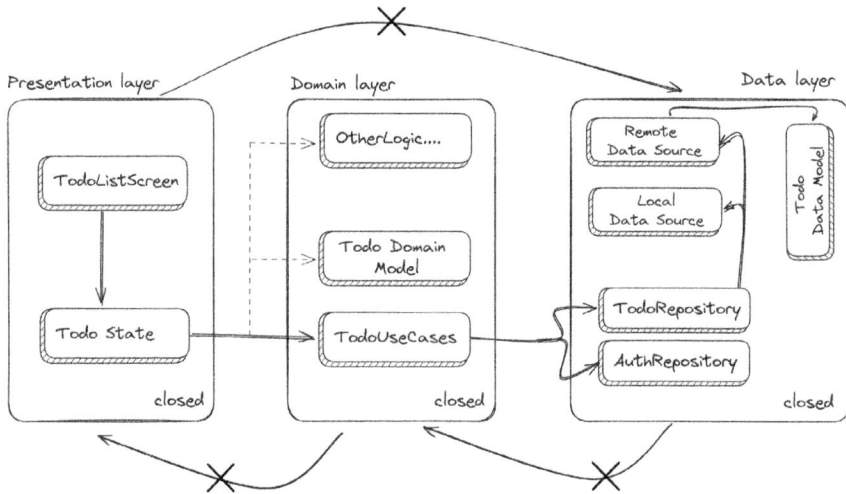

Figure 8.3: Todo App three-layer Architecture Pattern

8.2.2 BLoC

The **BLoC (Business Logic Component)** pattern is an architectural model in Flutter used to manage state and separate business logic from the UI (User Interface). Developed by the Google team, BLoC helps create reactive and maintainable applications. Do not get confused with `flutter_bloc` package, at this point, we are just talking about the pattern and the `bloc` package helps to implement this pattern easier.

Let's take a look at some of the core concepts of BLoC:

Separation of Concerns: BLoC distinctly separates business logic from UI components, ensuring that the UI and business logic aren't tightly coupled. This separation aids in more manageable and readable code.

Reactivity and Stream-Based: BLoC uses Dart's stream features to handle the flow of data within an app. This approach fits well with Flutter's reactive nature, ensuring the UI updates efficiently in response to state changes.

State Management: BLoC provides an organized way to manage the state, making it easier to track, debug, and maintain state changes across large and complex applications.

Scalability: As applications grow, BLoC scales well, making it suitable for large-scale applications due to its modular and reusable components.

The BLoC pattern draws inspiration from the event-driven and layered architecture styles and shares similarities with the three-layer architecture pattern. The key components of BLoC are located in the presentation layer, where your widgets dispatch an event and subscribe to a bloc stream to receive state changes.

To implement the Todo App using the BLoC pattern in Flutter, we will modify your previous implementation from a three-layer architecture to fit into the BLoC architecture pattern. Implementing the BLoC pattern using the `flutter_bloc` package, which is a standard package, is much easier than creating it from scratch.

This package has been used to create the example that follows. Here's how you can structure it:

Data Layer

This layer remains largely the same as in your previous implementation, with `LocalTodoDataSource` and `RemoteTodoDataSource` handling data-related operations.

```
// Local and Remote Data Sources
class LocalTodoDataSource implements TodoRepository { ... }
class RemoteTodoDataSource implements TodoRepository { ... }

// Data Model
class TodoDataModel { ... }

// Repository Implementation
class _TodoRepositoryImpl implements TodoRepository { ... }
```

Domain Layer

We keep the `Todo` domain model and use cases.

```
// Domain Model with Business Logic
class Todo extends TodoDataModel { ... }

// Use Cases Implementation
class _TodoUseCases implements TodoUseCases { ... }
```

Presentation Layer

The BLoC layer will replace your current state management implementation.

Events: Define events that represent user interactions or lifecycle events.

```
abstract class TodoEvent {}

class LoadTodos extends TodoEvent {}

class AddTodo extends TodoEvent {
  final Todo todo;
  AddTodo(this.todo);
}

class UpdateTodo extends TodoEvent {
  final Todo todo;
  UpdateTodo(this.todo);
```

```
}

class DeleteTodo extends TodoEvent {
  final String id;
  DeleteTodo(this.id);
}
```

States: Define states that represent different states of the UI.

```
abstract class TodoState {}

class TodosLoading extends TodoState {}

class TodosLoaded extends TodoState {
  final List<Todo> todos;
  TodosLoaded(this.todos);
}

class TodoError extends TodoState {}
```

Bloc: Implement the Bloc that processes events and emits states. This is a replacement for ChangeNotifier.

```
class TodoBloc extends Bloc<TodoEvent, TodoState> {
  final TodoUseCases todoUseCases;

  TodoBloc(this.todoUseCases)
      : super(
          TodosLoading(),
        ) {
    // Listen to an upcoming event
    on<LoadTodos>(_onLoadTodos);
    // Other event handlers...
  }

  // Handle coming events
  Future<void> _onLoadTodos(
    LoadTodos event,
    Emitter<TodoState> emit,
  ) async {
    try {
      // Access to Business Layer use cases
      final todos = await todoUseCases.getTodos();
      // emit a new state to notify all subscribers
      // to update the UI accordingly
      emit(TodosLoaded(todos));
    } catch (_) {
      emit(TodoError());
```

```
      }
    }
}

// typically, this would be a singleton
// or you must use a dependency injection framework
final todoBlocInstance = TodoBloc(
  todosUseCasesInstance,
);
```

Use BlocBuilder, BlocListener, or BlocConsumer to build your UI based on the Bloc's state in the presentation layer.

```
class TodoListScreen extends StatelessWidget {
  const TodoListScreen({super.key});

  @override
  Widget build(BuildContext context) {
    return Scaffold(
      appBar: AppBar(
        title: const Text('Todo List'),
      ),
      // listen to TodoBloc state change
      body: BlocBuilder<TodoBloc, TodoState>(//<---
        builder: (context, state) {
          if (state is TodosLoading) {
            return const CircularProgressIndicator();
          } else if (state is TodosLoaded) {//<---
            return ListView(
              children: state.todos
                .map(
                  (todo) => Text(
                    todo.title,
                  ),
                )
                .toList(),
            );
          } else {
            return Column(
              children: [
                const Text('Something went wrong!'),
                ElevatedButton(
                  onPressed: () {
                    // add another event if needed
                    BlocProvider.of<TodoBloc>(context).add(
                      LoadTodos(),
                    );
                  },
```

```
                child: const Text('Retry'),
              ),
            ],
          );
        }
      },
    ),
  );
  }
}
```

Main App Entry: Initialize and provide the `TodoBloc` in the main function.

```
void main() {
  runApp(MaterialApp(
    // Provide a block that is needed to TodoListScreen.
    home: BlocProvider(
      // Immediately add LoadTodos event to fetch data
      create: (context) => todoBlocInstance
        ..add(
          LoadTodos(),
        ),
      child: const TodoListScreen(),
    ),
  ));
}
```

In this setup, `TodoBloc` listens to events from the UI, interacts with the use cases, and emits states that the UI listens to and updates accordingly. This architectural pattern makes it easier to work with streams and utilize reactive programming.

This example illustrates how we refactored the presentation layer while leaving the other layers unchanged. You can perform the same operations with other state management.

Depending on your app, the layers and their components may change. For example, in many applications, I have seen that the presentation layer consists of UI and Bloc, which contain all the business logic within Bloc itself. The domain layer only consists of repositories, and the data layer only contains data sources.

As I have demonstrated, it's up to you to manage your layers, but I prefer to keep all logic out of state management and keep the repositories in the data layer. I think it's less coupled and makes it easier to replace a component of the architecture if needed.

8.2.3 MVVM

The Model-View-ViewModel (MVVM) pattern is a structural design pattern that separates objects into three distinct groups:

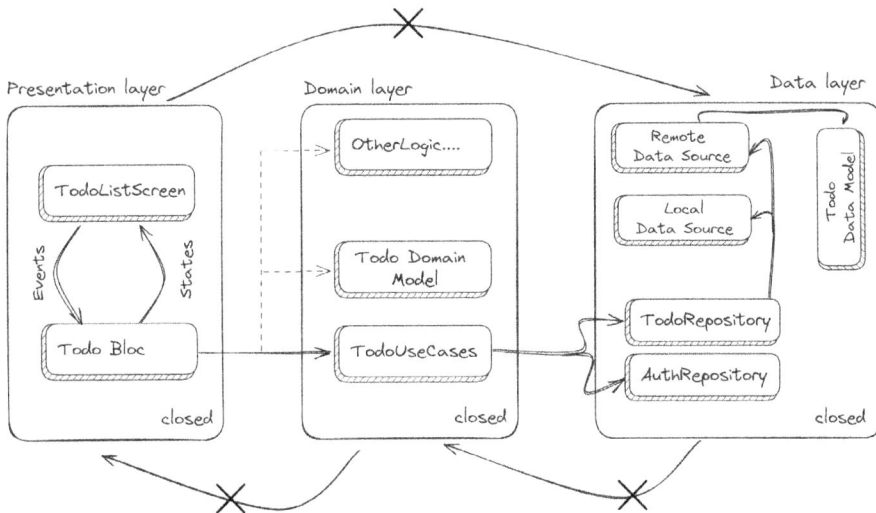

Figure 8.4: BLoC Pattern Inspired by Layered Architecture Style

Models: Represent the data and business logic of the application. They are responsible for fetching, storing, and manipulating data, often communicating with a backend system or database.

Views: Correspond to UI components. They display the data provided by the ViewModels and send user interactions back to the ViewModel. In Flutter, widgets play the role of views.

ViewModels: Act as a bridge between the Model and the View. They handle most of the view's display logic, transforming data from the Model into values that can be displayed on a View.

There are several benefits of using MVVM, including

- **Separation of Concerns**: MVVM enhances code organization by decoupling business logic from UI code. This separation simplifies the development process and improves code readability.
- **Data Flow**: The View interacts with the ViewModel to display information and capture user inputs. The ViewModel, in turn, communicates with the Model to fetch or update data. Any changes in the Model are communicated back to the ViewModel, which then updates the View accordingly.
- **Reactivity**: Flutter's reactive nature synergizes well with MVVM. The ViewModel can react to changes in the Model and automatically update the View.
- **State Management**: MVVM supports efficient state management, making tracking and managing changes in the application state easier.

We will now implement the Todo application using the MVVM architecture pattern, building on the Todo app from the previous section.

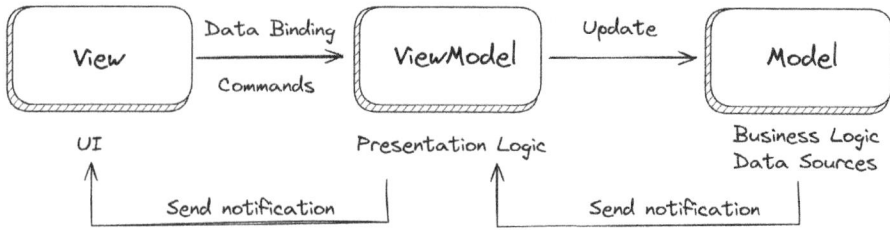

Figure 8.5: MVVM Pattern

Model

The model consists of the `Todo` class, the `DataSource` interfaces, and their implementations.

```
abstract class DataSource {
  Future<List<Todo>> fetchTodos();
  Future<void> addTodo(Todo todo);
  Future<void> updateTodo(Todo todo);
  Future<void> deleteTodo(String id);
}

class Todo {
  Todo({
    required this.id,
    required this.title,
    this.createdAt,
    this.updatedAt,
    this.isCompleted = false,
  });

  final String id;
  final String title;
  final bool isCompleted;
  final String? createdAt;
  final String? updatedAt;

  String get slug =>
      title.toLowerCase().replaceAll(' ', '-');

  factory Todo.fromJson(
    Map<String, dynamic> json,
  ) {
    return Todo(
      id: json['id'],
      title: json['title'],
      isCompleted: json['isCompleted'],
```

```dart
      createdAt: json['createdAt'],
      updatedAt: json['updatedAt'],
    );
  }

  toJson() {
    return {
      'id': id,
      'title': title,
      'isCompleted': isCompleted,
      'createdAt': createdAt,
      'updatedAt': updatedAt,
    };
  }
}
```

The different data sources are implemented.

```dart
class LocalTodoDataSource implements DataSource {
  @override
  Future<void> addTodo(Todo todo) {
    throw UnimplementedError();
  }

  @override
  Future<void> deleteTodo(String id) {
    throw UnimplementedError();
  }

  @override
  Future<List<Todo>> fetchTodos() {
    return Future.delayed(
      const Duration(seconds: 5),
      () => List<Todo>.generate(
        10,
        (index) => Todo(
          id: '$index',
          title: 'Todo $index',
          isCompleted: false,
          createdAt: DateTime.now().toLocal().toString(),
          updatedAt: DateTime.now().toLocal().toString(),
        ),
      ),
    );
  }

  @override
  Future<void> updateTodo(Todo todo) {
```

```
      throw UnimplementedError();
  }
}

// Remote Data Source
class RemoteTodoDataSource implements DataSource {
  // ...
}
```

ViewModel

The view model class receives commands, updates the model, and notifies the view model to update the UI upon receiving data.

```
class TodoViewModel {
  final RemoteTodoDataSource _remoteDataSource;
  final LocalTodoDataSource _localDataSource;
  List<Todo> _todos = [];

  // fetch command that is a notifier
  late final Command fetchTodosCommand;

  TodoViewModel(
    this._remoteDataSource,
    this._localDataSource,
  ) {
    // create and initialize fetch todo command
    fetchTodosCommand = Command(_fetchTodos);
  }

  List<Todo> get todos => _todos;

  // actually implementation of
  // the fetch todo to connect with data sources
  Future<void> _fetchTodos() async {
    _todos = [];
    try {
      _todos = await _remoteDataSource.fetchTodos();
    } catch (e) {
      _todos = await _localDataSource.fetchTodos();
    }
  }

  // Add more command methods as necessary
}

// Typically, this would be a singleton
// or you must use a dependency injection framework
final TodoViewModel todoViewModelInstance = TodoViewModel(
```

```
  RemoteTodoDataSource(),
  LocalTodoDataSource(),
);
```

The command is a change notifier. Upon execution, it updates the model and sends a notification to the UI upon completion.

```
typedef CommandAction = Future<void> Function();

class Command extends ChangeNotifier {
  final CommandAction _action;
  bool _isExecuting = false;

  Command(this._action);

  bool get isExecuting => _isExecuting;

  Future<void> execute() async {
    if (_isExecuting) return;
    _isExecuting = true;
    // Notify listeners when starting execution
    notifyListeners();

    try {
      await _action();
    } finally {
      _isExecuting = false;
      // Notify listeners when execution ends
      notifyListeners();
    }
  }
}
```

View

The TodoList has a dependency on the view model. Using `ListenableBuilder` does data binding and executes existing commands on the view model upon interaction, updating the UI accordingly.

```
class TodoListScreen extends StatelessWidget {
  TodoListScreen({
    super.key,
    required this.todoViewModel,
  }) {
    todoViewModel.fetchTodosCommand.execute();//<---
  }

  final TodoViewModel todoViewModel;
```

```dart
  @override
  Widget build(BuildContext context) {
    return Scaffold(
      appBar: AppBar(title: const Text('Todo List')),
      body: ListenableBuilder(
        // listen to notification of fetch command
        listenable: todoViewModel.fetchTodosCommand, //<---
        builder: (BuildContext context, Widget? child) {
          return Column(
            children: [
              Expanded(
                child: ListView.builder(
                  itemCount: todoViewModel.todos.length,
                  itemBuilder: (context, index) {
                    return Text(
                      todoViewModel.todos[index].title,
                    );
                  },
                ),
              ),
              ElevatedButton(
                onPressed: () {//<---
                  if (!todoViewModel//<---
                      .fetchTodosCommand.isExecuting) {
                    // execute fetch todo command to update the list
                    todoViewModel.fetchTodosCommand
                        .execute();
                  }
                },
                child: todoViewModel//<---
                        .fetchTodosCommand.isExecuting
                    ? const Text('Loading...')
                    : const Text('Refresh'),
              ),
            ],
          );
        },
      ),
    );
  }
}
```

Surprisingly, this pattern can also fit into layered architectural styles. In this approach, the presentation layer would consist of only View and ViewModel, and the Model would become the Data layer.

Although you may come across different variations of MVVM, this implementation is the foundation of the MVVM pattern. For example, instead of executing commands, you may see view models calling methods on themselves and acting as change notifiers. Alternatively, the model has a repository to aggregate data from different sources. All of these variations are valid, and which one you choose will depend on the size of your application and your specific needs.

8.3   Architectures Beyond Flutter Norms

As I mentioned, some patterns are more popular in Flutter development. However, we should continue learning. It's always nice to discover other patterns and learn how they work. This will help expand our knowledge and skills. In this section, I'll discuss a few more UI patterns that are popular in different ways and come with interesting concepts. I won't go into the details of their implementation, but I encourage you to experiment with them. Once you've implemented any of these patterns, feel free to share your work with me or others. I can't wait to see what you can build!

8.3.1   MVP, MVI, MVB, MVU/TEA

Each pattern offers unique approaches to structuring applications, and learning them can be valuable for developers looking to expand their architectural toolkit. However, many of these patterns can be implemented nearly the same with minor adjustments.

MVP (Model-View-Presenter)

The MVP architecture is a refinement of the traditional MVC (Model-View-Controller) pattern, focusing on improving the separation of concerns. This architecture is particularly popular in Android development due to its clear delineation of roles and responsibilities, which enhances maintainability and testability. The core components of the patterns consist of:

- **Model**: Handles data and business logic of the application. It's independent of the UI and can include functions like data retrieval, transformation, and persistence. Communicates with the Presenter to provide or store data.
- **View:** Represents the UI, displaying data to the user and capturing user inputs. Lightweight and empty of business logic. Receives data from the Presenter to display and sends user actions back to the Presenter.
- **Presenter:** Acts as an intermediary between the View and the Model. Contains the application's core logic, retrieving data from the Model and formatting it for the View. It also handles user interactions and updates the Model accordingly. Receives input from the View, fetches/updates data from/to the Model, and updates the View. The Presenter in MVP handles most of the logic, reducing the complexity of Views and ensuring that they remain as simple as possible.

In Flutter, MVP can be implemented by defining separate classes for Models, Views (Widgets), and Presenters. The View (Widget) communicates with the

Presenter to handle user inputs and display data, while the Presenter interacts with the Model to retrieve or update data. This separation facilitates independent development and testing of each component.

MVI (Model-View-Intent)

MVI, short for Model-View-Intent, is an architecture pattern popular in reactive programming environments. Used in functional and reactive programming paradigms, MVI is particularly well-suited for frameworks that embrace reactive data flows, like RxJava in the Android ecosystem. The core components of the patterns consist of:

- **Model**: Represents the state of the application or a particular feature. Immutable and fully represents the visible state of the UI at any given time. Generated as a response to Intents and provided to the View for rendering.
- **View**: Responsible for rendering the UI based on the state (Model) it receives. Passive, reflecting the current state without containing any business logic. Emits Intents based on user interactions and renders UI based on Models.
- **Intent**: Represents a user's intention to change the state, like clicking a button or pulling to refresh. It can be seen as a message or a command, triggering business logic and sent from the View to the underlying logic to request a state change.

MVI is one pattern that fits Flutter well to manage state in applications with complex UIs, especially when combined with reactive programming techniques. Its emphasis on unidirectional data flow and immutable state models leads to more predictable and manageable codebases. While it may require a shift in thinking, especially for those unfamiliar with reactive or functional programming, the benefits of clarity and maintainability can be significant.

Model-View-Binder (MVB)

MVB is a variation of architectural patterns aimed at enhancing the clarity and effectiveness of code, particularly in user interface (UI) development. It's less commonly discussed than more prevalent patterns like MVP, MVVM, or MVI, but it offers unique advantages. The core components and concepts of MVB are:

- **Model**: Represents the data and business logic of the application. It's similar to the model in other patterns and manages the application's data, rules, and logic.
- **View**: The View in MVB presents data to the user. It is typically a UI component that displays information and receives user interactions.
- **Binder**: The Binder is a distinctive component of MVB. It acts as a mediator between the Model and the View but differs from a Presenter or ViewModel in its operations. The Binder listens to changes in the Model and updates the View accordingly. It also handles user interactions from the View, translating them into actions or changes in the Model. The Binder is central to the MVB pattern, emphasizing the synchronization between the

View and the Model. Unlike MVP or MVVM, where the Presenter or View-Model might contain business logic, the Binder in MVB primarily focuses on data binding.

MVB provides a structured approach to UI development, focusing on the reactive synchronization between the Model and the View through the Binder. While it's less widely adopted than MVVM or MVP, MVB offers a viable alternative for developers leveraging reactive programming for more responsive and maintainable UI code.

Model-View-Update (MVU) / The Elm Architecture (TEA)

MVU is an architectural pattern that has gained popularity primarily in functional programming. It's known for its simplicity and effectiveness in building user interfaces, especially in web development with languages like Elm. The pattern is also used in other platforms and languages, adapting its core principles. The core components of MVU/TEA consist of:

- **Model**: Represents the state of the application. In MVU, the model is typically an immutable data structure that describes everything your application needs to know about its current state.
- **View**: A function that takes the model as an input and returns a user interface description based on that model. The view is purely declarative and does not contain any business logic.
- **Update**: A function that takes the current model and a message (an indication of what happened in the UI, like a user action) produces a new model. The business logic resides in the update function, handling changes to the application state in response to messages.

MVU/TEA stands out for its simplicity, unidirectional data flow, and emphasis on immutability and functional programming principles. You must separate all side effects from the UI logic in this pattern. This is worth trying if you want to adopt a different pattern that follows the Functional programming style.

8.3.2 VIPER

VIPER is an architectural pattern for View, Interactor, Presenter, Entity, and Router. It's primarily used in iOS development and is designed to address the common pitfalls of traditional MVC architecture by dividing an application into distinct layers of responsibility. Let's examine each component:

- **View**: This is responsible for presenting the UI (User Interface) and receiving user interactions. In Flutter, this corresponds to widgets or screens.
- **Interactor**: This layer contains the business logic of your application. It's where the app's main functionality lives: manipulating entities (models) and communicating with external data sources or services.

- **Presenter**: The Presenter takes information from the Interactor and formats it for presentation in the View. It acts as a middleman that handles presentation logic, but unlike traditional MVC, it doesn't handle user input directly.
- **Entity**: Entities are simple data models used by the Interactor. They represent the app's data and state but don't contain business logic.
- **Router**: In VIPER, the Router handles navigation logic, determining the flow of screens in an app. In Flutter, this can be managed by named routes or navigation functions.

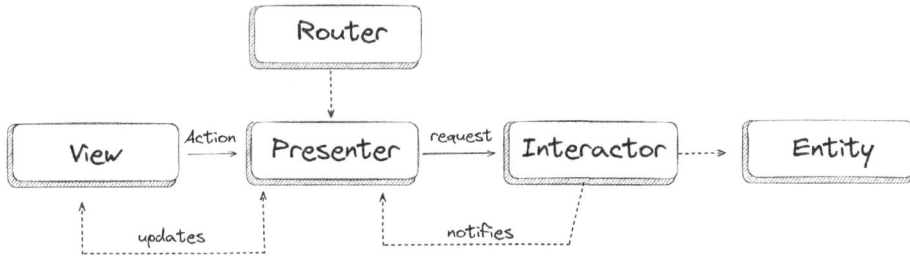

Figure 8.6: VIPER Flow Diagram

VIPER's distinct layers promote a clean separation of concerns, making each component easy to test and maintain. However, it also leads to a more complex structure than other architectures, which might be overkill for smaller or less complex Flutter apps.

8.3.3 RIBs

RIBs (Router, Interactor, Builder)[1] is an architectural framework developed by Uber that is tailored for complex and large-scale mobile applications. It enhances multi-platform collaboration, minimizes global states, and ensures high testability. Here's a detailed overview of its components:

- **Interactor:** Contains business logic, handles Rx subscriptions, state-altering decisions, data storage, and child RIB attachment.
- **Router:** Translates Interactor outputs into attaching and detaching child RIBs, acting as a Humble Object for easier testing of complex Interactor logic.
- **Builder:** Responsible for instantiating RIB's classes and the Builders for each child RIB. It's aware of the DI system used in the project.
- **Presenter (Optional):** Translates business models to view models and vice versa, facilitating testing of view model transformations.

---

[1]https://github.com/uber/RIBs

- **View(Controller):** Builds and updates the UI, including layout, user interaction, data display, and animations. Views are designed to be as "dumb" as possible.
- **Component:** Manages RIB dependencies, controls access to them, and provides access to external dependencies needed by the RIB.

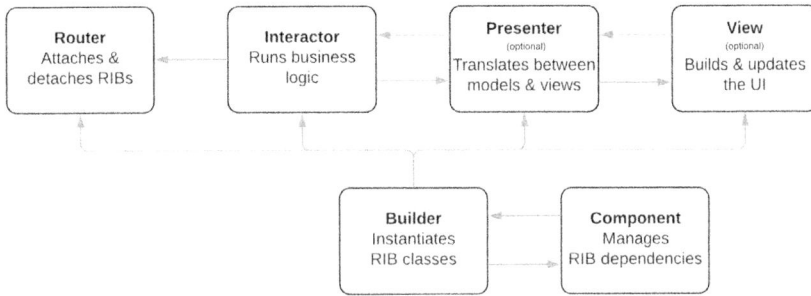

Figure 8.7: Original RIB Flow Diagram (credit to Uber/RIBs Github repository)

The application state is managed by the RIBs currently attached to the RIB tree in RIBs. Each RIB makes state decisions within its scope, which helps avoid global state issues. Any additional state, such as user profile settings, is stored in streams of immutable models.

When communicating between RIBs, downward communication is typically achieved through Rx streams or as parameters in a child RIB's build method. On the other hand, upward communication is accomplished via listener interfaces, allowing for a decoupled and memory-leak-free architecture.

RIB is designed for large-scale applications, and it comes with lots of boilerplate code, which probably code generation can help in Flutter if you decide to use this pattern.

8.4   Clean Architecture

Discussing Clean Architecture as a UI pattern is inappropriate since it's a blueprint of architecture with detailed implementation suggestions. However, the concept is beneficial to UI development. To understand clean architecture, it is essential to grasp the concept of domain-centric architecture.

8.4.1 Domain-centric architecture

Domain-centric architecture represents a paradigm shift in software design, much like the revolutionary change in astronomy when Nicolaus Copernicus[2] proposed that the sun, not the earth, was the center of the solar system. This analogy underlines a fundamental change in perspective from a database-centric to a domain-centric focus in software architecture.

Traditional three-layer database-centric architectures focus on the database, with the UI, business logic, and data access layer circling it. On the other hand, domain-centric architectures prioritize the domain model, treating databases and other external elements as implementation details. This approach aligns with Robert C. Martin's (also known as Uncle Bob) view[3] that architecture should prioritize usability over construction material.

The key types of domain-centric architectures are:

- **Hexagonal Architecture (Alistair Cockburn):** It's a layered architecture with an application layer at the center, surrounded by ports and adapters. These adapters allow the architecture to be independent of UI, databases, and external systems, enabling isolated testing.
- **Onion Architecture (Jeffrey Palermo):** This architecture also places the domain at its core, surrounded by an application layer. The outer layers include a thin UI layer and an infrastructure layer for persistence. It emphasizes that all dependencies should point inward toward the domain.
- **Clean Architecture (Robert C. Martin):** Similar to the other two, with entities at the center and use cases forming the application layer. The outer layer consists of ports and adapters for various external dependencies.

Domain-centric architectures are increasingly relevant in modern software development due to applications' high complexity and long lifecycles. This approach aligns with modern development practices and offers scalability, maintainability, and adaptability.

8.4.2 Clean Architecture Layers

Clean Architecture advocates dividing a system into layers, each with distinct responsibilities.

- **Entities Layer:** These objects represent the application's enterprise-wide policies and business rules.
- **Use Cases Layer:** Contains business logic and orchestrates data flow between entities and interface adapters.

---

[2]https://en.wikipedia.org/wiki/Nicolaus_Copernicus
[3]https://blog.cleancoder.com/uncle-bob/2011/09/30/Screaming-Architecture.html

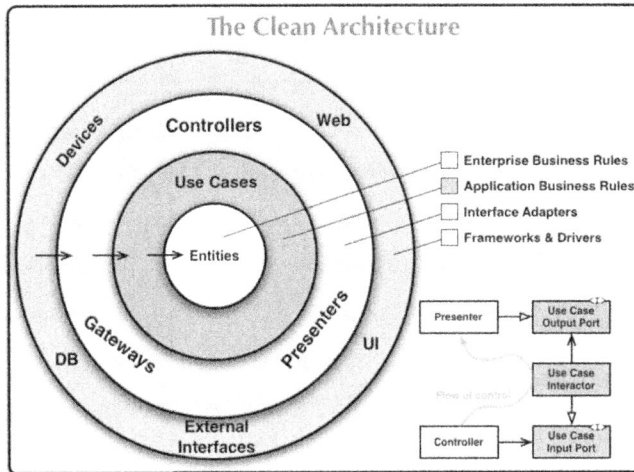

Figure 8.8: The Clean Architecture (credit to cleancoder.com)

- **Interface Adapters Layer:** Controllers, gateways, presenters, and views are part of the layer that converts data between the format needed for external layers and the format most convenient for use cases and entities.
- **Frameworks and Drivers Layer:** This layer includes databases and web and UI frameworks and focuses on implementation details, not business logic.

Clean Architecture is based on several principles, including the Dependency Rule. It states that dependencies must always point inward. This means that the inner layers of an application must be independent of the outer layers. For example, business rules should keep the database and the user interface a secret. This rule allows the system to be easily managed, adapted, and tested because each layer is responsible for its concerns.

8.4.3 Flutter And Clean Architecture

Now that we have seen the core concepts of Clean Architecture, it's easier to understand how it should be implemented in Flutter.

Clean architecture can have at least three layers, though more may be added depending on specific needs.

- The Presentation Layer contains the User Interface (UI) and the state holder.
- The Domain Layer contains the use cases, entities, and contracts that comprise the pure business logic. Both the UI and Data Layers have access to this layer.
- The Data Layer contains repositories, data sources, models, and mappers. The main role of the Data Layer is to convert data models to entities and vice versa. The Domain Layer doesn't know the data type or how it should

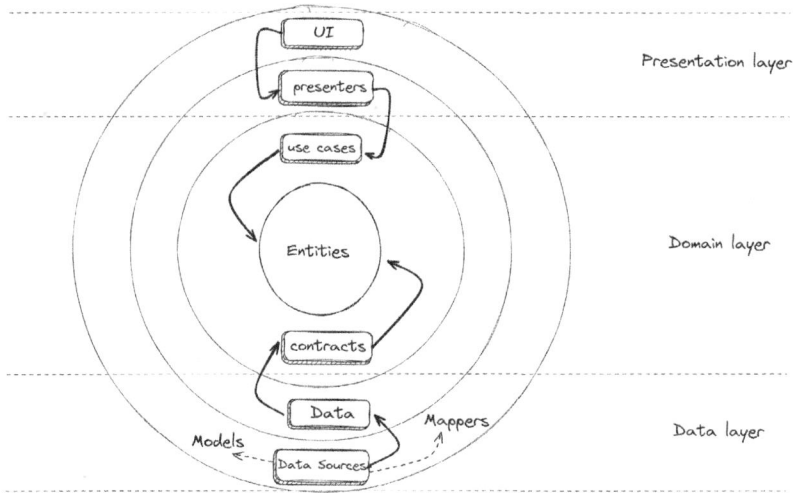

Figure 8.9: Clean Architecture in Three Layers for Flutter Implementation

be transformed. This is where the mapper in the Data Layer comes in, as it handles the data transformation based on the needs of the Domain Layer.

As you can see, we have already implemented a similar three-layer repository pattern in this chapter. The main difference is that the data and presentation layers focus on accessing the domain layer. Let's take a look at the code implementation.

Let's start with folder structure:

```
lib/todo_clean_architecture
 data
    data.dart
    datasources
       local_datasource.dart
       remote_datasource.dart
    models
       todo_mapper.dart
       todo_model.dart
    repositories
        todo_repository.dart
 domain
    contracts
       todo_data_contract.dart
    domain.dart
    entities
       todo.dart
    usecases
        delete_todo_usecase.dart
```

UI Architecture Patterns

```
        get_todo_usecase.dart
        get_todos_usecase.dart
main.dart
presentation
    presentation.dart
    presenters
        state.dart
    widgets
        ui.dart
```

Let's begin with the Domain Layer implementation, which is the most crucial one.

Domain Layer

Any business logic not connected to other layers should be placed here.

Entities: Your business entity with the required logic

```
class Todo {
  Todo({
    required this.id,
    required this.title,
    this.createdAt,
    this.updatedAt,
    this.isCompleted = false,
  });

  final String id;
  final String title;
  final bool isCompleted;
  final String? createdAt;
  final String? updatedAt;

  // example of business logic
  get slug => title.toLowerCase().replaceAll(' ', '-');
}
```

As you can see, the entity doesn't know how the data model is structured or derived.

Use cases: Use cases are crucial in encapsulating application-specific business rules and orchestrating data flow to and from the entities (business objects). They essentially represent the actions that can be performed within the system.

```
class GetTodosUseCase {
  GetTodosUseCase({
    required this.todoRepository,
  });

  final TodoRepository todoRepository;
```

```
  Future<List<Todo>> call() async {
    return todoRepository.fetchTodos();
  }
}
```

Contracts: The interface that repositories in the data layer must implement.

```
abstract interface class TodoRepository {
  Future<List<Todo>> fetchTodos();
  Future<void> addTodo(Todo todo);
  Future<void> updateTodo(Todo todo);
  Future<void> deleteTodo(String id);
}
```

We are now moving to the next data layer.

Data Layer

This layer retrieves data from various sources and maps data model objects to entity objects defined in the domain model.

Data Models: Data models received from various sources with different variations.

```
class TodoModel {
  TodoModel({
    required this.id,
    required this.title,
    required this.isCompleted,
    this.createdAt,
    this.updatedAt,
  });

  final String id;
  final String title;
  final bool isCompleted;
  final String? createdAt;
  final String? updatedAt;

  factory TodoModel.fromJson(Map<String, dynamic> json) {
    return TodoModel(
      id: json['id'],
      title: json['title'],
      isCompleted: json['isCompleted'],
      createdAt: json['createdAt'],
      updatedAt: json['updatedAt'],
    );
  }
```

```
  toJson() {
    return {
      'id': id,
      'title': title,
      'isCompleted': isCompleted,
      'createdAt': createdAt,
      'updatedAt': updatedAt,
    };
  }
}
```

Data Mappers transform the data model between the data layer and domain layer entities.

```
class TodoMapper {
  static Todo fromEntity(
    TodoModel todoModel,
  ) {
    return Todo(
      id: todoModel.id,
      title: todoModel.title,
      isCompleted: todoModel.isCompleted,
      createdAt: todoModel.createdAt,
      updatedAt: todoModel.updatedAt,
    );
  }

  static TodoModel toEntity(Todo todo) {
    return TodoModel(
      id: todo.id,
      title: todo.title,
      isCompleted: todo.isCompleted,
      createdAt: todo.createdAt,
      updatedAt: todo.updatedAt,
    );
  }

  static List<Todo> transformToModelList(
      List<TodoModel> models) {
    return models
        .map(
          (e) => fromEntity(e),
        )
        .toList();
  }
}
```

Data sources: There are various types of data sources available, such as local file management, databases, HTTP calls, and more.

```
class LocalTodoDataSource {
  Future<List<Todo>> fetchTodos() {
    return Future.delayed(
      const Duration(seconds: 5),
      () => List<Todo>.generate(
        10,
        (index) => TodoMapper.fromEntity(
          TodoModel(
            id: '$index',
            title: 'Todo $index',
            isCompleted: false,
            createdAt: DateTime.now().toLocal().toString(),
            updatedAt: DateTime.now().toLocal().toString(),
          ),
        ),
      ),
    );
  }
}
```

The data source doesn't necessarily need to have a relationship with contracts. However, it's a good practice to create an interface to ensure that the data source between local and remote data sources implements the same interface.

Repositories: They implement the domain contracts the data layer would require.

```
class TodoRepositoryImpl implements TodoRepository {
  const TodoRepositoryImpl({
    required this.localDataSource,
    required this.remoteDataSource,
  });

  final LocalTodoDataSource localDataSource;
  final RemoteTodoDataSource remoteDataSource;

  @override
  Future<List<Todo>> fetchTodos() async {
    try {
      return await remoteDataSource.fetchTodos();
    } catch (e) {
      return localDataSource.fetchTodos();
    }
  }
}
```

```
    // Implement logic combining
    // local and remote data sources
}
```

The abstraction level depends on the project's size and your team. The larger the team, the more important it is to abstract and make contracts.

Presentation Layer

This layer is responsible for storing the current state and updating the user interface to ensure it is rendered correctly.

State holders, Presenters, ViewModels: Managing state and invoking use cases.

```
class TodoState extends ChangeNotifier {
  TodoState({
    required this.getTodosUseCase,
  });

  GetTodosUseCase getTodosUseCase;

  List<Todo> _todos = [];

  @override
  List<Todo> get todos => _todos;

  @override
  Future<void> getTodos() async {
    _todos = await getTodosUseCase.call();
    notifyListeners();
  }
}
```

User Interfaces: They handle the rendering of the user interface (UI) by listening to updates on the state.

```
class TodoListScreen extends StatelessWidget {
  TodoListScreen({
    super.key,
    required this.todoState,
  }) {
    todoState.getTodos();
  }

  final TodoState todoState;

  @override
  Widget build(BuildContext context) {
```

```
    return Scaffold(
      appBar: AppBar(title: const Text('Todo List')),
      body: ListenableBuilder(
        listenable: todoState,
        builder: (BuildContext context, Widget? child) {
          return ListView.builder(
            itemCount: todoState.todos.length,
            itemBuilder: (context, index) {
              return Text(todoState.todos[index].title);
            },
          );
        },
      ),
    );
  }
}
```

Alright, now that you have everything set up, you can run the application.

```
main() {
  runApp(
    MaterialApp(
      // Need to use a proper dependency injection library
      home: TodoListScreen(
        todoState: TodoState(
          getTodosUseCase: GetTodosUseCase(
            todoRepository: TodoRepositoryImpl(
              localDataSource: LocalTodoDataSource(),
              remoteDataSource: RemoteTodoDataSource(),
            ),
          ),
        ),
      ),
    ),
  );
}
```

Now that you have seen the layered architecture in this chapter, it should be easier to understand how clean architecture works in the context of Flutter. This gives you great choices when implementing patterns in your application.

8.5   Balancing Trade-offs

In software architecture, choosing the right pattern is about balancing trade-offs. Each pattern has pros and cons, and there's rarely a one-size-fits-all solution. Key considerations include Suitability - ensuring the architecture fits the project's specific needs; Scalability - its ability to handle growth in users, data, or complexity; and Maintainability - how easily the system can be updated and extended.

Starting simple and scalable is advisable, as over-engineering can lead to unnecessary complexity. The chosen architecture should meet current requirements while being adaptable to future changes. The goal is to create a system that serves immediate needs and remains flexible for future developments, striking a balance between immediate functionality and long-term adaptability.

8.6 Customizing Architectures for Flutter

The most important factor to consider when developing with Flutter is the architecture. To create an effective architecture, you must focus on customization and adaptability. Drawing from various architectural styles allows you to design a structure that fits your project's specific needs. The key is to innovate and mix elements while ensuring that all components, data flow, and dependencies are clearly defined.

In today's software development landscape, it's important to have an iterative mindset. As Flutter and your project requirements continue to evolve, your architecture should be flexible enough to adapt to these changes. The best architecture is tailored to your specific needs while being agile enough to accommodate future growth and changes.

8.7 Conclusion

It is essential to explore and comprehend the various architectural patterns in Flutter to develop robust, maintainable, and scalable applications. Different architectural patterns, such as Layered Architecture, BLoC, MVVM, or Clean Architecture, have unique advantages and trade-offs.

Assessing project requirements, team expertise, and scalability needs is crucial to choose an architecture that best aligns with these factors. Adopting an adaptable and iterative approach to architecture ensures that your Flutter applications remain efficient and relevant in the ever-changing software development landscape.

The ultimate goal is to strike a balance between structure and flexibility, creating well-organized and adaptable solutions.

CHAPTER 9

Concurrency and Parallelism

Reviewer: Erick Zanardo

As you delve deeper into the app development world with Dart and Flutter, you might have come across the terms 'Concurrency' and 'Parallelism.' Though these concepts might initially sound complex and intimidating, they are required to create efficient and responsive applications. In this chapter, I will investigate the mysteries behind these terms, demonstrating how they enhance the user interface (UI) experience within Flutter applications.

In this chapter, I want to touch on the engineering aspect of these two concepts and their significance in UI development, especially with Flutter.

9.1 Demystifying Concurrency vs. Parallelism

Concurrency is about dealing with multiple tasks at once. It involves managing and executing several tasks in overlapping periods but not necessarily simultaneously. Think of it as a juggler tossing several balls in the air – the juggler handles one ball at a time but gives the impression of continuous motion. In programming, this translates to an environment where multiple processes share a single core, with the system rapidly switching between tasks to give the illusion of simultaneous execution. The key advantage of concurrency is that it can lead to more efficient use of system resources and improved responsiveness, especially in environments with limited computational power.

Parallelism, however, refers to the simultaneous execution of multiple tasks. This is possible in systems with multiple cores or processors, where each task can run on a separate core at the same time. Parallelism is like having several jugglers, each juggling their own set of balls simultaneously. In software, this leads to a significant boost in performance for tasks that can be divided and executed simultaneously. However, it requires a more complex architecture and careful management to avoid issues like data races or deadlocks.

In Dart, concurrency and parallelism are fundamental concepts that significantly influence application performance. Concurrency in Dart is about managing

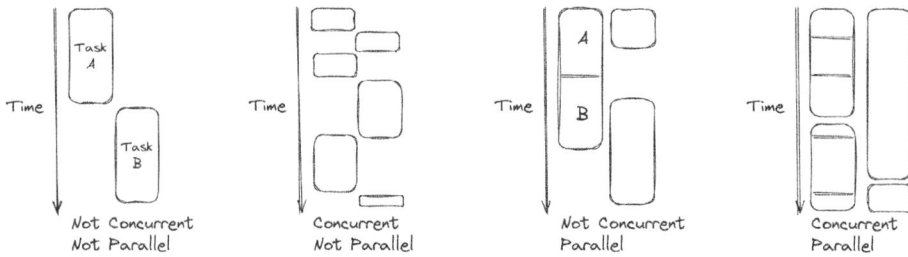

Figure 9.1: Four Different Scenarios with Concurrent and Parallelism

multiple tasks overlappingly without simultaneous execution, primarily achieved through its event-driven, single-threaded model. This approach ensures non-blocking operations, particularly in Flutter, for fluid UI experiences. In contrast, parallelism in Dart is implemented through **Isolates**, akin to independent threads that can execute simultaneously, often on different CPU cores. This allows for more efficient handling of computationally intensive tasks. Effectively utilizing concurrency and parallelism in Dart applications leads to enhanced performance, responsiveness, and a smoother user experience.

Focusing on Dart, these concepts become increasingly relevant. Dart is a single-threaded language, meaning it has one main execution thread. However, it efficiently handles concurrency through its event loop and Futures and Streams. These tools allow Dart to perform non-blocking operations, managing asynchronous events without halting the main thread.

The "main thread" is the central thread of execution in a program, handling key tasks like user interface updates. A thread is a sequence of instructions within a program that can be executed independently of other threads, allowing for concurrent operations within a single process.

This design is particularly beneficial in Flutter, where maintaining a responsive UI is critical.

9.2 The Importance of Efficient Task Handling

The efficiency of UI development in Flutter dramatically benefits from the strategic application of concurrency and parallelism, addressing key performance challenges in real-world app scenarios. Concurrency in Flutter enables the seamless handling of multiple tasks, such as user interactions and background data operations, without compromising the UI's responsiveness. This is particularly evident in scenarios like a social media app where new content loads as the user scrolls. While the app fetches new data from a server or database asynchronously, the user can continue interacting with the app, like liking posts or opening images, without experiencing any lag or stutter. This efficient handling of asynchronous tasks ensures the UI remains fluid and responsive.

On the other hand, parallelism is leveraged in Flutter through Dart's isolates to handle more compute-intensive tasks without affecting the main thread's performance. Consider a photo editing app developed in Flutter. When applying filters or processing high-resolution images, these resource-intensive operations are of-floaded to isolates. As a result, the main thread, which handles the UI, remains unburdened and continues to deliver a smooth experience, allowing users to seamlessly switch between tools or apply adjustments without any noticeable delay.

This division of labor optimizes the app's performance and significantly enhances the user experience, making it a crucial aspect of efficient UI development in Flutter.

9.3 Flutter's Single UI Thread Principle

In Flutter, the operation of the event loop is integral to the framework's efficiency and responsiveness. Each Dart code within Flutter runs in an environment known as an "isolate," which possesses its single-threaded event loop. This event loop is the backbone for processing many events occurring within the application. Events, from user interactions and I/O operations to repaint requests, are queued in the event loop. They are processed sequentially, ensuring the orderly execution of tasks. A crucial aspect of this event loop is handling repaint events, which are pivotal for the UI's smooth rendering. Flutter, aiming for a smooth 60 frames per second, adds repaint requests to the queue at this rate, approximately every 16 milliseconds. Timely processing of these requests is essential to prevent UI unresponsiveness and animation stutter, which are crucial to maintaining a fluid user experience.

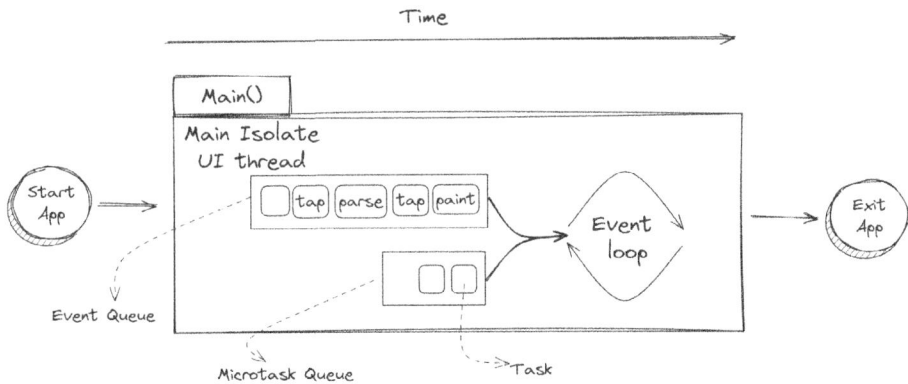

Figure 9.2: Flutter Main Isolate Event Loop

However, challenges arise when the application encounters long-running operations, such as file loading or intensive image processing. If these operations are performed synchronously, they can monopolize the event loop, leading to missed frames and a temporarily unresponsive UI.

Flutter's solution to this problem is the implementation of asynchronous operations. By utilizing asynchronous APIs and the `await` keyword in Dart, the primary isolate's event loop can continue to process other events, such as UI updates.

At the same time, the more extended operation is completed in the background. This approach ensures the UI remains responsive, even during intensive processing tasks.

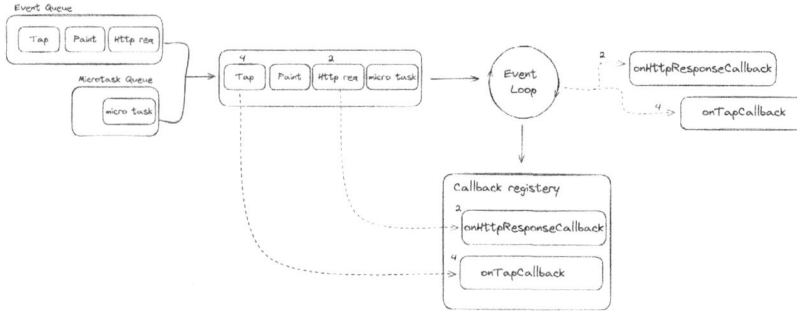

Figure 9.3: Event Loop and Callback Registry in Dart

Flutter advises offloading the work to a separate worker isolate for more demanding tasks. This strategy prevents blocking the main isolate dedicated to UI rendering.

9.4 The Asynchronous Programming Trio

In Dart and Flutter, the combination of `Future`, `async`, and `await` offers a streamlined approach to asynchronous programming.

```
Future<String> fetchData() async {
  await Future.delayed(Duration(seconds: 2));
  return 'Data retrieved';
}

Future<void> main() async {
  String data = await fetchData();
  print(data); // Outputs: Data retrieved
}
```

The `async` and `await` keywords work in tandem to enhance the usability of `Future`s. Marking a function with `async` transforms it into an asynchronous function, which, instead of blocking, returns a `Future`. This allows the function to perform lengthy operations while freeing the event loop to continue processing other events, a key aspect of maintaining responsive applications. The `await` keyword, used within `async` functions, pauses the execution until the associated `Future` completes, effectively unwrapping its value in a way that mimics synchronous code flow.

The `FutureBuilder` widget in Flutter is designed to build itself based on the latest snapshot of interaction with a Future. The `FutureBuilder` takes a `Future` and a `builder` function. The builder is designed to build the UI based on the Future's loading, success, or error state.

```
class MyApp extends StatelessWidget {
  @override
  Widget build(BuildContext context) {
    return MaterialApp(
      home: Scaffold(
        body: Center(
          child: FutureBuilder<String>(
            future: fetchData(),
            builder: (context, snapshot) {
              if (snapshot.connectionState ==
                  ConnectionState.waiting) {
                return const CircularProgressIndicator();
              } else if (snapshot.hasError) {
                return Text('Error: ${snapshot.error}');
              } else {
                return Text(
                    'Fetched Data: ${snapshot.data}');
              }
            },
          ),
        ),
      ),
    );
  }

  Future<String> fetchData() async {
    // Simulate a network request
    await Future.delayed(const Duration(seconds: 2));
    return 'Data loaded';
  }
}
```

In this example, `fetchData()` is a simulated asynchronous operation that returns a `Future<String>`. The `FutureBuilder` listens to this Future, and the `builder` function builds different UI states based on the Future's progress: a loading spinner while waiting, an error message if there's an error, and the actual data upon successful completion.

9.5   Managing Asynchronous Data Flows

A Stream is a sequence of asynchronous events. It is a data pipe that a listener can subscribe to and react to whenever a new piece of data comes down the stream.

In Flutter, this is particularly useful for widgets that need to update in response to changing data over time.

---

1. **Single-subscription streams** are like a radio station broadcast. They can have multiple listeners, but only one can be active. If a listener stops listening, the stream pauses and can be resumed later.

```
void main() {
  final controller = StreamController<int>();

  // Creating a single-subscription stream
  final Stream<int> stream = controller.stream;

  // Subscribing to the stream
  final subscription = stream.listen(
    (number) => print('Received number: $number'),
    onDone: () => print('Stream is closed.'),
    onError: (error) => print('Error: $error'),
  );

  // Adding data to the stream
  for (int i = 0; i < 3; i++) {
    controller.sink.add(i);
  }

  // Closing the stream
  controller.close();
}
```

1. **Broadcast streams** allow multiple listeners and will continue to emit events whether or not there are listeners.

```
import 'dart:async';

void main() {
  final controller = StreamController<int>.broadcast();

  // Creating a broadcast stream
  final Stream<int> stream = controller.stream;

  // First subscriber
  stream.listen(
    (number) => print('First subscriber received: $number'),
  );

  // Second subscriber
  stream.listen(
    (number) =>
        print('Second subscriber received: $number'),
  );
```

```
  // Adding data to the stream
  for (int i = 0; i < 3; i++) {
    controller.sink.add(i);
  }

  // Closing the stream
  controller.close();
}
```

Flutter leverages streams for handling user interface events and other asynchronous interactions. For instance, the `StreamBuilder` widget can listen to a stream and rebuild part of the UI based on the data received.

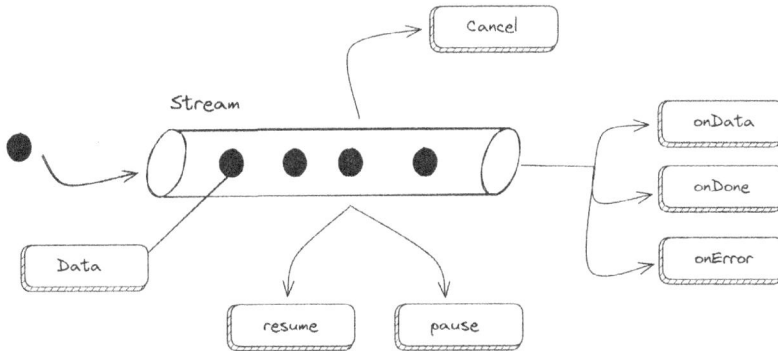

Figure 9.4: Streams in Dart

Delving further into Streams and Futures is beyond the scope of this book, but mastering these concepts is highly recommended to enhance your ability to create snappy and responsive UIs in Flutter significantly.

9.6 Expanding Horizons with Isolates

Isolates in Dart are independent workers, similar to threads but without shared memory, executing parallel to the main application thread. Each isolate has its memory heap, ensuring that the memory state is not shared, which leads to more predictable and safer code.

In Flutter development, achieving optimal performance and a smooth user experience often demands efficient task management, especially for CPU-intensive operations. This is where Dart's concept of isolates, complemented by Flutter's `compute` function, becomes invaluable.

First, look at a synchronous version of the JSON parsing function. This version will run on the main thread and can potentially block the UI if the JSON string is large:

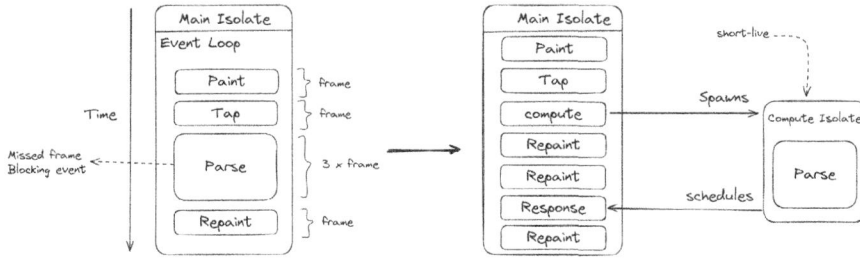

Figure 9.5: Spawning Isolated for Intensive Task to Avoid Non-blocking UI on Main Thread

```
Future<void> loadJsonDataSynchronously() async {
  setState(() => isLoading = true);
  final jsonString = await loadJsonString();
  final parsedJson = parseJson(jsonString); // <-----
  setState(() {
    jsonData = parsedJson;
    isLoading = false;
  });
}
```

The parseJson function is called directly within the main thread in this example. If parseJson is computationally intensive, it will block the main thread until the parsing is complete, leading to a frozen or unresponsive UI. Let's modify the function to use compute for parsing JSON.

```
Future<void> loadJsonDataAsynchronously() async {
  setState(() => isLoading = true);
  final jsonString = await loadJsonString();
  final parsedJson = await compute(
    parseJson,
    jsonString,
  ); // <---
  setState(() {
    jsonData = parsedJson;
    isLoading = false;
  });
}
```

In this version, compute(parseJson, jsonString) spawns a new isolate, passes the initial data (jsonString), and then runs the parseJson function in that isolate.

The compute function in Flutter is an intriguing aspect of how the framework handles concurrency and parallel processing. Let's delve deeper into its implementation.

```
// Flutter Source code
// packages/flutter/lib/src/foundation/isolates.dart
Future<R> compute<M, R>(...) {
  return isolates.compute<M, R>(...);
}
```

Interestingly, this function calls another `compute` function within the `isolates` namespace. The implementation of this inner `compute` function is as follows:

```
// isolates.compute
Future<R> compute<M, R>(
    // ...
    ) async {
  debugLabel ??=
      kReleaseMode ? 'compute' : callback.toString();

  return Isolate.run<R>(() {
    return callback(message);
  }, debugName: debugLabel);
}
```

Observing this code, it becomes evident that the core operation in `isolates.compute` involves invoking `Isolate.run`. When you use the `Isolate.run` method; it creates a new isolate that runs a provided function and immediately shuts down after sending back a single message to the main isolate. This mechanism is highly beneficial for executing short-lived background tasks in Flutter. By moving processing to a separate isolate, you can ensure that the main thread, responsible for UI rendering, remains unblocked and responsive.

However, it's important to consider that while short-lived isolates like this are convenient and easy to implement, they come with certain performance costs. Spawning new isolates and transferring objects between isolates involves overhead. This overhead is particularly noticeable when dealing with large objects or frequent isolate creation, as each spawn requires setting up a new execution context and memory allocation.

On the other hand, long-lived isolates, known as *background workers*, are used for tasks that require ongoing execution or need to communicate over time frequently. These isolates are ideal for continuous or repeated processes during an app's life-cycle. For example, in applications needing constant complex computations like image processing, using a long-lived isolate helps offload heavy tasks.

To establish communication between long-lived isolates in Dart, use two classes: `ReceivePort` and `SendPort`. These ports enable isolates to interact. `SendPort` acts like a `StreamController`, where you send messages using the `send()` method. `ReceivePort` works as the listener, triggering a callback with the message when a new one arrives.

Creating and managing isolates in Dart for concurrent processing can seem complex, but it becomes more straightforward with step-by-step guidance.

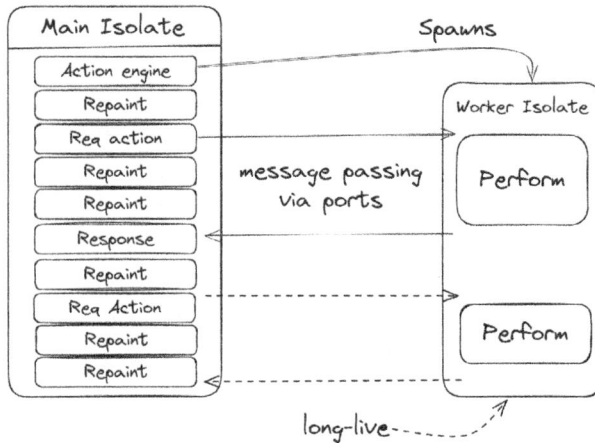

Figure 9.6: Long-lived background isolates

Here's a simplified explanation of the process, focusing particularly on the IsolateController class.

First, you define a data model to pass information to the isolate. In this case, ComputationModel holds data for a computation task.

```
class ComputationModel {
  final int iterations;
  final int factor;

  ComputationModel(this.iterations, this.factor);
}
```

Next, you create a computation function, computeSum, which performs intensive calculations using the data from ComputationModel.

```
int computeSum(ComputationModel model) {
  int sum = 0;
  for (int i = 1; i <= model.iterations; i++) {
    sum += i * model.factor;
  }
    return sum;
}
```

To establish communication between isolates, start with a worker task function, workerTask, executed in the new isolate. This function sets up a ReceivePort for communication and sends its SendPort back to the main isolate.

```
void workerTask(SendPort mainSendPort) async {
  // 1 initial message from
```

```
// the main thread would be mainSendPort
ReceivePort workerReceivePort = ReceivePort();
// 2, send to main thread the worker send port
mainSendPort.send(workerReceivePort.sendPort);

// 3. Check all messages
// and respond to what is needed
await for (final message in workerReceivePort) {
  if (message is ComputationModel) {
    //4. send the result of computing
    // back to the main thread
    mainSendPort.send(computeSum(message));
  }
}
}
```

In the main thread, you create a ReceivePort and spawn an isolate, passing
workerTask and the sendPort of the ReceivePort as arguments.

```
void main() async {
  ReceivePort mainReceivePort = ReceivePort();
final isolate = await Isolate.spawn(
    workerTask,
    mainReceivePort.sendPort, // initial message
  );
}
```

In this setup, Isolate.spawn requires two key arguments: a function to handle the
assigned task and an initial message. For the initial message, we pass the sendPort
from the main thread, which also serves as the argument for workerTask.

To establish a communication link with the worker isolate, we use a Completer.
This helps us retrieve the worker's sendPort, enabling communication from the
main isolate. We listen on the main receiver port, and upon receiving a SendPort
(initially sent by the worker), we know we've successfully connected with the
worker's sendPort, allowing us to start exchanging messages.

```
void main() async {
  ReceivePort mainReceivePort = ReceivePort();

  final isolate = await Isolate.spawn(
    workerTask,
    mainReceivePort.sendPort,
  );

  final completer = Completer<SendPort>();

  mainReceivePort.listen(
```

```dart
    (message) {
      if (message is SendPort) completer.complete(message);
      if (message is int) print(message);
    },
  );

  SendPort workerSendPort = await completer.future;

  workerSendPort.send(ComputationModel(10000, 5));

  await Future<void>.delayed(const Duration(seconds: 4));

  mainReceivePort.close();
  isolate.kill(priority: Isolate.immediate);
}
```

In this configuration:

- The primary isolate generates a `ReceivePort` and relays its `sendPort` to the subordinate isolate.
- The subordinate isolate responds by sending its `sendPort` back to the primary isolate.
- The primary isolate dispatches a message and `sendPort` to receive replies.
- The subordinate isolate accepts this message, executes the required task, and transmits the outcome to the primary isolate.

Additionally, it's crucial to grasp three essential functions for direct isolate management:

- `Isolate.kill()`: This function terminates an isolate before it completes its tasks.
- `Isolate.pause()`: This allows for the temporary suspension of an isolate's execution.
- `Isolate.resume()`: This function restarts an isolate's operations after being paused.

As an example, we'll demonstrate the use of `Isolate.kill()` in this context.

```dart
void main() async {
  ReceivePort mainReceivePort = ReceivePort();
  ReceivePort onExitPort = ReceivePort();

  final isolate = await Isolate.spawn(
    workerTask,
    mainReceivePort.sendPort,
    onExit: onExitPort.sendPort,
  );
```

```
    // ...

  onExitPort.listen((message) {
    exit(0);
  });

    // ...

  isolate.kill(priority: Isolate.immediate);
}
```

Once the isolate is terminated and concludes its operation, we can then proceed to exit the program.

Creating isolates becomes straightforward with a clear understanding. However, there may be better approaches for scaling. Isolates can function similarly to a `StreamController`. Thus, encapsulating the isolate within a controller or service makes it more versatile, reusable, and user-friendly for various applications. Here's an illustrative example:

```
typedef WorkerHandler<O, P> = O Function(P);

class CreateWorker<O, P> {
  CreateWorker(this.handler, this.sp);

  final WorkerHandler<O, P> handler;
  final SendPort sp;

  void call(SendPort _) {
    final rp = ReceivePort();
    sp.send(rp.sendPort);
    rp
        .takeWhile((msg) => msg is P)
        .cast<P>()
        .map(handler)
        .listen(sp.send);
  }
}

class IsolateController<O, P> {
  final ReceivePort mainReceiverPort;
  final ReceivePort onExitRp;
  final ReceivePort onErrorRp;
  final SendPort mainSendPort;
  final Isolate isolate;
  final Stream<dynamic> broadcastRp;
  final SendPort communicatorSendPort;
```

```dart
late Capability? _resumeCap;

IsolateController._({
  required this.mainReceiverPort,
  required this.onExitRp,
  required this.onErrorRp,
  required this.broadcastRp,
  required this.mainSendPort,
  required this.isolate,
  required this.communicatorSendPort,
});

static Future<IsolateController<O, P>> create<O, P>(
  WorkerHandler<O, P> handler,
) async {
  final mainReceiverPort = ReceivePort();
  final onExitRp = ReceivePort();
  final onErrorRp = ReceivePort();
  final mainRpSendPort = mainReceiverPort.sendPort;
  final communicator =
      CreateWorker(handler, mainRpSendPort);

  final isolate = await Isolate.spawn(
    communicator,
    mainRpSendPort,
    debugName: 'IsolateController',
    onExit: onExitRp.sendPort,
    onError: onErrorRp.sendPort,
  );

  final broadcastRp =
      mainReceiverPort.asBroadcastStream();
  final SendPort communicatorSendPort =
      await broadcastRp.first;

  return IsolateController._(
    isolate: isolate,
    onErrorRp: onErrorRp,
    onExitRp: onExitRp,
    mainReceiverPort: mainReceiverPort,
    mainSendPort: mainRpSendPort,
    broadcastRp: broadcastRp,
    communicatorSendPort: communicatorSendPort,
  );
}

void add(P payload) => communicatorSendPort.send(
      payload,
```

```dart
      );

  void dispose() {
    mainReceiverPort.close();
    isolate.kill(priority: Isolate.immediate);
  }

  void pause() {
    _resumeCap = isolate.pause(
      isolate.pauseCapability,
    );
  }

  void resume() {
    if (_resumeCap == null) return;
    isolate.resume(_resumeCap!);
    ping();
  }

  void ping() {
    final onPongMessage = ReceivePort();
    isolate.ping(
      onPongMessage.sendPort,
      response: 'pong',
      priority: Isolate.immediate,
    );
    onPongMessage
        .takeWhile(
          (e) => e is String && e == 'pong',
        )
        .take(1)
        .cast<String>()
        .first
        .then(
          stdout.writeln,
        );
  }

  Stream get onExit => onExitRp.asBroadcastStream();
  Stream get onError => onErrorRp.asBroadcastStream();

  Stream<P> get onData => broadcastRp
      .takeWhile(
        (element) => element is P,
      )
      .cast<P>();
}
```

Let's break down and explain this code, which demonstrates a structured approach

---

to handling Dart isolates.

1. **WorkerHandler Definition**:

```
typedef WorkerHandler<O, P> = O Function(P);
```

- This line defines a generic function type, `WorkerHandler`, that takes an input of type P and returns a result of type O.

2. **CreateWorker Class**:

```
class CreateWorker<O, P> {
  CreateWorker(this.handler, this.sp);

  final WorkerHandler<O, P> handler;
  final SendPort sp;

  void call(SendPort _) {
    final rp = ReceivePort();
    sp.send(rp.sendPort);
    rp
        .takeWhile((msg) => msg is P)
        .cast<P>()
        .map(handler)
        .listen(sp.send);
  }
}
```

- This class is designed to create a worker task for the isolate.
- `handler`: A function that processes messages of type P and returns results of type O.
- `sp`: The `SendPort` for communicating results back to the main isolate.
- The `call` method sets up a `ReceivePort` (`rp`) for incoming messages, sends its `SendPort` back to the main isolate, and listens for incoming messages. The handler processes each message of type P, and the result is sent back through `sp`.

IsolateController Class

1. **Class Properties**:

- Manages various `ReceivePorts` and a `SendPort` for communication.
- Holds a reference to the spawned `Isolate`.
- `broadcastRp`: A broadcast stream of messages from the main receiver port.
- `communicatorSendPort`: The `SendPort` sends messages to the worker.

2. `create` **Method**:

```dart
  static Future<IsolateController<O, P>> create<O, P>(
    WorkerHandler<O, P> handler) {
    // ...
  }
```

- This static method initializes an `IsolateController` instance.
- It spawns a new isolate with `CreateWorker` as its entry point, passing the `handler`.
- Sets up `ReceivePorts` for exit and error monitoring and retrieves the `SendPort` for communication with the isolate.

3. **Instance Methods**:

- `add`: Sends a payload to the worker isolate for processing.
- `dispose`: Terminates the isolate and closes communication ports.
- `pause` and `resume`: Control the execution of the isolate.
- `ping`: Sends a ping message to the isolate and listens for a response "pong," which is useful for checking if the isolate is responsive and alive.
- `onExit`, `onError`, `onData`: Streams for monitoring exit events, errors, and receiving data from the worker isolate.

This setup allows efficient and controlled communication between a main and worker isolates. It encapsulates the complexity of creating and managing isolates, providing a simpler interface for sending tasks to the worker and handling their responses.

The `IsolateController` can be instantiated with different inputs and outputs classes and with different handlers and may have several listeners on receiving data. It can offload intensive tasks to a background worker, improving performance and responsiveness in Flutter or Dart applications. An idea here is that you can now monitor the app's lifecycle and pause, resume, or dispose of workers accordingly to ensure that resources are freed up when they are no longer needed.

Remember, isolates are best used for CPU-intensive tasks to keep your application's main thread responsive.

Here is how you can now use this class.

```dart
// heavy computation
int sum(int end) {
  int sum = 0;
  for (int i = 1; i <= end; i++) {
    sum += i * 5;
  }
  return sum;
}

main() async {
  final isolateController =
      await IsolateController.create<int, int>(
```

```dart
      sum,
    );
    isolateController
      ..add(1000)
      ..add(200)
      ..add(500)
      ..ping()
      ..onData.listen(print)
      ..onError.listen((e) {
        print(e);
        exit(1);
      })
      ..onExit.listen((e) {
        print(e);
        exit(0);
      });

    Future.delayed(const Duration(seconds: 2), () {
      isolateController.pause();
    });

    Future.delayed(const Duration(seconds: 3), () {
      isolateController.ping();
    });

    Future.delayed(const Duration(seconds: 4), () {
      isolateController.resume();
    });

    Future.delayed(const Duration(seconds: 5), () {
      isolateController.ping();
    });

    Future.delayed(const Duration(seconds: 6), () {
      isolateController.add(100);
    });

    Future.delayed(const Duration(seconds: 7), () {
      isolateController.dispose();
    });
}
// console log
// pong -> first ping
// 2502500 -> first add
// 100500 -> second add
// 626250 -> third add
// pong -> ping after 3 seconds
// pong ->  ping after resume
```

```
// pong -> ping after 5 seconds
// 25250 -> add after 6 seconds
// null -> dispose after 7 seconds
```

9.6.1   Isolates on Web

While all Dart applications can use `async-await`, `Future`, and `Stream` for non-blocking operations, the web platform does not support isolates. However, Dart web apps can employ web workers for background thread processing, akin to isolates but with some differences. Keep an eye on this, as multiple requests to support these in Flutter may land at anytime.

9.7   Conclusion

Understanding Futures, Streams, Isolates, and the event loop is crucial for any Flutter developer aiming to build responsive and efficient applications. These concepts are fundamental to Flutter's architecture, enabling the creation of dynamic and interactive user interfaces.

To further enhance your skills in these areas, it's beneficial to delve into the official Dart and Flutter documentation and engage in hands-on practice through small projects.

CHAPTER 10

Offline Capabilities in Flutter

Reviewer: Muhammed Salih Güler

Adopting an offline-first architecture is extremely important for ensuring a seamless user experience, especially when internet connectivity is inconsistent or nonexistent. This approach not only addresses the challenges posed by slow or unreliable connections but also meets the growing expectations of users for apps to be fast and responsive at all times. Emphasizing offline-first functionality is not just about enhancing user experience; it's a strategic architectural decision that significantly impacts both the development process and end-user satisfaction.

Let's explore the capabilities of Flutter development, especially from an engineering and architectural point of view, and the significant responsibility that comes with it for app development.

10.1 The Dual-edged Sword: Challenges and Benefits

Adopting an offline-first architecture offers numerous benefits in mobile app development with frameworks like Flutter. One key advantage is the enhanced support for low-end devices, which operate on the periphery of networks and can leverage local data processing for improved performance. This approach ensures a **seamless user experience** with **fast and responsive** interactions, regardless of network conditions, which is crucial in areas with poor connectivity. By handling data locally, these applications achieve **quicker load times** and **smoother interactions**, as they are not restricted by server response times. This is particularly beneficial for edge devices that require immediate data processing and responsiveness. Furthermore, this architecture leads to **efficient data usage**, a vital aspect for users with limited data plans, and contributes to overall **user satisfaction** and **engagement**.

However, implementing an offline-first architecture in mobile apps, like those developed with Flutter, introduces significant challenges. The foremost is the **increased complexity** of the development process. Developers need help ensuring accurate **data synchronization** between local storage and servers, which becomes complicated with multiple user interactions. Managing "**data writes**" and resolving **conflicts and errors** during synchronization requires advanced strategies. This complexity extends to the need for **thorough testing** and **regular maintenance**, which is particularly important for ensuring functionality across various connectivity scenarios and maintaining data integrity. These challenges demand additional development effort, ongoing updates, and maintenance to utilize the benefits of this architecture effectively.

10.2 Embracing the Offline-first Philosophy

As an engineer, I have noticed that the benefits of adopting the offline-first approach are greater than the challenges that come with it. This is especially true with the help of modern tools and packages that can aid in overcoming the issues that arise during implementation. However, engineers need to assess and evaluate the implementation of this approach carefully, particularly from an architectural perspective, as we discussed earlier in this book.

In an offline-first design for Flutter applications, data modeling is critical in ensuring smooth data flow and consistency across local and network layers. Let's break down the design:

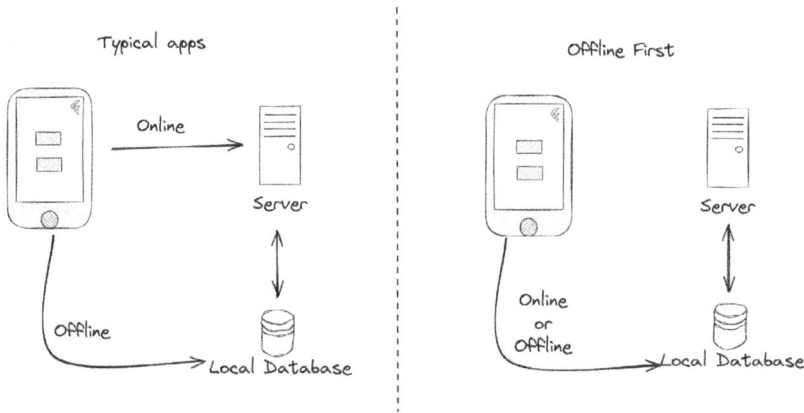

Figure 10.1: Offline-First Architecture

1. **Local and Network Data Sources**: In an offline-first Flutter app, every component interacting with network resources should have two data sources. A general code practice is having data access objects (DAOs) to map remote objects to local objects. I will not elaborate as we have seen data mappers in the Architecture Pattern Chapter. For example, In layered architecture where you have Repositories, each Repository must have the following:

   Local Data Source: This is the **primary source of truth** and should be the **exclusive** source for reading data in the app. It's often backed by

---

persistent storage. The database section often falls into the team decision based on the "best fit" for the entire architecture, whether it's SQL-based database or NoSQL.

```
class TodoLocalDataSource implements TodoService {
  TodoLocalDataSource(this.db);

  final TodoDatabase db;

  @override
  Future<List<Todo>> getAll() async {
    final List<Todo> todos = await db.getAll();
    return todos;
  }

  @override
  Future<void> save(Todo todo) async {
    return db.write(todo);
  }
}
```

Network Data Source: Represents the actual state of the app on the server. Depending on connectivity, it's synchronized with the local data source but might lag behind it or vice versa.

2. **Data Representation and Conversion**: The local and network data sources may have different representations of the same data. For example:

   - **Local Model**: Represents the data stored in the local database, often called "Entity."
   - **Network Model**: Represents the data received from or sent to the network.

3. **Exposing Resources**: It's good practice to have a third type of model that is exposed to the other layers of the app, protecting them from minor changes in the data layer.

In Flutter, using Isar and JsonSerializable packages, the model will look like:

```
@collection
@JsonSerializable()
class Todo {
  @JsonKey(includeFromJson: false)
  Id get localId => fastHash(id);

  @JsonKey(name: 'id')
  final String id;

  @Index(type: IndexType.value)
```

```
final String title;

Todo({
  required this.id,
  required this.title,
});
}
```

This simple Todo model will cover both TodoEntity and NetworkTodo using code generation.

Synchronization

In an offline-first Flutter app, data synchronization between local and network data sources is critical, involving two main strategies: **pull-based** and **push-based** synchronization. **Pull-based synchronization** is demand-driven, where the app fetches the latest data from the network as needed, often triggered by user navigation, making it suitable for scenarios with brief to intermediate periods of disconnection but potentially leading to heavy data use and stale caches. On the other hand, **push-based synchronization** proactively keeps the local data source in sync with the network, relying on server notifications to update stale data, thus allowing the app to remain functional for extended offline periods with minimal data use. While push-based synchronization excels in minimizing data use and supporting relational data, it demands sophisticated versioning for conflict resolution and a network source capable of synchronization.

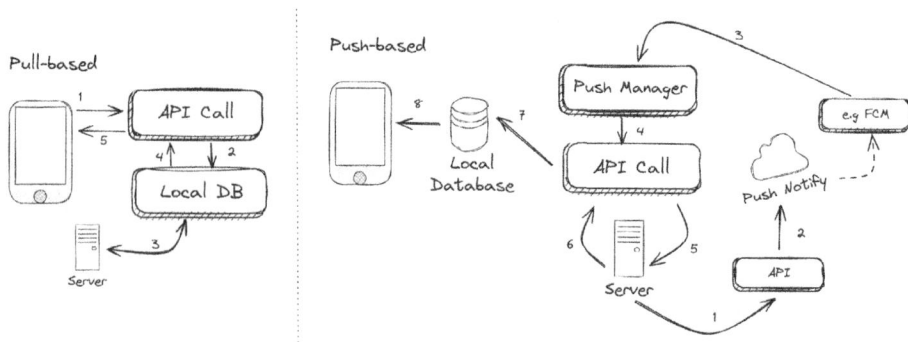

Figure 10.2: Pull-based vs. Push-based Synchronization in Offline First

Some apps may employ a **hybrid approach**, choosing between pull and push strategies based on the nature of the data, balancing the need for up-to-date information and efficient data usage according to the app's requirements and the constraints of its supporting infrastructure.

Conflict resolution

In a Flutter application that prioritizes offline functionality, it is important to handle conflicts that arise when local data modifications made while offline need to be synchronized with the network data source. This is a complex and extensive topic that even experts in the field specialize in. Therefore, I suggest exploring additional resources to understand the matter better.

One simpler way of looking at this topic is using a **versioning** system, where each local change is timestamped (though it is important to notice the timezone difference and errors that may occur here). The adopted **"last write wins"** strategy is utilized here: when the app reconnects to the network, it sends these timestamped updates to the server. The network data source resolves conflicts by comparing these timestamps and retaining the data from the most recent write, discarding older entries.

An alternative method is manual conflict resolution, where users are given prompts to resolve any conflicts that may arise.

One way to handle data conflicts is by assigning a build number to each data, comparing them, and ultimately selecting the data with the highest build number. However, this method could become tricky to manage if multiple users simultaneously work on the same data type.

Choosing an effective method to resolve conflicts can be complex and requires understanding the data type and database used. This is an important topic and must be considered while building offline-first apps.

Streams and Offline-First

Offline First architecture in Flutter significantly relies on the framework's reactive capabilities, and it's crucial to utilize Streams effectively. Streams are key in this context as they enable continuous data updates and synchronization. By having the UI components listen to these Streams, the app can dynamically and seamlessly display the most recent data to the user. Once connectivity is reestablished, this approach ensures that the UI remains up-to-date with the latest changes, whether from local data modifications or network updates. The use of Streams in Flutter not only facilitates real-time data management but aligns perfectly with the framework's emphasis on reactive and responsive design, making it an ideal choice for implementing an efficient and user-friendly offline-first strategy.

10.3   Monitoring and Handling Connectivity Changes

The **"read"** and **"write"** operations on data are the most important pieces in offline-first architecture. At a minimum, "reads" must be implemented; any app without **read** operation can't be considered offline capable. Both of these operations require careful consideration of the **Queue** to defer actions till the network is available and **Network monitoring** as a signal to drain the queue as soon as the network becomes available.

For instance, consider the process of handling read and write operations in an offline-first approach. For reads, the app queues the read request, waits for a network connection to become available, retrieves data from the network, and subsequently updates the local data source with the fetched information. In the

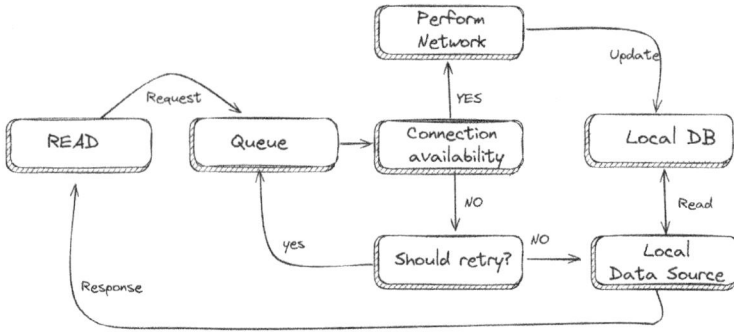

Figure 10.3: Read Operation in Offline First

case of writes, the app first records the changes in the local data source and then queues the write request for network transmission. Once a network connection is established, it executes the write operation on the server. If any conflicts arise during this synchronization process, the app must have robust mechanisms to detect and resolve these conflicts, ensuring data consistency and integrity.

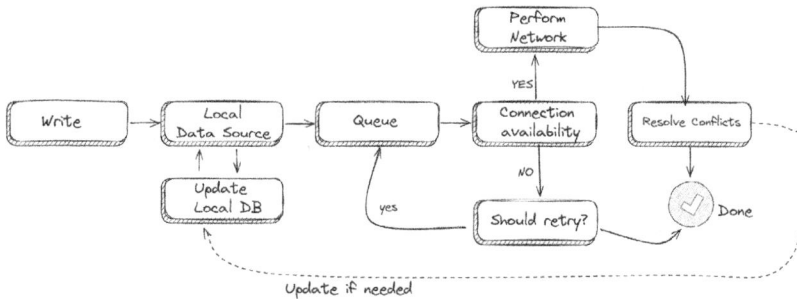

Figure 10.4: Write Operation in Offline First

Flutter provides the `connectivity` package to monitor network status changes. Integrating connectivity monitoring with a synchronization queue in a Flutter app allows efficient network operations management in an offline-first architecture.

10.4 Ensuring Data Integrity During Background Syncs

Data integrity, which maintains the accuracy and consistency of data during background syncs in an offline-first application, requires strategic planning and technical implementation.

Part of data integrity is conflict resolution, which we have seen earlier. Having a solid versioning system is important.

Furthermore, the synchronization process must be atomic; if any part of the operation fails, it should be rolled back entirely to prevent data inconsistency. For example, consider local databases for Flutter that provide ACID transactions. ACID transactions in databases refer to a set of properties that ensure reliable processing. **Atomicity** guarantees that transactions are all-or-nothing, either fully completed or not occurring. **Consistency** ensures that each transaction transitions the database from one valid state to another, maintaining data integrity. **Isolation** means concurrent transactions do not interfere with each other, and **Durability** ensures that once a transaction is committed, it remains so even in the event of a system failure.

Utilizing checksums or hash values to validate data post-sync is also an effective strategy to ensure that the data on the local database accurately mirrors that on the remote server.

10.5   Caching Patterns

Various caching patterns are employed in mobile and web development, particularly in systems designed with an offline-first approach. However, a key aspect in such architectures is understanding the patterns for invalidating cache, which I have briefly touched upon in earlier sections but will now summarize.

Among the critical elements of caching in an offline-first context is the implementation of effective cache invalidation strategies. A prevalent method used in Flutter applications is Time-Based Invalidation. This strategy assigns a predefined lifespan to cached data, ensuring its validity within this set timeframe. After the time expires, the cache is deemed invalid, prompting the application to fetch updated data from the server. This strategy strikes a balance between providing swift data access (by minimizing the number of server requests) and ensuring the freshness of information, thus safeguarding against the presentation of stale or outdated data to users.

Event-based invalidation is another cache invalidation strategy commonly utilized in Flutter apps. It is especially beneficial for handling data that experiences unexpected changes and requires immediate updates within the application. In this method, specific actions or events within the app act as triggers for invalidating the cache. This ensures the cached data aligns with the most recent information, significantly enhancing the user experience. For example, you can utilize push notifications to trigger updating cache.

While these strategies and other advanced patterns are critical to understand, a more detailed exploration is beyond the scope of this book.

10.6 Conclusion

Adopting an offline-first approach represents a strategic shift towards enhancing user experience and application reliability, especially in environments with inconsistent internet connectivity. This approach is particularly significant in Flutter due to the framework's ability to seamlessly integrate with various local storage solutions and its robust support for reactive programming models. An offline-first design ensures that users can access key functionalities of the app and view their data without a constant internet connection, thereby significantly improving app accessibility and usability. This is especially crucial in regions with limited network coverage or for users on the move.

This seamless transition between offline and online states enhances the overall user experience, making applications feel more responsive and reliable. In essence, the offline-first approach in Flutter is not just about coping with the absence of an internet connection; it's about redefining the user experience to be consistently effective and engaging, regardless of network availability.

CHAPTER 11

State Management

Reviewer: Carlo Lucera

State management is one of the most controversial topics in any application development, largely because it involves maintaining consistency and predictability in an application's behavior across various states. This challenge becomes even more pronounced in complex applications where multiple components must interact and stay synchronized. Effective state management ensures that data flows smoothly throughout the application, user interactions are handled gracefully, and the UI remains responsive and intuitive.

However, selecting the right state management strategy can be daunting due to the overload of available options, each with its trade-offs. Developers must consider scalability, maintainability, and ease of debugging when choosing a state management solution that aligns with their application's specific needs and architecture.

This chapter delves into the fundamental principles of state management and then explores how architectural thinking guides the selection of state management solutions.

11.1 Defining and Understanding State in Apps

In application development, "state" refers to an application's current status or condition at any given moment. This includes a wide range of information, from user inputs and application settings to the state of the user interface. The nature of the state is dynamic, constantly changing in response to user interactions or internal processes. The state can be either persistent, enduring across different app sessions, or transient, resetting when the application restarts. Additionally, the state can be categorized as either local (ephemeral), affecting specific widgets or sections of the application, or global (app), accessible, and mutable across the entire app.

The state is crucial in defining how an application behaves and appears to the user at any time. It is a snapshot of the application's memory, encompassing all the currently managed variables and conditions. For instance, the state includes items in a user's shopping cart, the active tab in a navigation menu, or the status of network requests and responses. The state of an application directly influences the user experience, playing a key role in the app's performance and functionality. Therefore, understanding and effectively managing the state is a key aspect of application development, requiring developers to thoughtfully design how the state is stored, updated, and passed throughout the app. This ensures that the app remains responsive, intuitive, and efficient.

11.2 Local vs. Global State: Effective Scoping Techniques

In application development, particularly in frameworks like Flutter, understanding the distinction between local and global states is vital for effective state management. Local state, or ephemeral or UI state, is data confined to a single widget or component. It's specific to a particular UI part and does not need to be shared across the entire application. This state is typically transient and does not require complex state management techniques. I usually manage this type of state within a `StatefulWidget`, using the `setState()` method to update the UI in response to events or user interactions.

On the other hand, global state, often referred to as app state, is data that needs to be accessed and potentially modified from multiple parts of the application. This state is more persistent and is crucial for functionalities that span the entire app, such as user preferences, login information, shopping cart contents in an e-commerce app, or the read status of articles in a news application. Managing the global state in Flutter requires more sophisticated state management solutions. This is where most of us would struggle to find the "Best State Management Solution."

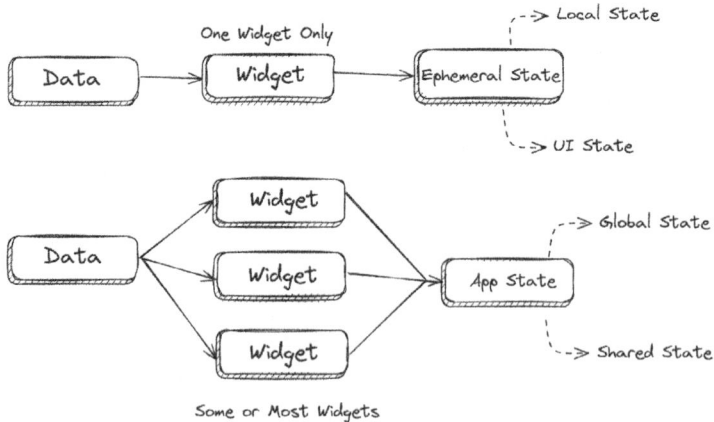

Figure 11.1: Two Types of State in Flutter

The Flutter framework provides flexibility in managing both types of states.

There's no strict rule for classifying a specific piece of data as ephemeral or app state. The decision often hinges on the specific requirements and context of the application. For simple, local states, a `StatefulWidget`, and `setState()` can suffice. However, as an application grows and its state management needs become more complex, developers might need to shift some of what was initially ephemeral state to app state, using more advanced state management techniques. This approach aligns with the overarching principle in Flutter development: choosing the method that feels most natural and least awkward for the specific scenario at hand.

11.3   Flutter's In-built Approaches

Flutter offers a variety of in-built state management techniques, equipping developers with the tools they need to manage application states effectively. While it's possible to delve into each of these methods, it's essential to remember the resources already at your disposal. The solution you seek is often within your team and Flutter's environment capabilities. This reminder underscores the importance of leveraging existing tools and functionalities in Flutter for efficient state management without necessarily searching for external solutions.

Let's review quickly.

The most fundamental approach in Flutter for managing state is through `StatefulWidget` combined with the `setState` method. This combination is particularly useful for managing local or ephemeral states confined to a single widget. When `setState` is called, it instructs Flutter to redraw the widget, reflecting any changes in the state.

For scenarios requiring state to be shared across multiple widgets, Flutter provides `InheritedWidget`. It allows data to be passed down the widget tree, enabling child widgets to access this data. Building upon this, `InheritedModel` is a specialized form of `InheritedWidget` that allows widgets to subscribe to specific changes in the inherited data, thus enhancing efficiency in state management.

For simpler state management scenarios, `ValueNotifier` is an effective tool. It wraps a single value and notifies listeners whenever this value changes. In tandem with `ValueListenableBuilder`, it provides a straightforward way to rebuild widgets in response to changes in the value notifier.

`ChangeNotifier` in Flutter is another simple yet powerful class designed for state management. It acts as a notifier that alerts all its listeners when the state changes. This mechanism is particularly useful in scenarios where different parts of an application need to stay updated with certain data changes. Developers use `ChangeNotifier` to encapsulate and manage the state of the app efficiently. When any state changes occur, `notifyListeners()` must be invoked to inform all listening widgets and update the UI accordingly.

From my experience in working with Flutter, I've found that while built-in solutions like `StatefulWidget` are often adequate for managing local states, handling app-wide state management can become increasingly complex and verbose with just these built-in tools. This complexity is why numerous popular external packages exist for state management in Flutter. On one hand, this diversity offers exciting options to cater to different needs and scenarios. On the other hand, it presents a challenge in determining the most suitable choice for a specific application. However, through the insights provided in this book, I hope you'll be equipped to decide on the best state management approach for your Flutter projects.

Nevertheless, you should still pay attention to the built-in solution. They have been built for a reason. Remember "Simplicity vs. Complexity" from Chapter 5.

11.4   Exploring Popular Solutions

In addition to Flutter's built-in state management tools, many external solutions are available to developers, each offering unique features and methods for handling state. It's impractical to delve into each one extensively in this book; realistically, each could justify its comprehensive guide. However, my focus here is to guide you on approaching these packages regarding selection, particularly when there's limited time for exploration. Does defaulting to the most popular option make sense? While popularity can be an indicator, it's not the sole criterion to consider.

Reflecting on the architectural thinking from Chapter 5, it's vital to recognize the knowns and unknowns in your toolkit. There are over 35 state management packages for Flutter, but it's not feasible, nor necessary, to test them all. You can narrow down your options based on certain criteria:

- **Active Open Source Repository**: A package abandoned for over a year is a red flag, given Flutter's rapid evolution. Check how actively issues are resolved and the level of ongoing community engagement.
- **Test and Test Coverage**: Look for packages with robust testing and coverage. While not exhaustive, they indicate the author's commitment to the package's reliability.
- **Single Responsibility**: I value the Unix philosophy of doing one thing well and doing it well, though sometimes a blend of state management and dependency injection is beneficial.
- **Number of Active Users**: Metrics like GitHub stars, likes on pub.dev, articles, social buzz, and Stack Overflow questions can indicate active use and community support, though this shouldn't be the sole deciding factor.
- **Documentation**: Comprehensive documentation, sample codes, or example apps significantly influence development efficiency and are crucial for team adoption.
- **Well-Documented APIs**: Packages with clear and well-documented APIs save time and reduce the learning curve, even if they require some digging into the source code.

Further, categorize these packages based on their integration with Flutter's built-in APIs, support for reactive programming, and other unique features. This step helps narrow down to a manageable selection, typically five or six options. A hands-on approach, like spending a day experimenting with these in an existing or new app, can provide practical insights into their fit.

Considering how each package aligns with your app's architecture is important. For example, if your app heavily relies on streams, a package that complements this methodology might be more suitable. Evaluate each option against architectural characteristics like simplicity, productivity, testability, scalability, maintainability, adaptability, agility, and deployability, translating these into terms understandable to both the business side and developers.

With these criteria in mind, I recommend exploring the following packages: Riverpod, BLoC/Cubit, MobX, GetIt with GetItMixin, Signal, and Redux. Remember, the final selection should come from a comprehensive analysis and prioritization of factors most crucial to your team and project's success.

Please note that the list I have provided is only a recommendation as of the writing of this book, which was published in January 2024. Your final list may differ, and the characteristics of the architecture that you choose may also be different from mine. The purpose of sharing this list is not for you to follow it exactly but to inspire you to create it anytime you or your team need to.

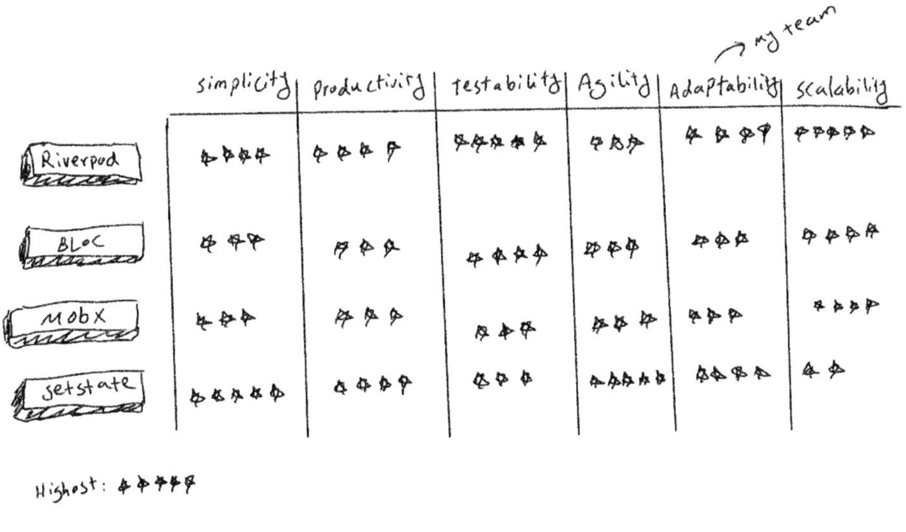

Figure 11.2: Example of Architecture Characteristics Table

As previously emphasized, there is no universal one-size-fits-all solution in state management for Flutter applications. However, this reality should not be a barrier to making swift decisions. While the suitability of a package often hinges on the specificities of your app, a solid architectural foundation, as explored in this chapter, greatly facilitates quicker decision-making in state management. This is because a well-structured architecture simplifies integrating and swapping different state management solutions.

11.5 The Flexibility of Flutter: Swapping and Iterating

In Flutter application development, embracing flexibility in architectural design is key, especially when considering the role of state management. It's essential to recognize that while state management is a crucial component of your architecture, it's just one piece of the puzzle. A solid architectural foundation provides the flexibility to swap out different state management approaches as needed. This adaptability is crucial because what might seem like the most integral component today could be replaced tomorrow with a more fitting solution as requirements evolve.

Maintaining an agile mindset is prominent in this rapidly changing software technology landscape, where Flutter and business requirements are constantly in flux. If a state management strategy selected a few months ago no longer aligns with current needs, it's feasible to phase it out gradually. The best approach often involves incrementally integrating a new state management solution. Implement it first in new features, and then, if a complete overhaul isn't practical, slowly refactor the older parts of your application. This gradual transition ensures that the app remains functional and responsive to the changing requirements without significant downtime or disruption.

The primary goal in your architectural strategy should be to create a highly decoupled application. In such a structure, the state management layer is solely responsible for conveying the state to the UI and does not intertwine with the business logic. This segregation ensures that the state management layer acts as a conduit, passing state data to the UI (widgets) above and accessing the application (Domain) layer below. By keeping these layers distinct, swapping or iterating over your state management solution becomes less costly and more manageable, even though it can still represent a significant technical debt in larger-scale applications.

Furthermore, it's important to continuously evaluate and reassess your state management strategy in the context of the entire app ecosystem. This includes considering the evolving Flutter capabilities, the scalability of your chosen state management approach, and its impact on the overall app performance and user experience. Keeping these factors in mind allows for a more dynamic and responsive development process, where adjustments in state management can be made in alignment with broader architectural and business objectives.

11.6 Conclusion

Understanding and effectively implementing state management in Flutter is a dynamic and critical aspect of building robust and responsive applications. As we've explored, there are multiple approaches, each with unique strengths and use cases. The key takeaway is the importance of flexibility and adaptability in architectural choices. By maintaining an agile mindset and being open to evolving technologies and requirements, you can ensure that your Flutter applications remain efficient, maintainable, and aligned with current and future needs.

The flexibility of Flutter's architecture offers the unique advantage of adaptability in state management strategies. By maintaining a decoupled and agile approach, adapting to evolving technologies and requirements becomes a streamlined and integral part of your development process. This adaptability fosters innovation and ensures your Flutter applications' long-term viability and competitiveness.

CHAPTER 12

Dependency Injection in Flutter

Reviewer: Marco Napoli

Dependency Injection (DI) is a technique that provides objects with their dependencies from the outside rather than having them construct themselves. This approach is fundamental in creating loosely coupled, testable, and maintainable code. By separating the creation of an object from its usage, DI enables a modular and flexible design, making it easier to manage and scale complex software systems. This is particularly important in frameworks like Flutter, where DI can significantly simplify development.

In Flutter, DI facilitates more efficient state management, better testability of widgets, and smoother integration of various services and providers, ultimately leading to more robust and easily maintainable mobile applications.

Let's explore DI from a Flutter engineer's point of view in this chapter.

12.1 The Principles Behind Dependency Injection

The primary goal of dependency injection (DI) is to achieve loose coupling, which reduces direct dependencies among components or classes. Rather than having components create their dependencies internally, DI injects them from an external source. This approach makes it easier to modify or replace dependencies without altering the components themselves, enhancing the flexibility and maintainability of the system. In the Flutter context, a widget can receive services or data it needs (like a network service) from external sources instead of creating them internally, leading to more reusable and maintainable widgets.

The mechanism of DI involves an external entity, such as a container or injector, providing dependencies to a component. These dependencies are typically services required by the component to perform its functions. By managing these dependencies externally, DI implements the Inversion of Control (IoC) principle, where the control flow is reversed compared to traditional procedural programming. I have explored D from S.O.L.I.D in Chapter 3, which is the base for this concept. This shift allows the system's runtime flow to be determined by an external container rather than the components themselves. In Flutter, this can manifest as using constructor injection to pass a model or ViewModel to a widget, separating UI from business logic and making the codebase more modular.

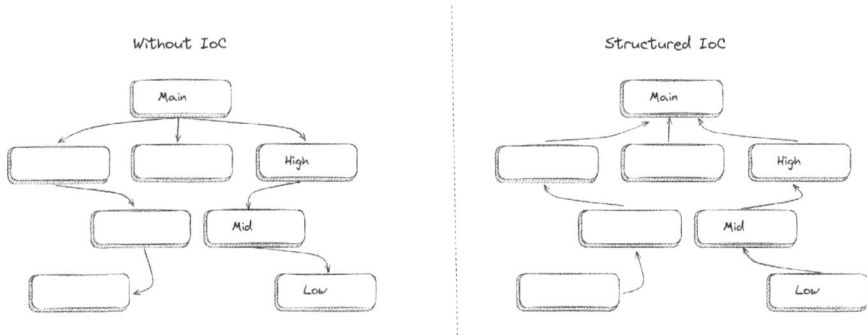

Figure 12.1: Dependency Inversion Concept

DI offers various methods for injecting dependencies, including constructor injection, setter injection, and interface injection. Constructor injection provides dependencies through a component's constructor, setter injection through setter methods, and interface injection allows a component to implement an interface to receive dependencies. This flexibility in dependency management leads to improved testability, as it becomes easier to replace real services with mocks or stubs during testing.

While DI injects dependencies, the Service Locator pattern involves a central registry where components fetch them. The choice between the two often depends on the specific needs and design of the application.

Additionally, DI supports a plugin architecture, allowing for easy replacement or updating of components, and reduces boilerplate code by handling object creation and binding. In Flutter, these advantages translate to easier testing of widgets, as dependencies like data providers can be swapped with mock versions and a cleaner, more focused codebase where widgets don't manage their dependencies.

Last but not least, while you read about DI, you may also see the IoC container term. An IoC (Inversion of Control) container is a tool that automates the creation of objects and managing their dependencies in an application. It acts as a central manager that handles the instantiation of classes and ensures that all their required dependencies are properly injected. This means **Automated Object Creation**: Instead of manually creating objects and their dependencies, the IoC container does it for you based on predefined configurations or conventions. **Dependency Resolution**: The container automatically identifies what dependencies an object has (other objects it relies on) and provides these dependencies to it, a process known as Dependency Injection. IoC containers require reflection for dependency injection, which can only be achieved in Dart for Flutter using code generation tools.

12.2   Benefits of Decoupled Code

Decoupling code using Dependency Injection (DI) provides a major benefit of enhancing the modularity of an application; I also mentioned that several times when I was explaining Dependency Inversion Principle (DIP) and Inversion of Control.

But what does it mean? Let me demonstrate the major benefits in an example.

This code might be familiar:

```
class EmailService {
  void sendEmail(String message, String receiver) {
    debugPrint(
      'Sending email to $receiver: $message',
    );
  }
}


class Notification {
  EmailService _emailService = EmailService();

  void notifyUser(String message, String emailAddress) {
    _emailService.sendEmail(
      message,
      emailAddress,
    );
  }
}

void main() {
  Notification notification = Notification();
  notification.notifyUser(
    'Hello, user!',
    'user@example.com',
  );
}
```

In this example, the `Notification` class directly depends on the `EmailService` class. If we decide to change the notification method (e.g., to SMS), we need to modify the `Notification` class, which could be better. Also, If I want to test the notification class, it would send an email as defined (depending) on this service, which I do not want to do. This is what we name it: coupled design.

Let's refactor it using an interface and demonstrate Dependency Inversion.

```
abstract interface class INotificationService {
  void sendMessage(String message, String receiver);
}
```

```dart
class EmailService implements INotificationService {
  @override
  void sendMessage(String message, String receiver) {
    debugPrint('Sending email to $receiver: $message');
  }
}

class SmsService implements INotificationService {
  @override
  void sendMessage(String message, String receiver) {
    debugPrint('Sending SMS to $receiver: $message');
  }
}

class Notification {
  final INotificationService _notificationService;

  Notification(this._notificationService);

  void notifyUser(String message, String receiver) {
    _notificationService.sendMessage(
      message,
      receiver,
    );
  }
}

// usage in a widget
@override
void initState() {
  super.initState();
  // Examples
  EmailService emailService = EmailService();
  emailService.sendMessage('message', 'receiver');
  EmailService().sendMessage('message', 'receiver');
  SmsService().sendMessage('message', 'receiver');
  Notification(emailService).notifyUser(
    'message',
    'receiver',
  );
  // Note: Without adding final
  // to INotificationService it can be modified
  // Notification(emailService)._notificationService =
  //    emailService;
}
```

This refactoring demonstrates the Dependency Inversion and Injection Principle. Let me break it down.

1. **Inversion of Control (IoC)**: Creating the notification service instance is removed from the `Notification` class and moved to the `main` function. This inverts the control - rather than the `Notification` class controlling which service to use, the control is external (in this case, the `main` function).
2. **Dependency Injection (DI)**: The specific notification service (`EmailService` or `SmsService`) is injected into the `Notification` class. This is an example of constructor injection, where the dependency (`INotificationService`) is provided to the `Notification` class through its constructor. The `Notification` class is no longer responsible for creating its dependencies; instead, they are provided from outside.

As you can see now, these small components are loosely coupled; therefore, it's easier to modify the application without touching any of these classes. This is one of the biggest benefits of decoupling.

Imagine we want to write a test now, so we have to fake our services for easier testing. I can create a fake class for testing purposes only without changing anything to the `Notification` service, as it's loosely coupled.

```
class FakeNotificationService
    implements INotificationService {
  @override
  void sendMessage(
    String message,
    String receiver,
  ) {
    debugPrint(
      'Fake service sending to $receiver: $message',
    );
  }
}
```

This approach demonstrates the benefits of decoupling and DI in testing. It makes unit tests more reliable (since they don't depend on external services) and faster (as no real communication is needed). It also highlights how easy it is to substitute different service implementations, a core advantage of using DI, and adhering to the Dependency Inversion Principle.

12.3   Implementing DI in a Flutter App

DI in Flutter can be implemented in various ways, each with advantages and limitations. Here, we'll explore two built-in methods: constructor injection and using InheritedWidget.

12.3.1   Constructor Injection

Constructor injection in Flutter involves passing dependencies down the widget tree via constructors. This method is straightforward and aligns well with Flutter's widget-centric architecture.

```
class API {}

class MyService {
  API api;
  MyService(this.api);
}

class MyWidget extends StatelessWidget {
  final MyService myService;

  const MyWidget({super.key, required this.myService});

  @override
  Widget build(BuildContext context) {
    return AnotherWidget(myService: myService);
  }
}

class AnotherWidget extends StatelessWidget {
  final MyService myService;

  const AnotherWidget({
    super.key,
    required this.myService,
  });

  @override
  Widget build(BuildContext context) {
    return const SizedBox();
  }
}

main() {
  final api = API();
  final myService = MyService(api);
  runApp(
    MaterialApp(
      home: MyWidget(
        myService: myService,
      ),
    ),
  );
}
```

While this works, it's great as it makes it more modular and testable and contributes to the basic principle of software engineering. It comes with several limitations.

- **Propagating Dependencies**: Dependencies must be manually passed down the widget tree, which can become cumbersome in deep widget hierarchies.
- **Widget Constructor Bloat**: Widget constructors can become bloated with numerous parameters as the number of dependencies increases.
- **Less Scalable for Large Applications**: Constructor injection may become unwieldy in larger applications with complex dependency trees.

Luckily, Flutter has another built-in mechanism that can be leveraged as an injector widget.

12.3.2 InheritedWidget

In Flutter, `InheritedWidget` is a specialized widget used to propagate information down the widget tree efficiently. It enables a form of implicit dependency injection, allowing child widgets to access shared data or services without the need to pass them explicitly through constructors. This approach can be particularly useful for providing access to objects like themes, localization, or shared services. `InheritedWidget` aims to provide a way to access data from ancestor widgets without manually threading it through every widget constructor. It works as an injector widget for DI, where dependencies can be provided at a higher level in the widget tree and accessed by descendant widgets.

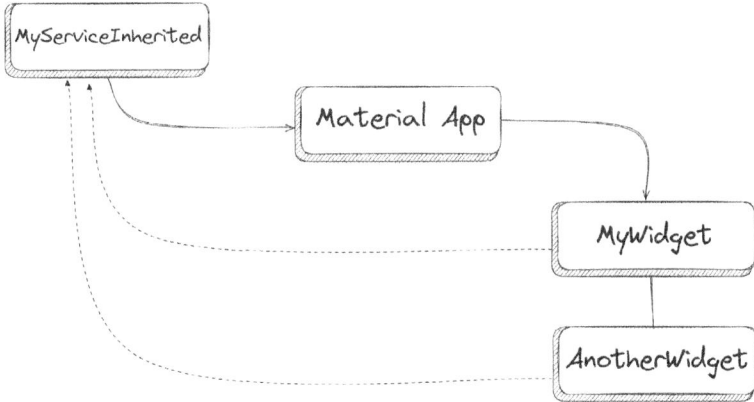

Figure 12.2: Inherited Widget Access Data Information Flow

Let's refactor the provided example to use `InheritedWidget` for DI. First, we create an `InheritedWidget` that will hold the `MyService` instance.

```
class MyServiceInherited extends InheritedWidget {
  final MyService myService;

  const MyServiceInherited({
    super.key,
    required super.child,
    required this.myService,
  });

  static MyService of(BuildContext context) {
    return context
        .dependOnInheritedWidgetOfExactType<
            MyServiceInherited>()!
        .myService;
  }

  @override
  bool updateShouldNotify(MyServiceInherited oldWidget) =>
      false;
}
```

MyServiceInherited takes MyService as a parameter and provides a static method of to access it from the context. Next, we use MyServiceInherited to provide MyService at a higher level in the widget tree.

```
void main() {
  final api = API();
  final myService = MyService(api);
  runApp(MaterialApp(
    home: MyServiceInherited(
      myService: myService,
      child: const MyWidget(),
    ),
  ));
}
```

Here, MyService is provided to MyWidget and its descendants via MyServiceInherited. Finally, we modify MyWidget and AnotherWidget to access MyService using MyServiceInherited.

```
class MyWidget extends StatelessWidget {
  const MyWidget({super.key});

  @override
  Widget build(BuildContext context) {
    final myService = MyServiceInherited.of(context);
    return const AnotherWidget();
  }
```

```
}

class AnotherWidget extends StatelessWidget {
  const AnotherWidget({super.key});

  @override
  Widget build(BuildContext context) {
      final myService = MyServiceInherited.of(context);
    return const SizedBox();
  }
}
```

`MyWidget` and `AnotherWidget` access `MyService` using the

`MyServiceInherited.of(context)` method. While this works, and you are not dependent on any packages to implement it, it could be challenging, especially in bigger applications such as:

- **Boilerplate Code**: Implementing an `InheritedWidget` can introduce an additional boilerplate. It requires creating a custom widget class and handling the `updateShouldNotify` method.
- **Complexity for Beginners**: Understanding how `InheritedWidget` works and how to use it effectively can be challenging for those new to Flutter.
- **Scoped Access**: `InheritedWidget` only works down the widget tree. Widgets higher up the tree or in parallel branches cannot access the data.

Now that I have explored the basics of implementing Dependency Injection in Flutter using constructor injection and InheritedWidget, I am setting the foundation for leveraging advanced packages to enhance DI mechanisms, particularly in large-scale applications. Let's find out what else we can do, especially for higher maintainability and scalability.

12.4 Exploring Flutter Dependency Injection Packages

In Flutter, while built-in mechanisms like constructor injection and InheritedWidget offer basic dependency injection (DI) solutions, leveraging third-party packages can provide more scalable and maintainable approaches. These packages simplify DI implementation, especially in large-scale applications, without reinventing the wheel.

Service Locator and the get_it Package

The concept of a service locator is a pattern where a central registry is used to obtain dependencies. `get_it` is a popular package in Flutter that implements this pattern, providing a simple way to access services from anywhere in your app.

```dart
import 'package:get_it/get_it.dart';

final getIt = GetIt.instance;

class API {}

class MyService {
  final API api;
  MyService(this.api);
}

void setupLocator() {
  getIt.registerLazySingleton<API>(() => API());
  getIt.registerFactory<MyService>(
    () => MyService(
      getIt<API>(),
    ),
  );
}

void main() {
  setupLocator();
  runApp(MyApp());
}

class MyApp extends StatelessWidget {
  @override
  Widget build(BuildContext context) {
    var myService = getIt<MyService>();
    // Use myService with API
    return MaterialApp(
      home: Text('Using GetIt'),
    );
  }
}
```

In this example, we register `API` and `MyService` with `get_it`. `MyService` depends on `API`, and `get_it` handles this dependency.

I recommend referring to the package document for more information, as it falls beyond the scope of this book.

12.4.1 Riverpod

In Riverpod, "providers" are pivotal objects that encapsulate and manage the application state, facilitating access and manipulation across different parts of an app. Providers in Riverpod replace conventional state management patterns like Singleton and InheritedWidget, making it easier to combine and optimize states. They enhance performance by minimizing unnecessary widget rebuilds and caching state computations, thereby increasing efficiency. Furthermore, providers greatly improve the testability of applications, simplifying test setups and teardowns and allowing for straightforward state behavior simulations during testing.

Let's adapt your previous example to use Riverpod for dependency injection. In the original example, we had an API class and a MyService class, with MyService depending on API. We'll now refactor this to use Riverpod to manage these dependencies.

```dart
import 'package:flutter/material.dart';
import 'package:flutter_riverpod/flutter_riverpod.dart';

// Defining the API class
class API {}

// Defining MyService which depends on API
class MyService {
  final API api;
  MyService(this.api);
}

// Creating a provider for API
final apiProvider = Provider((ref) => API());

// Creating a provider for MyService
final myServiceProvider = Provider((ref) {
  final api = ref.watch(apiProvider);
  return MyService(api);
});

// Main app
void main() {
  runApp(
    ProviderScope(
      child: MyApp(),
    ),
  );
}

// MyApp Widget
class MyApp extends ConsumerWidget {
  @override
  Widget build(BuildContext context, WidgetRef ref) {
    // Accessing MyService using Riverpod
    final myService = ref.watch(myServiceProvider);

    return MaterialApp(
      home: Scaffold(
```

```
    appBar: AppBar(
      title: const Text('Riverpod DI Example'),
    ),
    body: Center(
      child: Text(
        'Service is ${myService.api.runtimeType}',
      ),
    ),
  ),
);
  }
}
```

In the Riverpod implementation, we define two providers: apiProvider for the API class and myServiceProvider for the MyService class, with myServiceProvider utilizing apiProvider to resolve its dependency on API. Within the MyApp widget, a ConsumerWidget, we use WidgetRef to observe myServiceProvider, obtaining an instance of MyService with API already injected, showcasing Riverpod's capability in managing dependencies. The entire app is wrapped in ProviderScope in the main function, a necessary setup for enabling Riverpod's functionality.

You should read Riverpod documentation for more details and learn all types of Providers to simplify your DI mechanism and state management.

It's important to note that while the two packages mentioned are good dependency injection options, other packages that follow a similar approach are available. Choosing the right package for your application is an architectural decision that should not be based solely on someone else's recommendation. As you learned in previous chapters, you must evaluate your options and decide what's best for your app. As long as you follow software engineering principles and don't violate the Dependency Inversion and Injection principles with these packages, any package that fits your app is a good choice.

12.5 Conclusion

This chapter has explored the fundamental concepts and practical implementations of Dependency Injection (DI) in Flutter, an essential technique for building scalable, maintainable, and testable applications. Starting with basic approaches like constructor injection and InheritedWidget, we delved into how these built-in mechanisms provide initial pathways for managing dependencies. However, as applications grow in complexity, we observed the limitations of these methods, such as increased boilerplate and difficulty in managing deep widget hierarchies.

Ultimately, the key takeaway is the significance of DI in crafting a well-architected Flutter application. Developers can build more efficient, clean, and modular applications by understanding and appropriately applying these DI techniques and tools, leading to better development experiences and high-quality software.

Part III

Processes

CHAPTER 13

Rules and Style Guidelines

Reviewer: Alessio Salvadorini

The significance of these guidelines lies in their ability to enable clarity, consistency, and maintainability in software projects. Establishing a common language and format, these rules help teams avoid misunderstandings and errors, which are often costly and time-consuming to rectify. Consistent formatting, naming conventions, and best practices transform chaos into cohesion, making navigating, improving, and building upon each other's work easier because they create common patterns that are easier to follow and reduce cognitive overload when reading code written by others.

When starting a project, one of my initial steps is to set basic rules and guidelines, typically standard or community-approved ones. Gradually, I aim to enhance these by introducing best practices and rules. This is facilitated by well-crafted tools or scripts from the team and is enforced through automation to reduce friction.

In this chapter, I want to discuss this aspect, which might seem simple and easy to overlook. However, it greatly influences the maintainability and quality of the software introduced, as well as improves collaboration among team members and generally within the company in a healthier manner.

13.1   The Rationale Behind Rules

Having rules in software development is to enforce "good" behavior and avoid "bad" behavior. However, the definitions of good and bad can vary significantly from company to company, even among different teams within the same organization. This variability underscores the need for clearly defined, context-specific rules that align with each environment's unique goals, technologies, and culture. These rules act as a compass, a common language, guiding developers towards beneficial practices and steering them away from those deemed detrimental in their specific context, which everyone agrees, understands, and speaks.

A good example of such a rule could be the avoidance of certain functions or features that, although appealing, may not align with the team's agreed-upon practices. For instance, a team might decide to avoid using `print` statements for logging, instead enforcing the use of `debugPrint`. This practice ensures that debugging information is not inadvertently included in the production build, maintaining the app's performance and security. Another example is enforcing a specific folder structure that mirrors the app's architecture, such as separating business logic, UI components, and data models. This enhances code readability and makes it easier for team members to navigate and understand the codebase. Additionally, teams might implement rules for naming conventions, like ensuring that Class and Widget names follow a specific format, which can be automated for consistency checks.

The impact of such rationale behind rules on a team is significant. It leads to a more cohesive and simpler development process where all team members are on the same page regarding coding practices. This uniformity reduces the learning curve for new team members and enhances collaboration. It also simplifies code maintenance, as the standardized approach makes identifying and fixing issues easier. Ultimately, these rules, while they seem restrictive at first, enable the team to work more efficiently and produce higher quality, more maintainable Flutter applications.

13.2   Crafting Meaningful Guidelines

When defining a set of rules for software development, the foremost question is, "What goal are we trying to advance?"

Crafting meaningful guidelines in software development is a task that requires careful consideration of several factors. These principles emphasize the importance of consistency, brevity, and practicality in establishing rules and guidelines.

Emphasizing Consistency and Purpose

Guidelines should promote consistency across the codebase. This consistency is not just about formatting or naming conventions; it extends to how code behaves and is structured. For example, in Flutter development, consistency might mean adhering to the Scaffold-AppBar-Body pattern for screens or using a consistent method for state management across different modules. The purpose here is two-fold: to make the codebase intuitive and maintainable and to ensure that developers can easily understand and contribute to the project.

Brevity and Clarity

Dart's philosophy of being brief yet clear should be reflected in the guidelines. This means choosing the most concise way to express an intent without compromising readability. The aim is to avoid overly verbose or complex constructions that do not add clear value to the code. Remember that important rules must optimize the code for readers.

Practicality and Flexibility

While having a set of rules is important, acknowledging practicality is equally crucial. Rules should not be rigid to the extent that they hinder progress or innovation. For example, while a guideline might prefer certain widget structures in Flutter, there should be room for exceptions when a different approach better suits a specific requirement. This balance ensures that guidelines serve as a helpful framework rather than becoming an obstacle.

13.2.1   Types of Guidelines in Dart

Dart team organized their guidelines into several distinct sections for ease of comprehension and application:

Style Guide:[1] This guide[2] outlines the rules for formatting and organizing code, focusing on aspects not automatically handled by `dart format`. It details how to structure code layout and specifies naming conventions for identifiers, such as camelCase and using_underscores.

Documentation Guide:[3] This section[4] provides comprehensive instructions on effectively using comments in your code. It covers documentation and standard code comments, guiding what information should be included to make the code more understandable.

Usage Guide:[5] This guide[6] teaches you how to optimally utilize language features for implementing various functionalities. It encompasses guidelines for using statements and expressions effectively within your code.

Design Guide:[7] Though slight, this guide has the broadest scope. It encapsulates our insights on designing consistent and user-friendly library APIs. It includes guidance on type signatures and declarations.

Each guide is segmented into sections containing a list of specific guidelines. These guidelines are categorized as follows:

- **DO**: These are practices that should consistently be followed. Deviating from these guidelines is rarely, if ever, justified.
- **DON'T**: These are practices that are generally advised against. Due to Dart's streamlined nature, we aim to have fewer of these than other languages.
- **PREFER**: These guidelines are recommended practices. However, there might be situations where an alternative approach is more appropriate. If you do not follow these guidelines, be aware of the implications.
- **AVOID**: Unlike "prefer," these are practices you should generally not follow, except in rare circumstances where they make sense.

---

[1] https://dart.dev/effective-dart/style
[2] https://dart.dev/effective-dart/style
[3] https://dart.dev/effective-dart/documentation
[4] https://dart.dev/effective-dart/documentation
[5] https://dart.dev/effective-dart/usage
[6] https://dart.dev/effective-dart/usage
[7] https://dart.dev/effective-dart/design

- **CONSIDER**: These are practices you may or may not follow based on the specific context, existing precedents, and personal preference.

To assist in adhering to these guidelines, the **Dart analyzer** offers a linter. The linter helps you write consistent code that aligns with these and other standards. Where applicable, guidelines are linked to specific linter rules to facilitate their application.

This section is worth mentioning because it outlines good practices in software engineering that can inspire similar approaches for our projects. Depending on your team and project size, you can condense these guidelines. However, it's essential to understand the different sets and enforce them within your team. Read at least part of these guides to learn how to create similar ones for your team.

You don't necessarily need to reinvent the wheel or rewrite everything for a Flutter project. Instead, refer to these documents and incorporate your additional guidelines relevant to your team. This approach is more effective, especially for smaller teams and projects.

13.3   Ensuring Compliance with Rules

Once you have established and translated your project's rules into concrete guidelines, including your own lint rules, the question arises of ensuring everyone adheres to them. To maintain the project's integrity and quality, a mechanism must be in place to ensure these rules are followed. I have encountered several approaches to this problem, which I will explain below.

Automated Tools: One of the most effective ways to ensure adherence to coding standards is using automated tools. Tools like `flutter format` and `flutter analyze` are pivotal in Dart and Flutter projects.

Code Reviews: Besides automated tools, manual code reviews are essential. Code reviews by team members provide an opportunity to catch discrepancies that automated tools might miss and ensure that the code adheres to syntactical rules, best practices, and logical consistency.

Documentation and Training: Providing clear documentation of the coding standards and conducting regular training sessions can significantly boost compliance. When team members are fully aware of the coding guidelines and the rationale behind them, they are more likely to adhere to these standards.

Continuous Integration (CI) Checks: Implementing CI checks that run formatting and linting tools on every code commit can help catch issues early. Builds can be set to fail due to non-compliance to prevent merging code that doesn't meet the established guidelines.

Internal Tools: To maintain code quality, it is important to establish a set of scripts and tools or utilize available options like git hooks. These rules should be applied before any pull request is sent or before a commit is made. This is a crucial step that every team should follow. By introducing new processes, we can all learn from each other and improve the overall quality of the codebase. Remember, rules or patterns might be only for your team and project, so you must apply them correctly.

Contextual Consistency: This principle dictates that any new code introduced should align with the existing codebase. If the new code violates a particular rule, the relevant section should be revised in one go to ensure consistency.

Promoting a Culture of Quality: Lastly, cultivating a culture that values code quality and consistency is crucial. When the entire team understands the importance of adhering to coding standards and is committed to maintaining high-quality code, ensuring compliance becomes a collective effort and a shared goal.

Automation stands out as the clear winner. Automating tedious tasks and routine checks can save time and prevent human errors, improving your software's quality. If an error is discovered, you can learn from it and ensure it's automated the next time, preventing the mistake from recurring and creating a culture of constant improvement.

13.4   Leveraging Automation for Consistency

Automation is crucial for enforcing rules and ensuring adherence to patterns. I often advocate for creating internal tools and scripts that support the implementation of architectural patterns and compliance with rules and guidelines. It's particularly important to write these tools in a platform and environment-agnostic way, ensuring they can run on any machine, be it yours, a colleague's, or a continuous integration (CI) system.

While these tools may initially take time to create, as your app development progresses, you spend less time creating them and more time adjusting and maintaining them to adhere to your guidelines. However, these scripts and tools must serve as a canonical source of truth so they are well-maintained and used by everyone.

Let me illustrate this with two practical scenarios that are commonly encountered in development teams:

1. **Standardization of Code Structure**: Often, teams agree upon specific patterns for folder structures, file names, and class names, as outlined in their style guides. Additionally, there might be predefined requirements and design patterns for creating services or classes, along with a need for scaffolding test templates that align with these initial requirements. Automation can ensure these standards are consistently applied across the project.
2. **Quality Assurance Before Code Integration**: Before submitting a pull request (PR), it's essential to ensure that all tests, especially widget and unit tests, pass. Furthermore, code formatting and static analysis checks must be implemented to catch potential issues. It is important to receive automatic notifications about outdated dependencies to keep the project up-to-date.

Additionally, it is crucial to ensure that everyone follows a specific pattern and format for Git commits, as this may affect your CI or CD or generate good change logs automatically.

To address these scenarios, creating an internal Command Line Interface (CLI) tool or custom scripts can be highly effective and potentially written in Dart so that everyone in the team also understands it. Moreover, you can also leverage git hooks to establish more automated solutions via these scripts.

The great thing is that you don't have to start everything from scratch again. You can build on your initial foundation and use tools such as the mason[8] package, which is very useful. However, always be mindful of dependencies and how they affect your projects.

Here is a custom script to create a screen based on a specific architecture.

```
import 'dart:io';

void main(List<String> arguments) {
  if (arguments.isEmpty) {
    print('Please provide a screen name.');
    return;
  }

  String screenName = arguments[0];
  createMVVMScreen(screenName);
}

void createMVVMScreen(String screenName) {
  String screenDirectory = 'lib/screens/$screenName';
  Directory(screenDirectory).createSync(recursive: true);

  // Create View File
  String viewFileName = '${screenName}_view.dart';
  File('$screenDirectory/$viewFileName').writeAsStringSync(
    '''
import 'package:flutter/material.dart';
class ${capitalize(screenName)}View extends StatelessWidget {
  @override
  Widget build(BuildContext context) {
    return Container(); // TODO: Implement view
  }
}''',
  );
```

---

[8] https://pub.dev/packages/mason

```dart
  // Create ViewModel File
  String viewModelFileName =
      '${screenName}_view_model.dart';
  File('$screenDirectory/$viewModelFileName')
      .writeAsStringSync(
    '''class ${capitalize(screenName)}ViewModel {
      // TODO: Implement view model
    }\n''',
  );

  // Create Model or Service File
  String modelFileName = '${screenName}_service.dart';
  File('$screenDirectory/$modelFileName').writeAsStringSync(
    'class ${capitalize(screenName)}Service {\n'
    '  // TODO: Implement service or model\n'
    '}\n',
  );

  print(
    'MVVM screen structure created for $screenName.',
  );
}

String capitalize(String s) =>
    s[0].toUpperCase() + s.substring(1);
```

Run the script from your terminal, passing the screen name as an argument:

Replace my_screen with the name of your screen. The script will create a folder named my_screen inside lib/screens with the respective view, view model, and service/model files.

```
dart create_mvvm_screen.dart my_screen
```

Then you will have

```
lib/screens
 test
    test_service.dart
    test_view.dart
    test_view_model.dart
```

More than simply creating patterns and rules is required. Developers need tools to enforce and utilize them automatically.

Let me give another example. Create a Dart file, say code_check.dart, that runs different commands based on the hook triggered from.

```dart
import 'dart:io';
import 'dart:async';

Future<void> main(List<String> arguments) async {
  String hook =
      arguments.isNotEmpty ? arguments[0] : 'commit';

  if (hook == 'commit') {
    await _runFlutterFormat();
    await _runFlutterAnalyze();
  } else if (hook == 'push') {
    await _runFlutterTest();
  }
}

Future<void> _runFlutterFormat() async {
  print('Running Flutter Format...');
  await _executeCommand(
    'flutter',
    ['format', '.'],
  );
}

Future<void> _runFlutterAnalyze() async {
  print('Running Flutter Analyze...');
  await _executeCommand(
    'flutter',
    ['analyze'],
  );
}

Future<void> _runFlutterTest() async {
  print('Running Flutter Tests...');
  await _executeCommand(
    'flutter',
    ['test'],
  );
}

Future<void> _executeCommand(
    String executable, List<String> arguments) async {
  var result = await Process.run(executable, arguments);
  if (result.exitCode != 0) {
    print(result.stdout);
    exit(result.exitCode);
  }
}
```

This script checks for the type of hook executed and runs the appropriate Flutter commands, format, analysis upon committing, and tests upon pushing.

Git Hooks

Once you've your script `code_check.dart` in place, it's easy to trigger it with git hooks. Let's hook it to each commit and also to each push.

To hook it to each commit, create a file named `pre-commit` in your .git/hooks directory and add the following content:

```
#!/bin/sh
dart hooks/code_check.dart commit
```

This hook will trigger `flutter format`, and `flutter analyze` to ensure code formatting and static analysis checks are passed before each commit.

To hook it to each push instead, create a file named `pre-push` in your .git/hooks directory and add the following content:

```
#!/bin/sh
dart path/to/code_check.dart push
```

This hook will run `flutter test` to ensure all tests pass before any code is pushed to the repository.

Ensure both hook scripts are executable, typically for Linux and macOS:

```
chmod +x .git/hooks/pre-commit
chmod +x .git/hooks/pre-push
```

As you can see, the hooks can be written in shell or bash script. This means you can add a lot more to it for quality checks. However, I prefer to extract the implementation and add it all into your CLI or script written in Dart. This ensures that no matter where you run this script or who does it, it always runs the same things. This is where we can leverage CI by running this script again.

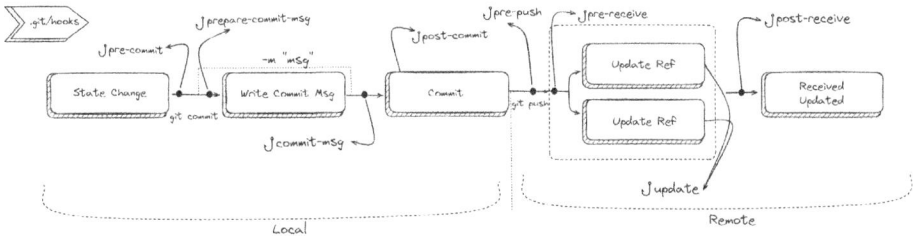

Figure 13.1: Selective Git Hooks In An Example Git Pipeline

Continuous Integration (CI) Systems

Continuous Integration (CI) systems are crucial in automating code integration. They ensure that every new code submission is immediately tested and reported to

---

the development team. In my opinion, your CI system should be agnostic around the commands you want to run. This approach provides a lot of flexibility to your project and team. For instance, you can run tests on a pre-push hook using the `code_check.dart` script. This can also be achieved on CI.

```
if (hook == 'commit') {
    await _runFlutterFormat();
    await _runFlutterAnalyze();
  } else if (hook == 'push') {
    await _runFlutterTest();
  } else if (hook == 'CI') {//<---
    await _runFlutterFormat();//<---
    await _runFlutterAnalyze();//<---
    await _runFlutterTest();//<---
  }
```

The same can be accomplished on CI; for instance, I am using GitHub Action, so a simple workflow is as follows:

```
name: Flutter Code Checks CI

on:
  push:
    branches: [ main ]
  pull_request:
    branches: [ main ]

jobs:
  flutter_checks:
    runs-on: ubuntu-latest

    steps:
    - uses: actions/checkout@v3

    - name: Set up Flutter
      uses: subosito/flutter-action@v2
      with:
        flutter-version: 'stable'

    - name: Get Flutter dependencies
      run: flutter pub get

    - name: Run code checks
      run: dart run path/to/code_checks.dart CI
```

That runs all checks via the script on push and pull requests on `main` branch.

Rules and Style Guidelines

This setup ensures that your specified code checks are automatically performed, helping maintain code quality and consistency both on CI and the developers' workstations.

Depending on your team and project requirements, this setup can be extended or customized differently. In some companies, a dedicated team may enforce rules and build tools that can be used across the organization, ensuring consistency.

As a Flutter engineer, creating solid tools and processes that enforce best practices within your team is not only important but extremely vital. Now, you should have a good idea of how to implement these practices in your team.

13.5   Linters and dartfmt

I noted that the Dart analyzer helps adhere to guidelines in Dart and Flutter. Lint rules are the criteria a **linter uses** to analyze and inspect your code. This analysis is done via static analysis, allowing you to find problems before executing a single line of code. In the Dart ecosystem, tools like the Dart Analysis Server utilize the analyzer package[9] for static analysis. This analysis can be tailored to identify various issues, including errors and warnings outlined in the Dart language specifications. Tools like `dart analyze`, `flutter analyze`, and various IDEs leverage the analyzer package for code evaluation.

It's a set of guidelines or style guides that the linter follows to identify potential issues in your program. These issues can fall into two main categories:

Programmatic Errors

These are mistakes in the logic or syntax of your code that could lead to bugs or malfunctions. Lint rules can help you catch things like:

- **Undeclared variables:** You're trying to use a variable that has yet to be defined.
- **Typos in function names:** You misspelled a function name so it won't be called correctly.
- **Missing semicolons:** This can break the flow of your code and cause unexpected behavior.
- **Misused operators:** You're using an operator like "=" instead of "==" for strict comparison.

Stylistic Issues:

Code formatting and consistency matters don't necessarily affect the program's functionality but can impact its readability and maintainability. Lint rules can help you enforce best practices like:

---

[9]https://pub.dev/packages/analyzer

- **Indentation:** Ensuring consistent indentation makes your code easier to read and understand.
- **Spacing:** Avoid unnecessary spaces or use consistent spacing around keywords and operators.
- **Line length:** Keeping your lines of code under a certain length for better readability.
- **Naming conventions:** Following agreed-upon naming conventions for variables, functions, and classes.

flutter_lints[10] is one such package. It takes recommended rules from the Dart lints package, incorporates Flutter's best practices, and provides them to us as developers. This customizable package allows you to tailor it to your specific needs.

Specifically, **flutter_lints** is designed to enhance code quality and consistency in Flutter projects. It does this by providing a collection of recommended lint rules that adhere to best practices in Flutter development.

You can use `flutter_lints` for recommended lint rules or customize the static analyzer through the `analysis_options.yaml` file. You should include `flutter_lints` in your `pubspec.yaml` under `dev_dependencies`. It is typically added when you create a new project. Then, in the project's root, next to `pubspec.yaml`, modify the `analysis_options.yaml` file to include `flutter_lints`:

```
include: package:flutter_lints/flutter.yaml
```

13.5.1 Customizing Static Analyzer with `analysis_options.yaml`

The `analysis_options.yaml` file is crucial for tailoring static analysis and linting in Flutter and Dart projects. It allows you to enforce stricter type checks and set specific linting rules.

Enabling Stricter Type Checks

For stricter type safety, you can enable specific modes in your `analysis_options.yaml` file:

```
analyzer:
  exclude: [build/**]
  language:
    strict-casts: true
    strict-inference: true
    strict-raw-types: true
```

---

[10]https://pub.dev/packages/flutter_lints

- exclude: This key allows you to specify files or directories that the analyzer should ignore. In the example, `exclude: [build/**]` tells the analyzer to ignore all files within the `build` directory. This is particularly useful for excluding generated files or third-party libraries you don't want to analyze. The `*` is a glob pattern that matches any directories and files.
- language: This section is used to enable specific language features or checks.
  - When `strict-casts` is set to `true`, this option enforces strict type casting in your code. This means the analyzer will flag any instances where there might be an implicit cast from a dynamic type to a more specific type, helping to catch potential runtime type errors.
  - When `strict-inference` is set to `true`, the Dart analyzer enforces stricter rules for type inference. This means the analyzer will flag any instances where the type of a variable, return value, or other elements cannot be inferred explicitly and would otherwise default to the `dynamic` type.
  - When `strict-raw-types` is set to `true`, this option makes the analyzer flag any usage of raw types in generic classes. For example, using `List` without specifying a type parameter (like `List<int>` or `List<String>`) will be flagged. This encourages the use of explicit type declarations, enhancing type safety.

Configuring Lint Rules with Linter

The linter rules can be customized to match your project's standards:

```
linter:
  rules:
    - always_declare_return_types
    - cancel_subscriptions
    - close_sinks
    # ... other rules ...
```

You can enable individual rules that align with your coding standards. To disable specific rules included in a default set, modify the rules with `false`:

```
linter:
  rules:
    avoid_shadowing_type_parameters: false
    await_only_futures: true
```

Rather than mixing rules enabled and disabled, a more effective strategy would be to set all linter rules[11] to `true` in a single file (for instance, `all_lint_rules.yaml`) and then selectively disable only specific ones that are not required or that conflict in `analysis_options.yaml`.

---

[11] https://dart.dev/tools/linter-rules/all

If you would like to create custom lints, you can also leverage the custom_lint package.[12]

Using Analyzer Plugins

For additional functionalities like new diagnostics or quick fixes, you can enable analyzer plugins:

```
analyzer:
  plugins:
    - your_favorite_analyzer_plugin_package
```

Add the plugin package as a dev dependency and enable it in the `analysis_options.yaml` file. Be cautious with plugins, as they can increase memory usage, especially in large projects or systems with limited memory.

It is possible to create your plugin by exploring the Dart Analyzer package API or by using packages that assist in creating such rules. I refrain from mentioning any specific package in this book as it may change over time. As an engineer, you must be aware of this possibility.

Once all lint rules are set according to the agreed style guide, `flutter analyze` and `flutter format` can be utilized to ensure their execution. In addition to some of your specific chosen rules, the Dart formatting rules[13] are primarily enforced through `dartfmt`, which automatically applies these standards to ensure consistency and readability. This includes using spaces for indentation, strategically placing newlines, and managing spaces around operators and brackets. `dart fix` is also under your control to automatically and programmatically make changes.

13.6   Conclusion

The significance of establishing robust tools and processes to support best practices within your team cannot be overstated. This chapter aims to provide a comprehensive overview of implementing such practices effectively. Now, equipped with this knowledge, you can apply these strategies within your team. By prioritizing and adopting these practices, you simplify your development process and contribute significantly to your projects' overall quality and maintainability. Embracing these methodologies is a step toward enhancing team efficiency, code consistency, and, ultimately, the success of your Flutter applications.

---

[12]https://pub.dev/packages/custom_lint
[13]https://github.com/dart-lang/dart_style/wiki/Formatting-Rules

---

✿ INVERTASE

Thanks to Invertase for sponsoring this chapter and for their contribution towards improving its quality.

Invertase is a software engineering firm that creates high-quality bespoke software with a focus on technical tools and obtain accurate. Tools such as Melos, Zapp, Globe and Open source packages such as Custom lints, Firebase SDK for Flutter (FlutterFire) and many more other built and maintained by invertase team.

www.invertase.io

CHAPTER 14

Collaboration in Development

Reviewer: Alessio Salvadorini

Collaboration in software development is critical for leveraging diverse skills and encouraging innovation. Effective communication is key, particularly in remote or culturally diverse teams. Utilizing digital platforms for regular meetings and clear documentation enhances this process. Version control systems like Git and project management tools are essential for coordinating efforts, allowing multiple team members to work on projects simultaneously without conflicts.

Adopting methodologies such as Agile and DevOps is vital in supporting teamwork. Agile emphasizes adaptive planning and continuous feedback, while DevOps blends development with IT operations, promoting shared responsibility and faster deployment. These approaches facilitate workflows and create a more inclusive and dynamic team environment, proving their effectiveness in real-world applications. It is important to let teams choose their tools. Otherwise, tools are set on them in a waterfall manner, leading to misunderstandings regarding their necessity. This can make people think they're doing Agile but follow a hidden waterfall approach.

In this chapter, I'd like to look at three main aspects of collaboration: using Version Controls, applying the DevOps mindset, and communicating via code review. Let's begin.

14.1 Version Control Essentials

Version control is the most adapted tool for software development. In my entire career, I have seen no project that has not used some form of version control, underscoring its universal importance. The two primary version control systems (VCS) types are centralized and distributed.

Centralized Version Control Systems (CVCS), like Subversion (SVN), store all files and their history in a single, central repository. This centralized structure means a developer must connect to this repository whenever they want to make changes. While this setup can simplify oversight and backup, it has its drawbacks.

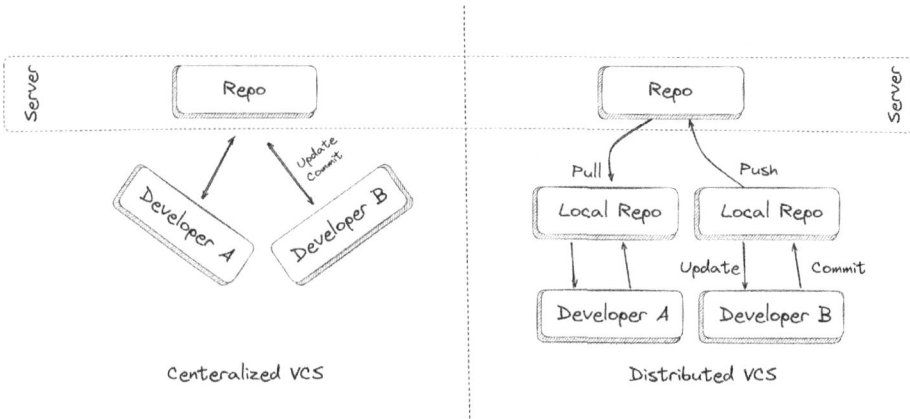

Figure 14.1: CVCS vs DVCS

The most notable is that if the central repository becomes unavailable, it can halt the entire development process.

Distributed Version Control Systems (DVCS), such as Git, Mercurial, or Bitbucket, offer a more flexible approach. In DVCS, the central repository is only a convention, as every developer has a local copy of the repository, complete with the full history of the project. This setup enables developers to work independently and even offline. Most of the time, changes are merged back into a central repository. Still, the distributed nature of these systems means that a failure in the central repository doesn't prevent developers from accessing the project history or continuing their work.

DVCS is the modern approach. DVCS, especially Git, is more dominant in the software industry. Platforms like GitHub and GitLab, built around Git, further illustrate this trend by offering integrated tools for collaborative development, such as issue tracking, code review, and continuous integration.

14.1.1 Trunk-Based vs. Feature-Based Approaches

Managing how code changes are integrated and deployed is crucial for the success of any project. Two widely adopted methodologies are Trunk-Based Development and Feature-Based Development. Each approach offers a distinct strategy for handling code modifications, merging, and release management, catering to different needs and workflows within development teams. Understanding each method's nuances, advantages, and challenges is essential for developers and project managers to choose the most suitable approach for their specific project requirements.

Feature Branch Workflow

The Feature Branch Workflow is a popular approach to software development where to introduce changes to the codebase, developers create a new feature branch instead of manipulating the codebase directly. In the Feature Branch Workflow, each new feature, bug fix, or enhancement is developed in a separate branch derived from the 'main' branch. This branching strategy ensures that the main codebase remains stable and unaffected by the ongoing development work. Once the feature is complete and tested, it's merged into the main branch, typically after a code review process. GitFlow[1] is a specific implementation of the Feature Branch Workflow, offering a structured model. It defines specific branch types like 'feature,' 'release,' 'develop,' and 'hotfix,' each serving a distinct purpose in the development lifecycle. This structured approach helps organize and manage complex development processes in a team environment.

Trunk-Based Development (TBD)

Trunk-based development is an approach to software development where developers manipulate the same branch directly to introduce changes into the codebase, often referred to as the 'trunk' or 'main' branch. This method emphasizes continuous integration and rapid iterations.

In Trunk-Based Development, developers work directly on the main branch of the codebase. They frequently commit small, incremental changes that are immediately integrated and tested. This approach minimizes the divergence between development work and the main codebase. Feature branches, if used, are short-lived and are merged back into the trunk as soon as the feature is stable and tested.

Here is a table that summarizes the key differences between TBD and FBD:

Feature	Trunk-based development	Feature-based development
Integration frequency	Frequent	Less frequent
Code isolation	Limited	Greater
Branch management	Simpler	More complex
Risk of conflicts	Lower	Higher
Suitability for frequent releases	Very suitable	Suitable
Merge Conflicts	Less frequent	Frequent

14.1.2 Git Branching with TBD

Trunk-based development is the preferred approach in this book, particularly as it fits the culture of continued delivery. It reduces the merge conflicts and helps improve team collaboration. Many big software companies have adopted this; **of course, this is my opinion**, and depending on the project, team, and company culture, you may have better choices. Let me explain more about it.

Bug Fixing in Trunk-Based Development: In Trunk-Based Development (TBD), bug fixing is facilitated, as there's only one mainline or trunk branch to

---

[1] https://nvie.com/posts/a-successful-git-branching-model/

focus on. When a bug is identified, it is addressed directly in the trunk. This approach ensures that the fixes are integrated quickly and reduces the risk of divergences between the main and release branches. If a bug is discovered in a release branch, it is first reproduced and fixed in the trunk. The fix is then cherry-picked into the release branch, maintaining consistency across branches and avoiding direct commits to the release branch.

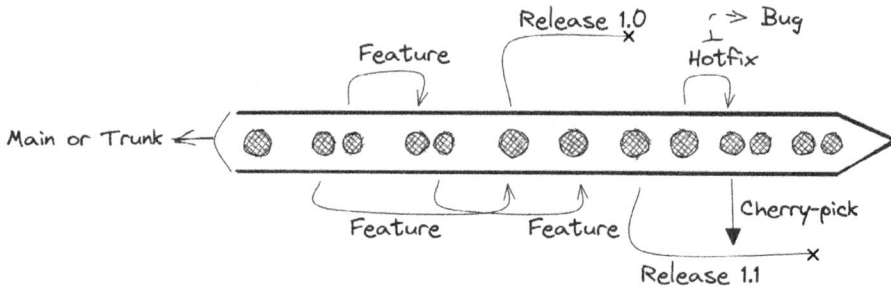

Figure 14.2: Truck Based Development

Release Management: Release management in TBD can vary based on the team's release frequency. A release branch is created for teams with less frequent releases for each minor version, allowing for quick hotfixes and version updates. For teams with high release cadence, releases can be made directly from the trunk using commit IDs or timestamps as version markers. This method eliminates the need for separate release branches, simplifying the release process and enabling rapid deployment.

Feature Flagging: Feature flags are a powerful technique in TBD, allowing developers to merge incomplete or experimental features into the trunk without exposing them to end-users. Feature flags control the visibility and activation of features, enabling selective testing and phased rollouts. They are particularly useful for A/B testing and managing long-term feature development. By toggling these flags, teams can manage which features are active in production, ensuring that only fully tested and approved functionalities are exposed to users.

Code Review: In TBD, code reviews are crucial for maintaining code quality and consistency. Since developers commit smaller, more frequent changes to the trunk, reviews tend to be more focused and manageable. The team's familiarity with the context and plan of each feature simplifies the review process, as reviewers primarily need to assess technical implementation rather than conceptual understanding. This approach promotes quick, efficient reviews and helps maintain a clean and stable mainline.

TBD is well suited for continuous integration and delivery (CI/CD) as it reduces conflicts and merges smaller pieces daily into a single source of truth, your main (trunk) lane.

14.1.3 Git Branching with Git Flow

Git Flow is a branching model for Git, a strategy that outlines a rigid branching structure designed around the project release. This widely used workflow defines a set of rules for creating, naming, and merging branches and is particularly useful for managing larger projects with scheduled release cycles. This approach is appropriate in cases where your product is explicitly versioned, or you need to support many different versions of your product for a long time.

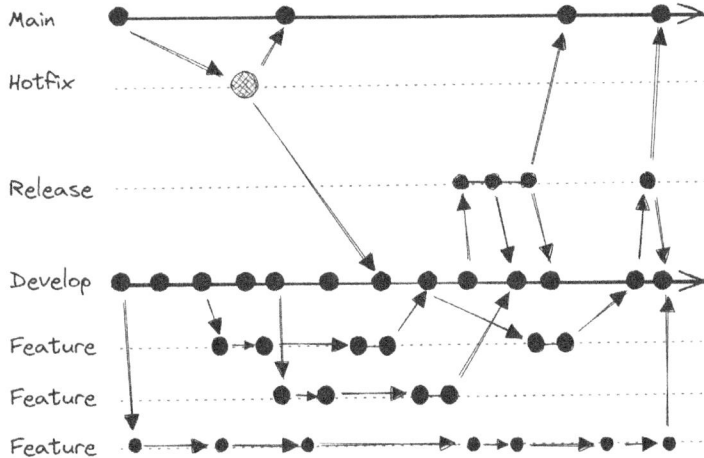

Figure 14.3: Feature-Based Development - Gitflow Model

How Git Flow Works:

1. **Main Branch:** This branch holds the official release history. It's the source of truth for the production environment.
2. **Develop Branch:** Derived from the main, this branch contains the work in progress before it's ready to be released.
3. **Feature Branches:** Each new feature is developed in a dedicated branch created from the develop branch and merged back once complete.
4. **Release Branches:** These are created from the development branch when it's ready to get released. They allow for last-minute tweaks and bug fixes.
5. **Hotfix Branches:** Created from the main branch, they are used to fix any bug present in production. Once fixed, these changes are merged into both the 'main' and 'develop' branches.

Feature management with Git flow involves isolated feature branches that exist for a long time, often leading to merge issues or conflicts. This doesn't mean it should be abandoned. This method is good for projects with a scheduled release cycle or requiring rigorous testing and stabilization phases before deployment, where continuous deployment or integration is not an issue.

Arguably, the feature branch approach fits less into a continuous integration framework, as you will have long-lived branches with much bigger changes to merge back from different branches. It's less problematic if the branches are orthogonal and the commits atomic, but if not, they can more easily conflict with each other.

14.2   Embracing CI/CD in Flutter Development

CI/CD, or continuous integration/continuous delivery, is a software development process that automates the building, testing, and deploying of code changes to production. This process is designed to reduce the time and effort required to release new features and updates to software products.

Integrating Continuous Integration and Continuous Delivery (CI/CD) as key components of DevOps into Flutter development significantly enhances team collaboration and efficiency. By automating key aspects of the development process, CI/CD facilitates the team workflow and promotes a more collaborative and cohesive working environment.

Continuous Integration (CI) for Collaborative Flutter Development: Continuous integration (CI) allows merging code changes from multiple developers into a central repository multiple times a day. This helps to detect and fix problems early in the development process before they can cause major issues.

CI plays a critical role in a collaborative Flutter development team. With team members constantly pushing new code to shared repositories, CI ensures that every integration is tested automatically.

This process includes:

- **Automated Testing:** Each code commit triggers a series of automated tests, including unit, widget, and integration tests, ensuring that new code doesn't break existing functionalities.
- **Immediate Feedback:** Developers receive instant feedback on their commits, enabling quick identification and resolution of issues.
- **Shared Codebase Integrity:** Regular, automated testing maintains the stability and integrity of the shared codebase, which is crucial for a collaborative environment.

Tools like **Jenkins** and **GitHub Actions** can be configured for Flutter projects to automate the testing workflows, making the process seamless and efficient.

Continuous Delivery (CD) for Flutter Releases: Continuous Delivery (CD) enables automatic deployment of code changes to targeted environment for example testing or production. This guarantees that code changes are promptly available to testers or even users, thereby ensuring that any issues are identified and resolved swiftly.

The CD takes collaboration a step further by automating the deployment process. For a Flutter team, this means:

- **Automated Deployments to Various Environments:** With CD, updates can be automatically deployed to testing, staging, or production environments, ensuring that the latest version of the app is always available for review, testing, and use.
- **Reduced Manual Processes:** Automating deployment reduces the need for manual intervention, minimizing the risk of human error and freeing up developer time for more critical tasks.
- **Enhanced Team Coordination:** CD ensures that all team members can access the latest builds, enhancing coordination, especially in teams distributed across different locations.

Platforms like **Codemagic**[2], which offer specialized support for Flutter, are ideal for setting up efficient CD pipelines.

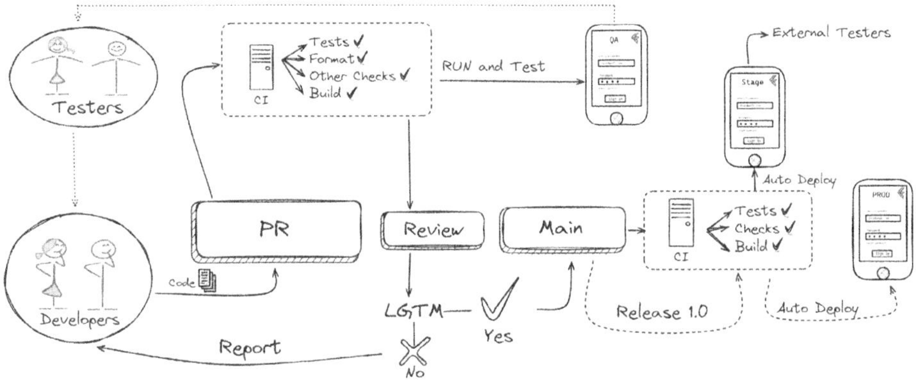

Figure 14.4: CD/CI in Flutter Development

By embracing CI/CD, Flutter development teams can achieve higher efficiency and collaboration. This approach not only automates and simplifies key development processes but also cultivates a culture of continuous improvement and shared responsibility among team members.

14.3 Effective Code Reviews

Effective code reviews are a cornerstone of high-quality Flutter development. They ensure code quality, enforce coding standards, and foster a collaborative environment. Through this process, teams can catch bugs early, share knowledge, and maintain a consistent approach to software development. This also follows one of the principles we discussed in Chapter 1, Shifting left.

What to Look for in a Code Review

---

[2]https://codemagic.io/

- **Design Appropriateness:** Assess if the new widget or function fits the existing Flutter app architecture well. For example, does a newly introduced state management solution align with the project's scale and complexity?
- **Functionality and Bug Checks:** Ensure the code does what it's supposed to do. If a new screen is added to the Flutter app, does it render correctly across different devices and orientations?
- **Efficiency:** Review for any redundant code or performance issues, particularly in resource-intensive operations like animations or data fetching. For example, is the JSON parsing done on an isolate?
- **Readability and Maintainability:** Check if the code is easy to understand and maintain. Is the class API well-designed and neat? Is the purpose of each function or widget clear and well-documented? Is all new code tested? Do the tests cover all scenarios? Is there anything missing?
- **Security Practices:** Ensure the code adheres to best practices, especially when handling user data or integrating network requests.
- **Consistency with Project Standards:** Verify that the code follows your project's conventions and patterns. This includes architectural patterns, file organization, naming conventions, etc.

Speed of Code Reviews

- **Promptness:** Aim to conduct reviews within a day to avoid bottlenecks. For example, quickly reviewing a pull request for a bug fix can accelerate the development cycle.
- **Balanced Approach:** Avoid interrupting your workflow for reviews. Schedule them at a natural break point in your working day, like after lunch or a meeting, to maintain personal and team productivity and reduce context switching.

Writing effective code review comments is crucial in guiding developers toward improving their code while maintaining a constructive and collaborative atmosphere. Here are some key points to consider:

- **Be Specific and Kind:** Instead of saying, "This function is too complex," suggest, "Consider breaking down this function for better readability and testability."
- **Be Clear and Constructive:** Suggest possible improvements instead of simply pointing out what's wrong. For instance, if a piece of code in Flutter could be optimized by using a different widget, provide that as a suggestion with an explanation.
- **Encourage Best Practices:** If a developer isn't using Dart's effective asynchronous features correctly, guide them on leveraging `Future` and `async-await` properly for better performance.
- **Explain Why:** Always provide a rationale for your suggestions to help the developer understand your perspective. For instance, "Using `ListView.builder` here can enhance performance when dealing with a large list of items."

Collaboration in Development

- **Use "Nitpick" for Minor Changes:** For small issues that don't impact the overall quality significantly, prefix your comment with "Nit:" This indicates that the comment is a nitpick, a minor suggestion that the developer can choose to address or not. For example, "Nit: Consider aligning the naming convention with our standard format for better consistency."
- **Focus on Code, Not the Developer:** Frame comments in a way that they address the code and not the developer. Say, "This function could be more concise by..." instead of "You didn't write a concise function."
- **Ask Questions:** Sometimes, posing questions can be more effective than direct statements. It can encourage the developer to think critically about their choices. For instance, "Could this be achieved with less complexity by using a different approach?"
- **Praise Good Work:** Recognize and appreciate good coding practices. A comment like "Great job optimizing such complex logic!" can boost morale.
- **Offer Contextual Learning:** If there's a teaching opportunity, like a new Flutter feature or a better way to handle a particular scenario, explain it briefly in the comments.
- **Be Respectful and Empathetic:** Always maintain a respectful tone. Understand that behind every written code, there's a human being who puts effort into it.

By incorporating these practices, code review comments become tools for collaborative improvement and learning rather than just a means of critique. At the end of the day, they are a unique occasion for learning on both sides.

Handling Pushback in Code Reviews

- **Dialogue and Compromise:** Discuss alternative solutions if a developer disagrees with a suggestion. For example, if there's a debate on whether to use `setState()` or a more advanced state management solution, weigh the pros and cons considering the project's scale.
- **Focus on Objectives:** Remind the team that reviews are about improving code quality and maintaining standards, not personal preferences.

Code walk-through, an alternative to code review

When asynchronous work is not mandatory, opting for a code walk-through instead of a code review is recommended. This is especially useful when there is a significant cultural gap between the PR author and the reviewers. Code walk-through is an interactive process that minimizes cognitive load transfer while explaining implicit assumptions. To conduct a code walk-through, the author can hop in on a video call with the reviewers and walk them through the PR, commit by commit. This allows reviewers to ask questions and interrupt in real-time, providing a comprehensive understanding of the code.

If the reviewers have doubts or need to check some details, they can easily review the PR.

Make Good Code Reviews Better

A few key strategies can be implemented to elevate the quality of code reviews from good to great. Start by encouraging a culture of continuous learning and growth.

For instance, in a Flutter project, this could involve sharing insights about new Dart features or Flutter widgets during reviews. Emphasize the importance of iterative progress over perfection; prioritize making significant code improvements that enhance functionality and maintainability while understanding that not every code has to be flawless in every review cycle.

Positive reinforcement plays a crucial role - acknowledge well-written code and commend developers for their improvements, as this boosts morale and motivates them to maintain high standards.

Additionally, tailor your review approach to fit the context of each submission. Consider the developer's experience level, the complexity of the changes, and the impact on the overall project. This personalized approach helps in providing more meaningful and impactful reviews. Finally, encourage an environment where feedback is not just one-way; encourage developers to voice their opinions and suggestions about the review process, creating a more collaborative and dynamic review culture.

14.4   Conclusion

The emphasis on teamwork and cooperative practices in Flutter development becomes unmistakably clear. This chapter has underscored the importance of cultivating a collaborative environment, highlighting that the collective effort in software development is just as important as individual contributions and that the code reflects the people who write it.

Through the lens of effective code reviews, we've explored how open communication, timely feedback, and a shared commitment to code quality can significantly enhance the development process. These practices are instrumental in improving the codebase and building a culture of mutual learning and respect, which is vital for any successful development team.

The essence of collaboration in Flutter development extends beyond the technical aspects of writing and reviewing code. It involves creating a shared vision, embracing diverse perspectives, and nurturing an environment where each team member feels valuable and heard.

This chapter doesn't cover everything; its subject could easily fill a book. However, I wanted to share my experiences and the knowledge I've gained over the years. It will prove useful for your journey towards becoming a proficient Flutter engineer.

codemagic

Thank you to Codemagic for sponsoring this chapter and helping improve its quality.

Codemagic is a cloud-based Continuous Integration/Continuous Delivery (CI/CD) product specifically designed for mobile developers building apps with Flutter, React Native, native iOS, native Android, Unity, Kotlin Multiplatform Mobile, and Ionic. Codemagic's API and versatile workflow configurations also provide a great platform for mobile development teams who are White labeling their apps.

www.codemagic.io

CHAPTER 15

The Art of Documentation

Reviewer: Alessio Salvadorini

One common issue developers frequently highlight is the need for adequate documentation or quality in existing documentation. Software engineers often find themselves responsible for the majority of documentation, though, in some organizations, project managers or technical writers may assist. Therefore, mastering the skill of creating effective documentation and doing so efficiently with the right tools is crucial.

Perhaps you have said or heard, "My code is self-documented" in your career. While clean code can provide a degree of comprehension, it needs to fully convey the purpose, intent, and context behind the code's creation, and it will anyhow contain some implicit assumptions. Proper documentation is a comprehensive guide, enabling developers to efficiently maintain, debug, and enhance the software's functionality. Utilizing code search in IDE is often useful to speed up development. This is one of the reasons we all love Flutter.

Flutter stands out as an exemplary model. Its exceptional documentation is a prime example of the importance engineers should place on producing high-quality documentation. Let's delve into the world of documentation through the lens of a Flutter engineer, exploring both the documentation itself and the art of crafting it effectively, taking the Flutter team documentation as a reference.

15.1 The Spectrum of Documentation in Software Development

Documentation in software development typically serves as a supplementary text, essential for engineers to perform their roles effectively. Documentation can manifest in various forms, from standalone documents to code docs to inline code comments.

Quality documentation facilitates knowledge sharing and transfer, ensuring that critical information about the software is accessible to both current and future team members. This is especially important for maintaining continuity when team members change. Documentation also aids collaboration, allowing developers to understand each other's work and maintain coherence across different project parts. It enhances the quality and maintainability of code, making it easier to understand, debug, and update. Additionally, well-structured documentation is crucial for the efficient onboarding and training of new team members.

How would we define 'poor' documentation? There are several factors contributing to it. Among all that I can recall, there are three that I experienced myself. One reason is that documentation benefits the engineer writing it initially, while its quality often can only be judged later. Another reason is that not all engineers are good technical writers as well. Last but not least, the target audience for the document may need to be adjusted when it's not appropriate.

15.1.1 Remember to Identify the Target Audience for your Writing

Understanding the audience is crucial in crafting effective software documentation. So, let's describe some key types to help identify the audience:

1. **Experience Level:** Tailor the documentation to the technical proficiency of the audience. Beginners need clear, jargon-free explanations, while advanced readers benefit from concise, detailed content focusing on complex functionalities.
2. **Domain Context:** Adjust the documentation based on the audience's familiarity with the specific industry or domain. Newcomers require more contextual information, whereas experts need specifics on how the software addresses domain-specific challenges.
3. **End-User Profile:** Differentiate documentation based on its intended use and end-user. User manuals are user-friendly for general end-users, technical specifications target developers with their in-depth technical details, and API documentation is designed for developers focusing on integration and extension aspects.

Often, you need to consider how these users interact with the documentation. Are they specialists who clearly understand what they are looking for, or are they novices who may need to know exactly what they need and have a vague idea, requiring more clarification and guidance?

Specialists often look for specific information, like a function's parameters or a certain feature's details. They benefit from well-organized, searchable documentation with clear indexing.

On the other hand, novices might explore the documentation to understand the software better or find solutions to problems they can't clearly define yet. Documentation with comprehensive overviews, tutorials, and easy-to-follow examples is more beneficial, helping them discover the necessary information through a more exploratory approach.

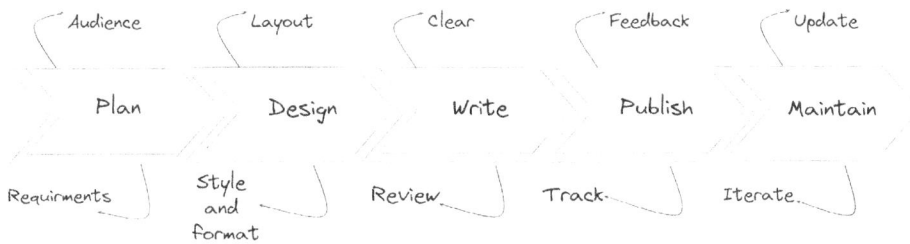

Figure 15.1: Life Cycle of Document Creation

Customers and Providers

In the documentation, it's key to distinguish between "customers" (end-users or API consumers) and "providers" (development team members). Customers need straightforward, practical documentation focusing on usage and application. Providers require more in-depth details, including technical specifications and design rationale. Therefore, documentation often includes references to more comprehensive materials like design docs, specifically catering to the needs of providers while maintaining user-friendly content for customers. This balance ensures that the documentation is relevant and useful for both groups.

15.1.2 Documentation Types

Each piece of documentation should have a clear, singular purpose, similar to the principle that a function should perform only one task exceptionally well.

There are several categories of documentation, but the most frequently written by engineers include reference documentation (including code comments), design documents, and tutorials. These forms of documentation play a distinct role in conveying information and guiding the development process and the user experience.

Reference Documentation

Reference documentation is among engineers' most frequently written types, often crafted as part of their daily work. This documentation encompasses any material that explains code usage within a codebase. The most prevalent form of reference documentation is code comments, which typically fall into two categories: API documentation and implementation documentation.

API documentation documents the signature of a class or a method. It focuses on how the code should be used externally, providing details on interfaces, parameters, return types, and thrown exceptions.

Implementation documentation, on the other hand, delves into the internal intricacies of the code, explaining the logic and mechanics behind the implementation, pointing out the corner cases, or documenting the rationales for implementing some specific details.

A significant aspect of reference documentation is that it is often generated directly from the codebase. Tools like Dartdoc for Dart are commonly used to automatically create comprehensive and up-to-date documentation from the annotations and comments embedded within the code.

AI tools like **ChatGPT**[1] and **GitHub Copilot**[2] transform software development by simplifying code writing and documentation. These tools provide intelligent and contextual code suggestions and automate documentation, allowing developers to focus on complex problem-solving and innovation. Utilizing AI solutions can significantly boost productivity and accuracy in software development, making them an essential tool.

They ease the writing of documentation, allowing the developers to generate it without investing too much time, providing a solid foundation to work with and build upon quickly.

Design Documentation

Design documentation outlines a software project's architecture, design choices, and overall plan. It's typically created during the planning and early stages of the development process. This documentation serves as a roadmap, guiding the development team and stakeholders by detailing how the system is structured, how components interact, and why certain design decisions were made. Ensuring everyone involved clearly understands the project's direction and goals is crucial, facilitating a consistent and coherent development.

Tutorials

Tutorials are step-by-step guides designed to teach users to perform specific tasks or use certain software features. They are typically straightforward, practical, and hands-on, and they are written to help users, especially beginners or newcomers, to understand and effectively use the software. Tutorials often include examples, screenshots, commands, and detailed instructions to facilitate learning and using the application.

Many companies choose to have dedicated technical writers who can assist developers in creating better tutorials and end-user guides that are not necessarily written by developers. However, when it comes to writing skills, in my opinion, all developers should possess a certain level of professionalism to excel in their jobs.

15.2 Embracing Flutter's Documentation Philosophy

Flutter's methodology for documentation is carefully structured, prioritizing clear, complete, and practical information. The characteristics I've observed in Flutter's documentation exemplify what is often regarded as 'good' documentation.

---

[1] https://chat.openai.com/
[2] https://github.com/features/copilot

Therefore, each element I discuss can serve as a guideline for crafting effective documentation.

Let's delve into the core components of this philosophy:

1. **Comprehensive Coverage:** Flutter insists on documenting all **library public members**, using tools like Dartdoc for Dart and similar technologies for other languages. This ensures that every aspect of the API is well-explained and accessible. If a decision needs documentation on private members, it's a good idea to write documentation for them.

2. **Immediate Documentation Updates:** If a question arises during development, add the answer to the documentation where it was first pursued. This creates a dynamic document that evolves with the project's understanding.

3. **Clarity Over Tradition:** The philosophy prioritizes clear, self-explanatory code and documentation (including all processes and conversions) over-reliance on 'oral tradition.' This approach makes the framework accessible to new contributors without insider knowledge.

4. **Quality Over Quantity:** Flutter advocates for meaningful documentation. Rather than filling pages with generic descriptions, it focuses on providing valuable insights, particularly for elements that are not self-explanatory.

   ```
   // BAD:

   /// The background color.
   final Color backgroundColor;

   // GOOD:

   /// The color with which to fill the circle.
   ///
   /// Changing the background color
   /// will cause the avatar to animate to the new color.
   final Color backgroundColor;
   ```

5. **Targeted Documentation:** The documentation is tailored to address real questions that users might have. It avoids generic descriptions and provides detailed, context-rich information, especially for complex or non-intuitive aspects.

6. **Layered Learning:** Flutter's documentation treats every piece as the first encounter for the reader with a particular concept. It avoids assuming prior knowledge, ensuring that terms are defined or linked to foundational documentation.

   ```
   // GOOD:

   /// An object representing a sequence
   ```

```
/// of recorded graphical operations.
///
/// To create a [Picture], use a [PictureRecorder].
///
/// A [Picture] can be placed in
/// a [Scene] using a [SceneBuilder], via
/// the [SceneBuilder.addPicture] method.
/// A [Picture] can also be
/// drawn into a [Canvas],
/// using the [Canvas.drawPicture] method.
///
/// See also:
///
/// * [FooBar], which is another way to peel oranges.
/// * [Baz], which quuxes the wibble.
abstract class Picture // ...
```

7. **Practical Examples and Use Cases:** Providing sample code, application samples, and practical examples is a core aspect of Flutter's documentation strategy. These examples help users understand how to implement and use various features in real-world scenarios.

   Combined with the possibility of Flutter running on the web, this allows the Flutter team to have code sample self-contained apps[3] to run in the context of the docs you're reading to showcase and demo the class itself in an interactive way.

```
/// Specify how a [MaterialBanner] was closed.
///
/// The [ScaffoldMessengerState.showMaterialBanner]
/// function returns a
/// [ScaffoldFeatureController].
/// The value of the controller's closed properly
/// is a Future that resolves to
/// a MaterialBannerClosedReason. Applications that need
/// to know how a [MaterialBanner]
/// was closed can use this value.
///
/// Example:
///
/// ```dart
/// ScaffoldMessenger.of(context).showMaterialBanner(
///    const MaterialBanner(
///      content: Text('Message...'),
///      actions: <Widget>[
```

---

[3]https://api.flutter.dev/flutter/material/FilledButton-class.html

---

The Art of Documentation

```
///        // ...
///      ],
///    )
/// ).closed.then((MaterialBannerClosedReason reason) {
///     // ...
/// });
/// ```
enum MaterialBannerClosedReason {
```

8. **Visual Aids:** For widgets and UI elements, Flutter includes diagrams, screenshots, and other visual aids in its documentation to give a clear idea of what the user can expect visually from the component.

```
/// Flutter widgets implementing Material Design.
///
/// To use, import `package:flutter/material.dart`.
///
/// {@youtube 560 315 https://youtu.be/DL0Ix1lnC4w}
///
/// See also:
///
/// ... More links here ...
library material;
```

9. **Canonical Terminology:** Flutter consistently uses terms such as "method" for class members, "function" for callable closures outside classes, "parameter" for variables in closure signatures, and "argument" for values passed to closures and uses "call" over "invoke" and "member variable" instead of "instance variable."

10. **Refactoring for Clarity:** If documentation becomes too complex or convoluted, the preference is to refactor the code to make it more understandable rather than over-complicating the documentation.

11. **Correct Grammar:** The documentation must have proper grammar in the chosen language, for example, proper English. Keeping a guiding, non-prescriptive tone in the documentation is also important. Prefer the passive voice and suggestions like "consider" instead of direct commands. Avoid using "you" or "we" and making value judgments. Recognize that readers come from diverse backgrounds and knowledge levels; avoid implying simplicity or ease, which can discourage those finding the material challenging.

```
// BAD

/// [foo] must not be null.

// GOOD

/// The [foo] argument must not be null.
```

12. **Avoiding Empty Prose:** Flutter's documentation philosophy emphasizes conciseness, avoiding unnecessary verbosity in favor of clear, to-the-point explanations.

```
// BAD:

/// Note: It is important to
/// be aware of the fact that in the
/// absence of an explicit value,
/// this property defaults to 2.

// GOOD:

/// Defaults to 2.
```

In line with Flutter's documentation philosophy, the focus should be on **clarity**, **thoroughness**, and **accuracy**. A good document should embody these principles to be truly informative, reliable, and user-friendly.

15.2.1 The 5W Approach

When creating great documentation, answering all 5W questions is crucial. While most documentation typically answers the question of "How," looking at examples from various software, such as Flutter, it's clear that a comprehensive approach is necessary.

1. **Who:** Identify the target audience. Understanding who will use the document helps tailor the content to their expertise and needs.
2. **What:** Clearly define what the document is about. This includes the scope, functionalities, and features of the software or code being documented.
3. **Where:** Provide context for where the document or its information applies. This could be specific environments, systems, or scenarios where the software is used.
4. **When:** Outline the appropriate timing or conditions for using the information. This could include version histories, update schedules, or relevant timelines.
5. **Why:** Explain the purpose or rationale behind the subject of the documentation. This includes the reasoning behind design choices, code logic, and the overall goals of the software.

Aim for comprehensive, meticulously accurate documents articulated clearly to communicate your message and engage your audience effectively.

15.2.2 Dartdoc - Dart Documentation Generator

Flutter predominantly uses `dartdoc` to generate its documentation. While other tools are available, `dartdoc` is highly recommended for both applications and libraries in the Flutter ecosystem. Dartdoc is a robust tool that facilitates the creation of high-quality documentation. To enhance your documentation skills, read Dartdoc[4] on pub.dev, and consider reading Effective Dart: Documentation[5].

Dartdoc supports Markdown through the markdown package[6], allowing for rich text formatting in documentation. An interesting aspect of Dartdoc in Flutter is its integration with the snippets package[7]. This package is instrumental in creating and managing code blocks within the Flutter API documentation, providing useful examples and starting points for using Flutter's APIs.

For instance, consider this snippet example in Flutter's documentation:

```
/// {@tool snippet}
///
/// If the avatar is to have an image,
/// the image should be specified in the
/// [backgroundImage] property:
///
/// ```dart
/// CircleAvatar(
///    backgroundImage: NetworkImage(userAvatarUrl),
/// )
/// ```
/// {@end-tool}
```

This snippet uses a special template (`snippet.html`[8]), found under

```
dev/snippets/config/skeletons/snippet.html
```

in the Flutter repository, to generate these informative code blocks.

15.3   Treating Documentation as a Living Entity

Treating documentation as a living entity is crucial for maintaining its relevance and usefulness over time. I have noticed that the Flutter team also follows this approach, which is why Flutter documentation is one of the best software documentation I have ever seen.

Here's a deeper look into this philosophy:

---

[4]https://pub.dev/packages/dartdoc
[5]https://dart.dev/effective-dart/documentation
[6]https://pub.dev/packages/markdown
[7]https://pub.dev/packages/snippets
[8]https://github.com/flutter/flutter/blob/master/dev/snippets/config/skeletons/snippet.html

Continuous Updates: Just like software, documentation requires regular updates. As new features are added, bugs are fixed, or user feedback is incorporated, corresponding changes should be made in the documentation to keep it updated.

Feedback Loop: Treat user feedback and queries as a source for improving documentation. If multiple users are confused about the same topic, it's a sign that the documentation in that area needs enhancement.

Version Control: Like code, documentation benefits from version control. Tracking changes over time allows for easy updates, reverts, and understanding of the evolution of the software.

Collaborative Effort: Encourage contributions to documentation from all team members, not just technical writers. Developers, testers, and even users can provide valuable insights and updates.

Accessibility and Clarity: Ensure that documentation is accessible and easy to understand. As the user base grows and diversifies, the documentation should be reviewed and revised to cater to a wider audience.

Integration with Development: Documentation should be an integral part of the development process, not an afterthought. This ensures that it remains in sync with the software at all stages. For example, when you have a PR, documentation should be treated like tests or other parts of the code. When you review a PR, make sure you focus on reviewing the documentation as well, checking not only the technical aspects and the accuracy of it but also whether it's clear enough for the targeted audience, its grammar, and spelling, and if the writing is correct and consistent, following the team's guidelines.

Tools and Automation: Utilize tools and automation for maintaining and updating documentation. This can include documentation generators, linters, and automated testing for code examples.

Periodic Reviews: Regularly review and audit the documentation to ensure it meets quality standards and remains aligned with the software's current state.

By treating documentation as a living entity, it becomes a valuable, evolving resource that enhances the usability and understanding of the software, benefiting both the users and the developers. The mindset should be to treat documentation as you treat code.

15.4 The Perils of Outdated Documentation

Just like outdated code can cause issues, so can outdated documentation. It's crucial to keep the documentation current and accurate, especially the ones defined outside of the codebase. Here are some effective strategies:

1. **Regular Refreshes:** Implement a system to refresh documentation regularly. While in-code documentation often gets updated with code changes, external documents need a defined update mechanism to ensure ongoing accuracy.

2. **Automation for Documentation:** Incorporate automation, particularly for code samples. Ensure that each release or pull request (PR) includes a documentation review, verifying that the documentation accurately reflects the released code.

3. **Documentation Freshness Tracking:** Create a system to track the freshness of documents. This could involve a periodic reminder or a review schedule to ensure documents are regularly updated.

4. **Tagging System for Updates:** Develop internal tools that tag documentation, allowing updates in the codebase to trigger notifications for relevant document owners. This ensures that changes in the code are reflected in the corresponding documentation.

5. **Minimizing Maintenance Effort:** Strive to keep documentation maintenance as effortless as possible. While it's only sometimes the most exciting task, reducing the effort through automation and tools can make it more manageable.

6. **Incentivizing Documentation Maintenance:** Different teams or companies might find incentivizing the update and maintenance of documentation effective. This can encourage teams to prioritize keeping documents up-to-date.

7. **Replacing Outdated Documentation:** In some cases, the best approach might be to completely overhaul or replace outdated documents. When documentation is no longer relevant or too cumbersome to update, starting fresh with new, accurate documentation is a practical solution.

Overall, the key is integrating documentation maintenance into the development workflow, using tools and strategies that make the process as efficient and low-effort as possible.

15.5   Conclusion

The significance of well-maintained documentation in software development must be considered. It serves as a vital guide for developers, a helpful resource for users, and a crucial tool for effective team communication. The practices and philosophies discussed, such as treating documentation as a living entity, treating it as you treat code, and the perils of outdated documentation, highlight the dynamic nature of software documentation. It's evident that keeping documentation up-to-date, clear, and accessible is not just a matter of good practices but a necessity for the success and longevity of software projects.

Embracing tools like Dartdoc, understanding the value of automation in documentation maintenance, and recognizing the importance of regular reviews and updates are key for achieving this. As software evolves, so should its documentation, reflecting changes, new features, and user feedback. Ultimately, well-crafted documentation ensures that software is usable, understandable, and continues to meet the needs of its diverse user base. This ongoing commitment to quality documentation sets apart successful, sustainable software projects.

CHAPTER 16

Testing in Flutter

Reviewer: Pooja Bhaumik

Testing is an integral part of programming. As soon as you start building any software, even by providing sample data to ensure that you can develop what is expected, you are essentially testing.

Automated testing helps prevent bugs from slipping through the cracks and affecting your users. Testing should be an integral part of a healthy code base, and tests must be maintained like any other code you write. They should follow the same guidelines and even have rules to ensure quality.

Companies can adapt quickly to code changes in the development cycle and gain a competitive edge by iterating faster and delivering better user features. Solid testing is essential to achieving this.

Writing tests can also improve the design of your system. As the first clients of your code, tests can tell you a lot about your design choices. For example, can your Flutter widget handle all edge cases? In this chapter, we will explore testing in software engineering, particularly in Flutter.

16.1 Why Testing Matters: Beyond Catching Bugs

I am frequently asked, "What should we test?" My straightforward answer is that you should write tests for everything you do not want to break or for which you want to be confident enough that it does not introduce undesirable behavior. So, this answer leads me to say that testing is more than catching bugs, especially in this context; we are talking about automated testing.

Defining what a test entails is essential to understand the importance of automated testing. In its simplest form, a test in the context of Flutter development should include:

- A single behavior is to be tested with specific input

- A visible output or behavior resulting from the input.
- A controlled environment for execution, such as an emulator, headless testing, or an isolated process.

In such a scenario, running tests allows developers to validate individual components of an application in a predictable and controlled manner. This methodical approach to testing identifies issues early and contributes to the concept of "shifting left" discussed in Chapter 1. Investing time early in the development process to discover and resolve problems significantly reduces the overall cost and complexity of fixing bugs later in the development lifecycle.

Furthermore, viewing tests as an integral part of the development lifecycle, covering an increasing portion of the codebase, aka code coverage, greatly reduces risks associated with changes. This attitude enables faster development cycles, quicker refactoring, adding new features, and updating existing ones. It also helps to speed up the code review. Consequently, this approach accelerates the time-to-market, promptly delivering products to customers and ensuring the product delivered is reliable and working according to design.

Regarding code coverage, it's common to hear that a specific percentage should be achieved, such as 80% or 90%. However, this approach should change in the Flutter ecosystem and software development in general. Instead of focusing on a target percentage, the goal should be to have enough tests to ensure the app is reliable and to provide confidence to the team and oneself. There is a greater chance of unintentionally breaking things when striving for a high code coverage percentage. A ceiling on code coverage can lead to writing tests that could be more valuable or of high quality but only written to reach that target percentage. Tests must have a purpose and bring value and quality to the app. Therefore, it's essential to ask oneself, "Have I done enough testing? Have I written enough tests to cover all scenarios? Am I confident that I have caught most cases? Can I change something in the app, and the tests will catch it if something goes wrong?"

Testing should be seen as an iterative process. When a bug is identified, writing a test to prevent its recurrence reduces the likelihood of the issue reappearing. It enhances the overall reliability and confidence of the application and the development team. This iterative nature of testing ensures continuous improvement and adaptation.

Lastly, an often-overlooked benefit of testing is its ability to highlight areas for improvement in software design. How often have developers written a function only to realize during testing that it's more complex than anticipated, incompatible with other system components, or that a better solution emerges during the testing process itself? Such instances underscore testing's role in refining and evolving software design.

In the following sections, we'll dig deeper into these aspects, illustrating how testing, particularly in the Flutter environment, is not just a tool for bug detection but a trigger for better software design, faster development, and a more reliable product.

16.2   Grasping the Testing Pyramid in Flutter

The Testing pyramid provides a framework for categorizing different tests based on their scope and the level at which they operate. In Flutter, the Testing Pyramid typically consists of three main layers: Unit Tests, Widget Tests, and Integration Tests.

However, often, we end up having more tests on large-scale apps, such as End-to-end (E2E) Tests, Golden Tests, and even manual testing. Each layer plays a distinct and vital role in the overall testing strategy.

1. **Unit Tests** focus on the application's smallest parts, such as individual functions, methods, or variables. These tests are conducted in isolation and are typically pure Dart tests without Flutter dependencies. They are particularly useful for verifying contract and business logic, offering quick and valuable feedback to developers, and enhancing their confidence in the code.

2. **Widget Tests** concentrate on single UI components. The key here is testing the widget sub-tree, not the rendered widget. This type of testing is crucial for evaluating UI components in isolation. While widget tests can encompass broader features, they should remain confined to individual components to ensure effectiveness.

3. **Integration Tests** bridge the gap between unit tests and end-to-end tests. They simulate an end-to-end experience with mocked dependencies, allowing developers to check how different app parts interact. These tests are particularly valuable for identifying any breaks in business logic and ensuring that various components of the application work together as intended.

4. **End-to-end (E2E)** Tests are comprehensive, involving the entire application with real backend and hardware, functioning as black box tests. These tests are vital for ensuring that the entire application functions correctly as experienced by the end-user. They help validate the full user experience from the start to the end of the application flow.

5. In addition to these automated tests, **Manual Testing** plays a significant role in Flutter development. Manual testing involves human interaction with the application to find bugs or unexpected behavior that automated tests might miss. It provides a real-world perspective on the application's user experience, usability, and overall feel. While more time-consuming, manual testing is essential for a holistic testing strategy, ensuring the application works technically and meets the user's needs and expectations.

Developers face a balancing act when deciding on the types of tests to use in Flutter development. They need to consider the benefits of having confidence and thoroughness in testing versus the costs associated with maintenance and execution speed. It is important to note that the higher up you go in the testing pyramid, the higher the level of confidence, but also the higher the chances of slowing down execution. Therefore, a strategic mix of unit, widget, and integration tests tailored to the app's specific needs and complexity is necessary to achieve a well-tested, reliable, high-quality Flutter application.

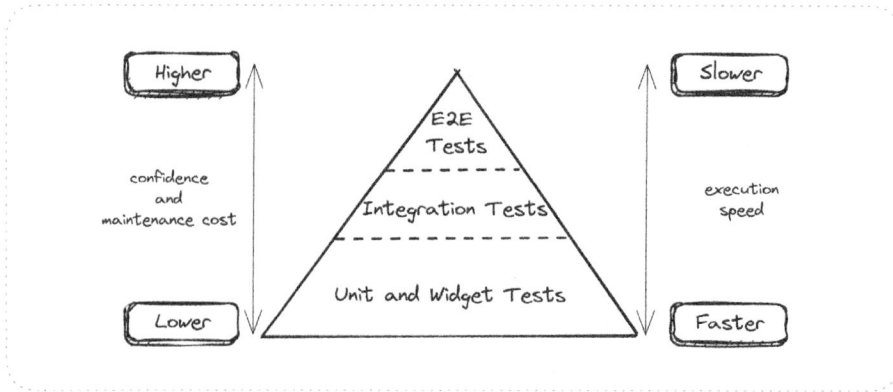

Figure 16.1: Flutter Tests Pyramid and Trade-Offs

An integration of different levels of testing in your continuous integration system can be beneficial.

Running unit and widget tests during the development and code review cycle is advisable. Running slower tests such as integration and end-to-end testing is recommended before merging or releasing your app. However, this decision ultimately depends on your team's mission and goals.

16.3   Unit and Widget Testing Essentials

The basics of how you can write tests can be found on official documents; I would rather focus on the engineering aspect of writing tests and best practices.

Let's start with the Arrange-Act-Assert pattern and then move through other principles.

16.3.1   Follow Arrange, Act, Assert

This is a structured approach for writing tests.

- **Arrange**: Set up the specific conditions for the test. This often includes creating objects, configuring mocks, or setting up any necessary state.
- **Act**: Perform the action that you want to test. This could be calling a method or triggering a user interaction in a widget.
- **Assert**: Check the results of the action. This involves verifying that the state or output is what you expect.

```
test('should add two numbers correctly', () {
  // Arrange
  final calculator = Calculator();
```

```
  // Act
  final result = calculator.add(2, 3);

  // Assert
  expect(result, 5);
});
```

16.3.2   Writing Clear and Complete Tests

Writing clear and complete tests in Flutter involves crafting easily understandable tests that are fully self-contained and independent of external factors.

- **Clarity**: The test name should state what behavior it's testing.
- **Completeness**: The test checks the `increment` method by executing it and then asserting the expected outcome. The test must be completed in any situation.
- **Independence**: The test does not rely on any external state. It creates its `Counter` instance. Nothing should block executing the tests.
- **Documentation**: The test demonstrates how the `increment` method should behave.
- **Failure Message**: The `expect` assertion is to provide a clear message if the test fails, aiding debugging. In the Flutter test, `expect` provides `reason` property you can optionally pass in case it helps clarify the test message.

```
class Counter {
  int value = 0;

  void increment() {
    value += 1;
  }

  void decrement() {
    value -= 1;
  }
}

void main() {
  group(
    'Counter',
    () {
      test('value should increment', () {
        // Arrange
        final counter = Counter();

        // Act
        counter.increment();
```

```
      // Assert
      expect(
        counter.value,
        1,
        reason: 'Counter value should increment by 1',
      );
    });

    // Additional tests for decrement
    // and the initial state
    // and edge cases can be added here
  },
  );
}
```

16.3.3   Follow DAMP over DRY in Tests

While DRY (Do Not Repeat Yourself) is a well-regarded principle in general software development to reduce redundancy, applying it strictly in testing can sometimes lead to obscure and hard-to-understand tests.

```
// DRY example
void main() {
  // Abstracted interaction method
  void enterCredentials(WidgetTester tester,
      String username, String password) async {
    await tester.enterText(
      find.byKey(Key('usernameField')),
      username,
    );
    await tester.enterText(
      find.byKey(Key('passwordField')),
      password,
    );
    await tester.tap(
      find.byKey(
        Key('loginButton'),
      ),
    );
    await tester.pump();
  }

  testWidgets(
    'successful login',
    (tester) async {
      await tester.pumpWidget(
        LoginWidget(),
```

```
    );
    await enterCredentials(
      tester,
      'validUser',
      'validPass',
    );
    expect(
      find.text('Login Successful'),
      findsOneWidget,
    );
  },
);

testWidgets(
  'failed login',
  (tester) async {
    await tester.pumpWidget(
      LoginWidget(),
    );
    await enterCredentials(
      tester,
      'invalidUser',
      'invalidPass',
    );
    expect(
      find.text('Login Failed'),
      findsOneWidget,
    );
  },
);
}
```

Tests often benefit from being explicit, even if that means repeating setup code or similar sequences in multiple tests often recognized as DAMP (**Descriptive And Meaningful Phrases**).

For instance, in Flutter, if you have several widget tests that require similar but slightly different setups, it's better to spell out these setups in each test rather than abstracting them into shared setup methods. This makes each test stand independently, clearly showing what's being tested and under what conditions without jumping around the codebase to understand shared setups or helpers.

```
// DAMP (Descriptive And Meaningful Phrases)
void main() {
  testWidgets('successful login', (tester) async {
    // Explicit setup and interaction within the test
    await tester.pumpWidget(LoginWidget());
    await tester.enterText(
      find.byKey(Key('usernameField')),
```

```
        'validUser',
    );
    await tester.enterText(
      find.byKey(Key('passwordField')),
      'validPass',
    );
    await tester.tap(
      find.byKey(Key('loginButton')),
    );
    await tester.pump();

    expect(
      find.text('Login Successful'),
      findsOneWidget,
    );
  });

  testWidgets(
    'failed login',
    (tester) async {
      // Repeating the setup and interaction for clarity
      await tester.pumpWidget(LoginWidget());
      await tester.enterText(
        find.byKey(Key('usernameField')),
        'invalidUser',
      );
      await tester.enterText(
        find.byKey(Key('passwordField')),
        'invalidPass',
      );
      await tester.tap(
        find.byKey(Key('loginButton')),
      );
      await tester.pump();

      expect(
        find.text('Login Failed'),
        findsOneWidget,
      );
    },
  );
}
```

Don't worry; being a bit repetitive in favor of clarity is a nice tradeoff that is worth it.

16.3.4 Do Not Put Logic in Tests (preferably)

This principle entails avoiding complex constructs like loops, conditionals, and computations within your test cases. The goal is to keep tests straightforward and predictable.

```
// a loop logic here
void main() {
  testWidgets(
    'List Widget displays multiple items',
    (tester) async {
      await tester.pumpWidget(
        ListWidget(
          items: ['Item 1', 'Item 2', 'Item 3'],
        ),
      );

      // Looping through items - introduces unnecessary logic
      for (var i = 0; i < 3; i++) {
        expect(
          find.text('Item ${i + 1}'),
          findsOneWidget,
        );
      }
    },
  );
}

// Or
void main() {
  testWidgets(
    'Greeting Widget displays correct message',
    (tester) async {
      String name = 'John';
      await tester.pumpWidget(
        GreetingWidget(name: name),
      );

      // Using string concatenation to build
      // the expected message - introduces logic
      String expectedMessage = 'Hello, $name!';
      expect(
        find.text(expectedMessage),
        findsOneWidget,
      );
    },
  );
}
```

While it is not a big deal, it sometimes introduces unintended bugs in tests that an eye cannot catch. Often, even a small piece of logic can reduce clarity.

```
// without any logic
void main() {
  testWidgets('List Widget displays multiple items',
      (tester) async {
    await tester.pumpWidget(
      ListWidget(
        items: ['Item 1', 'Item 2', 'Item 3'],
      ),
    );

    // Directly checking each item
    expect(find.text('Item 1'), findsOneWidget);
    expect(find.text('Item 2'), findsOneWidget);
    expect(find.text('Item 3'), findsOneWidget);
  });
}

// Or
void main() {
  testWidgets('Greeting Widget displays correct message',
      (tester) async {
    await tester.pumpWidget(
      GreetingWidget(name: 'John'),
    );

    // Directly checking the expected message
    expect(find.text('Hello, John!'), findsOneWidget);
  });
}
```

16.3.5   Shared Setup and Value in Flutter Tests

Shared setups are a widely used practice where you establish a specific state or create objects utilized in several tests. While this approach can enhance the efficiency of your tests, it is crucial to use shared setups carefully to ensure test clarity and autonomy.

1. **Use setUp() Wisely**: Flutter's testing framework provides the setUp() function to define a common setup that runs before each test. It reduces repetition but should only be used for the most common setup tasks to avoid confusion.

2. **Keep Tests Independent**: Each test should be able to run independently of others. Shared setups should not create dependencies between tests or assume a specific execution order.

3. **Clarity Over Convenience**: Avoid over-complicating the shared setup. If the setup is simple enough, it can make individual tests easier to understand. Prioritize making each test self-explanatory.

4. **Clean Up State**: If your shared setup modifies the global state, use `tearDown()` to reset that state after each test. This ensures that one test's setup does not affect another.

5. **Shared Constants**: Using shared constants for repeated values is usually fine as long as tests do not modify these values.

```
void main() {
  MyWidget myWidget;

  setUp(() {
    // Shared setup
    myWidget = MyWidget(title: 'Test Widget');
  });

  testWidgets('MyWidget has a title',
      (WidgetTester tester) async {
    await tester.pumpWidget(myWidget);
    expect(
      find.text('Test Widget'),
      findsOneWidget,
    );
  });

  testWidgets('MyWidget shows a specific item',
      (WidgetTester tester) async {
    await tester.pumpWidget(myWidget);
    expect(
      find.byType(ListTile),
      findsWidgets,
    );
  });

  // ... more tests
}
```

16.3.6   Test Behaviors and State

This approach ensures that your tests remain relevant and valuable even as the internal implementation details of your application change over time.

1. **Behavior over Methods**: Focus on what the application does (its behavior), not how it does it (the specific methods). This approach tests the functionality from the user's perspective.

---

2. **State over Interactions**: Verify the final state of the application or a component after an event or action rather than the specific sequence of interactions that led to that state.

Let's consider a `Counter` widget that increments a number each time a button is pressed.

```dart
void main() {
  testWidgets('Counter increments when button is pressed',
      (WidgetTester tester) async {
    // Arrange
    await tester.pumpWidget(CounterWidget());

    // Act
    await tester.tap(
      find.byType(FloatingActionButton),
    );
    await tester.pump();

    // Assert
    // Testing the state (displayed value), not the method
    expect(
      find.text('1'),
      findsOneWidget,
    );
  });
}
```

In this example, the test doesn't concern how the button tap increments the counter internally. Instead, it focuses on the behavior (button tap leads to increment) and the resulting state (the counter's displayed value). The test checks if tapping the button results in the counter displaying the number "1", which is the expected behavior from a user's perspective.

16.3.7 Be friends with Finder APIs

The `Finder` class helps locate widgets in the widget tree, which is essential in widget tests as it enables testers to interact with and verify the behavior of widgets. Flutter provides a variety of Finder methods to suit different testing needs.

Here are some of the commonly used ones:

- **find.byType(Type type)**: Finds widgets by their runtime type. It is useful when you want to interact with or check the existence of a widget of a specific type.

```dart
expect(find.byType(FloatingActionButton), findsOneWidget);
```

- **find.byKey(Key key)**: Locates widgets using a Key. This is particularly handy when you have multiple instances of the same widget type and must distinguish between them. You can learn about Key in Flutter in Chapter 2.

```
expect(find.byKey(ValueKey('loginButton')), findsOneWidget);
```

- **find.byText(String text)**: Searches for Text widgets that contain the given string. This is one of the most common finders used in UI tests.

```
expect(find.byText('Submit'), findsOneWidget);
```

find.byWidgetPredicate(WidgetPredicate predicate): Allows you to define a custom search criteria by providing a predicate function. This gives you the flexibility to write more complex and tailored search queries.

```
expect(
    find.byWidgetPredicate(
    (widget) => widget is Checkbox && widget.value == true),
    findsOneWidget,
);
```

- **find.byIcon(IconData icon)**: Finds Icon widgets that use the specified icon data. It is useful for testing if certain icons are present on the screen.

```
expect(find.byIcon(Icons.add), findsOneWidget);
```

- **find.descendant(of: Finder, matching: Finder)**: Finds widgets that are descendants of a widget identified by the 'of' finder and match the type specified by the 'matching' finder.

```
expect(
    find.descendant(
        of: find.byType(Row),
        matching: find.byType(Text),
    ),
    findsWidgets,
);
```

- **find.ancestor(of: Finder, matching: Finder)**: Opposite of `find.descendant`, it locates a widget that is an ancestor of the specified widget.

```
expect(
    find.ancestor(
        of: find.byType(Text),
```

```
        matching: find.byType(Column),
    ),
    findsWidgets,
);
```

- **find.bySemanticsLabel(String label):** Finds widgets with a specific `Semantics` label. This is useful for testing accessibility features, as screen readers use Semantics labels.

```
expect(find.bySemanticsLabel('Close Button'), findsOneWidget);
```

- **find.Semantics:** This is an important one frequently used for semantics. You will learn more about this in Chapter 20, Accessibility.

These `Finder` methods can be combined with `expect` statements to verify widgets' presence, absence, or properties within the widget tree.

16.3.8 Test Custom Painting Widgets (painterMatcher_)_

Often, because writing tests for custom painting widgets is difficult, they are abandoned. The `PaintPattern` class in Flutter is an abstract builder interface used for matching display lists, essentially sequences of canvas calls. This is particularly useful for testing custom painting and drawing in widgets.

`PaintPattern` comes with several methods:

- **Shapes (arc, circle, rect, RRect, etc.):** These methods specify expectations for drawing basic shapes. For example, `circle(...)` can be used to assert that a circle with specific properties is drawn.
- **Clipping (clipRect, clipRRect, clipPath):** These methods allow you to specify expected clipping operations.
- **Transformations (rotate, scale, translate, transform):** With these methods, you can assert that certain transformations are applied to the canvas.
- **Images and Text (image, drawImageRect, paragraph):** These are used to assert that specific images or text blocks are rendered.
- **Custom Matchers (everything, something):** These methods provide flexibility by allowing custom matchers for complex assertions.
- **Utility (save, restore, saveRestore):** These methods help assert the usage of canvas state-saving and restoring operations.

Suppose you have a `CustomPainterForTest` that draws a specific scene, and you want to test whether it correctly paints a circle and a rectangle with certain properties:

```
test(
  'CustomPainterForTest paints expected shapes',
  () {
    expect(
      // Painter widget
      find.byKey(const ValueKey('CustomPainterForTest')),
      paints // matching a PaintPattern
        ..circle(color: Colors.blue, radius: 30.0)
        ..rect(
          rect: const Rect.fromLTWH(10, 10, 100, 100),
          color: Colors.red,
        ),
    );
  },
);
```

In this test, `paints..pattern` is a matcher provided by Flutter's testing framework, and it uses `PaintPattern` to specify that the painter should draw a blue circle with a radius of 30.0 and a red rectangle at a specific position and size.

16.4 Test Doubles

In software testing, especially in Test-Driven Development (TDD), "test doubles" replace actual system components. This is done to simplify and control the system's behavior during tests. These doubles are important in isolating the System Under Test (SUT) from its dependencies, resulting in more dependable and easier-to-conduct tests.

Here are the common types of test doubles:

1. **Stubs**: Stubs are simplistic implementations that return hard-coded data. They are useful for tests where the SUT's behavior depends on the values it receives from external dependencies. Stubs do not simulate real-world complexities but provide specific answers to specific calls. Stubbing can usually be done with testing frameworks to reduce boilerplate codes. This should be familiar to you if you used packages that have `when(...).thenReturn(...)` methods call.
2. **Mocks**: Mock objects are pre-programmed with expectations and responses. They are used to **verify interactions** between the SUT and its dependencies. In other words, mocks contain two concepts: stubbing and interaction testing. You have seen stubs above, but interaction tests are when you validate 'how' a function is called. You probably have seen `verify(...)` method from mocking frameworks.
3. **Fakes**: A fake is a type of implementation of an API that mimics the behavior of a real implementation but is not intended for use in a production environment. For example, an in-memory database can be used as a fake. This approach can be effective as long as you understand the behavior of

---

the real implementation. However, if you are still getting familiar with how the real implementation works, it can take time to create an effective fake.

4. **Spies**: Spies are similar to mocks but are used to record information about how they were called, such as what methods were invoked and what parameters were passed. This information can then be used to make assertions about the SUT's behavior.

5. **Dummies**: Dummy objects are the simplest form of test doubles. They are placeholders and do not have any implemented functionality. They are used when a parameter is required by the SUT's method but are not used in the test context.

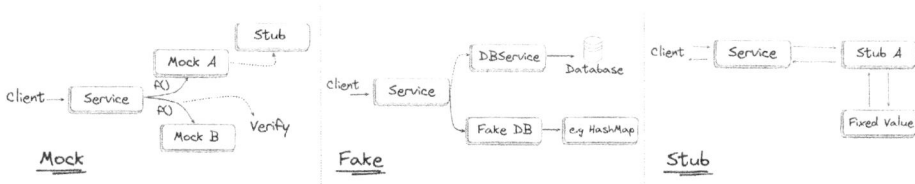

Figure 16.2: Main Test Doubles Illustrations

Each type of test double serves a specific purpose in testing scenarios, enabling developers to write more modular, maintainable, and reliable tests. In the upcoming section, let's explore how to use test doubles in Flutter testing.

16.5   Test Doubles in Flutter

Proper setting up of the test environment and test doubles is critical before writing tests in Flutter, especially when dealing with services for dependency injection to mimic real-world components. This often also requires creating dependencies for the implementations.

One of the general rules of thumb in Flutter is to test your code with real implementations as much as possible. Consider the following scenario where you may think using test doubles is a good idea.

```
final widget = MyWidget(
  WidgetA(
    WidgetB(
      WidgetC(
        WidgetD(),
      ),
    ),
  ),
);
```

It is always better to test the actual implementation as much as possible. Sometimes, trade-offs must be made when deciding between test doubles and real implementation. Instead of manually constructing objects in a test, the recommended approach is to use a factory method or automated dependency injection to reduce the cost of constructing dependencies.

When real implementation is not feasible, use one of the test doubles that suits your needs.

16.5.1   Preparing for Flutter Testing with Stubs

Stubbing can be useful when you want to concentrate on your code by providing reliable responses, such as fixed network data or hard-coded results. To ensure clarity, each stubbed function should directly relate to test assertions.

Assuming you have a complex app with a service that fetches user profiles from a network source, let's create a stub for this service:

```
class UserProfile {
  final String userId;
  final String name;
  final String email;

  UserProfile({
    required this.userId,
    required this.name,
    required this.email,
  });
}

abstract class UserProfileService {
  Future<UserProfile> getUserProfile(String userId);
}

class UserProfileWidget extends StatelessWidget {
  final UserProfileService userProfileService;

  const UserProfileWidget(
    this.userProfileService, {
    super.key,
  });

  @override
  Widget build(BuildContext context) {
    return FutureBuilder<UserProfile>(
      future: userProfileService.getUserProfile('123'),
      builder: (context, snapshot) {
        if (snapshot.hasData) {
          return Text(snapshot.data!.name);
        } else if (snapshot.hasError) {
          return Text('Error: ${snapshot.error}');
        } else {
```

```
      return const CircularProgressIndicator();
    }
  },
);
    }
}
```

Replace the real service with the stub when writing tests for a `UserProfileService` component. Typically, you can create a file to organize stubs, but it's up to you and your team to organize them in your test.

```
class UserProfileServiceStub implements UserProfileService {
  @override
  Future<UserProfile> getUserProfile(String userId) async {
    // Simulate network delay
    await Future.delayed(const Duration(seconds: 1));
    // Return a hardcoded user profile
    return UserProfile(
      userId: userId,
      name: 'John Doe',
      email: 'john@example.com',
    );
  }
}
```

This ensures your test is not affected by the actual implementation of the service.

```
main() {
  testWidgets(
    'User Profile Widget Test',
    (WidgetTester tester) async {
      final userProfileService = UserProfileServiceStub();

      // Inject the stub into the widget
      await tester.pumpWidget(
        MaterialApp(
          home: UserProfileWidget(
            userProfileService,
          ),
        ),
      );

      // Wait 1 second for the FutureBuilder to complete
      await tester.pumpAndSettle(
        const Duration(seconds: 1),
      );

      // Perform your test logic here
```

```
    // Example: Verify if the widget displays "John Doe"
    expect(
      find.text('John Doe'),
      findsOneWidget,
    );
  },
);
}
```

In a more advanced scenario, where state management or dependency injection is used, you may need to provide what is needed to the widget's parent before testing; here is a conceptual example.

```
testWidgets(
  'User Profile Widget with Provider Test',
  (WidgetTester tester) async {
    // Provide the UserProfileServiceStub
    // to the entire widget tree
    await tester.pumpWidget(
      ChangeNotifierProvider<UserProfileService>(
        create: (_) => UserProfileServiceStub(),
        child: MaterialApp(home: UserProfileWidget()),
      ),
    );

    // Add your complex testing logic here
  },
);
```

16.5.2   Preparing for Flutter Testing with Mocks

Mocks are invaluable. They not only simulate responses like Stubs but also allow us to verify interactions with these dependencies.

Mocks are best used when:

- You want to verify how a component interacts with its dependencies.
- The behavior of a component depends on the response from external services.
- You need to simulate complex scenarios that involve multiple method calls and interactions.

To effectively use Mocks in Flutter, mockito[1] or mocktail[2] packages are commonly utilized. It's recommended to use packages that allow you to create mocks,

---

[1]https://pub.dev/packages/mockito
[2]https://pub.dev/packages/mocktail

stubs, and fakes instead of manually creating everything. However, as an engineer, it is important to understand what's happening under the hood before using tools that abstract many concepts. I mentioned these packages because they can help you accomplish your tasks more efficiently.

Consider the previous example in which we had `UserProfileService`. This time, we can mock the service and not only stub with data but also verify if the component is interacting.

```
// 1.
class MockUserProfileService extends Mock
    implements UserProfileService {}

void main() {
  testWidgets('Should call getProfile on service',
      (tester) async {
    // 2.
    final mockService = MockUserProfileService();

    // 3.
    when(
      () => mockService.getUserProfile(
        any(),
      ),
    ).thenAnswer(
      (_) async => UserProfile(
        userId: '1',
        name: 'John Doe',
        email: 'john@example.com',
      ),
    );

    // Injecting the mock service
    // into the UserProfileWidget
    await tester.pumpWidget(
      MaterialApp(
        // 4.
        home: UserProfileWidget(mockService),
      ),
    );

    // Allow time for the UserProfileWidget
    // to rebuild with the new data
    await tester.pumpAndSettle();

    // Verify that the getUserProfile
    // method was called on the mock
    // 5.
    verify(() => mockService.getUserProfile(any()))
```

```
    .called(1);

  // Verify the widget displays the expected text
  // 6.
  expect(find.text('John Doe'), findsOneWidget);
});
}
```

1. This defines a mock class `MockUserProfileService`, which simulates the behavior of `UserProfileService` for testing purposes.

2. An instance of the mock class is created. This instance will be used to replace the real `UserProfileService` in the test.

3. Mock Behavior Setup with `when`:

   - `when`: It defines a condition or scenario for the mock object. This case specifies that whenever the `getUserProfile` method is called with any argument, the mock should react as defined in `thenAnswer`.
   - `any()`: A matcher that allows any argument to be passed.
   - `thenAnswer`: Used for more complex responses, especially when you need to perform asynchronous operations or return a Future. Here, it returns a `UserProfile` after a simulated delay.

   Alternatives to `thenAnswer`:

   - `thenReturn`: Immediately returns a specified value without any delay or additional processing. Useful for simple and synchronous responses.
   - `thenThrow`: Causes the mock to throw an exception when the specified method is called. Ideal for testing error-handling scenarios.

4. The `UserProfileWidget` is rendered in the test environment, with the mock service injected. This setup ensures that the widget uses the mock service instead of a real one.

5. Verifying Mock Interaction verifies that the `getUserProfile` method of the mock service was called exactly once during the test. It's a crucial part of the test that checks if the widget interacts with the service as expected.

6. This line asserts that the text 'John Doe' is present in the widget tree, indicating that the widget displays data as expected based on the mock's response.

16.5.3   Preparing for Flutter Testing with Fakes

Fakes are considered the best among other test doubles because they offer behavior closest to real implementations, often making it unnoticeable that you are testing with fakes.

Fakes are best used in testing scenarios when your test requires only a portion of the complex functionality of an actual object or service but must resemble the real implementation.

Here's an example of a typical unit test in Flutter and Dart. Imagine you have a repository implementation that loads user profile data from a database, which depends on the repository.

```
abstract class Database {
  Future<void> write(UserProfile user);
  Future<UserProfile> read(String userId);
}
class UserRepository {
  UserRepository(this.database);

  final Database database;

  Future<UserProfile> loadUserProfile(String userId) {
    return database.read(userId);
  }
}
```

Let's take a look at the test using a fake database implementation.

```
// 1.
class FakeDatabase extends Fake implements Database {
  final map = HashMap();

  @override
  Future<UserProfile> read(String userId) async {
    return map[userId]!;
  }

  @override
  Future<void> write(UserProfile user) async {
    map[user.userId] = user;
  }
}

void main() {
  test('should write and load user profile correctly', () async {
    // Arrange
    //2.
    final fakeDb = FakeDatabase();
    //3.
    final repository = UserRepository(fakeDb);

    // Act
```

```
    //4.
    await fakeDb.write(
      UserProfile(
        userId: '123',
        name: 'John Doe',
        email: 'jon@doe.dev',
      ),
    );
    final profile = await repository.loadUserProfile('123');

    // Assert
    //5.
    expect(profile.userId, equals('123'));
    expect(profile.name, equals('John Doe'));
    expect(profile.email, equals('jon@doe.dev'));
  });
}
```

1. Create a HashMap-based fake database that resembles the real implementation for reading and writing data.
2. Instantiate the fake database
3. Use this fake database in an actual class that is dependent on it.
4. Write a user in the database and then load a profile where under the hood is calling the read method from the database.
5. Finally, check all the results.

16.5.4   Preparing for Flutter Testing with Spies

Spies are very similar to Stubs; the main difference is that they also record extra information and call actual implementation. Imagine you have a `UserManager` class in your Flutter app that uses a `LoggerService` to log user activities. You want to verify that the `LoggerService` is being called correctly without altering its behavior.

```
class LoggerService {
  void log(String message) {
    // Actual logging logic
  }
}

class UserManager {
  final LoggerService logger;

  UserManager(this.logger);

  void deleteUser(String userId) {
    // User deletion logic
```

```
      logger.log('User $userId deleted');
  }
}

class SpyLoggerService extends LoggerService {
  int logCallCount = 0;

  @override
  void log(String message) {
    logCallCount++;
    super.log(message); // Calling the real log method
  }
}

void main() {
  test(
    'UserManager should call log when deleting a user',
    () {
      final spyLogger = SpyLoggerService();
      final userManager = UserManager(spyLogger);

      userManager.deleteUser('123');

      expect(
        spyLogger.logCallCount,
        1,
      ); // Verifying that log was called once
    },
  );
}
```

In this example, SpyLoggerService extends LoggerService and tracks the number of times the log method is called. This allows you to verify the interaction between UserManager and LoggerService without disrupting their real functionalities.

16.5.5   Preparing for Flutter Testing with Dummies

You have a UserProfileWidget in your Flutter app that requires a UserRepository for its constructor, but in your test, you're not interested in the UserRepository's functionality.

```
class UserRepository {
  // UserRepository methods
}

class UserProfileWidget extends StatefulWidget {
```

```dart
  final UserRepository userRepository;

  const UserProfileWidget(
    this.userRepository, {
    super.key,
  });

  @override
  State<UserProfileWidget> createState() =>
      UserProfileWidgetState();
}

class UserProfileWidgetState
    extends State<UserProfileWidget> {
  int count = 0;

  @override
  Widget build(BuildContext context) {
    // Widget build logic
    return const SizedBox();
  }
}

//1.
class DummyUserRepository extends UserRepository {}

void main() {
  testWidgets(
    'UserProfileWidget should render correctly',
    (tester) async {
      await tester.pumpWidget(
        MaterialApp(
          //2.
          home: UserProfileWidget(DummyUserRepository()),
        ),
      );
      //3.
      final widget = tester.state<UserProfileWidgetState>(
        find.byType(
          UserProfileWidget,
        ),
      );

      //4.
      expect(
        widget.count,
        0,
        reason: 'initial state must be 0 in this widget',
```

```
      );
    },
  );
}
```

1. A dummy version of `UserRepository` is created, serving as a placeholder without real functionality to fulfill dependencies in the widget test.
2. The widget is initialized in the test environment with the dummy object, isolating it from the real repository's behavior for focused testing.
3. The test accesses the internal state of the widget to verify its properties and behavior during the test execution. In this case, the initial value of the state is important for this test.
4. The test asserts to validate the initial state or behavior of the widget, ensuring it aligns with expected outcomes.

In this case, `DummyUserRepository` is a stand-in for `UserRepository`. It's used to satisfy the constructor requirement of `UserProfileWidget`, enabling you to test the widget without involving the `UserRepository`.

16.6   The World of Integration and Golden Tests

In Flutter, besides unit and widget tests, Integration and Golden tests ensure applications' overall quality and reliability. These testing types offer broader coverage, from user interaction flows to visual consistency.

16.6.1   Integration Tests in Flutter

Flutter's integration tests are crucial in testing the entire application as a cohesive unit. These tests mimic user interactions and verify the app's behavior under different scenarios. They link unit/widget tests and real-world usage, guaranteeing that the app operates correctly from beginning to end.

Setup and Usage

1. **Add Dependencies**: Include `flutter_test` and `integration_test` in your `pubspec.yaml` file. These packages provide the necessary tools and APIs for writing and running integration tests.
2. **Create Test Files**: In your project, create an `integration_test` directory. You'll write your integration test scripts here as Dart files (`<name>_test.dart`).
3. **Write Test Scripts**: Use `testWidgets` to define your tests. This function allows you to simulate user interactions like tapping buttons, entering text, navigating between screens, and verifying the expected outcomes.

Here's an example of an integration test in Flutter:

Testing in Flutter

```
void main() {
  IntegrationTestWidgetsFlutterBinding.ensureInitialized();

  testWidgets(
    'tap on the floating action button, verify counter',
    (tester) async {
      // Load your app's main widget
      await tester.pumpWidget(const MyApp());

      // Verify initial state or conditions
      expect(find.text('0'), findsOneWidget);

      // Simulate user actions
      final fab = find.byKey(const Key('increment'));
      await tester.tap(fab);

      // Trigger a frame to reflect changes
      await tester.pumpAndSettle();

      // Verify the app's response to the actions
      expect(find.text('0'), findsNothing);
      expect(find.text('1'), findsOneWidget);
    },
  );
}
```

In this example, the test loads the main widget of the app, simulates a user tapping a button, and then verifies that the app's state has changed as expected.

Considerations for Integration Tests

- **Resource Intensive**: Integration tests can be more resource-intensive than other tests, requiring more execution time and computational resources.
- **Flakiness**: They can sometimes be flaky, particularly in CI environments, due to dependencies on external factors like network conditions or third-party services.
- **Complex Setup and Maintenance**: Setting up integration tests can be complex, requiring a thorough understanding of the entire app's workflow. Maintaining these tests can also be challenging, especially as the app grows and evolves.
- **Device and Platform Variability**: Tests might produce different results on different devices or operating systems, necessitating testing across various devices for comprehensive coverage.
- **Balancing Test Coverage**: It's necessary to balance integration tests with unit and widget tests to ensure efficient and effective test coverage without unnecessary duplication of efforts.

When using the integration tests, it is important to consider using device farms such as Firebase Test Lab or AWS Device Farm. These tools help write interaction

---

tests on multiple devices with different settings and specifications in parallel. This increases the confidence that your app works perfectly on all devices. Selecting a wide range of devices is preferable to ensure that your app runs as expected on all devices in that range.

16.6.2 Golden Tests in Flutter

Golden tests in Flutter are an efficient way to verify the visual behavior of your widgets, ensuring that they are rendered correctly across different updates and conditions. These tests function by comparing the current rendering of a widget with a reference image that is considered 'golden', making them particularly useful for testing custom visuals such as charts or custom painters.

Golden tests compare the rendered output of your widgets against saved 'golden' image files. If the current rendering matches the golden file, the test passes; otherwise, it fails, indicating a visual discrepancy.

Setup and Usage

1. **Write Test Cases**: Similar to regular widget tests, golden tests in Flutter are written using the testWidgets function. Within these tests, you load the widget you want to test and then use the matchesGoldenFile matcher to compare the widget's rendering to the golden file.
2. **Creating and Updating Golden Files**: Run the test with the -update-goldens flag to create or update the golden files. This should be done whenever you intentionally change the appearance of a widget.

```
void main() {
  testWidgets(
    'ExamplePainter golden test',
    (tester) async {
      await tester.pumpWidget(
        SizedBox(
          width: 400,
          height: 400,
          child: CustomPaint(
            painter: ExamplePainter(100),
          ),
        ),
      );

      await expectLater(
        find.byType(CustomPaint),
        matchesGoldenFile(
          'goldens/example_painter_100.png',
        ),
      );
    },
```

```
    );
}
```

In this example, a `CustomPaint` widget with an `ExamplePainter` is rendered and compared against a golden file.

Advantages of Using Golden Tests

- **Visual Verification**: They are excellent for ensuring visual aspects like layout, colors, and text styles.
- **Documentation**: Golden files serve as a visual reference for how widgets are supposed to look, aiding in understanding and maintaining the code.

Considerations

- **Platform Differences**: There might be rendering differences across platforms, especially with fonts. Generating and checking golden files on the same platform as your CI environment is crucial.
- **File Management**: Golden files need to be managed carefully. They should be updated intentionally and reviewed as part of your code review process.

Using Alchemist with Golden Tests

Alchemist is an open-source package that enhances golden testing in Flutter. It addresses common challenges with built-in golden testing, like CI test flakes and font rendering inconsistencies.

- **Declarative API**: Alchemist provides a more readable and declarative API, improving test clarity.
- **Organized Tests**: It allows organizing multiple test scenarios in a single golden file using `GoldenTestGroup` and `GoldenTestScenario`.
- **CI Compatibility**: Alchemist generates CI-friendly golden files, reducing platform-specific rendering issues.

There is one important thing to keep in mind when creating Golden tests. Break down your widget into small pieces and test the most important ones. Otherwise, the cost of maintaining Golden tests can become high due to the many minor adjustments needed.

16.7   Conclusion

This chapter has been a journey over the pyramid of testing in Flutter. We started with unit tests, focusing on individual functions and classes. We moved on to widget tests for UI elements, then interaction and end-to-end tests for a more comprehensive application assessment.

Throughout this chapter, we've highlighted the significance of test doubles in enhancing engineering efficiency. They are instrumental in testing code quickly and efficiently. However, it's important to determine the appropriate context for each type of test double, as their misuse or overuse can lead to ambiguous, error-prone tests or tests that fail to make a meaningful contribution to robust software development.

While test doubles are beneficial, it's often preferable to test with real implementations, or at least those that closely mimic reality, typically achieved using fakes. Interaction tests may only sometimes yield significant benefits and can clutter the test suite if not used with good reason.

Our exploration of Flutter testing continues. There are myriad edge cases and nuances to discover, and I encourage you to delve into further resources, including books and official documentation. These will offer deeper insights into different types of tests and their strategic use in Flutter, enhancing your proficiency in crafting effective and efficient tests for Flutter applications.

CHAPTER 17

Environments and Flavors

Reviewer: Dominik Roszkowski

In this chapter, we will delve into the concept of environments from an engineering perspective, focusing on how this aspect of software development plays out in Flutter through flavors. It's important to note that what follows is an exploration of the underlying principles and the strategic importance of environments in software engineering rather than a step-by-step implementation guide. For detailed technical instructions on setting up and managing environments in Flutter, readers must consult the official documentation.

Environments in software engineering are similar to various stages in a play, each with its unique set of properties and behaviors. Development, testing, and production stages are essential for a software project's structured and efficient progression. These may vary from company to company to team, but the purpose remains the same. You may also need a different version of the app that you are building. In Flutter, this concept is elegantly handled through "flavors." Flavors allow developers to create distinct versions of an application under the same codebase, each tailored for specific environments.

Let's see why this is important and why you should prioritize it from the beginning of building your app.

17.1 The Need for Multiple Environments and Flavors

The distinction between "Environments" and "Flavors" lies in their application and scope. While these terms can sometimes be used interchangeably in Flutter, they have distinct meanings and applications. Environments are configurations for different stages of an app's lifecycle, such as development, testing, and production, mainly differing in settings like API endpoints and feature toggles but using the same codebase. On the other hand, Flavors are used to create distinct versions of the app (like free and paid versions), each with unique identifiers, assets, and potentially different features. While environments adjust how the same app behaves under different conditions, flavors result in separate builds of the app, each tailored for a specific purpose or audience.

17.1.1 Not Always Needing Flavors

A single Flutter flavor might suffice in some cases, especially for web or desktop applications, with different environments being set up for development, testing, and production. For instance, the same application could have configurations for a local development server, a staging server, and a production server. This setup can be efficiently managed using different environment configurations without creating multiple flavors.

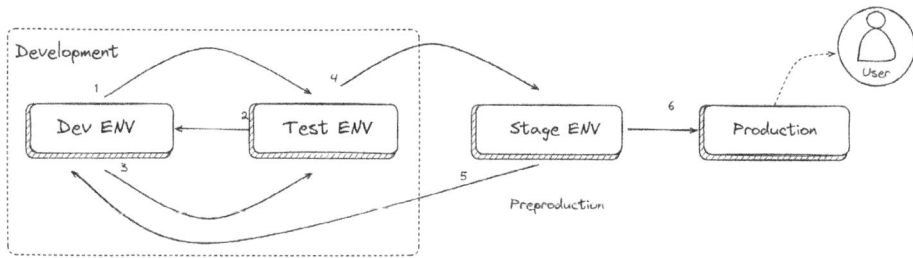

Figure 17.1: Typical Different Environments

17.1.2 The Case for Multiple Flavors

Flavors in Flutter offers a flexible approach to managing different aspects of mobile app development, particularly in environments like Android and iOS.

Flavors can be helpful in scenarios such as:

- Managing a next or beta version of the app that relies on vastly different dependencies, libraries, or target SDKs. This approach allows both the stable and experimental versions of the app to coexist on the same device, facilitating easier QA and team collaboration.
- White-labeling, where apps are customized with different names, bundle IDs, assets, and low-level configurations. This strategy is particularly useful for developing core functionalities while avoiding a codebase split that is too granular—implementing white-label solutions for various clients using a single codebase, enabling customized branding and features for different customers.
- Leveraging flavors for Proof of Concept (POC) projects and other experimental features not intended for public release.
- Utilizing distinct app icons for each flavor to facilitate easy identification by QA teams, managers, or investors. This helps differentiate between the production version and test versions of the app.

Each flavor, like `io.flutterengineering.beta` for the beta version and `io.flutterengineering.prod` for the production version, could be considered different applications. Multiple environments, such as development, staging, and production, can still exist within these flavors, leading to various configurations. For instance, a beta version of the app might have development, staging, and production environments similar to the main app.

It is also important to consider the associated costs and technical challenges. Some services may only readily support one environment. For instance, using Firebase with different flavors might necessitate setting up separate projects, each requiring its configuration files. Conversely, services like Intercom may require a different app ID to create a separate environment in the initialization process. Therefore, verifying whether your project's third-party services and libraries can accommodate multiple environments and, consequently, multiple flavors is crucial.

Flavors remain a unique and important feature in Flutter development. Once different flavors are set up, such as 'dev' and 'prod,' switching between them is straightforward. For example, running the development flavor of a beta version can be as simple as executing `flutter run --flavor dev-beta`. The implementation details are left for you to explore through official documentation. Let's delve into more advanced topics in this chapter.

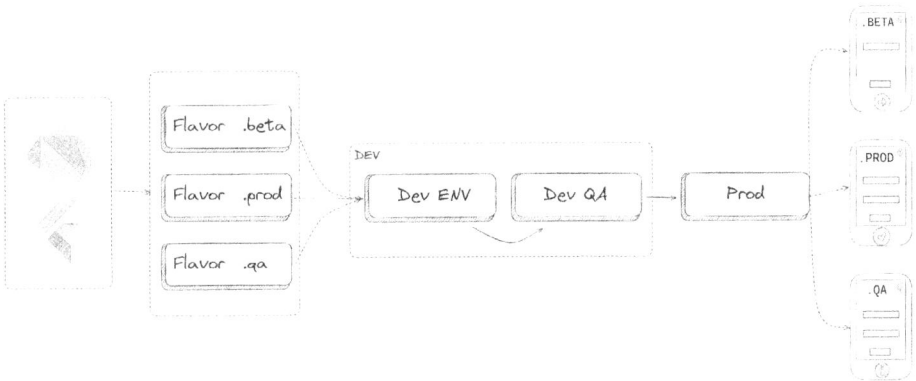

Figure 17.2: Multiple Flavors in Flutter, Different Icons for Different Flavors

17.1.3   Setting Up Environments via Entry Points

An alternative approach involves using different entry points for each environment. Typically, a Flutter app starts with `main.dart`, but you can have `main_dev.dart` and `main_prod.dart`, each configured for its respective environment. These files set up the app environment before running the app widget. You can target these different environments by executing commands like `flutter run -t main_dev.dart` for development and `flutter run -t main_prod.dart` for production. This is a suitable location to specify flavor-specific dependent configuration. For instance, if you want to inject distinct libraries for each flavor or initialize third-party SDKs such as Firebase for each flavor.

The example below shows how to leverage this approach to extend multiple-flavor development.

```
class EnvironmentConfig {
  EnvironmentConfig({
    required this.appFlavor,
    required this.bundleId,
    required this.apiUrl,
  });

  final String appFlavor;
  final String bundleId;
  final String apiUrl;

  factory EnvironmentConfig.betaFlavor() {
    return EnvironmentConfig(
      bundleId: 'io.fle.beta',
      appFlavor: 'Beta',
      apiUrl: 'https://api.beta.io',
    );
  }

  // other flavors and configs
}
```

Imagine if you do not have multiple flavors. For setting up environments in Flutter using entry points, you can define the `EnvironmentConfig` class in a Singleton pattern, which can be used via dependency injection and an `InheritedWidget` approach. Both methods serve to provide environment-specific configurations throughout the app.

In the `InheritedWidget` approach, `EnvironmentConfig` is an InheritedWidget that propagates environment settings down the widget tree.

```
class EnvironmentConfig extends InheritedWidget {
  const EnvironmentConfig({
    super.key,
    required this.env,                    .
    required this.label,
    required super.child,
  });

  final String env;
  final String label;

  static EnvironmentConfig of(BuildContext context) {
    final result =
        context.dependOnInheritedWidgetOfExactType<
```

```
              EnvironmentConfig>();
    assert(
      result != null,
      'No EnvironmentConfig found in context',
    );
    return result!;
  }

  @override
  bool updateShouldNotify(
    EnvironmentConfig oldWidget,
  ) =>
      false;
}
```

Usage in `main_dev.dart` and `main_prod.dart` would be as follows:

```
// main_dev.dart
void main() {
  runApp(
    EnvironmentConfig(
      env: 'dev',
      label: 'Development',
      child: MyApp(),
    ),
  );
}
// main_prod.dart
void main() {
  runApp(
    EnvironmentConfig(
      env: 'prod',
      label: 'Production',
      child: MyApp(),
    ),
  );
}
// app.dart
class MyApp extends StatelessWidget {
  @override
  Widget build(BuildContext context) {
    var config = AppConfig.of(context)!;

    return MaterialApp(
      title: config.appName,
      home: MyHomePage(),
    );
  }
}
```

17.1.4 Utilizing `dart-define`

Utilizing the `-dart-define` parameter in Flutter allows developers to inject environment-specific configurations at compile-time. This approach is particularly useful for setting variables that determine the app's behavior without exposing them in the codebase or requiring separate configuration files. Let's say you have an API URL and a feature flag that differs between development and production environments. You can set these using the `-dart-define` flag when running or building your app.

```
flutter run
--dart-define=API_URL=https://dev.example.com
--dart-define=FEATURE_ENABLED=true
```

You can now access this key and value using `String.fromEnvironment`

```
void main() {
  const apiUrl = String.fromEnvironment(
    'API_URL',
    defaultValue: '<https://prod.example.com>',
  );

  const featureEnabled = String.fromEnvironment(
      'FEATURE_ENABLED',
      defaultValue: 'false',
    ) ==
    'true';

  runApp(
    MyApp(
      apiUrl: apiUrl,
      featureEnabled: featureEnabled,
    ),
  );
}
```

This could be simplified by using separate files to load variables into the environment.

For example, you can also use `.json` or `.env` files to manage environment variables. Create *.env.dev* or *.env.prod* or *dev.json* or *prod.json*.

These files can be loaded using the `-dart-define-from-file` parameter.

```
// dev.json
{
  "API_URL": "<https://dev.example.com>",
  "FEATURE_ENABLED": "true"
}
```

Then load the entire file

```
flutter run --dart-define-from-file=dev.json
```

You can repeat the same things with .env files.

```
API_URL=https://dev.example.com
FEATURE_ENABLED=true
```

and load the entire file

```
flutter run --dart-define-from-file=.env
```

In both cases, accessing the variables in Dart code would be the same as shown earlier.

```
class EnvironmentConfig {
  EnvironmentConfig({
    required this.apiUrl,
    required this.featureEnabled,
  });

  final String apiUrl;
  final bool featureEnabled;

  static EnvironmentConfig fromEnvironment() {
    return EnvironmentConfig(
      apiUrl: const String.fromEnvironment(
        'API_URL',
        defaultValue: 'https://default.example.com',
      ),
      featureEnabled: const String.fromEnvironment(
          'FEATURE_ENABLED',
          defaultValue: 'false',
        ) ==
        'true',
    );
  }
}

void main() {
  final config = EnvironmentConfig.fromEnvironment();
  runApp(
    MyApp(
      config: config,
    ),
  );
}
```

Using -dart-define provides a flexible and secure way to manage environment-specific settings in Flutter, making it a popular choice for developers who want to maintain different configurations for different build environments.

When managing environments and configurations in Flutter, it's essential to prioritize security and maintain best practices for code management.

Firstly, be cautious with sensitive data; avoid storing keys and secrets directly in the app, which can lead to security vulnerabilities. To safeguard sensitive information, such as that found in .env or .json files, add these files to your .gitignore to prevent them from being checked into version control systems like Git. This step is crucial in avoiding accidental exposure of confidential data.

Additionally, for release builds, consider the practice of code obfuscation. While not a substitute for robust security measures, obfuscation adds an extra layer of difficulty for those attempting to reverse-engineer your app, helping to protect sensitive data. You can learn more about these techniques in the Security chapter.

17.2   Seamlessly Integrating CI/CD

In continuous integration (CI) and continuous deployment (CD), it's important to match different app flavors and environments with specific branches or tags for automated deployment. This method facilitates the deployment process, whether distributing apps across various app stores or rolling out web applications. This setup accurately detects different environments and flavors within the CI system. As a result, it enables targeted deployment, ensuring that the appropriate app versions are delivered to the relevant user groups or environments.

Let's envision an effective pipeline scenario:

We start with a CI step to verify successful builds and run automated tests in an isolated environment like Maestro[1]. To address the time-consuming nature of mobile app distribution, we batch changes from multiple PRs. This approach facilitates QA and regression testing, especially for minor updates, reducing deployment frequency and saving time. Once a batch passes QA, we deploy it to the appropriate environment, such as TestFlight for iOS for staging and external testers. This ensures a stable and thoroughly tested product, efficiently integrating different flavors and environments.

When it comes to deploying to the production environment, the process might vary. While some teams prefer an automated deployment as soon as changes are merged into the main branch, others opt for a more cautious approach, choosing manual deployment to production. This decision is typically based on the team's comfort level and the criticality of ensuring absolute stability in the production environment.

---

[1] https://maestro.mobile.dev/

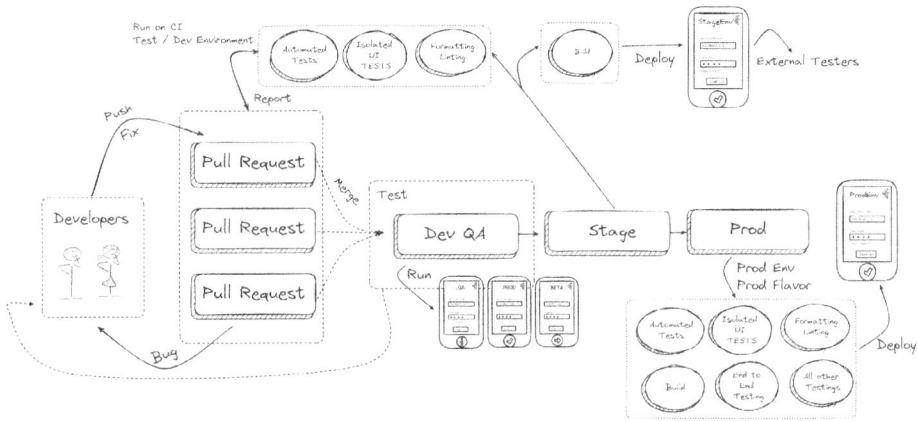

Figure 17.3: An Example of CI/CD with Flutter Environments

Adopting a platform-agnostic mindset is often beneficial regardless of the CI/CD tools your team uses. In this context, consider a tool like Fastlane.

Fastlane[2] is an open-source suite that simplifies and automates your app's release and deployment processes. It is a versatile and easy-to-integrate solution for handling various tasks, from code signing to deploying apps to different stores. It caters to a wide range of deployment needs efficiently and facilitated.

However, using Fastlane also has its disadvantages. It is only sometimes straightforward to use, and you need to manipulate and configure it with other external platforms specifically related to Fastlane. This can make it harder to maintain. Moreover, a team that needs to learn about the programming language, the tool itself, and its extensions can save time using Fastlane. As I always say, whether or not to use it depends on your team, project, and other factors that you need to consider. What's important is to try it out and add it to your skillset as a tool you are familiar with.

Although this book doesn't cover the complexities of Fastlane, it's critical to emphasize the significant advantages of creating a procedure that can be performed both locally and within a CI environment or by any team member to simplify the deployment pipeline. Whether you choose Fastlane or build a bespoke solution in Dart, ensuring the system has platform-agnostic capabilities is essential. This approach guarantees that the deployment process remains consistent and reliable across different platforms, enhancing the efficiency and adaptability of your team's workflow. Such a setup simplifies the deployment process and fosters a more collaborative and unified development environment.

Alternatively, based on the cons, I recommend choosing a tool that best suits

---

[2]https://fastlane.tools/

your requirements, such as Codemagic[3], Github, etc. After choosing the tool, you can use their specific configuration tools to create the build and test pipelines. Doing so will help you reduce the complexity of your setup, follow vendor-specific documentation, and get vendor support.

17.3 Conclusion

In this chapter, we've explored the pivotal role of flavors and environments in Flutter and how their integration with CI/CD processes can significantly enhance app development and deployment. Flavors allow us to efficiently manage different versions of an app from a single codebase, addressing diverse user needs and business objectives. The distinction between environments and flavors is crucial, enabling us to effectively handle various stages of the app development lifecycle, from development to production. This understanding is not just a convenience; it's a strategic approach that aligns with the needs of modern software development.

Incorporating these concepts into automated CI/CD pipelines underscores the importance of facilitating development workflows. Automation tools like Fastlane, or custom scripts in Dart, offer flexibility and robustness, facilitating automated testing, building, and deployment processes. This automation ensures consistency and reliability and allows development teams to concentrate on creative problem-solving and innovation rather than getting bogged down in repetitive tasks. As developers and teams in the Flutter ecosystem, embracing these practices will equip us to navigate the complexities of app development with greater efficiency and confidence.

---

[3]https://www.codemagic.io/

Part IV

Ethical Engineering

CHAPTER 18

Prioritizing Security in Flutter

Reviewer: Tomá Soukal

As the digital era advances, ensuring robust security measures in application development has become more critical. Despite its growing popularity for creating multi-platform applications, Flutter is not immune to cyber threats. The inherent risks, such as data exposure and the potential for reverse engineering, demand a proactive approach to security.

Incorporating these security measures in Flutter app development is not simply about adding layers of defense. It's about integrating security into the core of the development process, ensuring that each stage, from design to deployment, is approached with security in mind.

Flutter's multi-platform nature underscores the importance of addressing specific security needs across all targeted platforms: Android, iOS, macOS, Windows, web, or Linux. While the framework facilitates code reuse, developers must recognize and cater to the unique security considerations inherent to each platform.

By prioritizing security in Flutter development, you not only protect your application but also build trust with your users, ensuring they feel confident in the safety and reliability of your product.

18.1 Foundational Principles of Security

In Chapter 1, you have learned about the Flutter SDLC (Software Development Life Cycle). When it comes to security principles, it is essential to incorporate them into the life cycle from the first stage itself. Having this mindset is crucial. Let us explore what needs to be done in each stage to include security-focused tasks.

1. **Requirements Stage:** Involves risk assessment and understanding security needs based on the application's purpose and potential threats.
2. **Design Stage:** Focuses on threat modeling and design review, ensuring the architecture is robust against potential security vulnerabilities.

3. **Development Stage:** Utilizes static analysis and other security-focused development practices to build security into the app from the ground up.
4. **Testing Stage:** Employs security testing and code review to identify and rectify vulnerabilities before the application goes live.
5. **Deployment Stage:** Includes security assessment and configuration to ensure the application is resilient against real-world threats.

Regarding security, a shift in mindset during the development process is necessary, requiring collaboration from the entire team or organization.

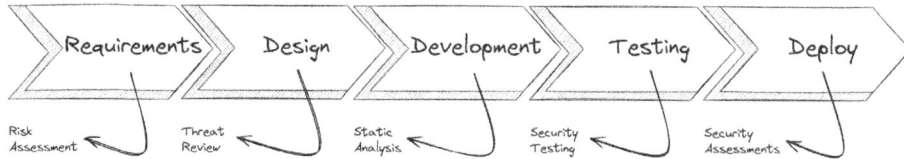

Figure 18.1: Secure Flutter SDLC

Flutter's security philosophy aligns with the broader concepts of security but is adapted to the unique aspects of developing in the Flutter environment.

The philosophy is centered around a comprehensive approach that includes:

1. **Identify:** The first step is recognizing the Flutter app ecosystem's essential assets, threats, and vulnerabilities. This includes understanding what needs protection and the potential risks it faces.
2. **Detect:** This involves employing tools and techniques to uncover vulnerabilities. For Flutter apps, this could mean utilizing static analysis tools to identify security weaknesses in the code.
3. **Protect:** Once risks are identified and assessed, the next step is implementing mitigation measures. This could involve coding practices that prevent data leaks, incorporating encryption, or using secure communication protocols.
4. **Respond:** A response plan is crucial when a security incident occurs. This includes procedures for reporting the incident, assessing the damage, and taking steps to resolve the issue.
5. **Recover:** The final step involves measures to recover from a security incident. This includes plans to restore services, data, and strategies to prevent future incidents.

Developers can create secure and reliable Flutter apps by grounding them in foundational security principles and adapting to unique requirements.

18.2 The CIA Triad: Confidentiality, Integrity, Availability

The CIA Triad is a fundamental concept in cybersecurity. It is the foundation for the strategies and measures to secure information systems and data. The triad comprises three crucial principles: Confidentiality, Integrity, and Availability. Understanding and applying these principles is important for developing secure Flutter applications.

Confidentiality

Confidentiality refers to ensuring that information is accessible only to authorized personnel. In the context of Flutter app development, it is vital to protect user data from unauthorized access and breaches. Various techniques, such as encryption, secure user authentication, and access controls, are employed to maintain confidentiality. The primary objective is to ensure that sensitive data, including personal information and payment details, remains private and secure.

Integrity

Data integrity is the degree to which data is accurate and consistent throughout its lifecycle. It guarantees that information is not changed or manipulated by unauthorized individuals. In Flutter applications, ensuring data integrity may necessitate the implementation of checksums, hash functions, or digital signatures. These precautions aid in detecting and preventing any unauthorized alterations to data, resulting in the app performing as intended and the data remaining reliable and trustworthy.

Availability

The principle of availability is essential for ensuring authorized users have access to information and resources when needed. This is particularly important for the efficient operation of Flutter apps. Maintaining hardware reliability, implementing network redundancy, and preparing for disaster recovery are some measures that can help ensure availability. By prioritizing this security aspect, apps can remain functional and accessible, even in system failures or cyber-attacks.

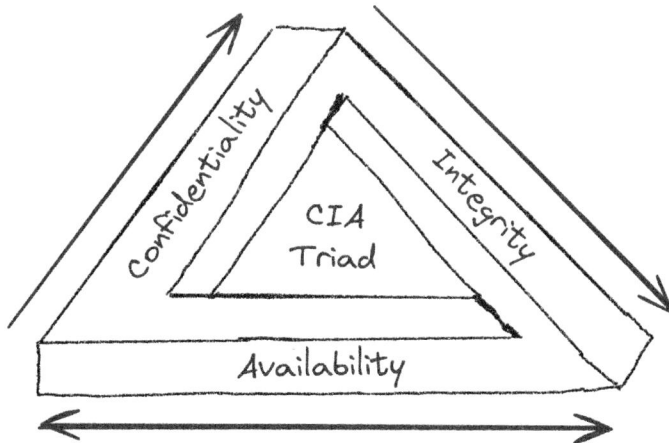

Figure 18.2: The CIA Triad

The CIA Triad is the foundation of application development security. Adherence to these principles for Flutter developers means creating secure apps that meet functional and aesthetic standards.

18.3   Addressing the OWASP Top 10

The OWASP[1] Top 10 is a guide that was first released in 2003 and is updated regularly. It is a crucial tool to raise awareness about software development's most significant security risks. This list is not just a set of opinions but a data-driven compilation of common vulnerabilities, categorized using the Common Weakness Enumeration (CWE) system and linked to real-world vulnerabilities cataloged by the Common Vulnerability Enumeration (CVE) project. A list of the top 10 web applications[2] was published in the past. However, a separate list of the top 10 mobile apps was created with the emergence of mobile apps. This does not mean that the top 10 for web apps is irrelevant for mobile apps, but rather that the top 10 for mobile apps is more specific. Therefore, I will be focusing on the Mobile Top 10 2023 Initial Release[3], which is the latest edition as of writing this book.

18.3.1   M1: Improper Credential Usage

In Flutter app development, improper credential usage typically involves issues like hardcoded credentials within the app's source code or configuration files, insecure transmission and storage of credentials, and weak user authentication mechanisms. These vulnerabilities can lead to unauthorized access to sensitive app functionalities, data breaches, and other security issues.

To prevent improper credential usage in Flutter apps, developers should:

1. **Avoid Hardcoded Credentials:** Never embed credentials directly in the code or configuration files. Hardcoded credentials are easily exploitable.
2. **Secure Credential Transmission:** Always encrypt credentials during transmission. Use secure protocols like HTTPS to ensure that data is encrypted in transit.
3. **Secure Credential Storage:** Avoid storing user credentials on the device. If storage is necessary, use secure solutions like the Flutter Secure Storage plugin, which stores data securely and encrypted.
4. **Implement Strong Authentication:** Use strong, multi-factor authentication protocols. Consider OAuth or similar mechanisms for user authentication.
5. **Regularly Update and Rotate Keys/Tokens:** Regularly update API keys and tokens and implement an effective rotation policy.

---

[1] https://owasp.org/
[2] https://owasp.org/www-project-top-ten/
[3] https://owasp.org/www-project-mobile-top-10

Collaboration between the backend and Flutter teams is required to implement all solutions.

```
class AuthService {
  final storage = FlutterSecureStorage();

  Future<void> authenticateUser(
      String username, String password) async {
    // Example of securely transmitting credentials
    var bytes = utf8.encode(password);
    var digest = sha256.convert(bytes);

    var response = await http.post(
      Uri.https('api.example.com', 'auth/login'),
      headers: <String, String>{
        'Content-Type': 'application/json; charset=UTF-8',
      },
      body: jsonEncode(<String, String>{
        'username': username,
        'password': digest.toString(),
      }),
    );

    if (response.statusCode == 200) {
      // Store the received token securely
      await storage.write( //<---
        key: 'auth_token', //<---
        value: response.body, //<---
      );
    } else {
      // Handle authentication failure
    }
  }
}
```

In this example, we use the `flutter_secure_storage` package to store the authentication token securely and the HTTP package to transmit the credentials securely. This approach avoids hardcoded credentials and ensures secure transmission and storage, adhering to best practices in Flutter app development.

18.3.2   M2: Inadequate Supply Chain Security

Inadequate supply chain security in Flutter development refers to vulnerabilities introduced through third-party libraries, SDKs, or during the app's build process. These can include malicious code injections, compromised certificates, or unvetted dependencies that could lead to data breaches, malware infections, unauthorized access, or system compromise.

To prevent Inadequate Supply Chain Vulnerabilities in Flutter:

1. **Evaluate Third-Party Components:** Carefully review and regularly update any third-party libraries or SDKs in your Flutter applications. Prefer libraries with a strong security track record.
2. **Secure Build Processes:** Protect your app's build and signing process. Ensure that continuous integration and delivery pipelines are secure and access to signing keys is restricted and monitored.
3. **Automated Testing and Code Reviews:** Implement automated security scanning and regular code reviews to detect vulnerabilities early in development.
4. **Awareness and Training:** Educate your development team about the risks associated with supply chain vulnerabilities and the importance of security best practices.
5. **Monitor and Audit Dependencies:** Regularly audit your app's dependencies for known vulnerabilities. Tools like AppSweep, Dependabot and Snyk can automate this process.

One of the most common issues I have seen is related to Git repositories and CI/CD, particularly around environment variables. Secure the CI/CD pipeline. Limit access to the built environment and use secure, encrypted channels for code distribution. Also, implement automated security scanning in your version control system. Tools like GitHub Advanced Security or GitLab's security features can identify vulnerable dependencies in pull requests.

18.3.3 M3: Insecure Authentication/Authorization

Security vulnerabilities in Flutter applications' authentication and authorization systems can lead to unauthorized access, data breaches, and the execution of restricted actions. Attackers can exploit these vulnerabilities in various ways, such as bypassing authentication processes or exploiting flaws in the authorization systems. Common issues include weak password policies, inadequate server-side validation, and insecure API endpoints.

To enhance security, it's essential to:

- **Implement Multi-Factor Authentication (MFA):** Introduce layers of authentication to add depth to security measures.
- **Avoid Local Storage of Sensitive Tokens:** Sensitive tokens or passwords should not be stored locally on the device. If necessary, use encrypted storage methods.
- **Enforce Strong Password Policies:** Discourage simplistic passwords like 4-digit PINs; instead, they require more complex and secure passwords.
- **Use Biometric Authentication Wisely:** Incorporate features like FaceID or TouchID, ensuring they are part of a multi-factor authentication strategy.
- **Server-Side Authorization Checks:** Perform all authorization checks on the server side, never relying solely on client-side validations.

- **Secure API Endpoints:** API endpoints must authenticate requests and verify permissions before processing any action.

Collaborating as a team to address these factors is crucial. It's not solely the responsibility of a Flutter developer, but they can detect and prevent these issues.

18.3.4   M4: Insufficient Input/Output Validation

Insufficient Input/Output Validation is the failure to properly check and sanitize data from external sources like user inputs or network data. This neglect can lead to security vulnerabilities, making the app susceptible to SQL injection, Command Injection, and cross-site scripting (XSS) attacks. It also includes inadequate output validation, leading to data corruption or exposure to malicious code injection.

To prevent Insufficient Input/Output Validation:

- **Implement Rigorous Input Validation:** All user inputs should undergo thorough validation. This includes checking input length, type, and format and ensuring it conforms to expected patterns.
- **Sanitize Output Data:** Outputs, especially those derived from user inputs, must be properly sanitized to prevent XSS attacks. Utilize output encoding techniques.
- **Use Context-Specific Validation:** Adapt validation strategies to the context, like handling file uploads or database queries differently to prevent path traversal or injection attacks.
- **Ensure Data Integrity Checks:** Implement checks to maintain data integrity, preventing unauthorized modifications or data corruption.
- **Adopt Secure Coding Practices:** Utilize secure coding standards, including parameterized queries and prepared statements for database access to prevent SQL injection.

```
import 'dart:convert';
import 'package:flutter/material.dart';

class SafeContentDisplay extends StatelessWidget {
  final String userContent;

  const SafeContentDisplay(
      {super.key, required this.userContent});

  @override
  Widget build(BuildContext context) {
    // Encoding user content to prevent XSS
    const htmlEscape = HtmlEscape(HtmlEscapeMode.attribute);
    final safeContent = htmlEscape.convert(userContent);

    return Text(safeContent);
```

```
    }
}
```

The `HtmlEscape` class in Dart is designed to convert characters to their respective HTML entities, primarily used for sanitizing text before inserting it into an HTML document. Its primary purpose is to prevent malicious code injection, such as Cross-Site Scripting (XSS) attacks, by converting characters that have special meanings in HTML (like &, <, >, ", ') into their corresponding HTML entities (like &, <, >, ", ').

```
// Here is an example using element mode
const htmlEscape = HtmlEscape(HtmlEscapeMode.element);
String unescaped = '<script>alert("XSS")</script>';
String escaped = htmlEscape.convert(unescaped);
print(escaped);
// &lt;script&gt;alert(&quot;XSS&quot;)&lt;/script&gt;
```

18.3.5   M5: Insecure Communication

Insecure communication in Flutter applications refers to the lack of data protection between the app, remote servers, or other devices during transit. This usually happens when data is transmitted in plaintext or when encryption is poorly implemented, making it susceptible to interception and modification by unauthorized parties. Common risks associated with insecure communication include exposure to man-in-the-middle attacks, data breaches, and identity theft.

To mitigate risks of insecure communication, it's essential to:

- **Enforce SSL/TLS:** Ensure all data transmitted by the app is over SSL/TLS channels. This encrypts the data during transit, protecting it from eavesdroppers.
- **Validate Certificates Properly:** Implement proper SSL certificate validation. Do not accept invalid or self-signed certificates.
- **Use Certificate Pinning:** To enhance security, consider using SSL certificate pinning, which ensures the app communicates only with the designated server.
- **Avoid Transmitting Sensitive Data over Insecure Channels:** Do not send sensitive information like passwords, personal data, or encryption keys over unsecured channels like SMS or MMS.
- **Implement Strong Cipher Suites:** Use strong, industry-standard cipher suites with appropriate key lengths to protect the data during transit.

Most tasks require collaboration between the backend and Flutter developers, with most of the implementation in the backend. However, there are certain things you can do as a developer to improve security. For instance, you can force your HTTP class always to use `https`.

```dart
import 'package:http/http.dart' as http;

Future<http.Response> fetchData(String url) async {
  // Ensure the URL uses HTTPS
  final uri = Uri.parse(url).replace(scheme: 'https');
  return await http.get(uri);
}
```

Another good practice is to ensure that both your development environment and production environment use secure mechanisms, not just production. This is particularly important when cultivating a security-minded culture within development teams and when your development environment closely mirrors the production environment. So, encourage your team to use secure TLS connections using a valid SSL certificate.

18.3.6 M6: Inadequate Privacy Controls

Inadequate privacy controls in Flutter applications refer to the need for more protection of **Personally Identifiable Information** (PII) such as names, addresses, and sensitive data like health or financial information. This data is valuable and vulnerable to misuse, leading to fraud, blackmail, or identity theft. Risks arise from data being leaked, manipulated, or blocked, violating confidentiality, integrity, or availability.

To effectively prevent inadequate privacy controls:

- **Minimize PII Collection:** Only collect necessary PII. Assess if all collected data is essential and if some can be replaced with less sensitive information.
- **Data Anonymization:** Where possible, anonymize or blur PII. Techniques like hashing or bucketing reduce risks associated with data breaches.
- **Secure Data Storage and Transmission:** Store and transmit PII securely. Use encryption and secure communication protocols like HTTPS.
- **Implement Strong Authentication and Authorization:** Ensure that strong authentication and authorization checks guard access to PII.
- **Regular Data Audits and Clean-up:** Regularly audit stored PII and delete unnecessary data. Implement data retention policies.
- **User Consent and Transparency:** Where optional PII usage enhances service, obtain explicit user consent, and inform users about the associated risks.
- **Secure Logging and Error Handling:** Avoid logging sensitive data. Ensure that error messages and logs are sanitized to prevent accidental data leaks.
- **Backup Data Security:** Use packages or techniques that store that data securely.

In Flutter, `debugPrint` is a safer alternative to `print` for logging in Flutter. It helps prevent excessive output, which can be risky if logs contain sensitive information. `debugPrint` also ensures that logs are only visible during development and not in release builds. Alternatively, you can use packages that help manage logs.

Carefully consider the app permissions your Flutter app requires. Only request permissions that are essential for the app's functionality. Over-requesting permissions can lead to unnecessary access to sensitive data. Packages such as `permission_handler` can help to manage the app's permission across platforms.

Flutter provides widgets like `Offstage` and `Visibility` that can help manage the display of sensitive information on the screen, preventing unnecessary data exposure.

18.3.7 M7: Insufficient Binary Protections

Insufficient binary protection in Flutter applications refers to the absence of security measures to protect app binaries against reverse engineering and tampering. Attackers may target these binaries to extract sensitive information such as API keys, discover vulnerabilities, or manipulate the app for malicious purposes. Popular apps are particularly vulnerable to such attacks since attackers can distribute modified versions of the app containing malicious code to exploit users.

To prevent Insufficient Binary Protection in Flutter:

- **Obfuscation:** Implement code obfuscation to make reverse engineering more challenging. Compiling sensitive parts of apps natively or using specialized code interpreters and virtual machines makes reverse engineering harder. You can utilize tools like O-MVLL[4], BlackObfuscator[5], DeClang[6], or javascript-obfuscator[7].
- **Strong Encryption for Sensitive Data:** Avoid hardcoding sensitive data like keys or credentials. If necessary, use strong encryption to protect such data within the binary. You can see more about it in the upcoming chapters.
- **Integrity Checks:** Implement runtime checks to verify the app's integrity. This can help detect if the app has been tampered with. Free and paid packages and services are available for integrity checks in Flutter.
- **Minimize Sensitive Code in Binaries:** Avoid directly placing critical business logic or sensitive algorithms in the app. Instead, consider handling such operations server-side.
- **Regular Security Audits:** Conduct regular security audits of your binaries to check for vulnerabilities and ensure your protection measures are up-to-date.

Flutter allows the obfuscation of Dart code, which is particularly important because Dart compiles easily readable and modifiable bytecode.

---

[4]https://obfuscator.re/omvll/introduction/
[5]https://github.com/CodingGay/BlackObfuscator
[6]https://github.com/DeNA/DeClang
[7]https://www.obfuscator.io/

Flutter supports several build targets, including Android Archive (AAR), Android Package (APK), Android App Bundle (appbundle), iOS, iOS Framework (ios-framework), iOS Application Archive (IPA), Linux, macOS, macOS Framework, and Windows. However, it's important to note that web apps do not support obfuscation. Instead, web apps can be minified, which achieves a similar outcome. When building the release version of your Flutter app, you can enable obfuscation using the `--obfuscate` flag with `flutter build` command. Beware, this process renames only classes and members to more obscure names.

18.3.8   M8: Security Misconfiguration

Security misconfiguration in Flutter apps refers to incorrect or incomplete settings, permissions, and controls that leave the app vulnerable to attacks. This can include using insecure default settings, improper access controls, weak encryption, or failure to use secure communication protocols. Attackers can exploit these weaknesses to gain unauthorized access to sensitive data or perform malicious actions.

To prevent Security Misconfiguration in Flutter:

- **Review and Secure Default Configurations:** Regularly review your app's configurations, particularly those set by default, to ensure they are secure.
- **Use Strong Encryption and Hashing:** Implement strong, up-to-date encryption and hashing algorithms for data protection.
- **Proper Access Controls:** Implement and regularly update access control mechanisms to ensure that only authorized users can access sensitive functionalities or data.
- **Disable Debugging Features in Release Builds:** Ensure that debugging tools and features are disabled in production versions of your app.
- **Keep Dependencies Updated:** Regularly update all dependencies, libraries, and frameworks used in your Flutter app to their latest, most secure versions.
- **Restrict File Permissions:** Avoid overly permissive file storage settings. Ensure that files are stored with appropriate permissions to prevent unauthorized access.

One common security issue is storing sensitive data or unencrypted configuration in shared preferences, which attackers can access with root permissions.

18.3.9   M9: Insecure Data Storage

Insecure data storage in Flutter applications refers to the inadequate protection of sensitive data stored within the app. This sensitive data can include passwords, user information, and other personal data. If this vulnerability is exploited, it can threaten the app's and its users' security. Using pre-built tools, various threat agents can exploit this vulnerability, including skilled adversaries, malicious insiders, cyber criminals, and even script kiddies. Therefore, ensuring that sensitive data is adequately protected within the app is crucial.

To mitigate risks associated with insecure data storage:

1. **Use Secure Storage Solutions:** Utilize Flutter's secure storage mechanisms, like `flutter_secure_storage`, `Isar`, `hive`, which store data in a secure, encrypted manner.
2. **Implement Strong Encryption:** Using strong, up-to-date encryption methods when storing sensitive data. Avoid storing sensitive data in plain text.
3. **Avoid Storing Sensitive Data on Shared Preferences:** Refrain from using shared preferences for storing sensitive data, as they are not designed for secure storage.
4. **Use Platform-specific Security Features:** Leverage platform-specific security features for data storage. For instance, on Android, use Keystore, and on iOS, use Keychain.

Luckily, in Flutter, we have several options to avoid the issue. We need to be aware of the concern and choose a package that can help with strong encryption and proper permissions in mind.

18.3.10   M10: Insufficient Cryptography

Insufficient cryptography in Flutter applications refers to situations where the cryptographic methods employed to safeguard sensitive data are inadequate or not correctly implemented. This can create weaknesses that attackers can exploit to decrypt sensitive information, tamper with cryptographic processes, or gain unauthorized access. Common problems include weak encryption algorithms, inadequate key management, and ineffective cryptographic protocol implementation.

I have dedicated a chapter (Chapter 18) to cryptography so that software and Flutter engineers can understand when to use it.

To prevent Insufficient Cryptography in Flutter:

1. **Use Strong Encryption Algorithms:** Implement strong and widely accepted encryption algorithms, such as AES (Advanced Encryption Standard) for symmetric encryption and RSA or ECC (Elliptic Curve Cryptography) for asymmetric encryption.
2. **Ensure Proper Key Management:** Securely generate, store, and manage cryptographic keys. Avoid hardcoding keys within the app's source code. Use secure storage like Android's Keystore or iOS's Keychain for key management.
3. **Use Secure Random Number Generators:** For generating keys or other cryptographic operations, use secure random number generators provided by the platform.

Prioritizing Security in Flutter

4. **Regularly Update Cryptographic Libraries:** Keep all cryptographic libraries updated to their latest versions to incorporate security patches and improvements.

5. **Avoid Deprecated Algorithms and Key Sizes:** Do not use outdated or weak cryptographic algorithms. Ensure that key sizes are sufficiently large to prevent brute-force attacks.

```dart
import 'package:encrypt/encrypt.dart';

class EncryptionService {
  // Replace with a secure key either
  // using secure-random or receive from the backend
  final key = Key.fromUtf8('16ByteSecretKey123');
  final iv = IV.fromLength(16);

  String encrypt(String plainText) {
    final encrypter = Encrypter(AES(key));
    return encrypter.encrypt(plainText, iv: iv).base64;
  }

  String decrypt(String encryptedText) {
    final encrypter = Encrypter(AES(key));
    return encrypter.decrypt64(encryptedText, iv: iv);
  }
}
```

We will explore cryptography in more detail in the next chapter.

18.4   Static and Dynamic Analysis

In software security, static and dynamic analyses are two fundamental approaches used to uncover vulnerabilities and enhance the security of applications. Understanding their differences and complementary nature is critical for a comprehensive security strategy.

1. **Static Analysis:** Static analysis, or "static code analysis", refers to examining an application's source code without executing it. Tools used for static analysis scan the codebase for potential security vulnerabilities, coding standards violations, and other quality issues. It analyzes the code and helps identify vulnerabilities early in the development lifecycle. Additionally, it can help enforce coding standards and best practices and can be integrated into IDEs and continuous integration pipelines for automated scanning. However, it may produce false positives and cannot detect runtime vulnerabilities or environment-specific issues. In Flutter, using custom lints or introducing rules that can be used during development is common.

2. **Dynamic Analysis:** Dynamic analysis is a process of evaluating and testing the application in a running state. It involves analyzing the software's behavior while it executes. Tools used for dynamic analysis interact with the application, monitor its operations, and simulate attacks to identify vulnerabilities that appear during runtime. Dynamic analysis can detect vulnerabilities that are only visible during the application's execution. It can also unveil runtime issues such as memory leaks, performance problems, and concurrency issues. A fully functional environment is often required for effective testing. Dynamic analysis is typically conducted later in the development lifecycle.

Static and dynamic analyses are not mutually exclusive but rather complementary. While static analysis can pinpoint issues during the coding phase, dynamic analysis can catch vulnerabilities that appear only when the application runs in a specific environment or state.

Mobile Security Framework (MobSF)[8] stands as an exemplary specimen, offering a static and dynamic analysis platform for Android and iOS applications. It caters to a range of use cases, including mobile application security, penetration testing, malware analysis, and privacy evaluation.

18.5   Flutter-Specific Security Best Practices

Most techniques and recommendations discussed in the previous section apply to Flutter. However, there are certain suggestions that Flutter developers should adhere to.

1. **Keep your Flutter SDK up to date:** Flutter frequently releases minor patches, some of which may include security fixes. It's nice to be always up to date.
2. **Application Dependencies:** It is recommended to regularly update application dependencies instead of pinning them to a specific version.
3. **Audit App:** It is important to regularly invite experts, especially those who know multiple platforms, to audit your application. This will help ensure that your application is secure and functioning properly.
4. **Leverage Active Security Monitoring Tools:** There are several packages and services that you can use in your app to address proactive defense and real-time analysis. One of the common security technologies is Runtime Application Self-Protection (RASP).
5. **Penetration Testing:** Thorough test of security involves a series of practices and tests designed to uncover security flaws and ensure the app's data and interactions are secure. Penetration Testing simulates cyberattacks to

---

[8]https://pub.dev/packages/freerasp

uncover weaknesses. It's important to encompass inspection of the **Software Bill of Materials** (SBOM) to identify and assess vulnerabilities associated with specific software components, like third-party libraries. A similar process called Security Auditing involves a comprehensive review of security policies and configurations, often done for compliance with regulations. One of the most popular web app scanner tools is Zed Attack Proxy (ZAP)[9], which can also be configured for Android and iOS and is suitable for Flutter.

RASP

Runtime Application Self-Protection (RASP) is an advanced security solution embedded within an application to detect and counter threats in real time. Unlike traditional security measures, RASP operates inside the app, offering immediate and context-aware protection against attacks. It actively monitors the app's behavior, identifies malicious activities, and can automatically block threats or alert administrators. This internal vantage point allows RASP to guard against known and unknown vulnerabilities effectively, including zero-day exploits, making it a crucial layer of defense for modern applications. Its integration into Flutter apps provides robust, proactive security, enhancing its capability to self-defend and maintain compliance with data protection standards.

The **freeRASP**[10] package is useful for implementing RASP in your Flutter application. It provides a free SDK for developers on Flutter targeting Android and iOS mobile platforms. The SDK is a community-driven initiative that aims to enhance app security and prevent various security threats, such as reverse engineering, app tampering, re-publishing, cloning, and operation on compromised OS environments. It also works towards combating malware and cybercrime. Some of the key features of freeRASP include root/jailbreak attempt detection (such as unc0ver and check1rain), detection of hooking frameworks (such as Frida and Shadow), and prevention of untrusted installation methods.

18.6   Conclusion

Security is always changing and developing, and new risks arise frequently. Therefore, developers need to remain alert and take proactive measures. By using guidelines such as OWASP or static and dynamic analysis, tools such as RASP, and following specific security testing methods, developers can significantly improve the security and robustness of their applications.

Adopting best practices like conducting regular code audits, scanning dependencies, and implementing rigorous testing regimes can ensure that applications are functionally robust and secure from various types of cyber threats. This approach

---

[9]https://www.zaproxy.org/
[10]https://pub.dev/packages/freerasp

is crucial for protecting sensitive user data, retaining user trust, and adhering to regulatory standards. Ultimately, it is the responsibility of developers and organizations to create secure applications. To do so, they must remain adaptable to changing security threats and embrace a security-first mindset throughout their development processes.

Talsec

Thank you to Talsec for sponsoring this chapter and helping improve its quality.

With Talsec, keep your application, business and customers secure with complete in-app and API protection SDK. Using multi-layered approach Talsec SDK combats reverse engineering, app cloning/republishing, rooting, API abuse, Frida hooking, MitM, and much more. Available for iOS, Android and Flutter apps.

www.talsec.app

CHAPTER 19

Cryptography in Flutter

Reviewer: Tomá Soukal

As we explore the world of software security, we come across a fundamental aspect: Cryptography. In the previous chapter, we learned about the vulnerabilities listed in the OWASP Top 10, many of which result from the incorrect use of cryptography. This highlights the critical importance of mastering cryptographic techniques. Cryptography involves creating and solving codes and is the primary means of protecting digital information.

This chapter delves into the details of various encryption methods and hashing algorithms. Flutter developers will find this chapter particularly valuable as it demonstrates the practical application of cryptographic principles in the Flutter framework.

Understanding these techniques is not only an academic exercise but a necessary step toward ensuring the security and integrity of software applications. The right cryptographic approach can make all the difference in protecting user data and securing communication channels.

19.1 Distinguishing Encryptions

In the complex field of cybersecurity, encryption plays a critical role in ensuring data privacy and security. Encryption involves converting plain and readable data, known as **plaintext**, into an unintelligible format called **ciphertext**. This process ensures that only individuals with the correct cryptographic key can access the information in its original form. Thus, understanding encryption is like having a master key that unlocks the secret code and protects confidential information from unauthorized access.

How Encryption Works

Imagine encryption as a sophisticated lockbox of data. When data is encrypted, it undergoes a mathematical transformation using an algorithm and a key. This process scrambles the data, making it unreadable to anyone who needs the key.

For instance, a simple message like "Hello" can be transformed into something unrecognizable, such as "Jgnnq," using a basic algorithm. This transformation is reversible only when the correct key is applied. Encryption can be applied to data at rest (stored data) and in transit (data being transmitted).

The Role of Keys in Cryptography

A cryptographic key is a string of characters integral to the encryption and decryption. It's like a physical key that locks (encrypts) and unlocks (decrypts) data. The complexity and length of this key are necessary to ensure the security of the encrypted data.

19.1.1 Symmetric and Asymmetric

Encryption is broadly categorized into Symmetric and Asymmetric (or Public Key).

Symmetric Encryption

Symmetric Encryption, often called secret key encryption, involves a single key for encrypting and decrypting data. This key must be shared among the parties involved, making the key exchange process as crucial as encryption.

Characteristics:

- **Speed**: Symmetric encryption algorithms are generally faster, making them ideal for encrypting large volumes of data.
- **Key Management**: A major challenge is the secure distribution and management of the key, as it must remain secret.
- **Common Algorithms**: AES (Advanced Encryption Standard) and 3DES (Triple Data Encryption Standard).

Flutter developers can use libraries like `encrypt` to implement symmetric encryption. For example, using AES in a Flutter app involves generating a key, encrypting data, and then using the same key for decryption.

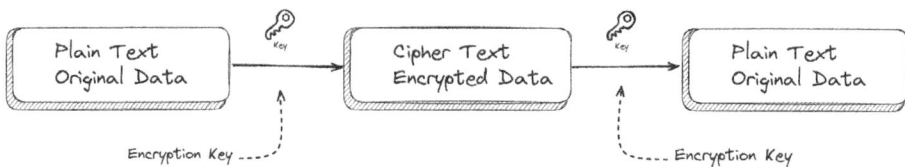

Figure 19.1: Symmetric Encryption

This is even more important when developing an app that requires users to save and utilize data locally or when implementing an offline-first approach where data is always stored locally.

Consider a note-taking or chat app where users can create and store personal or sensitive notes. We implement symmetric encryption to ensure the privacy and security of these notes. Each note is encrypted before it is saved locally or on a cloud server and decrypted when the user accesses it. The key for encryption/decryption is derived from a password entered by the user.

```
// --- all imports ---
class SecureDataService {
  final flutterSecureStorage = const FlutterSecureStorage();

  // 1. Derive a key from a password
  Future<encrypt.Key> deriveKey(
    String password,
    List<int> salt,
  ) async {
    // Argon2id is a password-hashing algorithm
    // that is resistant to side-channel attacks
    final algorithm = Argon2id(
      parallelism: 4,
      memory: 10000, // 10 MB
      iterations: 3,
      hashLength: 32,
    );

    // Derive a key from the password
    final secretKey = await algorithm.deriveKey(
      secretKey: SecretKey(utf8.encode(password)),
      // use salt as random bytes to make the key unique
      nonce: salt,
    );

    final secretKeyBytes = await secretKey.extractBytes();
    // get the key as a list of bytes
    return encrypt.Key(
      Uint8List.fromList(secretKeyBytes),
    );
  }

  // 2. Store the key in a secure storage for later use
  Future<void> storeSecretKey(
      encrypt.Key key, String keyName) async {
    await flutterSecureStorage.write(
      key: keyName,
      value: base64Encode(key.bytes),
    );
  }

  // 3. Retrieve the key from the secure storage when needed
  Future<encrypt.Key?> getSecretKey(String keyName) async {
    final keyString =
        await flutterSecureStorage.read(key: keyName);
    if (keyString == null) return null;
```

```dart
    return encrypt.Key(
      base64Decode(keyString),
    );
  }

  // 4. Generate a random salt
  List<int> generateSalt() {
    // always generate strong random
    return encrypt.SecureRandom(16).bytes;
  }

  //5. Encrypt and decrypt data
  // using the key you derived
  Future<String> encryptData(
      String data, encrypt.Key key) async {
    // IV Represents an Initialization Vector.
    final iv = encrypt.IV.fromLength(16);
    // Encrypter wraps an encrypt.
    // Algorithm in a Unique Container.
    // AES is a symmetric encryption algorithm
    // that uses the same key for
    // both encryption and decryption
    final encrypter = encrypt.Encrypter(
      encrypt.AES(key),
    );

    // Encrypt data using AES with the given key and IV
    final encrypted = encrypter.encrypt(data, iv: iv);
    return encrypted.base64;
  }

  // 6. Decrypt data using the key you derived
  Future<String> decryptData(
      String encryptedData, encrypt.Key key) async {
    final iv = encrypt.IV.fromLength(16);
    // Encrypter wraps an encrypt.
    // Algorithm in a unique Container.
    final encrypter = encrypt.Encrypter(
      // Same algorithm and key used for encryption
      encrypt.AES(key),
    );

    // Decrypt data using AES with the given key and IV
    return encrypter.decrypt64(encryptedData, iv: iv);
  }
}

void main() async {
```

```
  // --------------------------------------------------
  final secureDataService = SecureDataService();
  // Imagine Password is provided by the user
  const password = 'userPassword';
  // Implement this to generate a random salt
  final salt = secureDataService.generateSalt();

  // Derive and store the key
  final key =
      await secureDataService.deriveKey(password, salt);
  await secureDataService.storeSecretKey(
    key,
    'myEncryptionKey',
  );
  // --------------------------------------------------


  // --------------------------------------------------
  // Encrypt data
  final encryptedData = await secureDataService.encryptData(
    'Sensitive data',
    key,
  );

  // Decrypt data
  final decryptedData = await secureDataService.decryptData(
    encryptedData,
    key,
  );

  print('Encrypted Data: $encryptedData');
  print('Decrypted Data: $decryptedData');
  // --------------------------------------------------
}
```

The example above utilizes three packages - cryptography, encrypt, and flutter_secure_storage - to demonstrate how they work. This example will create a unique key for the encryption algorithm based on the user password, which is also hashed based on a secure algorithm and random salt to make it even more unique. Then, it provides encryption and decryption functions. This service can now be used anywhere the application needs to encrypt data. Even an in-memory database can store it safely.

Asymmetric Encryption

Asymmetric Encryption, or public-key cryptography, utilizes two keys – a public key for encryption and a private key for decryption. The public key is openly shared, while the private key is kept secret, thus solving the key distribution problem of symmetric encryption.

Characteristics:

- **Security**: Offers a higher level of security, particularly for key exchange over insecure channels.
- **Performance**: Typically slower than symmetric encryption due to its computational complexity.
- **Common Algorithms**: RSA (Rivest–Shamir–Adleman) and ECC (Elliptic Curve Cryptography).

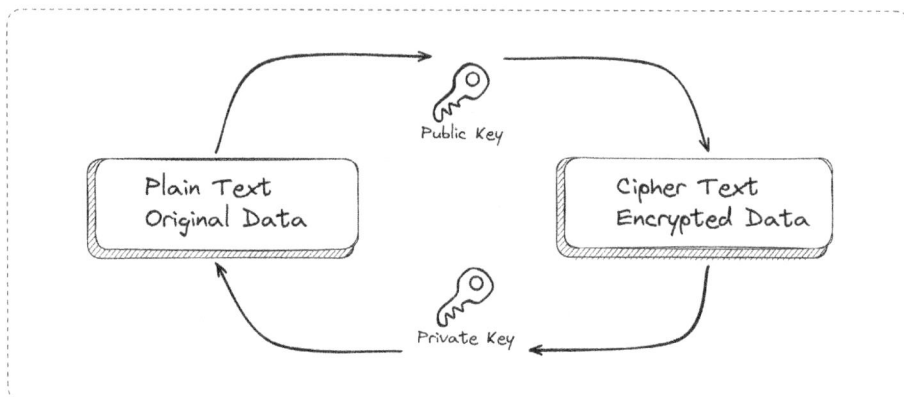

Figure 19.2: Asymmetric Encryption

Implementing RSA or ECC in Flutter involves using libraries that support asymmetric encryption. While generating public and private keys is not a complex process on different operation systems, you can still use packages to help you generate these keys and implement a proper encryption algorithm.

Choosing Between Symmetric and Asymmetric

The choice between symmetric and asymmetric encryption in a Flutter app depends on several factors:

- **Data Volume**: Symmetric encryption is more suitable for larger volumes of data due to its speed.
- **Security Needs**: Asymmetric encryption is preferred when secure key exchange is critical, especially over an insecure channel.
- **Use Case**: For instance, symmetric encryption is often used for encrypting stored data, while asymmetric encryption is used for secure communications and digital signatures.

19.1.2   Choosing Between Cryptographic Algorithms

When choosing the right cryptographic algorithm, several factors need to be considered:

- **Data Sensitivity**: The level of security required depends on the sensitivity of the data. High-value data may warrant stronger encryption like AES-256 or RSA.

- **Performance Requirements**: For applications where speed and resource efficiency are crucial, algorithms like Salsa20 or Blowfish might be more appropriate.
- **Data Size and Type**: Stream ciphers are typically better for real-time, continuous data streams, while block ciphers are suited for discrete data blocks.
- **Infrastructure Compatibility**: The algorithm should be compatible with existing systems and hardware. For instance, legacy systems might require 3DES for compatibility reasons.
- **Regulatory Compliance**: Certain industries have specific encryption standards that must be met, such as AES for government-related data.
- **Future-Proofing**: With the advancement of quantum computing, considering quantum-resistant algorithms might be prudent for long-term security planning.

Selecting a cryptographic algorithm is a balancing act between security needs, system performance, and operational constraints. It's essential to assess the specific requirements of the application environment and the data to be protected to make an informed decision. In this rapidly evolving field, staying updated with cryptographic trends and threats is crucial for maintaining effective data security.

19.1.3   Message Authentication Codes (MACs)

MACs are cryptographic protocols combining symmetric encryption or hash functions with a secret key. They ensure data integrity and authenticity by generating a code dependent on the message content and the secret key.

The same secret key must be shared among the involved entities to verify a MAC. Each entity with access to the key can generate and validate the MAC, ensuring that the message has not been altered and is authentic.

MACs are widely used in network communication and data storage to validate the integrity and authenticity of a message or file.

19.1.4   Consult With Experts

The most important point I emphasize here is that before choosing any algorithm, seek advice from an expert in the domain and have them review your decision. Although basic knowledge is important, expert review is key.

19.2   The Fundamentals of Hashing

Hashing is converting an input of any length into a fixed-size string of characters, which typically represents the data in a seemingly random sequence. Unlike encryption, hashing is a one-way process. This means that once data has been turned into a hash, it cannot be returned to the original data.

19.2.1 Characteristics of Hashing

- **Fixed Length**: No matter the input data size, the hash output is always fixed.
- **Unique**: Ideally, each unique input data should produce a unique hash. Even a small change in the input should result in a significantly different hash.
- **Irreversible**: Hashes cannot be reversed to reveal the original data, a fundamental difference from encryption.

19.2.2 Common Uses of Hashing

1. **Password Storage**: Hashing is commonly used for securely storing passwords. Instead of saving the actual passwords, systems store their hash values. When a user logs in, the system hashes the entered password and compares it with the stored hash.
2. **Data Integrity**: Hashing ensures the integrity of data. By comparing the hash of data sent and the hash of received data, one can verify if the data has been altered or tampered with during transmission.
3. **Digital Signatures**: Hashing is used in creating digital signatures, where a document hash is encrypted with a private key, allowing recipients to verify the document's integrity.

19.2.3 Hashing Algorithms

Hashing algorithms are necessary for various aspects of data security, including integrity verification, authentication, and digital signatures. Let's explore some of the widely used hashing algorithms, namely the SHA family, MD5, and the HMAC family, along with their use cases.

SHA Family (Secure Hash Algorithm): The SHA family includes several versions, each offering different hash lengths and security levels.

- **SHA-1:** Initially used for SSL certificates, software verification, and digital signatures. Due to vulnerabilities, it's mostly used for non-security purposes like Git repositories for integrity checks. The Hash Length is 160 bits.
- **SHA-256**: Ideal for securing sensitive blockchain technologies and digital signature data. Hash Length is 256 bits, offering a higher security level than SHA-1.
- **SHA-512**: Used in situations requiring enhanced security measures, like high-value cryptographic transactions. The hash Length is 512 bits, providing even stronger security.

MD5 (Message-Digest Algorithm 5): An older algorithm that produces a 128-bit hash value. Once popular for file integrity verification, it is now considered insecure for cryptographic purposes. It's still used for checksums in non-critical applications due to its speed.

Cryptography in Flutter

HMAC Family (Keyed-Hash Message Authentication Code): See next section.

19.2.4 Digest

In the context of cryptography, a "digest" is the output of a hash function. Essentially, it is the fixed-size string of characters that the hash function generates from an input. This digest represents the "fingerprint" or "summary" of the input data, and even a small change in the input will produce a significantly different digest.

19.2.5 HMACs (Hash-Based Message Authentication Codes)

HMACs are a specific MAC type that utilizes a hash function for message authentication.

They combine a secret key with the hash of a message, using the key in two phases of the hashing process. This dual usage of the key strengthens the security of the HMAC.

For example, HMAC-SHA256, a common HMAC variant, uses the SHA-256 hash function. It's frequently used in secure data transmission protocols and API authentication processes.

HMACs provide additional security over standard hashing due to the inclusion of a secret key. They ensure both the integrity and the authenticity of the message.

19.2.6 Key Derivation Functions (KDFs)

KDFs derive one or more secret keys from a secret value, such as a password or passphrase.

Unlike simple hash functions, KDFs are specifically designed to generate secret keys that are both secure and suitably random.

KDFs are used when keys need to be transformed or extended in length. They are crucial in multiple parties' protocols, like secure key exchange or password-based encryption.

KDFs must ensure that the derived keys appear random and are computationally infeasible to reverse-engineer. This randomness is vital in securing systems against various cryptographic attacks.

19.2.7 Implementing Hashing Algorithms in Flutter or Dart

Here's an example of how you might implement these hashing algorithms in Flutter using the `crypto` package:

```dart
import 'dart:convert';
import 'package:crypto/crypto.dart';

void main() {
  // Example String
  String text = 'Hello, world!';

  // SHA-256 Hash
  var bytes1 = utf8.encode(text); // data being hashed
  var sha256Result = sha256.convert(bytes1);
  print('SHA-256 hash: $sha256Result');

  // MD5 Hash
  var md5Result = md5.convert(bytes1);
  print('MD5 hash: $md5Result');

  // HMAC SHA-256
  var key =
      utf8.encode('secret key'); // secret key for HMAC
  var hmacSha256 = Hmac(sha256, key); // HMAC SHA256
  var hmacResult = hmacSha256.convert(bytes1);
  print(
    'HMAC SHA-256: $hmacResult',
  );
}
```

In this example, the `crypto` package generates SHA-256 and MD5 hashes of a given string and an HMAC SHA-256 hash. Note that while this code demonstrates basic usage, you should carefully manage and protect any secret keys used for HMAC in a real-world application.

Choosing the right hashing algorithm depends on the specific security, performance, and application requirements. While SHA-256 and SHA-512 from the SHA family are recommended for most security-sensitive applications, MD5 can still be used for basic checksums where high security is not a concern. HMAC, with its key-dependent security, is ideal for verifying data integrity and authenticity in applications like API authentication.

19.3 Ensuring Data Integrity with Digital Signatures

Let me start this section with a scenario I used to work on that could make sense to many Flutter developers. Imagine you are working on a smart application that resides on the user's mobile device and needs to communicate securely with the home hub. The user also has a hub, a device located in the user's home that controls various smart home functionalities. The hub holds the private key.

Imagine you have to communicate with the hub through an app, via the internet, or even a private local network. Using digital signatures that sign all messages between the app and hub can significantly improve security and verify data integrity.

Digital signatures are a cryptographic technique used to verify the authenticity and integrity of digital data. Much like a handwritten signature or a stamped seal, a digital signature offers a means of proving the origin, identity, and status of an electronic document, transaction, or message and confirming that it has not been tampered with.

19.3.1 How Do Digital Signatures Work?

Essentially, it has two steps:

1. **Creation**:
   - The sender of a message generates a hash of the data.
   - This hash is then encrypted with the sender's private key, creating the digital signature.
   - The original data and the digital signature are then sent to the recipient.

2. **Verification**:
   - The recipient uses the sender's public key to decrypt the digital signature, obtaining the hash value.
   - Simultaneously, the recipient generates a new hash of the received data.
   - If the two hashes match, it confirms the data integrity and authenticity.

So, the key components of digital signatures are

- **Private Key**: Used by the sender to create the digital signature. It must be kept secure.
- **Public Key**: Used by the recipient to verify the digital signature.
- **Hashing Algorithm**: Creates a unique hash of the data. Common algorithms include SHA-256.
- **Encryption Algorithm**: RSA is commonly used for encrypting the hash to create the digital signature.

19.3.2 Weak Cryptographic Algorithms

Inspect the app's source code to identify instances of weak cryptographic algorithms, such as DES, 3DES[1], RC2, RC4, BLOWFISH[2], MD4, MD5, and SHA1.

---

[1] https://www.enisa.europa.eu/publications/algorithms-key-size-and-parameters-report-2014

[2] https://www.enisa.europa.eu/publications/algorithms-key-size-and-parameters-report-2014

Keep an eye on trusted sources to ensure you are using something fixed. For example, OWASP has a mobile app cryptography[3] guide that can be checked regularly. In this source, you can also find recommended algorithms for different purposes.

19.4 Conclusion

Cryptography, though complex, is a fascinating and essential field. Its proper implementation in software applications like those developed with Flutter can significantly enhance security and trust. As technology continues to evolve, so do the challenges and opportunities in the domain of cryptography.

Developers and security professionals must continuously learn and adapt, ensuring their applications function effectively and safeguard user data with the highest security standards. This chapter provides the foundational knowledge and tools necessary to tackle this ongoing journey of learning and application in the dynamic world of cryptography. However, this was just a surface; please always check trusted resources and consult with experts before implementing.

---

[3]https://mas.owasp.org/MASTG/General/0x04g-Testing-Cryptography/

CHAPTER 20

Protecting User Privacy

Reviewer: Danielle Cox

In this new digital era, we are all vulnerable to data breaches, especially with the rise of mobile applications. These breaches compromise user data, leading to privacy violations. As a software engineer, it is essential to take this issue seriously as it affects both our users and ourselves. We also use apps developed by our colleagues or other developers, so we must prioritize user privacy to ensure we benefit from it.

Complying with legal requirements is essential to protect user privacy. Failure to do so may result in penalties and loss of customer trust in the app and brand.

In the previous chapter, we learned about using cryptography to protect user privacy. This chapter will explore other topics, such as regulations and design philosophy. Despite its theoretical nature, this brief chapter is very important for ethical software engineering.

20.1 Understanding Key Privacy Terminologies

A complete understanding of privacy terms is important in developing mobile applications, especially for platforms like Flutter. These terms describe the boundaries of privacy and data protection and help developers comply with legal and ethical standards. This section aims to simplify important privacy terms for Flutter developers, making it easier for them to incorporate these concepts into their application development process.

1. **Personal Data**: Any information relating to an identified or identifiable individual. In the context of mobile apps, this can range from basic personal details like name and email address to more sensitive data such as location, health information, and financial details.
2. **Data Processing**: Any operation performed on personal data, whether automated or manual. This includes collection, recording, organization, structuring, storage, adaptation, retrieval, consultation, use, disclosure, dissemination, or erasure.

3. **Data Controller**: The entity that determines the purposes and means of processing personal data. In app development, this could be the app developer or the company for whom the app is being developed.

4. **Data Processor**: A party that processes personal data on behalf of the data controller. This might include the app's third-party services, like analytics or advertising platforms.

5. **Consent**: Consent refers to a clear, informed, and unambiguous indication of the data subject's agreement to the processing of their data. It must be freely given, specific, informed, and clearly indicate the individual's wishes.

6. **Data Protection Impact Assessment (DPIA)**: A process to help identify and minimize the data protection risks of a project. It is particularly relevant for app developers when introducing new data processing processes or technologies.

7. **Encryption** is converting information or data into a code to prevent unauthorized access. We explore this in-depth in the previous chapter.

8. **Data Breach**: A security incident in which information is accessed without authorization. Developers must understand the protocols for responding to data breaches, including notification to authorities and affected individuals.

9. **Privacy by Design**: An approach where privacy and data protection are considered throughout the system engineering process. For Flutter developers, this means integrating privacy features and considerations from the ground up in app design and development.

From a developer's point of view, there are other terms, but the ones mentioned above are the most important.

20.2 Embracing the Privacy by Design Philosophy

Flutter developers must adopt the Privacy by Design (PbD) philosophy in today's ever-changing digital world. PbD is not just a compliance requirement; it's a mindset that integrates privacy into the core of app design and functionality in a proactive manner.

PbD urges developers to consider privacy at the initial design stages and throughout the app's lifecycle. This approach involves seven foundational principles that serve as the guiding pillars for developers:

1. **Proactive, not Reactive; Preventative, not Remedial**: The PbD philosophy encourages Flutter developers to anticipate and prevent privacy-invasive events before they happen rather than waiting for privacy risks to occur.

2. **Privacy as the Default Setting**: Apps developed with Flutter should automatically protect user privacy by ensuring that personal data is securely stored and accessed only on a need-to-know basis. Privacy should not be an opt-in feature; it should be ingrained in the app's default settings.

3. **Privacy Embedded into Design**: Privacy should be integral to the app's design and architecture. This means considering how data is collected, stored, and shared right from the start of the app development process.

4. **Full Functionality – Positive-Sum, not Zero-Sum**: PbD aims to balance privacy and app functionality, encouraging Flutter developers to enhance user privacy while maintaining full functionality.

5. **End-to-End Security – Full Lifecycle Protection**: Throughout the entire data lifecycle, privacy measures must be in place, from secure data handling during initial collection to eventual deletion, ensuring end-to-end security.

6. **Visibility and Transparency – Keep it Open**: Flutter developers must handle user data transparently. Users should be informed about data collection, usage, and access details.

7. **Respect for User Privacy – Keep it User-Centric**: The app's development process should prioritize user privacy preferences and expectations by providing clear consent mechanisms and easy-to-use privacy settings.

Embracing Privacy by Design (PbD) in Flutter development is about avoiding legal consequences and establishing a privacy-focused culture that respects and safeguards individuals' digital rights.

20.3   Best Practices to Support User Privacy

This section provides an overview of best practices focusing on technical implementation.

1. **Data Minimization**: Collect only the data necessary for the app's functionality. In Flutter, this can be managed by designing forms and data input fields that request minimal user information.

2. **User Consent Management**: Implement explicit user consent mechanisms. Before data collection or processing, this can be technically handled in Flutter through custom dialog boxes or consent forms.

3. **Data Encryption**: Utilize encryption for data at rest and in transit. We reviewed this in the previous chapter.

4. **Security Audits and Penetration Testing**: Regularly perform security audits and penetration testing. We explored these in the security chapter.

5. **Use of Secure Libraries and Dependencies**: Regularly update and audit libraries for security. Dependency management in Flutter can be maintained through careful monitoring of the `pubspec.yaml` file for any outdated or insecure packages. A security audit on open-source packages is a way to recognize whether they are secure.

6. **Robust Authentication Mechanisms**: Implement strong authentication methods such as OAuth multi-factor authentication (MFA) or biometrics authentication. When working with Flutter, it's important to handle foreground and background events to protect sensitive data. For example, if someone is using the app in front of others, hiding or partially showing certain data may be necessary. One way to achieve this is by displaying only a

portion of an email and providing an action for the user to reveal the rest. You can also implement a Privacy Screen, which technically hides or locks the entire app. When accessed again, it requires authentication, usually via biometrics, to unlock the app. There are even other packages that can help implement these features easily.

7. **Privacy Policy Transparency**: Communicate the privacy policy. This can be done by including a dedicated and easily accessible section within the app, developed using Flutter's UI components.

8. **User Data Control and Access**: Allow users to access, edit, and delete their data. This can be technically implemented in Flutter through user account management features that let users control their data. However, this also needs team collaboration from the backend team. Offering a delete option in the front end allows users to clear their data and respect their privacy.

9. **Limiting Third-Party Data Sharing**: Be cautious about integrating third-party services that might access user data. Evaluate each service or API integrated into your Flutter app for its data handling practices.

10. **Privacy Awareness for Development Team**: Ensure the development team is trained in privacy practices. This involves staying updated with Flutter's best practices and guidelines for privacy and security.

By embedding these practices into the development lifecycle, Flutter developers can build apps that are not only functional but also prioritize user privacy, ensuring a trustworthy and secure user experience.

20.4   International Data Protection Regulations

This section briefly overviews key international data protection laws and guidelines, highlighting their relevance to software engineers.

General Data Protection Regulation (GDPR) - European Union: Perhaps the most influential data protection legislation globally, the GDPR imposes strict guidelines on the collection, processing, and storage of personal data for individuals within the EU.

California Consumer Privacy Act (CCPA) - United States: Similar to GDPR, CCPA gives California residents more control over their personal information. It requires data collection and usage transparency and offers users the right to know about and opt out of their data being sold.

Personal Information Protection and Electronic Documents Act (PIPEDA) - Canada: PIPEDA governs how private sector organizations collect, use, and disclose personal information during commercial business.

Information Technology (Reasonable Security Practices and Procedures and Sensitive Personal Data or Information) Rules, 2011 - India: These rules require handling sensitive personal data with reasonable security practices.

Data Protection Act 2018 - United Kingdom: Post-Brexit, the UK's version of the GDPR virtually mirrors the EU regulation.

The Lei Geral de Proteção de Dados (LGPD) - Brazil: Similar to GDPR, LGPD is designed to protect the privacy and security of individuals' data.

The Privacy Act 1988 - Australia: This Act includes 13 Australian Privacy Principles (APPs) that govern standards, rights, and obligations around the collection, use, and disclosure of personal information. Flutter developers targeting Australian users need to adhere to these principles.

There are likely many data privacy protection laws specific to different countries. You can research to find out what the laws are in your country or region. It's important to know these laws if you're creating an app that will be used worldwide.

As a software engineer, knowing all the legal aspects of laws is optional. However, you should focus on how to address the legal concerns through technical means while building software. This is usually executed by a team of engineers, architects, designers, legal department, product owners, and other relevant members to ensure the application is approved.

20.5   Conclusion

Ensuring user privacy is a legal requirement and the foundation of reliable and long-lasting digital products. To achieve this, we must consider privacy terms, privacy by design principles, technical best practices, and global regulations. Equipped with this knowledge, you can create apps that comply with regulations, respect users' privacy, and contribute to a safer digital world that impacts yourself first.

Although privacy concerns are important, they are often given little attention by small development teams. However, as your team and product grow, it becomes more important to comply with regulations. Regardless of regulations, it's important to consider what can be done for the user (including yourself as a user of the app) and strive to implement those measures as an engineer.

However, learning and adapting never ends, and we must always keep user privacy at the forefront of every app we create.

CHAPTER 21

Ensuring Accessibility for All

Reviewer: Manuela Rommel

There is a misconception that accessibility is usually considered for impaired people. Accessibility in app development is critical for inclusivity, ensuring that apps are usable by everyone, including individuals with disabilities. Integrating accessibility is ethical, expands the app's reach, and complies with legal standards. An accessible app enhances the overall user experience, benefiting all users. Imagine a parent holding their child and trying to zoom in on an image in your app using a multi-pointer gesture. However, due to having only one hand free, they need help to act. In such situations, by incorporating accessibility features like enabling zooming by double-tap, you can provide a better user experience for parents and people with motor disabilities.

In Flutter app development, accessibility should be a core consideration. Flutter offers tools for accessible design, such as semantic widgets, but developers and project managers must prioritize these features from the beginning. Making accessibility a part of the engineering process in Flutter ensures a more universally usable and inclusive final product.

Let's explore accessibility from an engineer's perspective in this chapter and see how we can utilize it in any Flutter app.

21.1 Recognizing Various Disabilities

Recognizing various disabilities is important in creating inclusive environments in software development, education, healthcare, or workplace settings. Disabilities can be broadly categorized into several types, each with unique challenges and needs.

1. **Physical Disabilities:** For users with mobility or dexterity challenges, like those with paralysis or arthritis, app accessibility can include features like voice commands, larger clickable areas, and keyboard shortcuts. This ensures that users can navigate and interact with the app without relying solely on a touchscreen or mouse.

2. **Sensory Disabilities:** Users with visual impairments, such as blindness or low vision, benefit from screen readers, high-contrast color schemes, and text-to-speech functionality. For those with hearing impairments, apps can include subtitles or visual alerts as alternatives to audio cues, ensuring that all information is accessible.
3. **Cognitive Disabilities:** For individuals with cognitive disabilities, such as dyslexia or autism, apps should have a clear, consistent layout, straightforward navigation, and the option to customize text size and fonts. Simplifying language and providing easy-to-understand instructions can also make apps more accessible.
4. **Psychiatric Disabilities:** Users with mental health conditions like anxiety or PTSD may find overly stimulating interfaces overwhelming. Apps can offer a calm design, the ability to control sensory inputs like sounds or animations, and features that allow users to set their own pace without pressure or time constraints.
5. **Chronic Health Disabilities:** For those with chronic pain or fatigue, minimizing the need for prolonged interaction is important. Features like saving session states, easy-to-access controls, and low physical effort requirements can make apps more usable for these individuals.

Figure 21.1: Accessibility and A11y

Ensuring that apps and software are accessible means incorporating various features and design choices that cater to diverse needs. This often involves following established accessibility guidelines and standards and engaging with users from various disability communities for testing and feedback.

21.1.1 Accessibility Guidelines

The primary guidelines for web accessibility are the Web Content Accessibility Guidelines (WCAG), developed by the World Wide Web Consortium (W3C). WCAG is the gold standard for creating accessible web content applicable worldwide. It's structured around four key principles: content must be perceivable, operable, understandable, and robust. These guidelines ensure that web content is accessible to people with various disabilities, including visual, auditory, physical, and cognitive impairments. Compliance with these guidelines not only enhances accessibility but also aligns with legal standards in many regions, such as the ADA in the United States and the European Union's EN 301 549 standards. For mobile app accessibility, developers turn to platform-specific guidelines. Apple's **Accessibility Guidelines for iOS** and **Google's Accessibility Guidelines for Android** are pivotal in guiding developers. These guidelines include voice-over services, adjustable text sizes, and color contrast settings tailored to mobile devices' unique interfaces and interaction models. They focus on ensuring that mobile apps are accessible to users with various disabilities, including those affecting vision, hearing, motor skills, and cognition. Additionally, the principles of WCAG are also relevant and applicable in the mobile context, ensuring a unified approach to accessibility across different digital platforms.

21.2   The Tangible Benefits of Inclusive App Design

Inclusive app design is not just a moral imperative; it offers tangible benefits beyond compliance with accessibility standards. By embracing inclusivity, app developers and businesses can realize significant advantages.

Firstly, inclusive design expands market reach. By catering to the needs of people with disabilities, apps can tap into a wider audience, including approximately 16% of the global population who experience some form of disability, that is, 1.3 billion people. This inclusivity translates into a broader user base and, potentially, increased revenue.

Secondly, inclusive apps tend to have better overall usability. Designing for accessibility often results in cleaner layouts, clearer navigation, and simpler interfaces. These improvements enhance the user experience for all users, not just those with disabilities. A well-designed, accessible app reduces frustration and increases user satisfaction, leading to higher retention rates and positive word-of-mouth.

Moreover, inclusive design can lead to innovation. When designers and developers consider a wide range of abilities and experiences, they are often pushed to think creatively, leading to innovative design solutions that benefit all users. Features like voice commands and predictive text, initially developed for accessibility purposes, are now widely used and appreciated by a broader audience.

There's also a competitive advantage in inclusive design. As awareness of accessibility increases, users are more likely to choose apps that cater to a diverse audience. Companies prioritizing inclusivity can differentiate themselves in crowded marketplaces, appealing to socially conscious consumers and organizations.

In addition, inclusive design can mitigate legal risks. Many regions have laws requiring digital accessibility, and non-compliance can result in legal action and reputational damage. By integrating accessibility into the design process, businesses can avoid these risks.

These are the immediate benefits I can recall; perhaps there are local benefits you have experienced or can name.

21.3 The Four Pillars of Accessibility

Accessibility in digital design and development is grounded in four fundamental pillars: Perceivability, Operability, Understandability, and Robustness.

These pillars, derived from the Web Content Accessibility Guidelines (WCAG), provide a framework for creating accessible content for a wide range of people with disabilities. While extracted from WCAG, it can still apply to any digital product, whether on the web or mobile apps.

1. **Perceivability:** This pillar ensures that information and user interface components must be presentable to users in ways they can perceive. This means that users must be able to perceive the presented information regardless of their sensory abilities. For instance, this can include providing text alternatives for non-text content, ensuring that audio and video content is available in accessible formats, and designing for various visual abilities by using appropriate color contrast and resizable text.

2. **Operability:** User interface components and navigation must be operable. This pillar focuses on the functionality of an app or website, ensuring that all users can operate the interface. This includes making all functionality available from a keyboard for users who cannot use a mouse, providing enough time for users to read and use content, and not designing content in a way known to cause seizures.

3. **Understandability:** The information and the operation of the user interface must be understandable. This means that content should be clear and straightforward, avoiding unnecessary complexity. It includes providing instructions or labels for content, ensuring predictable navigation, and helping users avoid and correct mistakes.

4. **Robustness:** Content must be robust enough to be reliably interpreted by various user agents, including assistive technologies. This means creating content that can be interpreted reliably by various devices and tools, including screen readers, magnifiers, and other assistive technologies. It involves following standards and best practices to ensure compatibility and adaptability with current and future technologies.

There are three levels of compliance as outlined in the WCAG: A, AA, and AAA. These levels represent increasing degrees of accessibility:

1. **Level A (Basic Accessibility):** This is the foundational level, covering essential accessibility features. It includes basic requirements like text alternatives for images, keyboard navigability, and accessible content for assistive technologies. For mobile apps, this might mean ensuring that all essential functions are usable with a screen reader and support basic screen orientation and touch controls.

2. **Level AA (Enhanced Accessibility):** Targeted by most web and mobile apps, Level AA includes all Level A criteria plus additional requirements for improved usability. This includes better visual contrast, clearer labels, and error identification. For mobile apps, this level may involve more refined touch-target sizes and alternative input methods for complex gestures.

Ensuring Accessibility for All

3. **Level AAA (Advanced Accessibility):** The highest standard, Level AAA, includes all Level A and AA criteria, with even more stringent requirements. This level is often only partially achievable for all content but includes features like sign language interpretation and enhanced contrast. AAA compliance can be challenging for mobile apps due to the wide variety of user interactions and complex functionalities.

Generally, Level AA compliance is considered a robust target for web and mobile apps, ensuring high accessibility without the more challenging requirements of Level AAA.

21.4 Tools and Widgets Promoting Accessibility

It's time to start looking at our Flutter app from an accessibility angle. The **Semantics widget** in Flutter is fundamental for accessibility. It allows developers to annotate the app's UI with descriptions for screen readers. To visualize semantic nodes in Flutter, you can use the MaterialApp property `showSemanticsDebugger` and set it to true.

```
MaterialApp(
    showSemanticsDebugger: true,
)
```

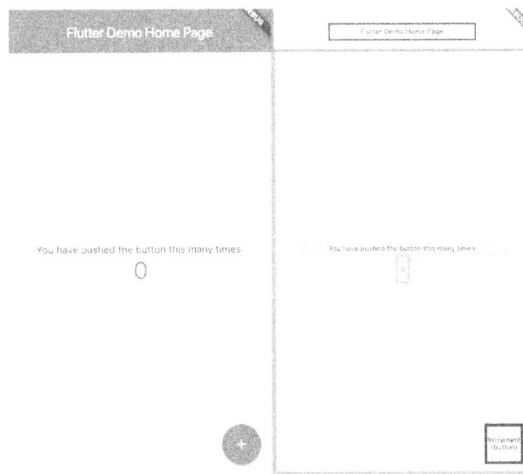

Figure 21.2: Flutter Semantics Debugger

21.4.1 Accessibility in Flutter

Flutter's approach to accessibility is deeply integrated within its architecture, primarily through a secondary tree, the Semantics Tree.

A unique aspect of accessibility in the web for Flutter is that the semantics tree is not built by default. When a user navigates to a Flutter web app using a screen reader, the screen reader will notify the user of an accessibility button that is not visible to the naked eye on the screen. The semantic tree is constructed only after activating this button, a measure taken to enhance the performance of the Flutter web.

This tree is critical in making apps accessible to assistive technologies like Android TalkBack and iOS VoiceOver. Flutter also supports accessibility across all platforms. Flutter maintains a Semantics Tree alongside the Widget tree, which is important for accessibility. This tree consists of `SemanticsNodes`, each corresponding to one or more Widgets. These nodes inform assistive technologies about describing and interacting with the UI. For example, a slider widget's `SemanticsNode` might include properties like `increasedValue` or `decreasedValue`, which define the values resulting from increased or decreased actions.

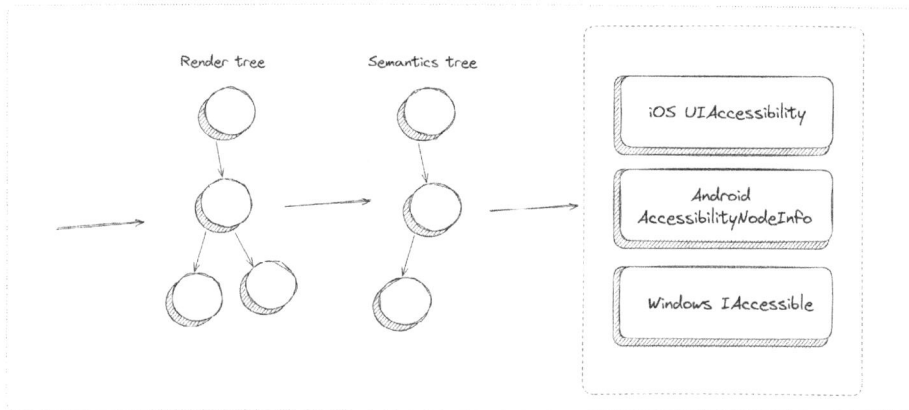

Figure 21.3: Semantics Tree in Flutter

In Flutter, there are several key widgets specifically designed to enhance accessibility. The four primary widgets are:

Semantics Widget

The Semantics widget is used to annotate the UI with descriptions that can be read by screen readers. It allows developers to create a custom accessibility experience for their widgets.

It provides many semantic parameters, including labels, hints, and text-to-speech descriptions for UI elements that may not be self-explanatory.

```
Semantics(
  label: 'Play Button',
  button: true,
    liveRegion: true,
  child: Icon(Icons.play_arrow),
)
```

In the code, `liveRegion` enables to read out the semantics as soon as the widget appears, so it is nice for stuff that needs to be read immediately.

MergeSemantics Widget

MergeSemantics is used when you have a group of widgets you want to be treated as a single semantic entity.

It combines the semantics of multiple widgets into a single node in the semantics tree. This is especially useful for complex widget compositions where you want to provide a unified semantic description.

```
MergeSemantics(
  child: Row(
    children: [
      Checkbox(...),
      Text('Accept Terms'),
    ],
  ),
)
```

ExcludeSemantics Widget

ExcludeSemantics excludes a widget and its children from the semantics tree.

This is particularly useful for hiding purely decorative widgets that do not contribute meaningfully to the app's content from screen readers.

```
ExcludeSemantics(
  child: Image.asset('decorative_image.png'),
)
```

BlockSemantics Widget

BlockSemantics is a widget used to omit the semantics of all widgets painted behind it in the same semantic container. This widget plays a crucial role in accessibility by controlling the visibility of certain UI elements to accessibility tools, like screen readers.

It's especially useful in scenarios where certain elements, like alerts or drawers, overlay other UI parts. For instance, when an alert dialog is on screen, it should typically prevent interaction with the elements behind it. BlockSemantics effectively hides these "behind" elements from assistive technologies, ensuring that the focus is kept on the primary interactive element, like the alert or drawer.

```
BlockSemantics(
  blocking: true,
  child: AlertDialog(
    // Alert dialog content
  ),
)
```

Along with the key accessibility widgets, Flutter provides several other features and tools to enhance accessibility:

Tooltip Widget Enhances understanding of icons and buttons for screen reader users.

```
Tooltip(
  excludeFromSemantics: false,
  message: 'Tap to open settings',
  child: IconButton(icon: Icon(Icons.settings),
  onPressed: () {/*...*/}),
)
```

TextButton Automatically include semantic labels for better screen reader support. isSemanticButton controls screen reader "button" announcements, and setting it to null avoids repetitiveness in menus.

```
TextButton(
    isSemanticButton: true,
  onPressed: () {/*...*/},
  child: Text('Submit'),
)
```

Slider Widget Accessibility Provides an accessible slider experience with value indicators.

```
Slider(
  value: _sliderValue,
  min: 0,
  max: 100,
  divisions: 10,
  label: '$_sliderValue',
  onChanged: (double value) {
    setState(() {_sliderValue = value;});
  },
)
```

ListView with Automatic Semantics Scrollable widgets like ListView automatically generate necessary scroll actions for accessibility.

```
ListView.builder(
  addSemanticIndexes: true,
  semanticChildCount: items.length,
  itemCount: items.length,
  itemBuilder: (context, index) => ListTile(
    title: Text(
      items[index],
```

```
    ),
  ),
)
```

CustomScrollView Widget

The `CustomScrollView` in Flutter is a versatile widget designed for creating custom scroll effects using an array of slivers. `CustomScrollView` supports accessibility features like Talkback/VoiceOver, which is essential for visually impaired users. It can provide announcements about scroll state changes, such as the number of items visible and the position within a list or grid. To facilitate accessibility, widgets within slivers should be wrapped in `IndexedSemantics` to associate each item with a semantic index. This helps convey accurate information about lists or grid positions to accessibility tools. For certain layouts like `ListView.separated`, where not all items contribute to the semantic information, the semantic index may differ from the widget index. This needs to be handled correctly to provide accurate semantic information.

```
CustomScrollView(
  slivers: [
    ...
  ],
)
```

Text.rich() Widget Allows for text with multiple styles and scales, enhancing readability for important information.

```
child: const Text.rich(
      TextSpan(
        text: 'Do not forget to',
        children: [
          TextSpan(
            text: 'save',
            style: TextStyle(fontWeight: FontWeight.bold),
          ),
          TextSpan(text: ' your work!'),
        ],
      ),
    ),
```

Focus Traversal and Screen Reader Order Manage focus traversal for keyboard and screen reader navigation. It's worth noting that focus traversal won't work for screen reader navigation to change the order in which widgets are read; one must use the Semantics sortKey property.

```
// Block for Screen Reader Order (Semantics Sort Key)
Column(
```

```
  children: [
    Semantics(
      sortKey: const OrdinalSortKey(2),
// First in screen reader order
      child: const TextField(),
    ),
    Semantics(
// Second in screen reader order
      sortKey: const OrdinalSortKey(1),
      child: const TextField(autofocus: true),
    ),
  ],
)
```

Accessibility Announcements Make custom announcements to the user using `SemanticsService`, although implicit mechanisms like Semantics are preferred whenever possible.

Use `SemanticsService.announce` for custom announcements not triggered by UI changes (e.g., camera object detections). The assertiveness level will determine the priority in which the announcement should be made. This only applies currently to the web.

```
SemanticsService.announce(
    'Accessibility',
    TextDirection.ltr,
    assertiveness: Assertiveness.assertive,
);
```

Incorporating these accessibility features into a Flutter app ensures a more inclusive and user-friendly experience, catering to a diverse user base, including individuals with disabilities. These features highlight Flutter's capability to build accessible applications efficiently and provide an essential foundation, sometimes out of the box.

21.5   Flutter Accessibility Audit

An Accessibility Audit is a critical evaluation process to ensure that a Flutter application is accessible to all users, including those with disabilities. This audit involves examining various aspects of the app, from visual elements to interactive functionalities, to identify and rectify potential accessibility barriers.

In Flutter, this process is especially important due to the framework's unique capabilities and widgets. The audit typically focuses on key areas such as **fonts and text**, **colors and contrast**, **screen readers**, **gestures**, **and animation**.

21.5.1 Fonts and Text Accessibility in Flutter

In Flutter, ensuring text accessibility involves a few key practices. A crucial feature is the framework's ability to automatically adapt to the user's preferred font sizes in their device's system settings. This means that when a user chooses larger or smaller text sizes for better readability, Flutter's text widgets automatically adjust their font sizes accordingly. However, developers must design their app layouts to be flexible and accommodating to these changes. This is particularly important for visually impaired users who rely on larger text. Testing the app on devices with small screens and the font size set to the largest option is a good way to ensure that the layout remains functional and the text is legible under various conditions.

Readability: For text legibility, selecting clear, readable fonts is essential. Standard, non-stylized fonts are preferred for their ease of reading.

```
Text(
  'Readable Text',
  style: TextStyle(fontFamily: 'Roboto'),
)
```

Additionally, high contrast between text and background colors is vital for readability. This can be achieved by using contrasting color schemes for text and backgrounds. Tools can be utilized to check contrast ratios, ensuring compliance with accessibility guidelines.

```
Text(
'High Contrast Text',
    style: TextStyle(
      color: Colors.white,
      backgroundColor: Colors.black,
    ),
)
```

Dynamic Font Sizing: As a developer, it's important to ensure that your app's layout remains functional and the text legible when the font size changes. Testing devices with small screens and maximum font size settings effectively validates this adaptability.

```
double scaleFactor = MediaQuery.textScalerOf(context);
Text(
  'Sample Text',
  style: TextStyle(fontSize: 16 * scaleFactor),
)
```

Semantic Labels for Non-Textual Elements: Another important aspect is using semantic labels for icons or elements representing non-standard text. For example, an icon that acts should have a descriptive label so that screen readers can convey its meaning effectively. The `Semantics` widget in Flutter is used for this purpose.

```
Semantics(
  label: 'Settings Icon',
  child: Icon(Icons.settings),
)
```

Constrained Text and Automatic Adjustments: Managing constrained text and ensuring it adjusts automatically is a critical aspect of accessibility in Flutter. This involves designing your app's layout to accommodate varying text sizes without breaking or losing content, ensuring readability across various user settings. For example, Flexible and Wrap Widgets allow text to expand or wrap according to the available space, preventing overflow.

```
Flexible(
  child: Text(
    'Long text that might need to wrap or adjust',
    overflow: TextOverflow.ellipsis,
  ),
)
```

By addressing these aspects, developers can significantly enhance the text and font accessibility in their Flutter applications, making them more inclusive for users with different visual needs.

21.5.2   Colors and Contrast in Flutter Accessibility

Effective use of colors and contrast is paramount in creating an accessible app in Flutter. Proper color schemes and contrast ratios make your app more visually appealing and ensure that it is usable by individuals with visual impairments, such as color blindness or reduced vision.

Although this section often should be done in the phase of UI design, the developer can run an audit to ensure that the app and design follow accessibility best practices.

Color Selection

Choose colors that provide sufficient contrast between text and background elements. Avoid using color as the only means of conveying information. Combine colors with text labels or icons.

Contrast Ratios

Ensure that text and interactive elements meet the minimum contrast ratios defined by the Web Content Accessibility Guidelines (WCAG). By the end of this chapter, I will introduce tools you can use to test color combinations for sufficient contrast.

The W3C recommends[1]:

- At least 4.5:1 for small text (below 18 point regular or 14 point bold)
- At least 3.0:1 for large text (18 points and above regular or 14 points and above bold)

Adapting to User Preferences and Respecting Accessibility Settings

In Flutter, you can query the system's accessibility settings and adapt your app's color scheme accordingly, like switching to a darker or lighter theme based on user preferences.

Considerations for Interactive Elements

Ensure that interactive elements are easily distinguishable by using color contrasts and other indicators like underlines for links or distinct shapes for buttons.

21.5.3 Screen Reader Accessibility in Flutter

This is one of the most important sections that enable users to navigate and interact with the app using audible cues. Let's see what you can do.

Implementing Screen Reader Support

Use the `Semantics` widget to provide descriptive labels for all interactive elements, images, and non-text content.

```
Semantics(
  label: 'Share Button',
  child: IconButton(
    icon: Icon(Icons.share),
    onPressed: () { /*...*/ },
  ),
)
```

As I mentioned earlier, certain widgets can also aid in achieving this goal. It's important to note that `Semantics` has numerous properties, and providing a comprehensive explanation of all of them is beyond the scope of this book. However, I can say that the information covered so far should suffice for most accessibility implementation scenarios.

Ensure Semantics

In Flutter, `SemanticsBinding.instance.ensureSemantics()` is a crucial method for enabling and verifying the generation of the semantics tree, a key

---

[1] https://www.w3.org/TR/UNDERSTANDING-WCAG20/visual-audio-contrast-contrast.html

component for accessibility features in the app, particularly for screen readers. This method ensures the necessary semantic information is properly constructed and updated, allowing screen readers to interpret and narrate the UI elements accurately. Typically managed automatically by Flutter, this call is especially useful in custom widget development or during accessibility testing.

```
void main() {
  SemanticsBinding.instance.ensureSemantics();//<--
  runApp(MyApp());
}
```

Custom Actions and Hints

Beyond basic labels, you can provide custom actions and hints using the Semantics widget to guide screen reader users in interacting with certain elements.

```
Semantics(
  label: 'Play',
  hint: 'Double tap to play',
  child: PlayButton(),
)
```

Navigational Feedback

Ensure your app provides clear feedback as users navigate different screens or complete actions.

```
Navigator.of(context).push(MaterialPageRoute(
  builder: (context) => NewScreen(),
));
SemanticsService.announce(
  'Navigated to New Screen',
  TextDirection.ltr,
);
```

Handling Dynamic Content

For dynamic content such as live updates or notifications, use tools like SemanticsService.announce() to verbally communicate changes to the user. Another option would be to use semantics widgets liveRegion property, which we have seen earlier in this chapter.

By prioritizing screen reader accessibility in Flutter app development, you can make your app more inclusive, ensuring that users with visual impairments have a seamless and independent user experience.

21.5.4 Gestures Accessibility in Flutter

Accessibility in gesture navigation ensures that the app's interactive elements are usable by everyone, including users with motor impairments or those who rely on assistive technologies.

Simplifying Gestures

Flutter apps should offer simple, easy-to-perform gestures for common actions. Complex gestures like multi-finger swipes or long presses might be challenging for some users. Provide alternative ways to perform actions that typically require complex gestures wherever possible.

Custom Gesture Detectors

Use Flutter's `GestureDetector` widget to create custom gestures that are more accessible.

```
GestureDetector(
  onTap: () { /* Handle tap */ },
  onDoubleTap: () { /* Handle double tap */ },
  child: /* ... */,
)
```

This allows for the creation of tailored gestures catering to a wider range of users.

Feedback for Gestures

Providing immediate visual or auditory feedback for gestures helps users understand that their actions have been recognized. Use animations, haptic feedback, or sound effects to confirm gesture interactions. Please note that when using animations, announce this to users using screen readers.

Accessible Drag-and-Drop

For features like drag-and-drop, consider implementing alternative methods for users who might find direct interaction difficult.

```
LongPressDraggable(
  data: /* Data to be dragged */,
  feedback: /* Widget representing the drag */,
  child: /* Widget to drag from */,
)
```

Offer buttons or simpler interactions as alternatives to drag-and-drop actions.

21.5.5 Flutter Animations Accessibility

Animations can significantly enhance the user experience in an app, but they can also pose accessibility challenges, particularly for users with certain disabilities like visual impairments or motion sensitivity. In Flutter, it's important to consider how animations are used and provide options to accommodate users with different needs.

Reduce Motion

Some users are sensitive to motion and prefer reduced motion settings. Flutter apps can respect the system's reduced motion settings using the `AccessibilityFeatures` in `MediaQuery` or from the `PlatformDispatcher`

```
bool disableAnimations = MediaQuery.disableAnimationOf(
    context,
  );
  bool reducedMotion = WidgetsBinding
      .instance
      .platformDispatcher
      .accessibilityFeatures
      .reduceMotion;
```

Use this flag to adjust or disable animations for users who prefer reduced motion.

```
AnimationController(
  duration: reducedMotion
      ? Duration.zero
      : const Duration(
          seconds: 1,
        ),
  vsync: this,
)
```

Multiple variables are useful for handling accessibility features on both MediaQuery and PlatformDispatcher, such as

- `accessibleNavigation`: Indicates if an accessibility service that modifies the device's interaction model is active. Services like Android's TalkBack or iOS's VoiceOver will trigger this feature.
- `invertColors`: Detects if the platform has enabled color inversion for the application.
- `disableAnimations`: Determines if the platform has requested the disabling or simplification of animations.
- `onOffSwitchLabels`: Identifies if the platform has requested the inclusion of on/off labels within switch controls. This feature is mainly supported on iOS.
- `highContrast`: Determines if the platform has requested the UI to be rendered with higher contrast, usually involving darker colors. This feature is primarily supported on iOS.

You can also listen to the change of these features if needed

---

Ensuring Accessibility for All

```
WidgetsBinding.instance.platformDispatcher
    .onAccessibilityFeaturesChanged = () {
  print('reduceMotion: ');
};
```

Descriptive Labels for Animated Elements

When using animations to convey information, ensure that this information is also accessible through screen readers. Use the `Semantics` widget to provide descriptions for elements involved in animations.

Avoid Flashing and Rapid Movements

Avoid animations with flashing or rapidly moving elements, as these can trigger seizures in users with photosensitive epilepsy and cause discomfort for others.

Pause, Stop, Hide Controls

Provide controls to pause, stop, or hide animations. This empowers users to control their experience and reduces potential issues with motion or distraction.

Test With and Without Animations

Regularly test your app with and without animations to ensure it remains functional and accessible in either mode.

21.5.6   Flutter Accessibility Testing

Flutter offers specific guidelines and tools to facilitate this process.

Accessibility Guidelines in Flutter An accessibility guideline in Flutter describes a set of recommendations an application should meet to be considered accessible. These guidelines cover target size, contrast, and labeling, aligning with standard accessibility practices.

Using the `meetsGuideline` Matcher The `meetsGuideline` matcher is a powerful tool in Flutter's testing suite that asserts whether a screen or widget meets specific accessibility guidelines. It's used in conjunction with Flutter's unit testing framework to validate various aspects of accessibility.

Testing Tap Target Size and Labeling:

```
testWidgets(
  'HomePage meets *',
  (WidgetTester tester) async {
    final SemanticsHandle handle =
        tester.ensureSemantics();
    await tester.pumpWidget(
      const MaterialApp(
        home: HomePage(),
      ),
    );
```

```
    await expectLater(
      tester,
      meetsGuideline(androidTapTargetGuideline),
    );
    await expectLater(
        tester, meetsGuideline(iOSTapTargetGuideline));
    await expectLater(
      tester,
      meetsGuideline(labeledTapTargetGuideline),
    );
    handle.dispose();
  },
);
```

This test checks that the tappable nodes in the `HomePage` widget meet the minimum size requirements for Android and iOS platforms and are properly labeled.

Testing Text Contrast

```
testWidgets(
  'Text contrast meets guidelines',
  (
    WidgetTester tester,
  ) async {
    final SemanticsHandle handle =
        tester.ensureSemantics();
    // Your widget setup
    await expectLater(
      tester,
      meetsGuideline(textContrastGuideline),
    );
    handle.dispose();
  },
);
```

This test verifies that text elements in your widget meet the minimum contrast levels specified by WCAG.

Accessibility Guidelines and Their Purposes

1. `androidTapTargetGuideline`: Ensures tappable semantic nodes have a minimum size of 48x48 pixels based on Android's accessibility guidelines.
2. `iOSTapTargetGuideline`: Checks that tappable nodes on iOS have a minimum size of 44x44 pixels, adhering to iOS human interface guidelines.
3. `textContrastGuideline`: Validates that text contrast meets the minimum values required for readability, as specified by WCAG.
4. `labeledTapTargetGuideline`: Enforces that all interactive nodes with tap or long-press actions are accompanied by proper labeling.

SemanticsController in Flutter

The `SemanticsController` class in Flutter plays a role in interacting programmatically with the Semantics tree. This class enables developers and testers to examine and manipulate the Semantics tree directly, facilitating thorough testing of how an app would be interpreted by assistive technologies, search engines, and other software that relies on semantic analysis to understand the app's content and structure.

Using `simulatedAccessibilityTraversal` in Flutter Tests: This method simulates the traversal of the currently visible semantics tree as if by assistive technologies, such as screen readers. It ensures the semantics tree is navigated in the expected order and all necessary elements are accessible.

```
testWidgets(
  'MyWidget',
  (WidgetTester tester) async {
    await tester.pumpWidget(
      const MyWidget(),
    );

    // Simulate screen reader
    // traversal (using SemanticController)
    final traversalResult = tester.semantics
        .simulatedAccessibilityTraversal();

    // Verify the order and
    // properties of the elements in the traversal
    expect(
      traversalResult,
      containsAllInOrder(
        <Matcher>[
          containsSemantics(label: 'My Widget'),
          containsSemantics(
            label: 'is awesome!',
            isChecked: true,
          ),
        ],
      ),
    );
  },
);
```

In this test:

- `simulatedAccessibilityTraversal` simulates the traversal of the semantics tree.
- `expect()` checks that the elements are encountered in the correct order with the expected semantic properties (like labels and states).

- `containsAllInOrder` ensures that the elements in `traversalResult` match the specified matches in the given order.
- `containsSemantics` is used to specify the expected properties of the semantic nodes, like labels and other attributes.

This approach is effective for validating the accessibility of your Flutter app, ensuring that the semantic content is correctly structured and navigable for users with assistive technologies.

Checking Semantics with `tester.getSemantics` The `tester.getSemantics` method can retrieve the semantics tree for a given widget. This allows you to inspect the semantic information that screen readers use to read out loud. You can check if the correct labels, hints, and actions are provided for interactive elements. This test checks if a button has the correct semantic properties, such as the tap action and an appropriate label.

```
testWidgets(
  'Check semantics on a button',
  (WidgetTester tester) async {
    await tester.pumpWidget(MyApp());
    final SemanticsHandle handle =
        tester.ensureSemantics();

    // Assuming you have a button with a key 'submitBtn'
    final Finder submitButton = find.byKey(
      const Key('submitBtn'),
    );
    expect(
      tester.getSemantics(submitButton),
      matchesSemantics(
        hasTapAction: true,
        isButton: true,
        label: 'Submit',
      ),
    );

    handle.dispose();
  },
);
```

By combining these methods with the standard accessibility guidelines checks, you can create a comprehensive testing strategy for your Flutter app's accessibility, ensuring that it is fully usable by screen reader users and adheres to best practices.

Writing tests using the matchesSemantics matcher can be a demanding task due to its non-fuzzy nature (meaning every semantics information must exist as it is expected). If the tests fail consistently, you can troubleshoot by inspecting all the semantic nodes using debugDumpSemanticsTree().

Testing Accessibility on the Web For web applications, Flutter allows you to debug accessibility features by visualizing semantic nodes. This can be enabled using the command line flag

```
--dart-define=FLUTTER_WEB_DEBUG_SHOW_SEMANTICS=true
```

In profile or release modes, we provide a visual overlay of the semantic nodes on top of the widgets.

21.5.7 Accessibility Tools

When developing Flutter applications, it's crucial to leverage various accessibility tools to ensure the application is usable and friendly for all users, including those with disabilities. Here's a breakdown of specific tools for Flutter, categorized by platform and functionality:

iOS (macOS)-Specific Tools

1. **VoiceOver:** Apple's built-in screen reader, VoiceOver, is essential for testing how an app is navigated and read aloud to users with visual impairments. Use VoiceOver to ensure your Flutter app's UI components are labeled and navigable.
2. **Accessibility Inspector:** Part of Xcode, this tool helps audit iOS apps for accessibility, including checking voiceover feedback, touch target sizes, and color contrast ratios.

Android-Specific Tools

1. **TalkBack:** Google's screen reader, TalkBack, is similar to VoiceOver but for Android devices. Testing with TalkBack is key to ensuring your Flutter app is accessible on Android.
2. **Accessibility Scanner:** A tool by Google that scans your app and suggests improvements for accessibility, such as enlarging small touch targets, increasing contrast, etc.

Windows Accessibility Tools

1. **Narrator:** Windows' built-in screen reader. It's useful for testing how applications are read and navigated by users with visual impairments on Windows platforms.
2. **Magnifier:** A screen magnification tool that helps test the app's usability for low-vision users.
3. **Color Contrast Analyzer:** Tools like the Colour Contrast Analyser can be used on Windows to check if your app meets the required contrast ratios.

Linux Accessibility Tools

1. **Orca Screen Reader:** A popular screen reader for Linux that provides spoken feedback and Braille output, useful for testing applications on Linux platforms.
2. **Magnification Tools:** Linux distributions often include built-in or downloadable magnification tools, like KMag in KDE, which are useful for testing visual accessibility.

Cross-Platform Tools

1. **Flutter Widget Inspector:** Built into Flutter's dev tools, it's useful for inspecting the widget tree and layout, ensuring the semantics are correctly implemented for accessibility.
2. **Flutter Testing:** Flutter's integration testing framework can automate the testing of accessibility features in your app.
3. **Color Contrast Analyzers:** Tools like the WebAIM Color Contrast Checker can be used to ensure that your app has adequate color contrast ratios as per WCAG guidelines.
4. **Manual Testing:** Manually testing your app with various accessibility features enabled on Android and iOS devices is crucial.

Packages

1. `accessibility_tools` **Package:** Available at pub.dev, this package provides tools and utilities to help develop accessible applications in Flutter. It includes functionalities like checking color contrasts, ensuring text sizes comply with accessibility standards, and more.

21.6   Conclusion

In this chapter, I had one simple message to convert: "to create digital experiences that are inclusive and accessible to everyone, regardless of their abilities or disabilities."

The tools and practices discussed throughout this chapter are not just guidelines but are fundamental components of ethical and responsible software development. By incorporating accessibility considerations from the outset, we developers can ensure our applications comply with legal standards and are universally usable and appreciated. This approach enhances the overall user experience and broadens the application's reach to a diverse audience.

It's also important to recognize that the field of digital accessibility is continuously evolving, and staying informed about the latest trends, tools, and guidelines is crucial. Developers, designers, and content creators are encouraged to consult major websites and resources dedicated to accessibility regularly. Websites like the Web Accessibility Initiative (WAI), the A11Y Project, and the WCAG guidelines provide invaluable insights and updates on accessibility standards and best practices. Engaging with these resources and incorporating their recommendations into your work will improve your skills as a developer and contribute positively to the inclusivity and accessibility of the digital world.

Let's strive to build a more accessible and inclusive digital future for everyone.

Ensuring Accessibility for All

Part V

Advancing UI Development

CHAPTER 22

Crafting Adaptive UIs

Reviewer: Verena Zaiser

Adaptive User Interfaces (AUIs) represent a transformative approach in application development, key for the ever-evolving ecosystem of devices and user needs. Imagine a scenario where a user, familiarized with a desktop application's expansive view and input methods, switches to a mobile device. The experience can be harsh if the app does not adapt to the smaller screen and touch-based interaction. This is where the significance of adaptive design in Flutter comes into play. By leveraging Flutter's capabilities, we can create applications that intelligently adjust not only to varying screen sizes but also to different input methods like touch, mouse, and keyboard.

Adaptive design goes beyond mere responsive layouts; it encompasses a nuanced understanding of platform-specific expectations and user interactions. The benefits are manifold: enhanced user experience, increased app usability, and greater engagement across diverse platforms. This adaptiveness in Flutter allows a single codebase to cater to multiple platforms efficiently, saving time and resources while ensuring a consistent and intuitive user experience.

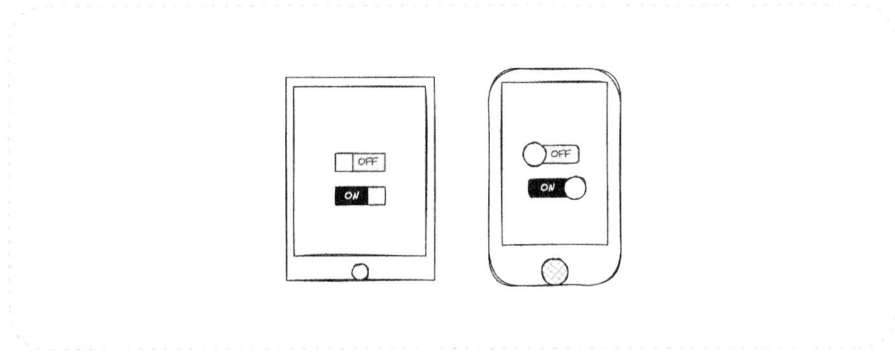

Figure 22.1: Adaptive UI Switch Example

As a Flutter developer, you have likely implemented some adaptive UI elements such as `Switch.adaptive` or `AdaptiveTextSelectionToolbar.buttonItems`.

However, building UIs in Flutter can present several challenges, particularly when supporting multiple platforms. In this context, it would be useful to have a comprehensive list of potential issues developers can consult to ensure their UIs function correctly across all platforms. In this chapter, I aim to provide a list and help developers tackle these issues using built-in features.

22.1   Platform-Specific UI Considerations

When crafting adaptive UIs in Flutter, it's essential to consider how various platform-specific elements influence user experience. These considerations ensure that your app feels intuitive and efficient on any device. Here, I categorize and explore these crucial aspects:

22.1.1   Screen Size and Resolution

Different devices feature a variety of screen sizes and resolutions, significantly impacting the user interface and experience. In Flutter, If you are targeting more than smartphones, it's important to design flexible UIs responsive to these variations. For instance, a spacious and user-friendly layout on a large screen might feel cramped on a mobile device. To address this, you can use Flutter's `MediaQuery` class to detect screen dimensions and adjust the layout dynamically. A practical implementation could involve switching from a detailed `GridView` on a tablet or desktop to a more compact `ListView` on a smartphone, ensuring that content is presented in an accessible and visually appealing manner on every device. In the upcoming chapter, Chapter 22, Responsive UI, I will delve further into this topic.

22.1.2   Input Methods

When developing adaptive Flutter apps, an aspect to consider is the variety of input methods across different devices and platforms. Each input method offers unique interaction capabilities and user expectations, from touch to mouse and keyboard.

Key Aspects to Consider

1. **Touch Input**: Predominant on mobile devices, touch input requires UI elements to be finger-friendly. This means larger tap targets and gesture-based navigation (like swipes and long presses) should be implemented.
2. **Mouse Input**: Common in desktop environments, mouse input enables precise control. Features like hover effects, right-click context menus, and scroll wheel interactions are expected in a desktop UI.
3. **Keyboard Input**: Keyboard input is crucial for both mobile and desktop apps. It includes text input, keyboard shortcuts, and navigation (using tab keys, arrow keys, etc.).

4. **Hybrid Devices**: Consider devices that support touch and mouse/keyboard inputs (like tablets with keyboards or touch-enabled laptops).

Let's explore how to implement these varied input methods in Flutter, ensuring your app is fully equipped to interact with users in their preferred way.

GestureDetector for Touch

Use Flutter's `GestureDetector` widget to handle tap, double-tap, drag, and other touch gestures.

```
GestureDetector(
  onTap: () { /* Handle tap */ },
  onLongPress: () { /* Handle long press */ },
    onDoubleTap: () { /* Handle double tap */ },
    onVerticalDragStart: (_){}
    onHorizontalDragStart: (_){},
    onPanUpdate: (_){},
  // Other gestures...
)
```

MouseRegion for Mouse Interactions

Employ `MouseRegion` for detecting mouse hover states and changing mouse cursors. Imagine creating custom rollover and hover effects.

```
MouseRegion(
  onEnter: (PointerEnterEvent event) {
      /* Handle hover enter */
    },
     onHover: ( PointerEnterEventevent) {
      /* Handle hover */
    },
  onExit: (PointerEnterEvent event) {
      /* Handle hover exit */
    },
  cursor: SystemMouseCursors.click,
  child: /* Your widget */,
)
```

An interesting widget that might be handy is the `FocusableActionDetector`. This widget in Flutter bundles the power of `Actions`, `Shortcuts`, `MouseRegion`, and `Focus` into one package, simplifying the creation of custom controls. It lets you define key bindings, manage focus changes, and handle hover highlights. This convenient helper keeps your code clean and ensures your custom controls behave consistently under keyboard, mouse, and touch interactions.

```
FocusableActionDetector(
    actions: <Type, Action<Intent>>{
```

```
    ActivateIntent: CallbackAction<Intent>(
      onInvoke: (intent) => print('Action triggered'),
    ),
  },
  shortcuts: _shortcuts,
  onShowFocusHighlight: _handleFocusChanged,
  onShowHoverHighlight: _handleHoverChanged,
  child: /* Your widget */,
)
```

Listener for Advanced Mouse Control

The `Listener` widget offers more detailed control over mouse events, like tracking movement or scroll wheel use.

```
Listener(
  onPointerSignal: (event) {
    if (event is PointerScrollEvent) {
      // Handle scroll event
    }
  },
  // Child widgets...
)
```

Widgets that can be scrolled, such as `ScrollView` or `ListView`, are already equipped to support the scroll wheel functionality by default.

Tab Traversal and Focus Interactions

In Flutter, effectively managing tab traversal and focus interactions is crucial for ensuring an accessible and user-friendly application. This involves two main components:

Traversal Management dictates the order and logic of moving focus between widgets using the keyboard, and **Focus Highlights** provide visual indicators to show which widget is currently focused. Users who rely on keyboard navigation, particularly those with motor or vision impairments, need these features.

In Flutter, built-in buttons and text fields automatically support focus traversal and highlights. For custom widgets, the `FocusableActionDetector` can be used. It combines `Actions`, `Shortcuts`, `MouseRegion`, and `Focus` functionalities, allowing for custom focus and hover interactions.

The default algorithm in Flutter for focus traversal is `ReadingOrderTraversalPolicy`, which intelligently guides keyboard focus through your app, mimicking natural reading order. It identifies the node rectangle with the highest top position on the screen. It then looks for other nodes intersecting the horizontal band created by the top and bottom edges of this highest rectangle. Finally, it selects the node closest to the beginning of the reading order among the intersecting nodes.

Focus Management

Utilize Flutter's focus management system to enable keyboard-based navigation and control, which is especially important for accessibility.

To control the focus order in Flutter, `FocusTraversalGroup` is used to group widgets, dictating the tab order. For instance, in a form, you can set the tab order to navigate through all input fields before reaching the submit button. While Flutter defaults to the `ReadingOrderTraversalPolicy` for focus traversal, this can be customized with other predefined policies or by creating a custom policy.

```
FocusTraversalGroup(
    child: MyFormWithMultipleColumnsAndRows(),
);
```

Keyboard Accelerators

Keyboard accelerators, or shortcuts, are essential for enhancing user experience, especially on desktop and web platforms. These shortcuts, like 'Delete' for quick deletions or 'Control+N' for creating new documents, are expected by users for efficient navigation and interaction.

In Flutter, several widgets and classes are designed to handle keyboard interactions and accelerators, enhancing the application's usability and accessibility. These include `RawKeyboardListener`, which listens to low-level keyboard events; `Shortcuts`, a widget for defining keyboard shortcuts for an entire widget subtree; `FocusableActionDetector`, which combines focus and action detections; and `FocusTraversalGroup` for managing the focus order. Additionally, Flutter provides `RawKeyboard` for global keyboard event listening and `Actions` binding specific actions to user-defined or system-defined intents. Each plays a vital role in creating an intuitive and accessible keyboard navigation experience in Flutter apps.

Considerations for Hybrid Devices Your app should gracefully handle the switch between touch and non-touch inputs for devices supporting multiple input methods. For instance, it shows a scrollbar that works with both the mouse wheel and touch swipes or buttons that are large enough to be tapped but also offer hover effects.

22.1.3   Visual Design and Density

Visual elements such as size, spacing, and density must be adapted to the platform's characteristics. Desktop interfaces often afford more space and can handle higher information density than mobile devices, with limited screen real estate. In Flutter, this can be managed by adjusting the `VisualDensity` property in your Material Components. This adjustment can make UI elements more compact for desktop applications or spaced out for mobile apps, enhancing readability and interaction quality across different devices.

```
main() {
  final touchMode = Platform.isIOS; // example
```

```
  final densityAmount = touchMode ? 0.0 : -1.0;
  return MaterialApp(
    theme: ThemeData(
      visualDensity: VisualDensity(
        horizontal: densityAmount,
        vertical: densityAmount,
      ),
    ),
    home: MyApp(),
  );
}
```

The `horizontal` and `vertical` arguments must be in the interval between `minimumDensity` (-4.0) and `maximumDensity` (4.0), inclusive.

The term `minimumDensity` and `maximumDensity` refer to the bounds within which you can set the visual density. Specifically:

- `minimumDensity` is `-4.0`, meaning this is the most expanded or least dense the components can be.
- `maximumDensity` is `4.0`, representing the most compact or most dense configuration.

22.1.4   Navigation Patterns

Navigation within an app should be intuitive and fit the platform's standards. Luckily, this comes out of the box for Flutter in most cases, although some adjustments on specific platforms may need to be made.

22.1.5   Platform Conventions and Components

Each platform has its unique conventions and preferred UI components. For instance, date pickers, switches, and dialog boxes have different appearances and behaviors on iOS and Android. In Flutter, you can cater to these differences by using Cupertino widgets for an iOS look and feel and Material widgets for Android. This adherence to platform-specific design languages ensures that your app aligns with user expectations and feels native to the platform, improving the overall user experience. Flutter also has built-in widgets, such as `Switch.adaptive()` and `Slider.adaptive()`.

22.2   Leveraging Unique Platform Features

Understanding the subtleties of each platform's user interface norms and behaviors creates an intuitive and engaging user experience. This approach requires a mindset shift from a one-size-fits-all design to a more subtle, platform-specific strategy. It involves not only considering the typical functionalities and design elements of each platform but also embracing the perspectives of native users. This is not easy, though. This big teamwork and effort should have been cultivated already in your team and company. But what can you do to ensure that each platform's unique feature is properly used?

One way to solve this problem is by having dedicated platform advocates; you can obtain invaluable insights and feedback, ensuring your app resonates well with the specifics of each platform. While aligning with these platform-specific standards, it's also important to maintain a unique and consistent brand identity across all platforms, striking a balance between harmony and distinctiveness. It's important to note that advocates don't need to be part of the development team. Anyone within the company who is familiar and willing to help and external advocates who can occasionally run manual adaptiveness tests can be helpful.

Maintaining uniqueness across different platforms is essential for several reasons: it reduces cognitive load by aligning with users' existing mental models, thus simplifying interaction and navigation; it builds trust as users feel more comfortable with apps that meet platform-specific expectations, potentially leading to better ratings and perceived quality; and it allows for customized experiences, leveraging each platform's unique strengths to enhance user engagement. This balance between conformity to platform norms and distinctiveness is key to creating successful, user-friendly applications.

22.2.1   Unique Features

While working with various Flutter apps, I noticed a few essential platform features that one should consider using. These are not the only features but the most common ones.

Scrollbars for Platform-Specific Behavior Adapt the scrollbar behavior to fit the platform norms. On mobile, opt for auto-hiding scrollbars; on desktop, use more prominent, always-visible ones.

```
Scrollbar(
  thumbVisibility: DeviceType.isDesktop,
  child: ListView(/* Your content */),
);
```

Multi-select Interactions with Keyboard and Touch Support Multi-select functionality in applications varies significantly between keyboard-driven and touch-based interactions. For desktop environments, multi-select is often enabled through keyboard shortcuts, such as Shift and Ctrl. This allows users to select multiple items in a list or grid seamlessly. Conversely, on touch devices, multi-select is typically handled through gestures, such as long presses, which are more intuitive for touch interactions. In this scenario, detecting which keys are down plays a unique role in each platform. Consider this condition:

```
if (Platform.isMacOS) {
  isDown = isKeyDown(
    {
      LogicalKeyboardKey.metaLeft,
      LogicalKeyboardKey.metaRight
    },
  );
} else {
  isDown = isKeyDown(
    {
      LogicalKeyboardKey.controlLeft,
      LogicalKeyboardKey.controlRight
    },
  );
}
```

Selectable Text for Enhanced User Interaction Ensure text is selectable on web and desktop platforms for user convenience.

```
SelectableText('Your selectable text here');

// or
SelectionArea(
  child: Scaffold(
    body: Center(
      child: Column(
        mainAxisAlignment: MainAxisAlignment.center,
        children: <Widget>[
          Text('Row 1'),
          Text('Row 2'),
          Text('Row 3'),
        ],
      ),
    ),
  ),
)
```

The `SelectionArea` widget is designed to provide users with an area to select. It features adaptive selection controls that can adjust to the user's preferences.

Context Menus and Tooltips for Intuitive Interactions Implement context menus for desktop apps with right-click functionality and simpler tap-based menus for mobile.

```
PopupMenuButton(
  onSelected: (Object? value) {/* Handle selection */},
  itemBuilder: (BuildContext context) {/* Build items */},
);
```

```
// Or
Tooltip(
  message: 'Tooltip',
  child: Text('Hover over the text to show a tooltip.'),
);
```

Drag and Drop Adapted for Input Methods

Drag and drop is a key interaction in apps, differing significantly between touch-based and pointer-based (mouse) inputs. Touch users often rely on visible drag handles or long-press gestures to initiate a drag, as the same finger is used for scrolling and dragging. Conversely, mouse users can easily differentiate between dragging and scrolling, typically using the mouse cursor for drag operations and the wheel or scrollbar for navigation.

In Flutter, drag and drop functionalities can be customized for different input methods:

- **For Touch Input**: Implement visible drag handles or activate drag with a long press.
- **For Mouse Input**: Allow direct item dragging without additional indicators.

```
// Using Draggable and DragTarget
// for custom drag-and-drop
Draggable(
  data: itemData,
  child: YourItemWidget(),
  feedback: YourItemDragRepresentation(),
);
DragTarget(
  onAccept: (receivedItemData) {
    // Handle the received data
  },
  builder: (context, candidateData, rejectedData) =>
      YourDropAreaWidget(),
);
```

This task can be challenging and require extensive logic. Alternatively, pre-made packages can handle many details for you. You can find some packages for this purpose on "pub.dev".

22.3 Conclusion

The fundamental aspects of creating adaptive applications in Flutter were explored, focusing on utilizing and enhancing the platform-specific features to craft a more intuitive and engaging user experience. From handling multi-select inter-actions to customizing UI elements like menu bars and scrollbars, we've covered a range of techniques to make your app feel at home on any device.

However, it's important to note that the scope of Flutter's adaptiveness is so vast that it cannot be fully encapsulated in just one chapter of a book. While this chapter provides a solid foundation, remember there's much more to discover and implement. You should now understand what adaptiveness means in Flutter, how to leverage its built-in features, and how to build upon these to tailor your application to meet both the platform standards and your creative vision.

CHAPTER 23

Responsive UI Techniques

Reviewer: Çaatay Ulusoy

Responsive Design, traditionally associated with adapting user interfaces to screen sizes, has evolved considerably from its web-centric origins. With mobile technology, this concept now encompasses a wider array of challenges. Users operate devices with varied screen specifics, and applications must seamlessly run across different operating systems, each offering unique experiences.

Flutter addresses the varying screen dimensions and ensures compatibility and optimal user experience across multiple platforms.

In the previous chapter, you learned about adaptive elements in Flutter. The only element that needed to be added was the responsive design. To remind us, adaptive design in Flutter refers to creating apps with layouts and features specifically tailored for different platforms (like iOS, Android, web, and desktop). In contrast, responsive design focuses on building a single layout that adjusts gracefully to fit various screen sizes and orientations.

In this chapter, you'll learn about the engineering aspect of responsive design and how to use it in Flutter.

23.1   Principles of Responsive Design

Responsive design principles pave the way for implementing multi-device layout patterns tailored to the Flutter framework. These principles are included, but not limited to:

1. **Flexibility**:   Emphasizing flexible layouts with Flutter's widgets like `Flexible` and `Expanded` allows UI elements to resize dynamically based on screen size.
2. **Adaptability**:   Employing breakpoints through Flutter's `MediaQuery` to create different UI representations for various screen dimensions, enhancing readability and user interaction.

3. **Consistency**: Keeping a consistent design language across devices using Flutter's theme system, ensuring a familiar user experience on every device.

4. **Performance Optimization**: Leveraging Flutter's performance features, such as efficient asset loading and custom widget rendering for different screen resolutions, to enhance app performance.

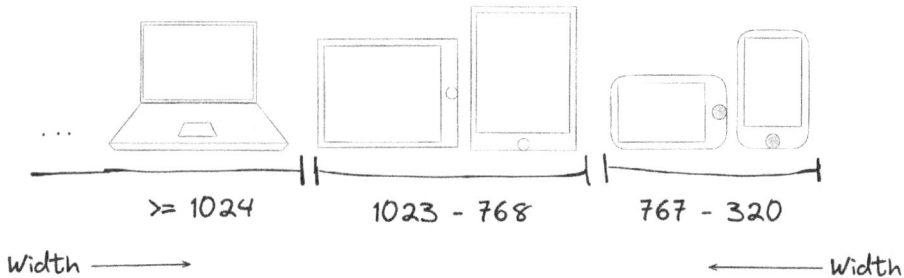

Figure 23.1: Devices Size Variations

Incorporating these principles into Flutter development, specific layout patterns emerge as effective solutions for multi-device compatibility:

1. **Mostly Fluid**: This pattern involves minor adjustments to the layout and spacing as the screen size changes, maintaining a fluid and consistent appearance across devices. Using widgets such as `GridView` , `Wrap` is an example of adapting this pattern in Flutter.

2. **Layout Shifter**: One of the most responsive patterns, it involves significant changes in layout across different breakpoints. This can include rearranging content blocks, altering navigation positioning, and implementing different layouts for different screen sizes or orientations using conditional statements with MediaQuery, for example, switching between a `Row` and `Column` layout.

3. **Off-Canvas**: Frequently used for navigation elements, this pattern hides secondary content off-screen, accessible through interactions like swiping or tapping a menu icon, saving screen space on smaller devices. Adapting the off-canvas pattern, using Flutter's `Drawer` widget for navigation on smaller screens, which can be hidden or shown based on the screen size or user interaction.

Moreover, in Flutter, three major considerations must be made: size, orientation, and device features such as density.

Let's explore how to achieve these principles and patterns in Flutter.

23.2 Approaches to Responsiveness in Flutter

In Flutter, achieving responsiveness in app design typically involves two main approaches: using `MediaQuery` based on device screen size and incorporating the `LayoutBuilder` widget. Both methods offer unique advantages and can be used separately or in combination to create highly adaptive and flexible user interfaces.

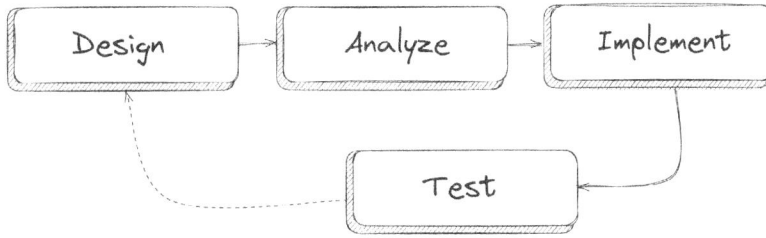

Figure 23.2: Responsiveness Design Flow

23.2.1 Responsiveness Based on Media Query Size

The first approach to creating a responsive UI in Flutter is using the `MediaQuery` class. This method primarily focuses on the device screen size to determine how the UI should adapt.

How It Works:

- MediaQuery provides information about the device's current configuration, such as screen size, orientation, and pixel ratio.
- Developers can define different layouts or styles based on these parameters. For example, a grid layout with two columns on a mobile device might change to four columns on a tablet or desktop.

```
Widget build(BuildContext context) {
  var screenWidth = MediaQuery.sizeOf(context).width;

  if (screenWidth < 600) {
    // Mobile layout
    return mobileLayout();
  } else {
    // Tablet/Desktop layout
    return tabletDesktopLayout();
  }
}
```

23.2.2 Incorporating LayoutBuilder

The second approach involves using the `LayoutBuilder` widget. `LayoutBuilder` provides the dimensions of the parent widget, allowing for more granular control over the layout based on the space available to the widget.

How It Works:

- LayoutBuilder passes the parent widget's constraints to its builder function, enabling the child to adapt its size and layout accordingly.

Responsive UI Techniques 463

- This approach is particularly useful when the widget's size depends on its parent rather than the screen size, allowing for more dynamic and flexible layouts.

```
Widget build(BuildContext context) {
  return LayoutBuilder(
    builder: (BuildContext context,
        BoxConstraints constraints) {
      if (constraints.maxWidth < 600) {
        // Layout for smaller width (like mobile)
        return mobileLayout();
      } else {
        // Layout for larger width (like tablet or desktop)
        return tabletDesktopLayout();
      }
    },
  );
}
```

23.2.3   Flutter Responsive Considerations

When building a responsive application in Flutter, there are several key considerations to ensure your app adapts effectively to various screen sizes and orientations. Here's a detailed approach:

Grid Model and Layout Strategy: Conceptualize your UI grid model for different screen sizes. This involves planning what content and elements to show on each screen size and orientation. Design your grid to be flexible and adaptive to ensure a consistent device experience.

Define Breakpoints: The breakpoint concept in responsive design involves defining specific screen sizes at which a layout adjusts to provide an optimal viewing experience across different devices. Consider defining a set of breakpoints representing different screen sizes. Using an enum or a class to encapsulate these breakpoints can simplify adapting your UI to various screen dimensions. Here's a common set of breakpoints:

```
enum ScreenSize {
  // Phone in portrait
  compact(maxWidth: 600),
  // Tablet in portrait or Foldable in portrait (unfolded)
  medium(maxWidth: 840),
  // Phone in landscape or Tablet in landscape or
  // Foldable in landscape (unfolded) or Desktop
  expanded(maxWidth: 1200),
  // Desktop, TV
  large(maxWidth: 1600);
```

```
const ScreenSize({required this.maxWidth});

final double maxWidth;

bool isSmallerThan(double screenWidth) =>
    screenWidth < maxWidth;

static ScreenSize getScreenSize(double screenWidth) {
  if (ScreenSize.compact.isSmallerThan(
    screenWidth,
  )) {
    return ScreenSize.compact;
  } else if (ScreenSize.medium.isSmallerThan(
    screenWidth,
  )) {
    return ScreenSize.medium;
  } else if (ScreenSize.expanded.isSmallerThan(
    screenWidth,
  )) {
    return ScreenSize.expanded;
  } else {
    return ScreenSize.large;
  }
}
}
```

Break Down to Smaller Widgets: Modularize your UI by breaking it down into smaller, reusable widgets. This enhances readability and maintainability and allows for a more flexible composition of layouts for different screen sizes.

Creating a Responsive Builder Widget: Implement a widget that uses LayoutBuilder to render different UIs based on the screen size. Here is an example based on Strategy design patterns:

```
abstract class LayoutStrategy {
  Widget build();
}

class MediumLayoutStrategy implements LayoutStrategy {
  @override
  Widget build(BuildContext context) {
    return const Center(
      child: Text('MediumLayoutStrategy'),
    );
  }
}

class ExpandedLayoutStrategy implements LayoutStrategy {
  @override
```

```
  Widget build(BuildContext context) {
    return const Center(
      child: Text('ExpandedLayoutStrategy'),
    );
  }
}

class LargeLayoutStrategy implements LayoutStrategy {
  @override
  Widget build(BuildContext context) {
    return const Center(
      child: Text('LargeLayoutStrategy'),
    );
  }
}
```

Then, create the ResponsiveLayout widget to accept layout strategies:

```
class ResponsiveLayout extends StatelessWidget {
  final LayoutStrategy compactLayoutStrategy;
  final LayoutStrategy mediumLayoutStrategy;
  final LayoutStrategy expandedLayoutStrategy;
  final LayoutStrategy largeLayoutStrategy;

  const ResponsiveLayout({
    super.key,
    required this.compactLayoutStrategy,
    required this.mediumLayoutStrategy,
    required this.expandedLayoutStrategy,
    required this.largeLayoutStrategy,
  });

  @override
  Widget build(BuildContext context) {
    return LayoutBuilder(
      builder: (BuildContext context,
          BoxConstraints constraints) {
        final layoutStrategy =
            _getLayoutStrategy(constraints.maxWidth);
        return layoutStrategy.build(context);
      },
    );
  }

  LayoutStrategy _getLayoutStrategy(double width) {
    final screenSize = ScreenSize.getScreenSize(width);

    switch (screenSize) {
```

```
      case ScreenSize.compact:
        return compactLayoutStrategy;
      case ScreenSize.medium:
        return mediumLayoutStrategy;
      case ScreenSize.expanded:
        return expandedLayoutStrategy;
      case ScreenSize.large:
        return largeLayoutStrategy;
    }
  }
}
```

In this design, ResponsiveLayout is more versatile. Different layout strategies can be defined and injected as needed, allowing customization of the responsive behavior per use case.

23.2.4 Widgets Beyond Basic

Crafting a responsive UI requires going beyond basic layout widgets to leverage advanced widgets. Let's explore these widgets in detail, providing practical examples and scenarios to illustrate their importance in responsive Flutter development.

Each widget plays a specific role in achieving a fluid, adaptable design, such as:

CustomSingleChildLayout

Perfect for custom positioning or sizing a single child within its parent, especially when standard widgets don't suffice. This is particularly useful when you need to position or size a child widget in a way that standard layout widgets like Container, Column, or Row cannot achieve.

```
class MyCustomLayout extends StatelessWidget {
  const MyCustomLayout({super.key});

  @override
  Widget build(BuildContext context) {
    return CustomSingleChildLayout(
      delegate: MyCustomDelegate(),
      child: Container(color: Colors.blue),
    );
  }
}

class MyCustomDelegate extends SingleChildLayoutDelegate {
  @override
  BoxConstraints getConstraintsForChild(
      BoxConstraints constraints) {
    // Custom constraints for the child
    return constraints;
```

```
  }

  @override
  Offset getPositionForChild(Size size, Size childSize) {
    // Position child at the bottom-right corner
    return Offset(size.width - childSize.width,
        size.height - childSize.height);
  }

  @override
  bool shouldRelayout(MyCustomDelegate oldDelegate) =>
      false;
}
```

The layout logic is handled by a delegate class that extends `SingleChildLayoutDelegate`. This delegate provides the flexibility to define custom rules for how the child should be sized and positioned. Since `CustomSingleChildLayout` performs layout calculations at runtime, it's more performance-intensive than standard widgets. It's recommended to use it when necessary and avoid overuse for simpler layout tasks.

This example demonstrates how `CustomSingleChildLayout` works; however, remember that the Stack widget is more appropriate for simple cases, such as aligning a widget to one edge.

CustomMultiChildLayout

It is ideal for complex layouts involving multiple children whose positions and sizes are interdependent. This is common in custom UI designs where standard layout widgets like `Row`, `Column`, or `Grid` fall short.

```
class MyComplexLayout extends StatelessWidget {
  const MyComplexLayout({super.key});

  @override
  Widget build(BuildContext context) {
    return CustomMultiChildLayout(
      delegate: MyComplexLayoutDelegate(),
      children: <Widget>[
        LayoutId(
          id: 'first',
          child: Container(
              color: Colors.red, width: 100, height: 100),
        ),
        LayoutId(
          id: 'second',
          child: Container(
              color: Colors.green, width: 100, height: 100),
        ),
      ],
```

```
    );
  }
}

class MyComplexLayoutDelegate
    extends MultiChildLayoutDelegate {
  @override
  void performLayout(Size size) {
    // Position 'first' widget
    layoutChild('first', BoxConstraints.loose(size));
    positionChild('first', Offset.zero);

    // Position 'second' widget to the right of 'first'
    if (hasChild('second')) {
      Size firstSize =
          layoutChild('first', BoxConstraints.loose(size));
      layoutChild('second', BoxConstraints.loose(size));
      positionChild('second', Offset(firstSize.width, 0));
    }
  }

  @override
  bool shouldRelayout(
          MyComplexLayoutDelegate oldDelegate) =>
      false;
}
```

The layout logic is managed by a delegate that extends `MultiChildLayoutDelegate`. This delegate defines the positioning and sizing rules for each child. The delegate offers a canvas where each child can be placed and sized based on custom rules.

It's worth noting that you need to understand what you're doing inside `performLayout`. This is because the handling of this part is typically done by `RenderObjects` for standard widgets. If implemented incorrectly, it could result in performance issues. Moreover, utilizing `shouldRelayout` logic can help optimize calculations.

FittedBox

Automatically scales and positions a child widget within its parent, maintaining the child's aspect ratio. This is crucial for elements like images or videos, where maintaining the original proportions is essential for visual integrity.

Imagine a scenario where you have a profile picture that needs to fit within a circular avatar. The picture should cover the entire avatar space without getting distorted when the screen size changes.

```
FittedBox(
  fit: BoxFit.cover,
  child: Image.network('https://example.com/image.jpg'),
)
```

The `fit` property of `FittedBox` allows you to define how the child should be scaled and positioned. Options include `BoxFit.fill`, `BoxFit.contain`, `BoxFit.cover`, and others provide a different scaling behavior.

FractionallySizedBox

Instead of using absolute dimensions, `FractionallySizedBox` allows for relative sizing, which is crucial for responsive layouts. It ensures that the child widget scales proportionately to its parent's size. You can specify the width and height factors as fractions, giving you fine-grained control over the size of the child widget relative to the parent.

Consider a scenario where you need a button that always occupies a certain percentage of the screen width, regardless of the device size, to ensure consistent usability and aesthetics.

```
FractionallySizedBox(
  widthFactor: 0.5, // 50% of parent's width
  heightFactor: 0.3, // 30% of parent's height
  child: Container(color: Colors.purple),
)
```

The `widthFactor` and `heightFactor` properties determine what fraction of the parent's width and height the child should occupy, respectively.

AspectRatio

`AspectRatio` is ideal for scenarios where the child widget needs to maintain a specific width-to-height ratio. It automatically adjusts the child's size while keeping the ratio constant, vital in responsive layouts where the available space can vary significantly.

Consider a scenario where a gallery of images must retain their aspect ratio regardless of the screen size or device orientation.

```
AspectRatio(
  aspectRatio: 16 / 9,
  child: Container(color: Colors.orange),
)
```

The `AspectRatio` property is a double value representing the width-to-height ratio. For example, an aspect ratio of `16 / 9` is common for widescreen videos.

Expanded and Flexible

These widgets allow for flexible space distribution among children within `Row` and `Column`.

```
Row(
  children: <Widget>[
    Expanded(
```

```
      flex: 2,
      child: Container(color: Colors.blue),
    ),
    Expanded(
      flex: 3,
      child: Container(color: Colors.red),
    ),
  ],
)
```

Or using in Column

```
Column(
  children: <Widget>[
    Flexible(
      flex: 1,
      child: Container(color: Colors.green),
    ),
    Flexible(
      flex: 1,
      child: Container(color: Colors.yellow),
    ),
  ],
)
```

Key differences:

Expanded: Forces its child to fill the available space along the main axis (horizontally in Row, vertically in Column). Expanded is a shorthand for Flexible with a flex factor of 1 and fit set to FlexFit.tight, meaning it doesn't allow its children to shrink.

Flexible: More versatile than Expanded, it allows more fine control over allocated space. The flex factor determines the proportion of each child's available space. The fit property (FlexFit.loose or FlexFit.tight) determines whether the child is forced to take up all the available space (FlexFit.tight, similar to Expanded) or can be smaller (FlexFit.loose).

Wrap

Wrap is ideal for situations where you have a collection of elements that need to adjust to the screen width, such as a group of chips, buttons, or tags. It ensures the layout remains clean and uncluttered, regardless of the screen size or orientation. Unlike Row or Column, which might overflow if their children do not fit in the available space, Wrap automatically transitions its children to the next line or column, making it highly effective for responsive layouts.

Imagine creating a responsive layout where you must display a set of chips representing selectable options. These chips should be wrapped on smaller screens to ensure they are visible and accessible.

```
class ResponsiveChips extends StatelessWidget {
  final List<String> options;

  const ResponsiveChips({
    super.key,
    required this.options,
  });

  @override
  Widget build(BuildContext context) {
    return Wrap(
      alignment: WrapAlignment.spaceBetween,
      direction: Axis.horizontal,
      spacing: 8.0, // gap between adjacent chips
      runSpacing: 4.0, // gap between lines
      children: options
          .map(
            (option) => Chip(label: Text(option)),
          )
          .toList(),
    );
  }
}
```

Key Features:

Direction: The `direction` property allows you to specify the direction in which the children are laid out (either horizontally or vertically).

Spacing and Run Spacing: You can control the spacing between the children in a run (`spacing`) and the spacing between the runs themselves (`runSpacing`).

Alignment: `Wrap` provides various ways to align children along the main axis (`alignment`) and the cross axis (`crossAxisAlignment`).

Understanding and effectively utilizing these advanced widgets is key to developing responsive Flutter applications that provide a seamless experience across various devices and screen sizes.

23.2.5   Flutter Responsiveness Tips

Engineers should consider a few important things when designing a responsive app with Flutter.

1. Avoid using hard-coded values for dimensions, font sizes, and other properties in your widgets. Instead, use relative sizes or define these values centrally and adjust them based on screen size or other conditions.
2. As you learned, responsive design concerns layout, content sizing, and other considerations. Therefore, it is essential to define proper sizing in the theme.

In chapter 25, Theming in Flutter, you will see how to use ThemeExtension. Using that, you can define your customized size based on the device. You can also define different themes using `.copyWith` to override the proper sizes for theme components.

3. Modern devices often have notches, cutouts, or rounded corners, which can obscure UI elements. For example, you can use `MediaQuery.paddingOf(context);` to detect the safe areas of the screen where content can be displayed without being hidden by these features or use the `SafeArea` widget, which automatically applies padding based on the device's physical constraints.

4. The on-screen keyboard can affect the layout by reducing the visible space. Utilize `MediaQuery.viewInsetsOf(context);` to adjust your layout when the keyboard is visible.

5. Test manually; it's just important that you test your UI.

6. Respect your user settings; some users may use an orientation lock designed for a good default experience.

There is one more thing left, especially on mobile, and that is orientation. Let's explore it in the next chapter.

23.3   Adapting UI to Screen Orientation

Managing the UI layout for different screen orientations, portraits, and landscapes is necessary in Flutter to ensure a flexible and adaptive user experience. I have seen users locked on specific orientations, and designing to consider different organizations is important to enhance their experience.

23.3.1   Utilizing Orientation in Flutter

In Flutter, there are two ways to determine the orientation.

1. **Detect Orientation with MediaQuery**: Determine the device's current orientation using `MediaQuery.orientationOf(context)`. It returns either `Orientation.portrait` or `Orientation.landscape`.

2. **Dynamic Layouts with OrientationBuilder**: This widget listens for orientation changes and rebuilds its child with an appropriate layout for the current orientation.

As you can see, these are very similar to determining the size. To create distinct layouts for portrait and landscape orientations, you can do similar to `LayoutBuilder`

```
Widget build(BuildContext context) {
  return OrientationBuilder(
    builder: (context, orientation) {
      return orientation == Orientation.portrait
```

```
        ? buildPortraitLayout()
        : buildLandscapeLayout();
    },
  );
}
```

The tips given in the previous section can also be applied here. For example, you can use adaptive widgets such as `Grid` to respond to orientation or size changes.

```
class GalleryApp extends StatelessWidget {
  const GalleryApp({super.key});

  @override
  Widget build(BuildContext context) {
    return MaterialApp(
      home: Scaffold(
        body: OrientationBuilder(
          builder: (context, orientation) {
            return GridView.count(
              crossAxisCount:
                  orientation == Orientation.portrait
                      ? 2
                      : 3,
              children: List.generate(20, (index) {
                return Center(
                  child: Text(
                    'Item $index',
                  ),
                );
              }),
            );
          },
        ),
      ),
    );
  }
}
```

23.3.2   Using LayoutBuilder and OrientationBuilder

Refactoring the `ResponsiveLayout` also considers the device orientation can significantly enhance its adaptability. By incorporating `OrientationBuilder` and `LayoutBuilder`, the layout can respond dynamically to screen size and orientation changes. Here's how the refactored `ResponsiveLayout` might look:

```
class CompactLayoutStrategy implements LayoutStrategy {
  @override
```

```
  Widget build(BuildContext context) { //<---
    return MediaQuery.orientationOf(context) == //<---
            Orientation.portrait //<---
        ? const Text('MobilePortraitLayout') //<---
        : const Text('MobileLandscapeLayout'); //<---
  }
}
```

In this refactored version, `OrientationBuilder` is used to determine the current orientation (portrait or landscape), and `LayoutBuilder` is used to provide the constraints. The `ResponsiveLayout` decides which specific layout to render based on these two factors. This allows for more nuanced control over the UI, ensuring the layout remains optimal and user-friendly across different screen sizes and orientations.

23.3.3 Locking device orientation

Flutter provides the flexibility to control the device orientation for your app. This can be particularly useful when maintaining a specific orientation is crucial for the app's functionality or user experience.

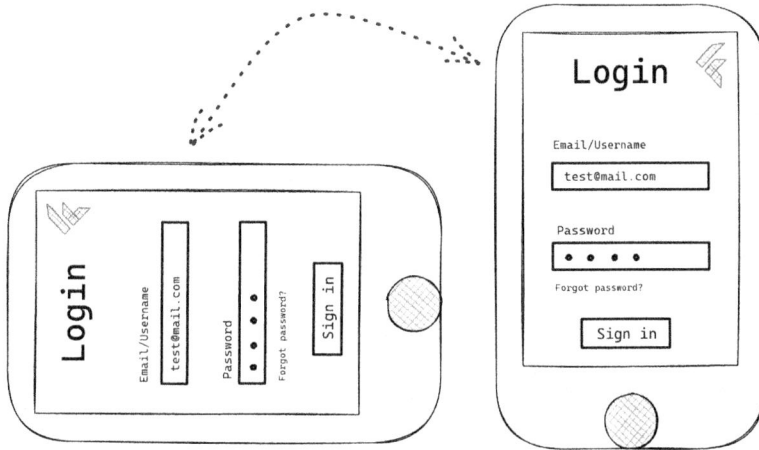

Figure 23.3: Locking Device Orientation

If your app is designed to work exclusively in one orientation (like portrait or landscape), you can lock the device to that orientation. This is often used in games or media apps where the orientation impacts the user interaction and experience.

Alternatively, you can specify multiple supported orientations while excluding others. For instance, you should allow both portrait orientations but not landscape.

To set the preferred orientations, use `SystemChrome.setPreferredOrientations()` method. This is typically done in the `main()` method before the app is run.

```
void main() {
  WidgetsFlutterBinding.ensureInitialized();
  SystemChrome.setPreferredOrientations([ //<---
    DeviceOrientation.portraitUp, //<---
  ]).then((_) { //<---
    runApp(const MyApp());
  });
}
```

In this implementation, `SystemChrome.setPreferredOrientations()` is called with a list containing `DeviceOrientation.portraitUp`. This ensures that the app will only be displayed in the portrait-up orientation. You can customize this list based on your app's specific needs, choosing from various `DeviceOrientation` values to define your app's supported orientations.

23.4   Conclusion

By utilizing Flutter's powerful layout widgets, such as `OrientationBuilder`, `LayoutBuilder` developers can build interfaces that adapt elegantly to different screen sizes and orientations. Combining these tools and approaches creates dynamic, flexible, and visually appealing UIs that maintain functionality and aesthetic integrity, regardless of the device used.

As a result, embracing these responsive design principles is essential for any Flutter developer looking to create versatile and robust mobile applications.

CHAPTER 24

i18n and l10n

Reviewer: Dominik Roszkowski

The concepts of translation (t9n), localization (l10n), internationalization (i18n), and globalization (g11n) play roles in shaping user experiences across diverse geographies and cultures. These terms, often abbreviated numerically for their lengthy character count, are not only about translating text but involve a comprehensive approach to making apps adaptable to various languages, regions, and cultural nuances.

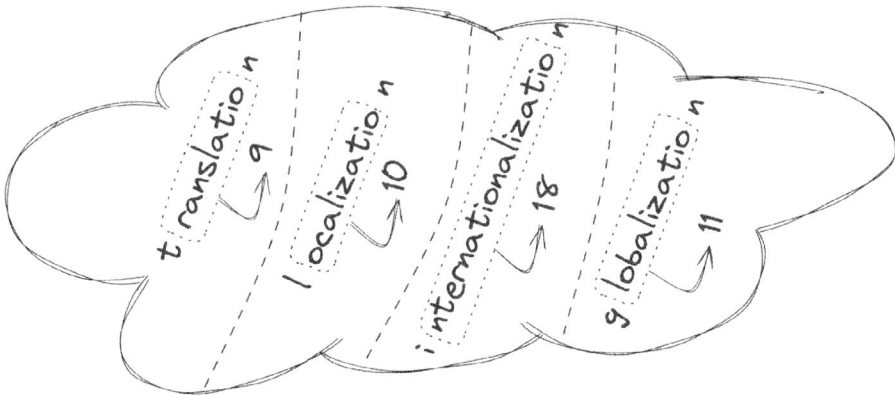

Figure 24.1: t9n, l10n, i18n, g11n letter counts

This chapter delves deep into the engineering aspects of i18n and l10n within the Flutter ecosystem. Moving beyond the basics, we will explore advanced strategies and best practices that enable developers to integrate these critical components into their applications, ensuring a truly global and inclusive user experience.

24.1   i18n vs. l10n: Key Differences

Internationalization (i18n) and Localization (l10n) are two sides of the same coin in the app development world, yet they serve distinct purposes. Understanding their differences is crucial for developers creating apps with a global reach.

Internationalization (i18n) is designing and building an application to make it adaptable to various languages and regions without requiring significant changes in the source code. It's about creating a flexible framework that can handle multiple languages, character sets, date formats, currencies, and other region-specific elements. In Flutter, this means designing your app's layout and functions to support different languages and cultural norms seamlessly.

Localization (l10n), on the other hand, is the process of adapting your application to a specific region or language. This goes beyond mere text translation; it includes adapting graphics, adapting to local customs and regulations, and even changing the layout to suit different reading directions. Localization is tailoring the experience to a specific audience, ensuring the app feels natural and intuitive to users from a particular region or language group.

Even within the same country, needing different locales in your app is typical. Regional variations in language, cultural references, legal requirements, and even date and number formats can significantly impact user experience. However, apps only sometimes require multiple localizations within a single nation. For example, Norway typically has two main languages, Bokmål and Nynorsk. Many speak both; this does not include English, which almost everyone speaks. So, it's typical that even if your app is supposed to be only regional in Norway, you still need different language variations.

I have seen many apps that must adopt this concept from the beginning, even if they don't need it initially. Preparing your app for localization from the outset can be a wise strategy. Anticipating future expansion and user diversity allows smoother transitions as the app grows and enters new markets. Furthermore, the effort required to retrofit an app for localization at a later stage can be considerably more than during the initial development phase.

Preparing your app from the beginning for internationalization and localization is good practice, especially if the process is manageable.

24.2 Implementing Internationalization in Flutter

There are two approaches to i18n in Flutter. You can go *the official* way, and it will provide you with most of the things you need, but there are some quite popular *unofficial* solutions. It's typically enough to use the official approach, but in teams that have origins in native or web development, folks sometimes decide to use some more custom approaches.

Implementing internationalization (i18n) and localization (l10n) in Flutter is straightforward in an official way. You'll require the `flutter_localizations` package from the Flutter SDK and the `intl` package.

```
// pubspec.yaml
dependencies:
```

```
flutter:
  sdk: flutter
flutter_localizations:
  sdk: flutter
intl: any
```

Create a `l10n.yaml` file in your Flutter project's root directory to specify the template and output file names. The properties are self-explanatory.

```
arb-dir: lib/l10n
template-arb-file: app_en.arb
output-localization-file: app_localizations.dart
```

Next, populate your `lib/l10n` directory with `.arb` files, starting with the `app_en.arb` template file. For instance:

```
// app_en.arb
{
  "helloWorld": "Hello World!",
  "@helloWorld": {
    "description": "Give as much context as possible here"
  }
}
```

Create corresponding `.arb` files like `app_no.arb` for additional languages like Norwegian.

```
// app_no.arb
{
  "helloWorld": "Hallo Verden!",
}
```

Execute `flutter pub get` or `flutter run` or later `flutter gen-l10n` for automatic code generation. In your project's `.dart_tool/flutter_gen/gen_l10n` directory, you'll find the `app_localizations.dart` file. This file can be utilized as follows:

```
import 'package:flutter/material.dart';
import 'package:flutter_gen/gen_l10n/app_localizations.dart';

main() {
  runApp(const MaterialApp(
    title: 'Localizations Sample App',
    locale: Locale('en'),
    localizationsDelegates:
        AppLocalizations.localizationsDelegates,
```

```
      supportedLocales: AppLocalizations.supportedLocales,
      home: MyHomeIntl(),
  ));
}

class MyHomeIntl extends StatelessWidget {
  const MyHomeIntl({super.key});

  @override
  Widget build(BuildContext context) {
    return Scaffold(
      body: Column(
        children: [
          Text(AppLocalizations.of(context).helloWorld),
        ],
      ),
    );
  }
}
```

AppLocalizations automatically generates all necessary locales and delegates.

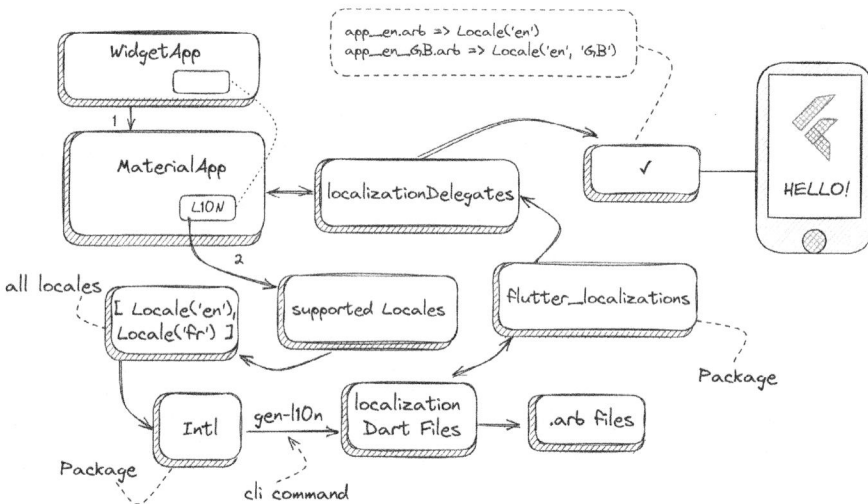

Figure 24.2: Flutter i18n and l10n Essential Components

24.2.1   Application Resource Bundle (ARB)

ARB is a localization resource format based on JSON, making it simple, extensible, and easy to use. Understanding it will help you implement advanced concepts. Let's explore more.

Defining your resource ID properly and adding attributes to the main file is important. This will ensure that there is enough context and description for the resource. In addition to the resource ID and resource value, a resource can also have a set of additional attributes. These attributes are embedded in an attribute item, keyed by the original resource ID and a prefix character '@.'

```
"helloWorld": "Hello World!",
"@helloWorld": {
    "type": "text",
    "context": "HomePage",
    "description": "Give as much context as possible here"
},
```

I can include type to support my variable in this code. If you use VS code, you can use the ARB Editor plugin from Google, which can be very useful in formatting and editing these files.

Placeholders, plurals, and selects are essential components in ARB (Application Resource Bundle) files, especially when dealing with complex localization scenarios in Flutter. These features allow for dynamic and context-sensitive translations, catering to various languages and grammatical rules.

Placeholders in ARB files are used to insert dynamic values into localized strings. They are marked with curly braces and can be either positional or named. Use descriptive names inside curly braces (e.g., {username}, {date}). This makes the code more readable and maintainable. You can define types for the placeholder variables, and Flutter's code generation will make sure to use the correct type (String, DateTime, double, int, num).

```
{
  "greetingMessage": "Hello, {username}! Today is {date}.",
  "@greetingMessage": {
    "placeholders": {
      "username": {
                "type": "String",
        "description": "Name of the user"
      },
      "date": {
                "type": "String",
        "description": "Current date"
      }
    }
  }
}
```

In Flutter

```
Text(
  AppLocalizations.of(context)!.greetingMessage(
```

```
    'username',
    'date',
  ),
)
```

Pluralization in ARB files is handled using ICU syntax, accommodating different plural forms based on the number.

ICU Message Syntax, part of the International Components for Unicode (ICU) project, is a widely used standard for handling complex message patterns in software localization. It's particularly useful for formatting messages in a way sensitive to various languages' grammatical rules.

This is crucial for languages with complex plural rules.

```
{
  "emailCount":
  "{count, plural, =0 {no emails} =1 {one email} other {{count} emails}}",
  "@emailCount": {
    "placeholders": {
      "count": {
                "type": "num",
        "description": "The number of emails"
      }
    }
  }
}
```

In Flutter

```
Text(AppLocalizations.of(context)!.emailCount(1)),
Text(AppLocalizations.of(context)!.emailCount(0)),
Text(AppLocalizations.of(context)!.emailCount(5)),

// Jeden e-mail
// Zero e-maili / Brak e-mali
// 5 e-maili
```

Selects in ARB files are used for conditional strings based on a key's value. This is particularly useful for gender-based translations or other conditional scenarios.

```
{
  "greeting":
"{gender, select, male {Mr.{name}} female {Ms.{name}} oth {Hi{name}}}",
  "@greeting": {
    "placeholders": {
      "gender": {
        "description": "Gender of the user"
```

```
      },
      "name": {
        "description": "Name of the user"
      }
    }
  }
}
```

In Flutter

```
Text(
  AppLocalizations.of(context)!.greeting(
    'male',
    'name',
  ),
)
```

Providing clear file context, with types and examples, eases maintenance, especially with external translators or teams.

```
"costText": "Your pending cost is {COST}",
    "@costText": {
        "type": "text",
        "context": "Subscription:MainPanel",
        "description": "balance statement.",
        "placeholders": {
            "COST": {
                "type": "num",
                "example": "$123.45",
                "description": "cost presented with currency symbol"
            }
        }
    }
```

In Flutter's ARB files, escaping syntax includes characters like {, }, and ' as literals in your translations, especially when using ICU Message Syntax.

```
{
  "literalBracesExample": "Hello! '{Isn''t}'! wonderful day?"
}
```

These characters are normally reserved for defining placeholders and special formatting. Make sure you enable the **use-escaping** flag by adding the following to l10n.yaml:

In Flutter, the `intl` package provides the `NumberFormat`[1] and `DateFormat`[2] classes for localizing numbers, currencies, and dates according to various locales. The `NumberFormat` class has several constructors to format numbers in different styles. For example, `decimalPattern` can be used to format currency values compactly.

```
{
  "formattedCurrency": "Total: {value}",
  "@formattedCurrency": {
    "description": "Currency value formatted compactly",
    "placeholders": {
      "value": {
        "type": "double",
        "format": "decimalPattern",
        "optionalParameters": {
          "decimalDigits": 2
        }
      }
    }
  }
}
```

In Flutter

```
Text(
  AppLocalizations.of(context)!.formattedCurrency(1200000),
  // 1,200,000
)
```

Similarly, the `DateFormat` class handles the localization of date strings. You can specify formats like `yMd` for year, month, and day.

```
{
  "formattedDate": "Date: {date}",
  "@formattedDate": {
    "description": "Formatted date",
    "placeholders": {
      "date": {
        "type": "DateTime",
        "format": "yMd"
      }
    }
  }
}
```

---

[1] https://api.flutter.dev/flutter/intl/NumberFormat-class.html
[2] https://api.flutter.dev/flutter/intl/DateFormat-class.html

and in Flutter

```
Text(
  AppLocalizations.of(context)!.formattedDate(
    DateTime.utc(1959, 7, 9),
  ),
)
```

In Flutter, when dealing with DateTime values in placeholders, the `DateFormat` class from the `intl` package is utilized for formatting. This class offers 41 format variations, each corresponding to a specific DateFormat factory constructor. These formats adapt to the app's locale settings, displaying dates in the appropriate local format. For instance, in the US English locale (`en_US`), a date might be formatted as "7/9/1959", while in a Russian locale (`ru_RU`), the same date would be formatted as "9.07.1959".

To explicitly format dates according to a specific locale, regardless of the user's device settings, you can use the `initializeDateFormatting` function from the `intl` package. For example, initializing with `de_DE` would format dates according to German conventions:

```
// Initialize German locale
initializeDateFormatting('de_DE', null);
// Use German date format
var formatter = DateFormat.yMd('de_DE');
```

This approach ensures that your app consistently uses the specified locale for date formatting.

24.2.2 Advanced tips and tricks

While using these packages with other users, I've come across several tips and tricks that I think are worth sharing with you.

Generated files

When using Flutter's `gen_l10n` tool for localization, the generated files are typically part of a synthetic package and are not included in version control systems like Git. If you need to track these localization files in your version control system, you can modify your `l10n.yaml` file with specific configurations.

```
# l10n.yaml
synthetic-package: false
output-dir: lib/l10n/generated
```

The **output-dir** parameter specifies the directory where the generated localization classes will be placed. You can set this option to generate the localization code in a location different from the default. If `output-dir` is not specified, the generated files will be placed in the same directory as your ARB files, as defined by arb-dir. The **synthetic-package** flag is set to true by default, meaning the generated output files are part of a synthetic package and are not placed in the project's directory structure. However, if you set synthetic-package to false, the localization files will be generated directly in the directory specified by arb-dir or output-dir if it's specified.

Avoid null checking

You noticed that we used ! in the example code above. In Flutter's l10n.yaml configuration, you can set nullable-getter to false to ensure that getters in the generated localizations class are non-nullable. This change removes the need for repeated null checks when accessing localization messages.

```
# l10n.yaml
nullable-getter: false

// in Flutter
AppLocalizations.of(context).helloWorld
```

Override the locale

Sometimes, you may need to override the current locale for a specific application part, which is entirely possible. You can use the Localizations.override factory constructor. Here's an example where the helloWorld message is displayed in both the default locale and an overridden Spanish locale:

```
@override
Widget build(BuildContext context) {
  return Column(
    children: [
      // Display message in the default locale
      Text(
        AppLocalizations.of(context)!.helloWorld,
      ),

      // Override locale to Spanish for the next Text widget
      Localizations.override(
        context: context,
        locale: const Locale('es'),
        child: Builder(
          builder: (BuildContext context) {
            // Display message in the overridden locale
            return Text(
              AppLocalizations.of(context)!.helloWorld,
            );
          },
        ),
      ),
```

```
      ],
   );
}
```

In this code, the first Text widget uses the default locale, while the second Text widget, wrapped in Localizations.override, displays the same message but in Spanish (es locale).

Requires resource attribute

You have seen throughout this chapter how important it is to pass along context and metadata via attributes to clarify the context. You can make it a requirement.

Use required-resource-attributes: true in your l10n.yaml file, and you get an error when running the flutter gen-l10n command if attributes are missing.

Output class name

If you want to change the output class name, use the **output-class** parameter with your class name in the l10n.yaml file.

```
output-class: S
```

For example, S here is shorter. S.of(context)!.helloWorld

Extracting Localization Data

When localizing an app with the Dart intl package, one of the steps is to extract and generate localization files. The process of doing this may vary depending on the version being used.

Missing Translations

It's always nice to know what has been missed in translation so you can force the gen-l10n command to give you a report.

```
# l10n.yaml
untranslated-messages-file: l10n_errors.txt
```

You can use this file to check for any missing content or translation errors. This is particularly useful for CD/CI or **pre-push** git hooks.

Understanding Localizations Widget in Flutter

In Flutter, the Localizations widget plays a key role in setting the locale for its child widgets and determining the localized resources they use. When the system's locale changes, the WidgetsApp widget, which creates a Localizations widget, automatically rebuilds it to reflect these changes.

To retrieve the current locale of an app, you can use the Localizations.localeOf() method:

```
Locale myLocale = Localizations.localeOf(context);
```

This code snippet allows you to access the locale currently used by the app.

Naming Conventions for .arb Files in Flutter Localization

In Flutter localization, .arb files are named following a convention that includes ISO language and regional codes. The file names should contain underscores and adhere to the ISO 639-1 language codes, with the option to add ISO 3166 regional codes for different language regions.

- **English Locales**:
    - US English: `app_en.arb`
    - Great Britain: `app_en_GB.arb`
    - Australia: `app_en_AU.arb`

- **Other Languages**:
    - France (French): `app_fr.arb`
    - French Canada: `app_fr_CA.arb`
    - For a project supporting multiple English-speaking regions, you might have:

- Base fallback (US default): `/lib/l10n/app_en.arb`
- Australia: `/lib/l10n/app_en_AU.arb`
- Great Britain and Ireland: `/lib/l10n/app_en_GB.arb`

You'd only need the base file `app_en.arb` if only supporting English across all regions.

Always make sure your template file exists as the default file to fallback. Otherwise, your project will not compile.

In Flutter's .arb files, the `@@locale` key, although optional, serves as a validation tool to ensure the file is named correctly according to its locale. For instance, in `app_en.arb`, the presence of `@@locale: "en"` confirms that the file is appropriately named for the English locale, with `_en` being the crucial part of the file name. An incorrectly named file not matching its `@@locale` value will result in an exception.

```
// /lib/l10n/app_nb_NO.arb
{
    "@@locate": "nb_NO",
    "helloWorld": "Hallo Verden!",
}
```

Additionally, in Flutter, the order of locales in `supportedLocales` is critical for accurate locale resolution, using the `basicLocaleListResolution` algorithm. This prioritizes matching locales by language code (`languageCode`), script code (`scriptCode`), and country code (`countryCode`). For languages with multiple scripts, specifying `scriptCode` is crucial.

```
supportedLocales:<Locale>[
  Locale.fromSubtags(languageCode: 'zh'), // Generic Chinese
  Locale.fromSubtags(
    languageCode: 'zh',
    scriptCode: 'Hans',
  ), // Simplified Chinese
  Locale.fromSubtags(
    languageCode: 'zh',
    scriptCode: 'Hant',
  ), // Traditional Chinese
  Locale.fromSubtags(
    languageCode: 'zh',
    scriptCode: 'Hans',
    countryCode: 'CN',
  ), // Mainland China
  Locale.fromSubtags(
    languageCode: 'zh',
    scriptCode: 'Hant',
    countryCode: 'TW',
  ), // Taiwan
  Locale.fromSubtags(
    languageCode: 'zh',
    scriptCode: 'Hant',
    countryCode: 'HK',
  ), // Hong Kong
]
```

This approach ensures precise locale matching for diverse user settings, preventing issues like a Simplified Chinese user defaulting to Traditional Chinese in Taiwan.

Tools

It can be helpful to use certain tools when working with ARB files. This is not because you need help to handle them alone, but because as a project grows, it can quickly become overwhelming. Some useful tools include `arb_utils`, `poEditor`, or similar tools designed to assist with .arb files.

Real-time uptime mechanism

It is always advisable to have a tool or a process to help you add translations on the fly. This is because there may be instances where someone may want to change the translation quickly, and you would want to immediately start the next app release or delay the app release due to a small translation error. Therefore, it's best to have a solution that can help you handle such situations efficiently.

Defining a class for the app's localized resources

If you need to make multiple customizations, it's best to begin creating your Localization class and utilize the built-in text extraction feature from the `intl` package. This doesn't prevent you from using ARB files and the underlying mechanism, but you'll have to include the localization class that meets your specific needs.

Assets

last but not least, always make sure you are also supporting `assets` for different languages.

```
assets
|--- en
|----- flag.png
|--- fr
|----- flag.png
|--- fr_CA
|----- flag.png
|--- en_GB
|----- flag.png
```

24.3   Catering to Right-to-Left Languages

Supporting Right-to-Left (RTL) languages in Flutter apps opens the door to a broader global audience. RTL languages, used by about 1 billion people worldwide, include Arabic, Hebrew, and Persian/Farsi and are read from right to left, contrasting with the more common left-to-right (LTR) languages like English.

Figure 24.3: Right-to-Left vs Left-to-Right

When designing for RTL languages, it's essential to flip the UI layout horizontally, including navigation elements and text alignment. For instance, UI components and text in an RTL app are aligned to the right and flow from right to left. This might also involve mirroring icons and adjusting the placement of graphics to ensure proper alignment with the RTL layout.

Flutter simplifies the implementation of RTL support through its localization and directionality widgets. The `MaterialApp` widget in Flutter, for example, can be set to an RTL locale, automatically adapting the text direction and UI elements to RTL:

```
MaterialApp(
  locale: const Locale('fa'), // Farsi locale
  supportedLocales: const [Locale('fa'), Locale('en')],
  // Other properties...
);
```

In this setup, the `Directionality` widget plays a crucial role by setting the appropriate text direction. Flutter also offers directional versions of common widgets like `PositionedDirectional` and `Align` (using `AlignmentDirectional`), facilitating the development of layouts that adapt to RTL without extensive modifications.

Moreover, Flutter's `Icon` widget and packages like `flutter_svg` for SVG images have properties like `matchTextDirection`, which automatically mirror icons and images in RTL layouts. Packages like `auto_direction` can dynamically adjust text directionality for handling mixed-direction texts, ensuring consistency in the app's user interface.

Embracing globalization by integrating RTL layouts in Flutter apps is remarkably manageable and advantageous for connecting with a broader audience. Flutter's innate support and extensive range of widgets designed for RTL adaptation make this process efficient and user-friendly.

24.4   Conclusion

It is necessary to include internationalization (i18n) in the development of any application. However, it can be a complicated and resource-intensive process to add support for multiple languages and cultural norms later on. Therefore, it is recommended to use Unicode for encoding since it supports various characters and symbols from different languages.

Additionally, developers should design software architecture to easily adapt to different language inputs, text directions (such as right-to-left scripts), and varied character sets. This forward-thinking approach not only saves time in the long run but also broadens the potential user base from the initial release of the application.

Regarding localization (l10n), it's not just about translating text; it's about adapting your app to meet your target audience's cultural and linguistic expectations. This requires understanding your target region's local customs, cultural nuances, legal requirements, and preferences. Pay attention to local conventions such as date formats, currency formats, number representations, and even color meanings, as these can significantly differ from one culture to another.

Furthermore, consider working with native speakers or localization professionals for accurate and culturally sensitive translations. Effective localization can dramatically enhance user experience and satisfaction, increasing the app's acceptance and success in different markets.

CHAPTER 25

Embracing Theming in Flutter

Reviewer: RydMike

Theming in Flutter is more than just a cosmetic choice; it's a foundational aspect of app development that ensures a cohesive and intuitive user experience. By defining a consistent set of design rules, such as colors, fonts, and widget styles, theming helps maintain visual harmony throughout the app. This consistency strengthens brand identity and enhances user navigation and interaction. Effective theming in Flutter allows for a seamless experience where users can intuitively understand and interact with the app's features and content.

When multiple developers work on a shared codebase, there's no need to teach new developers how to use custom-wrapped and composed UI widgets such as `BrandCheckbox` to get the desired style. Instead, they can use the default `Checkbox` with confidence that it, and all other built-in components are already styled to match the application's theme and brand via the global theme. Applications may still require custom UI widgets outside the standard library. Fortunately, theming does not prevent adding these components. To ensure a consistent theme throughout the application, it is recommended also to style custom components using a `ThemeExtension`. This can give custom components a themed style that matches the rest of the application.

This chapter is designed to provide Flutter developers, whether novices or experts, with the essential knowledge and skills to implement effective and efficient theming strategies in their apps.

25.1 Flutter Themes

Flutter offers two primary widgets for setting the stage of any application: `MaterialApp` and `CupertinoApp`. These cater to Material Design, commonly used in Android apps, and Cupertino design, tailored for iOS apps. `MaterialApp` and `CupertinoApp` come equipped with a `theme` property, where you can define their `ThemeData` and `CupertinoThemeData`, respectively.

The CupertinoApp and its style can only be customized to a limited extent using CupertinoThemeData, mainly colors, brightness, and text theme.

ThemeData in the MaterialApp is flexible enough to cater to various custom UI design needs. It is based on Google's Material design and defaults to the Material-3 design specification, but you can modify its visual appearance significantly. It is worth noting that CupertinoApp is best suited for apps that follow Apple's HIG design guide. Here is an example to set up your theme in a MaterialApp might look like this:

```dart
class ThemeDataExampleApp extends StatelessWidget {
  const ThemeDataExampleApp({super.key});

  static final ColorScheme _colorScheme =
      ColorScheme.fromSeed(
    seedColor: Colors.indigo,
  );

  @override
  Widget build(BuildContext context) {
    return MaterialApp(
      title: 'ThemeData Demo',
      theme: ThemeData(
        colorScheme: _colorScheme,
        floatingActionButtonTheme:
            FloatingActionButtonThemeData(
          backgroundColor: _colorScheme.tertiary,
          foregroundColor: _colorScheme.onTertiary,
        ),
      ),
      home: const Home(),
    );
  }
}
```

Once your theme is established, accessing and modifying these styles across your app is seamless. By leveraging Theme.of(context), you can retrieve the current ThemeData within any widget and use its properties to style other widgets based on the ambient theme. This approach ensures that your app maintains a consistent look and feel. For instance, to apply the primary color defined in your theme to a widget, you would use:

```dart
Container(
  color: Theme.of(context).colorScheme.primary,
  child: Text(
    'Themed Text',
    style: TextStyle(
      color: Theme.of(context).colorScheme.onPrimary,
```

Embracing Theming in Flutter

```
    ),
  ),
)
```

In Flutter, while `MaterialApp` and `CupertinoApp` are commonly used for their built-in theming capabilities, there's also `WidgetsApp` for those needing a more granular control level. `WidgetsApp` is a lower-level widget that offers the essential functionalities needed for building an app without the pre-built theme structure of `MaterialApp` or `CupertinoApp`. Here's a basic example of using `WidgetsApp`:

```
WidgetsApp(
  color: Colors.blue,
  onGenerateRoute: (settings) {
    return MaterialPageRoute(
      builder: (context) {
        return Scaffold(
          appBar: AppBar(title: Text('Home')),
          body: Center(child: Text('Welcome to WidgetsApp')),
        );
      },
    );
  },
)
```

`WidgetsApp` is set up in this example with a basic route and a default color. However, it's important to note that when using `WidgetsApp`, developers are responsible for managing many aspects of the app's design, including theming, which are automatically handled in `MaterialApp` and `CupertinoApp`.

It's essential to consistently use themes for styling widgets for typography and coloring. This practice ensures a cohesive look across your app and simplifies maintenance and scalability. Relying on the theme makes applying changes universally and maintaining consistency easier. Overriding styles directly in widgets can lead to a fragmented appearance, making implementing a comprehensive theming strategy challenging.

Let's see an example where we directly apply a color to a widget without using `ThemeData`:

```
MaterialApp(
  home: Scaffold(
    appBar: AppBar(
      title: Text('Directly Styled App'),
    ),
    body: Center(
      // Directly apply a color to the text style
      child: Text(
        'Hello, Direct Styling!',
        style: TextStyle(color: Colors.purple),
```

```
      ),
    ),
  ),
);
```

Rather than directly setting colors and text styles in each widget, it's better to define them in your `ThemeData` and then use `Theme.of(context)` to apply them.

```
// Define ThemeData with a custom primary color
main() {
  runApp(
    // Define ThemeData with a custom primary color
    MaterialApp(
      theme: ThemeData(
        colorScheme: ColorScheme.fromSeed(
          seedColor: Colors.teal,
          primary: Colors.teal,
        ),
      ),
      home: const MyThemeApp(),
    ),
  );
}

class MyThemeApp extends StatelessWidget {
  const MyThemeApp({super.key});

  @override
  Widget build(BuildContext context) {
    return Scaffold(
      body: Container(
        color: Theme.of(context).colorScheme.primary,
        child: Text(
          'Themed Text',
          style: TextStyle(
            color: Theme.of(context).colorScheme.onPrimary,
          ),
        ),
      ),
    );
  }
}
```

This approach ensures that all widgets adhere to the same design guidelines and simplifies updating the app's look and feel.

In this chapter, I will focus on `MaterialApp`, which is widely used. Widgets and theming in `MaterialApp` are highly customizable, so you can make it look like anything you want.

25.1.1　Material-2 versus Material-3

Flutter version 3.16 introduced a significant change in ThemeData, which uses Material-3 mode by default. The Material-3 design language is visually significantly different from the previous Material-2 design-based defaults.

If you have an old app that was designed to depend on the previous Material-2 defaults visually, you can still, in Flutter 3.16 and, for at least versions released one year after it, use the Material-2-based defaults by in ThemeData defining that you do not want to use Material-3.

```
main() {
  runApp(
    // Define ThemeData that is forced
    // to used old Material-2 styles.
    MaterialApp(
      theme: ThemeData(
        useMaterial3: false,
      ),
      home: const MyThemeApp(),
    ),
  );
}
```

Material-2 support will be deprecated in Flutter. After it is marked as deprecated, it will still be available and work for about a year after it was deprecated. After that, the flag and support for Material-2 will be removed from the Flutter framework. Material-3-based ThemeData is very configurable, and you can, in Material-3 mode, define a custom theme that looks very similar to the older Material-2 styles if you so desire.

25.2　Custom Theming Techniques

Custom theming in Flutter is an essential aspect of UI design, allowing developers to create a unique look and feel for their applications. Flutter provides several ways to customize and create your own ThemeData.

25.2.1　ThemeData Customization

You can create a ThemeData object with the ThemeData() factory and specify properties such as colorScheme, textTheme, elevatedButtonTheme, iconButtonTheme, and many more. This is useful for defining a complete theme from scratch using a lot of built-in convenience logic in the ThemeData() factory. Here's an example:

```
final themeData = ThemeData(
  colorScheme: ColorScheme.fromSeed(
    seedColor: Colors.teal,
    primary: Colors.teal,
  ),
  textTheme: const TextTheme(
    displayLarge: TextStyle(
      color: Colors.teal,
    ),
  ),
  elevatedButtonTheme: ElevatedButtonThemeData(
    style: ButtonStyle(
      backgroundColor: MaterialStateProperty.all<Color>(
        Colors.teal,
      ),
    ),
  ),
);
```

To understand the `ThemeData` class, we must examine its source code closely. It's a versatile class with multiple factories and constant constructors. The `const ThemeData.raw()` constructor is the named constructor that creates the actual `ThemeData` object, while other factory constructors provide unique factory methods for creating `ThemeData` instances.

```
@immutable
class ThemeData with Diagnosticable {
  factory ThemeData({...}) {...}
    const ThemeData.raw({...}){...}
  factory ThemeData.from({...}) {...}
  factory ThemeData.light({...}){...}
  factory ThemeData.dark({...}){...}
  factory ThemeData.fallback({...}){...}
}
```

Here's a breakdown of each constructor:

- `factory ThemeData({...})`: The main factory constructor. It provides a flexible way to create a `ThemeData` object, allowing developers to specify various parameters to customize the theme, including all component themes.
- `const ThemeData.raw({...})`: Is the named constant constructor of the class. `ThemeData.raw()` requires all properties to be explicitly defined. Other constructors use it internally or indirectly to create a `ThemeData` object with precisely specified values. Typically, you would not use this constructor directly, as it would require recreating the logic provided in the different factory constructors.
- `factory ThemeData.from({...})`: This constructor creates a `ThemeData` instance based on a `ColorScheme`. It's particularly useful when you use

Material-2, have a predefined `ColorScheme`, and want to create a theme that aligns with it.

- `factory ThemeData.light({...})`: This creates a predefined light theme. It sets up a `ThemeData` instance with a light color scheme. It is a convenient way to implement the default light theme in an application
- `factory ThemeData.dark({...})`: Similar to `light`, this constructor provides a quick way to set up the default dark theme. It pre-configures `ThemeData` with a dark color scheme.
- `factory ThemeData.fallback({...})`: This is used as a last resort when no other theme data can be obtained. It provides a basic default theme to ensure the app has some styling. It is typically only used as an internal fallback theme.

Each constructor serves a unique purpose, allowing for broad and specific theme customizations. Understanding the distinctions and appropriate use cases for each constructor can significantly enhance the theming capabilities of your Flutter application.

25.2.2   Using ThemeData.from()

This method was and is useful when creating a theme based on a `ColorScheme` where the produced `ThemeData` adheres to the Material-2 color system specification. It ensures consistency in your color palette in a way that conforms to the Material-2 design guidelines. You can also define your text theme but not specify any component themes in the same factory definition; you must add them with `copyWith` when using this factory.

Using this factory constructor to create Material-3-based themes is possible but optional.

```
ThemeData themeLight = ThemeData.from(
  colorScheme: const ColorScheme.light(
    primary: Colors.blue,
    secondary: Colors.green,
  ),
  textTheme: const TextTheme(
    displayLarge: TextStyle(
      color: Colors.black,
      fontSize: 30,
    ),
  ),
);
```

25.2.3   Leveraging Color Schemes

Color schemes are at the core of Flutter Material theming, providing a systematic approach to applying consistent colors throughout an application. Based on Material Design, a Color Scheme encompasses various color properties to harmonize UI components.

You can make a `ColorScheme` object by manually defining color values for all its color properties. Doing so requires an understanding of the Material color system and how all the colors should be defined concerning their contrasts, tones, and relations to each other.

While you can do all this manually to define a light and dark color scheme, you may prefer to use `ColorScheme` factory constructors that assist with the creation of the color scheme by using default values for not-defined color values or by using computational color scheme generation.

In **Material-2,** the correct baseline defaults were provided by the factories `ColorScheme.light()` and `ColorScheme.dark()`. You only needed to provide color values for `primary` and `secondary` colors that you wanted to override and differ from the defaults. You used it, e.g., like this:

```
// Defining a light color scheme
ColorScheme myLightScheme = ColorScheme.light(
    primary: Colors.blue,
    secondary: Colors.amber,
    onPrimary: Colors.white,
);
// Defining a dark color scheme
ColorScheme myDarkScheme = ColorScheme.dark(
    primary: Colors.blueGrey,
    secondary: Colors.teal,
    onPrimary: Colors.black,
);
```

`ColorScheme.fromSeed()` is an advanced computational factory method that generates a harmonious color scheme from a single seed color. This is useful for maintaining thematic consistency that adheres to the **Material-3 color system.** To create a color scheme that matches the light and dark schemes, you use the same seed color for both the light and dark color schemes and only change the brightness value.

```
// Defaults to brightness light,
//  we do not have to define it.
ColorScheme myLightScheme =
    ColorScheme.fromSeed(seedColor: Colors.blue);
// If we want a dark scheme
// we have to specify Brightness.dark
ColorScheme myDarkScheme = ColorScheme.fromSeed(
  seedColor: Colors.blue,
  brightness: Brightness.dark,
);
```

Once the color scheme is defined, either with ColorScheme.ligh/dark or ColorScheme.fromSeed, you can create a ThemeData object using the ThemeData() factory using Material-3. If you still use Material-2, prefer using ThemeData.from() and passing in your ColorScheme. This ties your color scheme to the app's overall theme:

```
ThemeData lightTheme = ThemeData(colorScheme: myLightScheme);
ThemeData darkTheme = ThemeData(colorScheme: myDarkScheme);
```

To apply the themes to your Flutter app, assign them to the theme and darkTheme properties of the MaterialApp widget:

```
MaterialApp(
    theme: lightTheme,
    darkTheme: darkTheme,
    home: MyHomePage(),
);
```

ColorScheme.fromImageProvider() is a method for creating a color scheme based on an image's dominant color. Here's a conceptual example:

```
ColorScheme myLightScheme = ColorScheme.fromImageProvider(
    AssetImage('assets/my_image.jpg'),
);
```

This approach is particularly effective for apps that want to create dynamic themes based on visual content, such as photo gallery apps or theme-based social media platforms. The fromImageProvider method finds the most prominent color in an image and uses that color as the seed color to generate a matching color scheme.

The flexibility of Flutter's theming system, particularly through color schemes, opens up a world of possibilities for creative and effective app design.

25.2.4   Using ThemeData copyWith

The copyWith method in ThemeData and all its component themes is a standard immutable data class copyWith method. It is ideal for tweaking an existing theme. It allows you to copy the object while changing some property values of an existing ThemeData without redefining the entire theme.

```
ThemeData newTheme = existingTheme.copyWith(
    colorScheme: themeData.colorScheme.copyWith(
      primary: Colors.red,
    ),
);
```

Typically, the `themeData` value above would be the `ThemeData` object value obtained via `Theme.of(context)`, but can, of course, be any defined `ThemeData` value.

It is worth noticing that `ThemeData.copyWith` operates on the object properties as defined by the `ThemeData.raw` object constructor. Any logic included in the `ThemeData()` factory will not be re-applied when you use `copWith`. You can, for example, not make a light theme dark by setting the `brightness` to `Brightness.dark` using `copyWith`. The brightness property, stored in the `ColorScheme` object, only provides information about whether the scheme is intended for a light or dark theme. What makes a theme look light or dark are all the color value definitions in `ThemeData` and its `colorScheme`.

Sometimes, you also need to copy the nested component themes deep. Let's look at an example:

```
ThemeData newTheme = themeData.copyWith(
  // Customizing the text theme,
  // particularly the 'displaySmall' style
  textTheme: themeData.textTheme.copyWith(
    displaySmall:
        themeData.textTheme.displaySmall!.copyWith(
      // Setting the text color to red
      color: Colors.red,
    ),
  ),
  // Customizing the ElevatedButton theme
  elevatedButtonTheme: ElevatedButtonThemeData(
    style: themeData.elevatedButtonTheme.style!.copyWith(
      // Setting the overlay color to red for all states
      overlayColor:
          MaterialStateProperty.all<Color>(Colors.red),
    ),
  ),
);
```

In the deep `copyWith` example, we're creating a new `ThemeData` instance called `newTheme` based on an existing `themeData`. We use `copyWith` to customize specific parts:

1. The `textTheme` is modified, particularly the `displaySmall` style. Here, we're changing the text color to red.
2. The `elevatedButtonTheme` is also customized. We alter the `style` of the `ElevatedButtonThemeData`, setting the `overlayColor` to red for all states of the button using `MaterialStateProperty.all<Color>`.

This approach ensures targeted changes to the theme while retaining the remaining `themeData` properties unchanged.

25.2.5 What is `MaterialStateProperty`?

`MaterialStateProperty` is a specialized class in Flutter's material library that allows for the creation of properties that can resolve to different values depending on the state of a material component. It's part of Flutter's extensive material design system. It defines how certain visual aspects of a widget should change in response to state changes, such as being pressed, hovered, focused, or disabled.

The key feature of `MaterialStateProperty` is its ability to associate different values with different widget states. This is particularly useful for styling material design widgets so they can visually respond to user interactions or changes in their state.

Here are some important points about `MaterialStateProperty`:

1. **State-Specific Values**: It allows you to define different values for different widget states. For instance, you can specify a color for a button when it's in its normal state and a different color when it's pressed.
2. **Use with Material Widgets**: `MaterialStateProperty` is commonly used with material design widgets like buttons, checkboxes, radio buttons, etc., to customize their appearance based on their state.
3. `resolveWith` **Method**: One of the common ways to use `MaterialStateProperty` is through the `resolveWith` method. This method takes a callback function that returns the property's value based on the states passed.
4. **Enhancing User Experience**: By providing visual feedback to the user through state changes, `MaterialStateProperty` helps enhance the user experience.

Here's a simplified example to illustrate its use:

```
ElevatedButton(
  style: ButtonStyle(
    backgroundColor:
        MaterialStateProperty.resolveWith<Color>(
      (
        Set<MaterialState> states,
      ) {
        if (states.contains(MaterialState.pressed)) {
          return Colors
              .green; // Color when the button is pressed
        }
        return Colors.blue; // Default color
      },
    ),
  ),
  onPressed: () {},
  child: const Text('Elevated Button'),
)
```

In this example, the `backgroundColor` of the `ElevatedButton` is set using `MaterialStateProperty.resolveWith`. The color changes to green when the button is pressed and remains blue otherwise. This dynamic and state-aware styling is a core aspect of material design in Flutter. It is important to notice that the order of resolved states is relevant to the resolution of the value.

You can also use more involved logic in the resolution and combine states that should resolve to the same value. A good way to learn how Material state properties are and can be used is to study the source code for default resolution logic used by component themes.

I am often asked how to add properties to theme data. Let's move on to the next section and see how.

25.2.6   Theme Extensions

If you are working on a Flutter project and need to add custom properties to your theme, `ThemeExtension` is very useful. It lets you extend the existing theme system with your properties. This is very useful when you want to include design elements not covered by the default theme properties.

Create a class that extends `ThemeExtension` and defines your custom properties. In this simple example, we only have one property called `customColor`.

```
class CustomThemeExtension
    extends ThemeExtension<CustomThemeExtension> {
  final Color customColor;

  CustomThemeExtension({
    required this.customColor,
  });

  @override
  CustomThemeExtension copyWith({
    Color? customColor,
  }) {
    return CustomThemeExtension(
      customColor: customColor ?? this.customColor,
    );
  }

  @override
  CustomThemeExtension lerp(
    ThemeExtension<CustomThemeExtension>? other,
    double t,
  ) {
    if (other is! CustomThemeExtension) {
      return this;
    }
```

```
  return CustomThemeExtension(
    customColor: Color.lerp(
      customColor,
      other.customColor,
      t,
    )!,
  );
  }
}
```

Add your custom theme extension to your `ThemeData` and access it using `Theme.of(context).extension<CustomThemeExtension>()`.

```
ThemeData theme = ThemeData().copyWith(
  extensions: <ThemeExtension<dynamic>>[
    CustomThemeExtension(customColor: Colors.red),
  ],
);
```

```
// Usage
CustomThemeExtension customTheme
  = Theme.of(context).extension<CustomThemeExtension>()!;
```

There is a YouTube video (youtu.be/8-szcYzFVao) by the Flutter team that explains theme extensions well.

Adding Multiple Theme Extensions

In more complex applications, you can define multiple theme extensions for different custom components. This allows each component to have its own set of customizable properties. The theme extensions also work well for adding **semantic colors** and **content text style**.

Semantic colors

Semantic colors refer to colors with specific meanings in your application that may be relevant to your application's domain or be more general. `ColorScheme` contains many colors, but almost all of these colors are related to styling visual elements, with colors representing the app's style and brand. Only one color in `ColorScheme` is semantic: the `error` color, its container version, and its contrast colors (`onColors`). The error colors are typically different shades of red.

Your application may need other obvious semantic colors, such as **OK** and **Warning**. You may have other semantic colors that represent domain colors for **order status**. An application that displays code may have semantic colors used by keywords for **code highlighting**. You may have **charts** with properties that should have **semantically meaningful color legends,** not app theme-based ones. These colors, with meaning, fall outside what the `ColorScheme` is intended to be used for. They are very well suited for being added to your app via theme extensions.

Suppose your application offers multiple user-selectable theme color options or gets the theme from the host system or images. In that case, consider harmonizing your semantic colors towards the effective theme's primary color. This ensures that semantic colors adjust their color temperature slightly to fit better with the application's primary color. To do this, look into the `blend` function in the **Material Color Utilities**[1] package.

Content Text Styles

If your app displays a lot of text content that should be styled separately, outside of the text themes in `ThemeData` and text styles in component themes, add them as theme extensions. All `ThemeData` text styles are intended to provide the text styles for components used by your application. They may be better suited for styling additional text content in your app, like text styles and formatting notes in a note-taking app, text in an auditing app, or blog content styling.

Sometimes, the built-in text styles may fit with others you need, but often they do not. To support content styles without the need to modify any `ThemeData` text styles used as defaults by components that could create style conflicts with them, add the needed content text styles as their theme extensions.

Fallback values

Suppose you are making an app where you can guarantee that you have included your custom theme extensions in the `ThemeData` and that the extensions always have values defined for all their properties. Then, your custom widgets can always safely look up the widget tree for these values.

However, suppose you are making a package that includes a custom theme extension for the package. In that case, users may optionally add it to their app's `ThemeData` when needed, but there is no guarantee that they have done so. Your package should then provide internal fallback default values. Consider using the same default value fallback strategy that Flutter widgets use: widget property value theme property value default property value.

Use hard-coded value tokens or make it more elegant by adding a named constructor that defines suitable default values, maybe also defined via const value tokens, that may differ depending on theme mode brightness. This is useful if any color properties need their defaults for light and dark mode to be different, which they typically do.

```
final CustomThemeExtension defaults =
    CustomThemeExtension.defaults(
  Theme.of(context).brightness,
);


final CustomThemeExtension? customTheme =
    Theme.of(context).extension<CustomThemeExtension>();
```

---

[1]https://pub.dev/packages/material__color__utilities

```
final Color myColor = widget.customColor ??
    customTheme?.customColor ??
    defaults.customColor;
```

Benefits of Theme Extensions

This is in addition to extending `ThemeData` with your custom properties and providing access to them via the standard inherited theme. Theme extension properties also animate their value changes with the rest of the theme when it changes. This includes changing a theme extension property value in the same light or dark mode. It applies not only to colors but also, e.g., to shape radius, edge insets, material elevations, font sizes, and any other custom property values you define.

If you use such custom properties in your extensions and dynamically change a theme property value in your theme extension. Like, e.g. in a custom text style's font size, all components and elements using this text style will animate the font size transition change. This happens together and in sync with any other properties you modified in your `ThemeData`.

This makes your custom theme properties fully integrated with the rest of the built-in `ThemeData` for nicely animated change transitions. This is also why every theme extension property needs the `lerp` function override.

Using these techniques, developers can craft a theme that perfectly aligns with their app's branding and design requirements, providing a coherent and immersive user experience. Whether tweaking existing themes or crafting something entirely new with `ThemeExtension`, Flutter offers the flexibility needed for comprehensive theming.

25.2.7   Visual Density in Flutter

Visual Density in Flutter's `ThemeData` is a concept that refers to the vertical and horizontal "compactness" of UI components. Defining the spacing and layout density of various Material Design components within an app's UI is crucial without altering text sizes, icon sizes, or padding values. But let's understand it better:

- **Unitless Measure**: Visual density is unitless, meaning it doesn't translate directly to specific measurements like pixels or ems. Instead, it adjusts the density of components relative to their default state as specified in the Material Design guidelines.
- **Default Density**: The default visual density is zero for vertical and horizontal densities. This default corresponds to the standard component spacing defined in Material Design.
- **Component Spacing**: Visual density affects the spacing around and within components. For instance, buttons alter the space around the button's child, while in lists, it changes the gap between entries.

Several Material widgets respond to changes in visual density settings:

- Components like Checkbox, Radio, IconButton, and various button types (ElevatedButton, OutlinedButton, TextButton, etc.) adjust their spacing.
- InputDecorator, which underlies widgets like TextField, responds to density changes by altering the spacing around the text field.
- ListTile and Chip also adapt their spacing based on the visual density settings.

Visual density can be specified in ThemeData to set a baseline horizontal and vertical density for Material components in an app.

```
ThemeData(
  visualDensity: VisualDensity(
    horizontal: VisualDensity.standard,
    vertical: VisualDensity.standard,
  ),
)
```

In this example, the VisualDensity.standard is used, but you can adjust these values to make UI components more or less compact, as needed.

Adjusting visual density can impact the accessibility and comfort of the app for users. More compact layouts might suit power users or those using larger screens, while a less dense layout could be better for accessibility and touch targets. Consistency in applying visual density across different components ensures the app's unified look and feel.

Understanding and Customizing Visual Density in Flutter

Flutter automatically adjusts the VisualDensity of your application's UI based on its running platform. This feature enhances the user experience by optimizing the spacing and size of the UI elements for different devices.

By default, Flutter uses VisualDensity.defaultDensityForPlatform(platform). This function sets the VisualDensity to VisualDensity.standard for Android, iOS, and Fuchsia platforms. In contrast, for desktop platforms like Linux, macOS, and Windows, it opts for VisualDensity.compact. The compact density is more suitable for mouse-based interactions, as it offers tighter and more efficient spacing of UI elements.

Customizing Visual Density for Touch-Enabled Desktops

In scenarios where your app runs on touch-enabled desktops, like certain Linux and Windows devices, the default compact visual density might not be the most user-friendly option. To cater to such cases, consider implementing a custom function to determine the VisualDensity. For instance, you could use VisualDensity.comfortable on touch-enabled Linux and Windows devices. This setting provides more spacious and touch-friendly UI elements, making interactions more comfortable for users with touch screens.

Here's an example of how you can implement this:

```
VisualDensity adaptiveVisualDensity(
  BuildContext context,
) {
  var platform = Theme.of(context).platform;

  if (platform == TargetPlatform.linux ||
      platform == TargetPlatform.windows) {
    // Check for touch screen
    if (isTouchScreen) {
      return VisualDensity.comfortable;
    }
    return VisualDensity.compact;
  }

  return VisualDensity.standard;
}
```

It's important to note that `VisualDensity` subtly affects the spacing between UI components like buttons and text fields and significantly impacts elements like padding and alignment. This fine-tuning can greatly improve your app's usability and aesthetic appeal, especially when dealing with diverse screen sizes and interaction modes (touch vs. mouse and keyboard). By thoughtfully customizing the `VisualDensity`, you can ensure that your Flutter app offers an optimal user experience across various devices, from mobile phones to touch-enabled desktops.

25.3   Managing Dark and Light Themes

In the previous section, I also defined dark mode colors. Flutter's theming system simplifies the process of implementing dark and light themes. You can define separate `ThemeData` instances for light and dark themes to cater to this need. You assign the light theme to the `MaterialApp` property `theme` and the dark mode theme to the property `darkTheme`. You can then use the `MaterialApp.themeMode` enum property to define which one to use.

Use `ThemeMode.light` to use the theme defined by `theme` and `ThemeMode.dark` to use the theme defined by `darkTheme`. By default, `themeMode` uses `ThemeMode.system`, which means that the application will use the light or dark mode as specified by user preferences in the host device system settings. Consider allowing users to select between all these choices in the app. Sometimes, users may want a different brightness setting in some apps than the one they use for their general system device mode.

In Flutter, the `MaterialApp` class includes properties to accommodate users who need or prefer high-contrast modes, often due to accessibility needs. These properties, `highContrastTheme`, and `highContrastDarkTheme`, are particularly used to ensure that your app is accessible to a broader range of users, including those with visual impairments.

The high contrast theme properties in `ThemeData` are specifically designed to be used when the system requests a **high contrast** mode. This is common in many host platforms, such as iOS, where users can increase contrast through an accessibility setting. This setting enhances the visual legibility of text and UI elements, which is crucial for users with certain visual impairments.

When you define `highContrastTheme`, you provide a version of your app's `theme` with increased contrast. This doesn't necessarily mean altering the color scheme completely but adjusting it to ensure that elements are more distinguishable and readable. For instance, this could mean using darker text on lighter backgrounds and vice versa or increasing the contrast between different UI elements.

Like `highContrastTheme`, the `highContrastDarkTheme` is used when the system requests a theme that is both **dark mode** and **high contrast.** This theme should have its `ThemeData.brightness` set to `Brightness.dark`, ensuring that the overall theme is dark but with enhanced contrast compared to the standard dark theme. This might involve using brighter or less saturated colors against dark backgrounds, ensuring that text and key UI elements stand out clearly.

```
main() {
  runApp(
    MaterialApp(
          themeMode: usedMode,
      theme: CustomTheme.light,
      darkTheme: CustomTheme.dark,
      highContrastTheme: CustomTheme.highContrastLight,
      highContrastDarkTheme: CustomTheme.highContrastDark,
    ),
  );
}
```

Creating high-contrast color schemes in Flutter to support Apple platforms (and others that offer similar accessibility settings) involves defining themes with more pronounced color differences.

At the time of writing, only the iOS platform supports the system request to use the higher contrast themes provided in `highContrastTheme`, `highContrastDarkTheme`. This will change in later Flutter versions. Newer Android versions already support and offer high-contrast theme versions. The Material-3 design system also includes specifications on how to create them to fit the used color system.

In both cases, for other than iOS platforms, you would need to use in-app user settings where the user selects a higher contrast version of the theme and `ThemeData` versions, made using these color scheme strategies, must then be swapped into `theme` or `dark theme` properties instead of the normal ones. This is needed since the system high contrast request has not been recognized on any platform other than iOS. This will change; you should check; a later Flutter version than 3.16 may support it.

Good color scheme design for accessibility may be complex and needs collaboration with your UI and UX designer to help you find the best scheme.

25.4 MaterialApp Theming Steps

Now that we know the tools available to create `ThemeData` let's consider a workflow and steps for setting things up:

1. Determine the main colors of the application for light and dark mode.
2. Define light and dark color schemes based on these colors.
3. Define the overall `textTheme` and `primaryTextTheme` for your application.
4. Define component theme styles so they match your design goal.
5. Add a theme extension with any semantics and additional colors you need.
6. Add a theme extension with any additional content text styles you need.
7. Add theme extensions for more advanced custom components that need their themes.

Let's discuss a bit more what is involved in some of these steps that we did not cover earlier already.

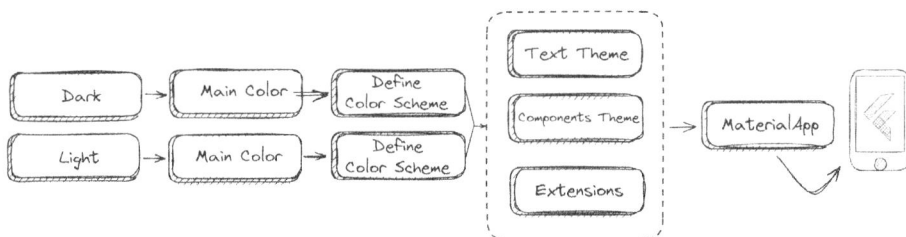

Figure 25.1: MaterialApp Theming steps

25.4.1 App main colors

When you style your application, you may be given or have selected a main app identity color or brand color. Typically, you want this as your application's `ColorScheme.primary` color.

You often also have one, or sometimes even two, supporting colors. You can use these as `secondary` and `tertiary` colors in your application's `ThemeData.colorScheme`. If you have only one supporting color, you should prefer using `tertiary` color in the `ColorScheme` over the `secondary` color. The secondary palette in the Material-3 color system is typically a more muted version of the primary palettes, basically primary with less chrome. It does not have to be, but the default color mappings on components assume this is the case in some mappings. So, if you only have one supporting accent brand color, you prefer assigning it to the `tertiary` palette with no such assumptions. It is better suited to work as an accent color, much like a `secondary` color was used in the Material-2 color system.

If we are talking about company brand colors, they are typically designed to work well on a light background, as they traditionally appear on white paper. Many

---

companies may have yet to define brand colors designed to work well on digital media in dark mode.

The colors used in dark mode typically need to be of lower saturation than the light mode colors to offer good contrast against the dark or black background. If they are not predefined, you can often use the result from `ColorScheme.fromSeed` with dark brightness when using the primary color as seed. You can, of course, also define less saturated versions of the light mode color manually.

25.4.2   ColorScheme from token color values

You can define the input color values as token color values, either as top-level constants or wrapped in a class with static color values. Below is an example with two colors: one main brand color and one supporting brand accent color.

```
class ColorTokens {
    AppColors._();
  // Dark deep purple
    static const Color brandMain = Color(0xFF4527A0);
  // Dark meadow green
    static const Color brandAccent = Color(0xFF006E51);
}
```

We can now use these colors for our light and dark color scheme definitions. If we only care about the main brand color, this setup would be fine:

```
ColorScheme brandLightScheme = ColorScheme.fromSeed(
    seedColor: ColorTokens.brandMain,
    primary: ColorTokens.brandMain,
);

ColorScheme brandDarkScheme = ColorScheme.fromSeed(
    brightness: Brightness.dark,
    seedColor: ColorTokens.brandMain,
    primaryContainer: ColorTokens.brandMain,
);
```

Since the `brandMain` color is a dark purple value with good contrast on white, it works well as our primary color in light mode. To ensure we keep it as our `primary` color, we must also override the `primary` color in the `fromSeed` factory. Without it, a color based on the computed tonal palette from this brand seed color would be used instead. It would be close but different from our brand color.

In dark mode, we did not, in this case, have a predefined color for the main primary color. We can accept the computed value based on the seed color, where we used the same brand color.

This means it will get a higher tonal value based on the brand color, which is less saturated. In this case, we want to add the saturated dark purple brand color to the dark theme. Typically a good place for it is the `primaryContainer` color in dark mode since its role is to be a less prominent version of the `primary` color. The light mode `primary` color often works well as the `primary` color in dark mode. You may need to verify this though. You can use the computed container color if it does not work.

Above, we can see that we have not yet used our brand's accent color, the dark meadow green color. We now notice a limitation of `ColorScheme.fromSeed`; it only accepts one color as seed color. Based on this input, it computes the tonal palettes for the `primary` colors based on the seed's hue and chroma. It assigns different tones from the resulting tonal palette to the different primary colors in `ColorScheme`, using different tones for light and dark modes.

It does the same for the secondary palette but locks the chroma value to 16 to make a much less saturated palette that still uses the hue of the seed color. For tertiary colors, the hue of the seed color is rotated 60 degrees, and the chroma is locked to 24. We cannot provide any seed inputs with their hue or without chroma limitations and locks to the `fromSeed` factory.

If we use `ColorScheme.fromSeed`, we must override the color properties `tertiary`, `onTertiary`, `tertiaryContainer`, and `onTertiaryContainer` separately for both the light and dark color schemes. Since we only had one brand accent color, we must also define or compute six missing suitable color tones for these colors; our `brandAccent` color is only usable directly for the `tertiary` color in light mode and for the `tertiaryContainer` color in dark mode. The other missing color values for tertiary in light mode and dark mode must thus be manually defined.

This can be tedious and difficult to dial in properly. To automate it, we can consider going lower in the Material computational color system and use the **Material Color Utilities**[2]package[3]that Flutter is also using for its `fromSeed` factory and use it to compute a tonal palette based on our `brandAccent` color and assign appropriate tones from this palette to the tertiary `ColorScheme` colors.

A more convenient way to do this is to use the FlexSeedScheme package[4], which allows you to use different seed colors for each color palette in the `ColorScheme` and adjust how colorful the produced palettes are.

```
// Make ColorSchemes from
// brand based primary and tertiary seed keys.
final ColorScheme brandLightScheme =
    SeedColorScheme.fromSeeds(
  brightness: Brightness.light,
  primaryKey: ColorTokens.brandMain,
  // Lock primary to brand main
  primary: ColorTokens.brandMain,
```

[2]https://pub.dev/packages/material_color_utilities
[3]https://pub.dev/packages/material_color_utilities
[4]https://pub.dev/packages/flex_seed_scheme

```
    // You can add optional own seeds for
    // secondary and tertiary key colors. Here
    // we only use tertiary and let secondary
    // be computed and related to primary,
    // as it is by default in the M3 color system.
    tertiaryKey: ColorTokens.brandAccent,
    // Lock tertiary to brand accent
    tertiary: ColorTokens.brandAccent,
    // Tone chroma config and tone mapping
    // is optional if you do not add it
    // You get the config matching Flutter's Material 3
    // ColorScheme.fromSeed.
    // Here, we use strategy that uses the chroma
    // from our provided seeds and is
    // less aggressive on primary tint
    // on the surface colors. There are many
    // other predefined tone strategies
    // available used to make the tonal palettes,
    // and you can also define your own
    // FlexTones class to customize it.
    tones: FlexTones.chroma(Brightness.light),
);
final ColorScheme brandDarkScheme =
    SeedColorScheme.fromSeeds(
  brightness: Brightness.dark,
  primaryKey: ColorTokens.brandMain,
  // Lock primaryContainer to brand main
  primaryContainer: ColorTokens.brandMain,
  tertiaryKey: ColorTokens.brandAccent,
  // Lock tertiaryContainer to brand accent
  tertiaryContainer: ColorTokens.brandAccent,
  tones: FlexTones.chroma(Brightness.dark),
);
```

25.5   Theming Tools

Flutter applications are simple but can be laborious and somewhat complicated
at some points. Fortunately, various third-party tools and packages can simplify
the process or allow for more advanced theming and color scheme generation.

- **Color Scheme Generation Tools:**

    - A **web-based theme builder** from the Material Design team for creating color schemes (Material Theme Builder[5]).

  – Official **Figma ColorScheme kit** by the Material Design team for UI design based on Material-3 (Material Theme Builder Figma Plugin[6]).

  – **Material-3 design kit** for UI creation in Figma (Material-3 Design Kit[7]).

- **Deep Dive into Material-3 Color System**:

  – Material-3 guide for understanding the Hue Chroma Tone (HCT) based color space (Material-3 Guide[8]).

  – **Material Color Utilities (MCU) package** for low-level operations with HCT color space (MCU Package[9]).

- **Advanced Color Scheme Generation**:

  – **FlexSeedScheme (FSS) package** for seed-generated color schemes with more control (FlexSeedScheme Package[10]).

- **FlexColorScheme (FCS) Package**:

  – A Flutter Favorite package for defining complex `ThemeData` with built-in color schemes and a compact API (FlexColorScheme Package[11]).

  – Includes support for advanced color scheme generation based on FlexSeedScheme.

  – FlexColorScheme allows defining themes with platform adaptive properties.

25.6 Conclusion

Theming in Flutter stands out for its remarkable flexibility, particularly with `ThemeExtension`, `ColorScheme`, and component themes with many configuration options.

These features have changed how themes are created and managed in Flutter, offering improved customization and control. `ColorScheme` delivers a cohesive color palette throughout an application, while `ThemeExtension` opens up possibilities for adding custom properties to themes. This flexibility is pivotal in crafting user interfaces that are visually appealing and uniquely tailored to an app's specific branding and design needs.

As Flutter continues to evolve, so does its theming system, with the potential for introducing new features and enhancements. Developers working with Flutter are

---

[5]https://m3.material.io/theme-builder#/custom
[6]https://www.figma.com/community/plugin/1034969338659738588/material-theme-builder
[7]https://www.figma.com/community/file/1035203688168086460/material-3-design-kit
[8]https://m3.material.io/styles/color/system/overview
[9]https://pub.dev/packages/material_color_utilities
[10]https://pub.dev/packages/flex_seed_scheme
[11]https://pub.dev/packages/flex_color_scheme

encouraged to stay updated with these changes to leverage the full potential of Flutter's theming capabilities.

To master theming in Flutter, it's recommended to experiment with different aspects of `ThemeData`, understand the impact of visual density, embrace high-contrast themes for accessibility, and keep an eye on community forums and Flutter's official documentation for the latest updates and best practices.

Whether you are a beginner or an experienced Flutter developer, mastering theming is key to building more engaging, responsive, and visually appealing applications.

CHAPTER 26

Custom Painters and Shaders

Reviewer: Renan C. Araújo

The world of custom painting and shaders in Flutter is vast and limitless. It offers remarkable flexibility that goes beyond conventional frameworks. The purpose of this chapter is not only to help you become a professional Flutter developer who can use canvas and shaders to create generative animated art but also to provide a comprehensive understanding of the engineering aspects of these features. We will explore when and how you can utilize these powerful tools in Flutter to enhance your applications while balancing technical ability with creative expression. It would require a book or more to thoroughly cover these topics, which could be the focus of my next book. Alternatively, please email me if you know these areas and would like to collaborate with me on writing about them.

Let's begin now.

26.1 The Art of CustomPainter

CustomPainter is a canvas for drawing custom designs in a Flutter application. The CustomPaint widget in Flutter is a gateway to creating visually stunning and unique user interfaces. At its core, CustomPaint is a widget that provides a canvas to draw custom graphics. It bridges the high-level world of Flutter widgets and the low-level operations of drawing and rendering.

But why and when should you use CustomPainter? The key lies in its flexibility and control. It's ideal for scenarios where you must create complex, custom graphics that can't be achieved with standard widgets. This includes scenarios like generating dynamic shapes, creating intricate animations, or implementing custom UI elements that must be visually distinct and interactive. CustomPainter shines in applications that require a high degree of customization in the UI, such as games, data visualization tools, or any app that wants to stand out with a unique visual identity.

Sometimes, you may need to use CustomPainter to optimize your application's UI. For instance, if you have a complex UI that can be created using standard widgets, but it might cause lags or consume a lot of energy and CPU. Using lower-level APIs in `CustomPainter` can help you optimize your app even more, though this may come at the cost of higher complexity in understanding and writing code. So, if you need to improve your app's performance, `CustomPainter` is an excellent option.

In short, CustomPainter is about painting points on the screen as desired. CustomPainter performs better than other widgets in Flutter because it bypasses the complex widget layout mechanism that Flutter usually uses. This allows you to control what the canvas will do. A similar concept can be found in fragment shaders, where you bypasses the Flutter framework and engine. But remember, as Winston Churchill once said: "Where there is great power, there is a great responsibility."

26.1.1   CustomPaint widget

To better understand CustomPaint in Flutter, let's review its fundamental structure and usage. The foundation is built upon a custom class that extends `CustomPainter`, as shown in the snippet:

```
class AwesomePainter extends CustomPainter {
  const AwesomePainter();

  @override
  void paint(Canvas canvas, Size size) {}

  @override
  bool shouldRepaint(
    covariant CustomPainter oldDelegate,
  ) =>
      false;
}
```

This `AwesomePainter` class grants access to a `Canvas` object, your playground, for custom drawing. The `paint` method is where all the magic happens. Here, you can draw anything from simple shapes to complex graphics on the canvas using various drawing methods provided by the `Canvas` API. The size parameter gives you the dimensions of the area you have for drawing.

The `shouldRepaint` method, the other method, is crucial for optimizing the widget's performance. It determines whether the `CustomPainter` should repaint itself. For instance, returning `false` means the canvas will not repaint unless explicitly told, which is beneficial for static graphics.

Now, to use this custom painter, you wrap it within a `CustomPaint` widget, like so:

```
CustomPaint(
  painter: const AwesomePainter(),
)
```

Custom Painters and Shaders

The CustomPaint widget integrates your custom drawing (AwesomePainter in this case) into the Flutter widget tree. When you use CustomPaint and pass in your AwesomePainter, Flutter knows to call the paint method of AwesomePainter whenever it needs to render the widget.

26.1.2 Drawing App

In this example, I want to ensure you understand how easy it is to use Canvas, even if it is your first use. Don't be afraid to try!

Step 1: Define the Custom Painter (DrawingPainter)

```
class DrawingPainter extends CustomPainter {
  List<Offset> points;

  DrawingPainter(this.points);

  @override
  void paint(Canvas canvas, Size size) {
    final pencil = Paint()
      ..color = Colors.black
      ..strokeWidth = 4
      ..isAntiAlias = true
      ..strokeCap = StrokeCap.round;

    for (int i = 0; i < points.length - 1; i++) {
      canvas.drawLine(
        points[i],
        points[i + 1],
        pencil,
      );
    }
  }

  @override
  bool shouldRepaint(
    DrawingPainter oldDelegate,
  ) => true;

  @override
  bool shouldRebuildSemantics(
    DrawingPainter oldDelegate,
  ) => false;

  @override
  bool? hitTest(Offset position) {
    return super.hitTest(position);
  }
}
```

DrawingPainter extends CustomPainter and is responsible for rendering the drawing on the canvas. The Constructor takes a list of Offset points, representing the positions where the user has touched the screen.

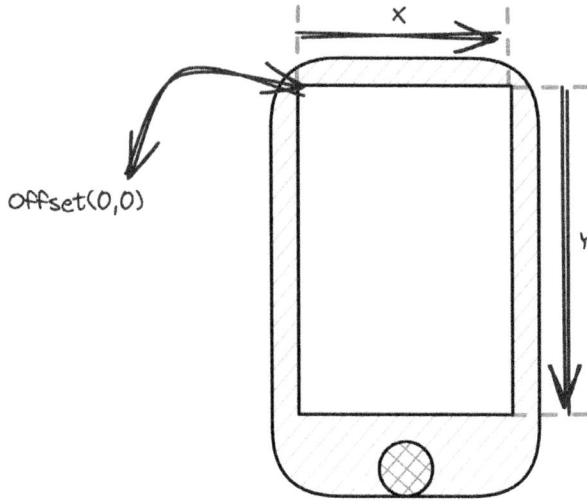

Figure 26.1: Start Point (0,0) Top Left Corner Screen

The paint method iterates through the points, drawing a line between each consecutive points. The Paint object defines the appearance of the lines (color, stroke width, anti-aliasing, and stroke cap); you can think of it as your pencil. And finally, the drawLine method is used, which draws a line between the given points using the given paint.

The shouldRepaint **method** returns true, ensuring the canvas repaints whenever the points list updates, and shouldRebuildSemantics and hitTest methods are related to accessibility and hit-testing, respectively. These work similarly to what you learned in Part 1 of the book while building custom RenderObject.

Step 2: Define the Widget (DrawingPage)

```
class DrawingPage extends StatefulWidget {
  const DrawingPage({super.key});

  @override
  DrawingPageState createState() => DrawingPageState();
}

class DrawingPageState extends State<DrawingPage> {
  List<Offset> points = <Offset>[];

  @override
  Widget build(BuildContext context) {
    return Scaffold(
```

```
      appBar: AppBar(
        title: const Text('DrawingPage'),
      ),
      body: GestureDetector(
        onPanStart: (details) =>
            points.add(details.localPosition),
        onPanUpdate: (
          DragUpdateDetails details,
        ) {
          points.add(details.localPosition);
          setState(() {});
        },
        onPanEnd: (DragEndDetails details) {
          points.add(Offset.infinite);
        },
        child: SizedBox(
          width: double.infinity,
          height: double.infinity,
          child: CustomPaint(
            painter: DrawingPainter(points),
            child: Container(),
          ),
        ),
      ),
    );
  }
}
```

This state class maintains a list of `Offset` points, updated whenever the user draws on the screen, which is given by `onPan` callbacks via `GestureDetector`.

```
GestureDetector(
  onPanStart: (details) => points.add(details.localPosition),
  onPanUpdate: (DragUpdateDetails details) {
    points.add(details.localPosition);
    setState(() {});
  },
  onPanEnd: (DragEndDetails details) {
    points.add(Offset.infinite);
  },
  // ... [CustomPaint]
)
```

The `onPanStart` Listener adds a new point to the list when the user starts dragging. TheonPanUpdate Listener Continuously adds points to the list as the user moves their finger and calls `setState` to trigger a rebuild. The `onPanEnd` Listener adds a special `Offset.infinite` point, signaling the end of a continuous stroke.

Figure 26.2: Simple Drawing App with Flutter

The current list of points is passed to `DrawingPainter`, who draws the lines on the canvas.

Nothing too fancy is happening here, just a few basic lines of code. And voila! You now have a canvas that can be used to paint anything on. I am showing you how to combine some basic elements to create an interesting concept using a powerful API in Flutter. Now, let's explore more advanced best practices.

26.1.3 Optimize

In the example provided, there are several key improvements and best practices that I would like to highlight for a more efficient implementation.

Firstly, let's consider the `CustomPainter` class in Flutter:

```
abstract class CustomPainter extends Listenable {
  const CustomPainter({Listenable? repaint})
      : _repaint = repaint;

  final Listenable? _repaint;

  // ...
}
```

In this snippet, it's noteworthy that `CustomPainter` can automatically manage repainting when provided with a `Listenable`. This feature enables us to simplify our widget structure by transitioning from a `StatefulWidget` to a `StatelessWidget`, utilizing a `ValueNotifier`:

```
class DrawingPage extends StatelessWidget {
  DrawingPage({super.key});

  final pointsListenable = ValueNotifier<List<Offset>>([]);
  // ...
}
```

Within this stateless widget, changes to the drawing can be easily managed by updating the `ValueNotifier` in response to user gestures:

```
class DrawingPage extends StatelessWidget {
  //...
  body: GestureDetector(
    onPanStart: (details) => pointsListenable.value = [
      ...pointsListenable.value,
      details.localPosition
    ],
    onPanUpdate: (DragUpdateDetails details) {
      pointsListenable.value = [
        ...pointsListenable.value,
        details.localPosition
      ];
    },
    onPanEnd: (DragEndDetails details) {
      pointsListenable.value = [
        ...pointsListenable.value,
        Offset.infinite,
      ];
    },
    //...
  );
  // ... ;
}
```

Additionally, we can optimize the repaint process by passing this notifier to the custom painter and wrapping the painter with `RepaintBoundary`.

I suggest you review the official documentation and source code to learn about `RepaintBoundary`. Explaining the details would take a lot of pages. However, I can tell you that to display a colored border around each widget; you need to set the `debugRepaintRainbowEnabled` property to `true`. These borders will change color as the user scrolls through the app. To set this flag, add `debugRepaintRainbowEnabled = true;` as a top-level property in your app. If you see that static widgets rotate through colors after setting this flag, consider adding repaint boundaries to those areas.

```
main() {
  debugRepaintRainbowEnabled = true; //<---
```

```
  runApp(MyApp());
}
```

RepaintBoundary ensures that the repainting is contained and does not affect other parts of the Flutter widget tree unnecessarily:

```
child: RepaintBoundary(
        child: CustomPaint(
          painter: DrawingPainter(pointsListenable),
          child: const SizedBox.expand(),
        ),
      ),
```

Furthermore, the implementation of the CustomPainter itself is crucial. Here's how it can be adapted to leverage the ValueNotifier:

```
class DrawingPainter extends CustomPainter {
  ValueNotifier<List<Offset>> points;

  DrawingPainter(this.points) : super(repaint: points);
  // ...
  @override
  void paint(Canvas canvas, Size size) {
    for (int i = 0; i < points.value.length - 1; i++) {
      canvas.drawLine(
        points.value[i],
        points.value[i + 1],
        pencil,
      );
    }
  }

  @override
  bool shouldRepaint(DrawingPainter oldDelegate) =>
      oldDelegate.points != points;
  // ...
}
```

This modification greatly enhances performance, especially in larger-scale applications. It's an important optimization technique for a more efficient and effective Flutter development experience.

This is the perfect moment to introduce you to the next section on best practices.

26.1.4   Best Practices

CustomPainter offers immense flexibility for crafting custom visuals in Flutter, but mastering its efficiency and maintainability requires thoughtful practice. Let's dive into essential best practices with code examples for a deeper understanding:

Custom Painters and Shaders

Minimize Rebuilds with `shouldRepaint`:

Imagine your CustomPainter draws a dynamic chart. Every data tweak triggers a complete redraw, impacting performance. `shouldRepaint` come to the rescue!

```
class ChartPainter extends CustomPainter {
  final List<double> data;

  ChartPainter(this.data);

  @override
  bool shouldRepaint(ChartPainter oldDelegate) {
    // Compare only data changes
    return !listEquals(
      data,
      oldDelegate.data,
    );
  }

  @override
  void paint(Canvas canvas, Size size) {
    // ... draw chart based on data
  }
}
```

With this code, the chart repaints only when the data changes, not for minor UI tweaks, boosting performance.

Cache with `PictureRecorder` **for Smooth Animations:**

Think of a complex animated scene with static background elements. Repainting them every frame is redundant. Enter `PictureRecorder`:

```
class AnimatedPainter extends CustomPainter {
  PictureRecorder recorder = PictureRecorder();
  Picture? picture;

  AnimatedPainter() {
    _initializePicture();
  }

  void _initializePicture() {
    // Start recording drawing commands with our recorder
    final canvas = Canvas(recorder);

    // Perform drawing commands
    final paint = Paint()
      ..color = Colors.blue
      ..style = PaintingStyle.fill;
```

```
    canvas.drawCircle(Offset(100, 100), 40, paint);

    // End recording and produce a Picture
    picture = recorder.endRecording();
  }

  // ... other methods

  @override
  void paint(Canvas canvas, Size size) {
    if (picture == null) {
      return;
    }
    canvas.drawPicture(picture!);

    // ... draw dynamic animation elements on top
  }

  @override
  bool shouldRepaint(covariant CustomPainter oldDelegate) {
    // ...
  }
}
```

Here, the static background gets recorded once and reused repeatedly, making animations smoother and less resource-intensive.

Separate Logic with Mixins for Code Reuse:

Sometimes, your painting logic becomes complex. Mixing it with widget management can get messy. Mixins to the rescue!

```
mixin ShapePainterMixin on CustomPainter {
  @override
  void paint(Canvas canvas, Size size) {
    // ... common painting logic for drawing shapes
  }
}


class MyPainter extends CustomPainter
    with ShapePainterMixin {
  // ... other properties and methods
}
```

This mixin encapsulates reusable shape-drawing logic, keeping your MyPainter class focused on specific details and facilitating code reuse across other painters.

Modularize with Reusable Painters for Large Compositions:

Large, intricate visuals benefit from a divide-and-conquer approach. Enter modular painters:

```
class ChartPainter extends CustomPainter {
  // ... paint the chart
}

class GaugePainter extends CustomPainter {
  // ... paint the gauges
}

class LabelPainter extends CustomPainter {
  // ... paint the text labels
}

class DashboardPainter extends CustomPainter {
  @override
  void paint(Canvas canvas, Size size) {
    ChartPainter().paint(canvas, size);
    GaugePainter().paint(canvas, size);
    LabelPainter().paint(canvas, size);
  }
}
```

Here, individual painters handle specific elements; the DashboardPainter combines them seamlessly for a complete picture. This promotes modularity and simplifies maintenance.

Enhance Accessibility with Semantics:

Accessibility ensures everyone can use your app. Semantics help screen readers understand your custom visuals:

```
class ChartPainter extends CustomPainter {
  // ...

  @override
  void paint(Canvas canvas, Size size) {
    // ... draw chart elements

    for (int i = 0; i < data.length; i++) {
      final rect = Rect.fromLTWH(
        i * 10,
        0,
        10,
        data[i] * 50,
      ); // Example rect for data point
      CustomPainterSemantics( //<---
        rect: rect,
        properties: SemanticsProperties( //<---
          label: 'Data point ${i + 1}',
          value: '${data[i]}',
```

```
        ),
      ).paint(canvas, size);
    }
  }
}
```

With semantics, screen readers can interpret data points and values, making your custom charts accessible to everyone.

Reuse Paint Objects:

Instantiate `Paint` objects outside of the `paint` method and reuse them. This practice conserves resources as creating a new `Paint` instance on each repaint can be costly.

```
final paint = Paint()
  ..color = Colors.blue
  ..style = PaintingStyle.stroke;

void paint(Canvas canvas, Size size) {
  // use existing paint object
  canvas.drawLine(
    Offset.zero,
    Offset(size.width, size.height),
    paint,
  );
}
```

Handling High-DPI Screens:

Ensure your custom painting code scales correctly on high-DPI screens for a consistent visual experience across devices.

```
final pixelRatio = MediaQuery.of(context).devicePixelRatio;

void paint(Canvas canvas, Size size) {
  // Scale your drawing based on pixelRatio
}
```

Profiling and Optimization:

Regularly profile your custom painter code, especially when dealing with complex drawings or animations, to identify and optimize performance bottlenecks.

Utilizing RepaintBoundary for Performance Optimization:

`RepaintBoundary` is a widget that isolates its child from the rest of the widget tree in terms of painting. This can significantly improve performance, especially for widgets that are expensive to paint and only change sometimes. By using `RepaintBoundary`, you tell Flutter to handle the painting of this widget separately, reducing the overall repaint cost.

```
RepaintBoundary(
  child: CustomPaint(
    painter: ExpensivePainter(),
    isComplex: true,
    willChange: false,
  ),
)
```

This code wraps `ExpensivePainter` in a `RepaintBoundary`, optimizing its rendering performance. The `isComplex` and `willChange` properties further inform the rendering system about the nature of the painting operation, allowing for more efficient handling.

Vertices - Advanced Shape Rendering with high performance:

In graphics programming, vertices are the cornerstone of rendering shapes and models. A vertex is a point in either 2D or 3D space, defined by coordinates, and serves as the fundamental unit for constructing more complex geometrical shapes. Vertices are crucial in defining the outlines of polygons, particularly triangles, which are the basic building blocks for most graphical objects in two-dimensional and three-dimensional environments. These points can also carry additional attributes such as color, texture coordinates, and normals, essential for creating detailed and visually rich graphics.

In Flutter, the `Vertices` class is crucial for custom shape rendering, especially when dealing with intricate designs or the need for high-performance graphics. This class allows developers to define a series of points and how they should be connected and colored. When used with the `Canvas.drawVertices` method, it enables the drawing of complex shapes that are not achievable with standard widgets.

The shapes drawn using `Vertices` are primarily based on triangles, the simplest polygon in graphics programming, and can be combined to form any complex shape. The way these triangles are formed and rendered depends on the mode specified:

1. **Triangles:** Each set of three vertices forms an independent triangle.
2. **Triangle Strip:** Vertices are connected in a strip-like fashion, where each new vertex forms a triangle with the previous two.
3. **Triangle Fan:** All triangles share the first vertex, fanning out from this common point.

The `Vertices` class can be instantiated using either its default constructor or the `Vertices.raw` constructor for more direct control over the data. Here's a basic overview of how to use each:

```
Vertices(
  VertexMode mode,
  List<Offset> positions, {
    List<Color>? colors,
```

```
    List<Offset>? textureCoordinates,
    List<int>? indices,
})
```

This constructor is more straightforward and uses lists of `Offset` and `Color` objects, making it user-friendly but slightly less efficient.

```
Vertices.raw(
  VertexMode mode,
  Float32List positions, {
    Int32List? colors,
    Float32List? textureCoordinates,
    Uint16List? indices,
})
```

`Vertices.raw` is a more performance-oriented constructor using typed data arrays like `Float32List` and `Uint16List`. This approach is closer to the low-level data format the rendering engine uses. It is ideal for performance-critical applications or when working with data already in a raw format.

One example in the source code provided in this book allows you to navigate to `/lib/custompainters/snowfall.dart`. Once you run the application, you can turn `Vertices.raw` implementation on and off and fall back to standard canvas drawing to observe the difference in performance.

26.2 Exploring Shaders

Shaders are small but powerful programs that run on the graphics processing unit (GPU), responsible for rendering the intricate details of light and color that bring digital images to life.

Shaders operate within the graphics pipeline, a sequence of steps that a computer graphics system uses to render 3D objects onto a 2D screen. This pipeline includes stages like vertex processing, rasterization, and fragment processing, with shaders playing a vital role at various points. There are several types of shaders, each with its unique function:

1. **Vertex Shaders**: These process each vertex of a 3D model, transforming 3D coordinates into 2D screen coordinates and passing per-vertex data down the pipeline. They are essential for manipulating vertex positions and creating effects like animations.
2. **Fragment (Pixel) Shaders**: These calculate the final color of each pixel, factoring in lights, shadows, and textures. They are key to achieving detailed surface effects and realistic rendering of materials.
3. **Geometry Shaders**: Operating between vertex and fragment shaders, they can generate new vertices and shapes, adding complexity and detail to objects.

4. **Tessellation Shaders**: Used for adjusting the level of detail of 3D models, these shaders enhance efficiency and visual quality by adapting to the camera's distance.

5. **Compute Shaders**: These handle general-purpose computing tasks within the GPU, like physics simulations or post-processing effects, separate from the direct image rendering process.

The graphics pipeline is a conceptual framework describing the steps to render a 3D object onto a 2D screen. It starts with processing the 3D coordinates (vertex processing), then turning the object into pixels (rasterization), and finally coloring these pixels (fragment processing). Shaders are integral to this process, providing the flexibility to create complex visual effects.

26.2.1   Understanding Shader Language (GLSL)

OpenGL Shading Language (GLSL) is a high-level shading language used widely in computer graphics for writing custom shaders. Shaders are small programs that dictate how to graphically render each pixel, vertex, or geometry on the screen. They are executed directly on the graphics processing unit (GPU), making them incredibly efficient for graphics computations.

GLSL is an integral part of the OpenGL graphics API, a standard specification defining a cross-language, cross-platform API for rendering 2D and 3D vector graphics. The language closely resembles C and, in essence, Dart-like syntax, making it familiar to Flutter developers.

The primary types of shaders in GLSL include **vertex shaders**, which process vertex data, and **fragment shaders**, which determine each pixel's color and other attributes. Other types, like geometry and tessellation shaders, offer additional control over rendering. I will focus on Fragment shaders as Flutter only supports that.

A typical fragment shader, which usually has `.frag` or `.glsl` extension in GLSL, includes:

Version Declaration: Specifying the GLSL version. This is optional.

Output Variable: A variable to store the color output for the pixel.

```
out vec4 fragColor;
```

`vec4` is the most common output variable type used in fragment shaders. It represents a four-component vector corresponding to the color's RGBA (Red, Green, Blue, Alpha) components. Sometimes, you might encounter `vec3` if the alpha component is not needed or is handled separately. It represents a three-component vector for the RGB components of the color. In cases where only a single color channel or a grayscale output is needed, a `float` can be used.

Main Function: Where the color calculation happens.

```
void main() {
    fragColor = vec4(1.0, 0.0, 0.0, 1.0);  // Red color
}
```

Here, `fragColor` is set to a static red color for every pixel.

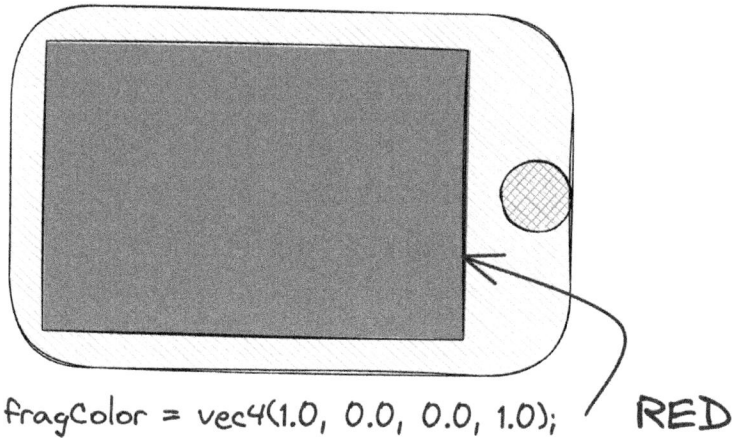

fragColor = vec4(1.0, 0.0, 0.0, 1.0);   RED

Figure 26.3: Demonstrate Red for Every Pixel

Incorporate Uniform Variables: In GLSL, uniform variables are a type of variable that you can use to pass data from your main application (running on the CPU) to your shader program (running on the GPU). Uniforms are global and remain constant for all vertices and fragments processed during a single draw call. They are a key way to make your shaders dynamic and responsive to what's happening in your application.

For example, you can pass the time elapsed to create animations.

```
uniform float u_time;
out vect fragcolor;
void main() {
        // The **sin** function creates a wave-like pattern,
        // and **abs** ensure the value is positive.
    float red = abs(sin(u_time));
    fragColor = vec4(red, 0.0, 0.0, 1.0);
}
```

The fragment shader will produce a pulsating red color on the rendered object, with the intensity of red changing over time in a sinusoidal pattern[1].

---

[1] https://www.shadertoy.com/view/XclSWr

Manipulate Coordinates: Use the coordinates of each pixel (gl_FragCoord) to create gradients or patterns. gl_FragCoord provides the coordinates of the current fragment (or pixel).

In the following example, these coordinates are divided by u_resolution, a uniform variable passed to the shader representing the resolution of the rendering window or texture. The result is a normalized coordinate st (with both x and y values ranging from 0 to 1) across the rendered surface.

```glsl
uniform vec2 u_resolution;
out vec4 fragColor;

void main()
{
    vec2 st = gl_FragCoord.xy / u_resolution;
    fragColor = vec4(st.x, st.y, 0.0, 1.0);
}
```

This shader will produce a gradient effect[2] across the rendered surface, smoothly transitioning in color based on the pixel's position. The gradient will blend from black at the bottom-left corner to red and green at the top-right corner.

Figure 26.4: Manipulate Coordinates to Create Gradient Effect

Complex Lighting and Color Effects: Here, we're calculating the diffuse component of lighting based on a light direction and surface normal.

---

[2]https://shadertoy.com/view/4csSWr

```
uniform vec3 u_lightDirection;
uniform vec3 u_normal;
void main() {
    float diff = max(dot(u_normal, u_lightDirection), 0.0);
    // Diffuse lighting effect
    vec3 diffuse = diff * vec3(1.0, 0.5, 0.3);
    fragColor = vec4(diffuse, 1.0);
}
```

So, as you can see, there are also available helper functions. You can also create a function to define `const` variables.

Texture Sampling: In shaders, textures are images that add surface details like color, patterns, or bumps to 3D models.

In the example, `sampler2D` uniform in a shader is used to pass a 2D texture from your application to the shader. The term "sampler" refers to the functionality in a shader that allows it to read or sample data from a texture. The shader then samples colors from this texture to apply to the rendered surface.

```
uniform sampler2D u_texture;
void main() {
    vec4 texColor = texture(u_texture, gl_FragCoord.xy);
    fragColor = texColor;
}
```

There are also other sampler types for different kinds of textures, like `sampler3D` for 3D textures and `samplerCube` for cube map textures, each used for specific rendering techniques.

This should give you an overview of how to read the shader's GLSL code. However, we have just touched the surface, and the best is to read a few shader examples, particularly fragment shaders, to get more familiar with the concept.

26.3   Using Shaders in Flutter

Now that you understand what shaders are and how they play a role in computer graphic programming let's explore how Flutter leverages them. Flutter incorporates Fragment shaders for enhanced visual effects. As a Flutter engineer, understanding how to integrate and use shaders can significantly elevate the visual appeal of your applications.

26.3.1   Adding a Fragment Shader to Flutter

In Flutter, you primarily work with fragment shaders. Here's how you can add a `.frag` shader file to your Flutter project:

Custom Painters and Shaders

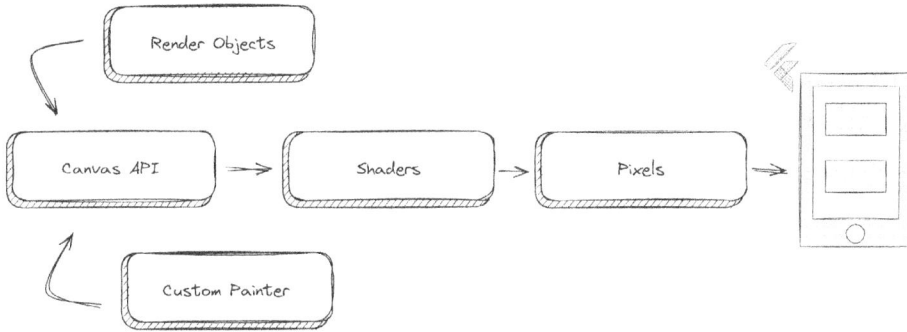

Figure 26.5: Widgets to Pixels Simple Pipeline in Flutter

Creating the Shader File (`simple.frag`): Create a fragment shader file with your GLSL code. Here's an example shader that creates a gradient using Flutter's brand colors:

```glsl
#version 460 core

#include <flutter/runtime_effect.glsl>

uniform vec2 u_surfaceSize;

out vec4 fragColor;

vec3 flutterBlue = vec3(5, 83, 177) / 255;
vec3 flutterNavy = vec3(4, 43, 89) / 255;
vec3 flutterSky = vec3(2, 125, 253) / 255;

void main() {
  vec2 st = FlutterFragCoord().xy / u_surfaceSize.xy;

  vec3 color = vec3(0.0);
  vec3 percent = vec3((st.x + st.y) / 2);

    color = mix(
    mix(flutterSky, flutterBlue, percent * 2),
    mix(flutterBlue, flutterNavy, percent * 2 - 1),
    step(0.5, percent));

  fragColor = vec4(color, 1);
}
```

- Any GLSL version from 460 to 100 is supported in Flutter, though some available features are restricted.
- #include <flutter/runtime_effect.glsl>: This line includes declarations for using Flutter-specific features in your shader.

- `FlutterFragCoord()`: A Flutter-specific function that provides the fragment coordinates. Unlike `gl_FragCoord` in traditional GLSL, `FlutterFragCoord` is adjusted for Flutter's coordinate system.
- This Shader needs two `floats` that define surface size, which we can pass from Flutter.

Adding Shader to `pubspec.yaml`: Include your shader file in the `pubspec.yaml` file of your Flutter project:

```
flutter:
  shaders:
    - shaders/simple.frag
```

Loading Shaders at Runtime

One way to use shaders in Flutter is by loading them at runtime:

```
void loadMyShader() async {
  final program = await FragmentProgram.fromAsset(
    'shaders/snow.glsl',
  );
  final program2 = await FragmentProgram.fromAsset(
    'shaders/simple.frag',
  );
}
```

- `FragmentProgram.fromAsset`: Loads the shader from assets.
- You may see both `.frag` and `.glsl` extensions for fragment shaders.

Using Fragment Shaders with Canvas APIs

In Flutter, fragment shaders can be used with Canvas APIs by setting the `Paint.shader` property:

```
void paint(Canvas canvas, Size size) {
  shader.setFloat(0, size.width);
  shader.setFloat(1, size.height);
  final paint = Paint()..shader = shader; //<---

  canvas.drawRect(
    Rect.fromLTWH(0, 0, size.width, size.height),
    paint,
  );
}
```

- In this case, we are just cascading the shader with the `fragment shader` that must be passed down to the custom painter class.

Custom Painters and Shaders

- Shaders can be applied to various shapes and paths drawn on the canvas, offering versatile possibilities for custom graphics. Shaders, in combination with blend modes, can have effects, too!
- Last but not least, since we have to define surface size to float, now we can define it as the max with height—the setFloat sets the float uniform at [index] to [value].

Now, we can use everything together in our Flutter app.

```
void main() async {
  // 1
  final fragmentProgram = await FragmentProgram.fromAsset(
    'shaders/simple.frag',
  );
  // 2
  runApp(MyApp(shader: fragmentProgram.fragmentShader()));
}

class MyApp extends StatelessWidget {
  const MyApp({super.key, required this.shader});

  // 3
  final FragmentShader shader;

  @override
  Widget build(BuildContext context) {
    return MaterialApp(
      title: 'Simple Shader Demo',
      theme: ThemeData(
        colorSchemeSeed: Colors.blue,
        useMaterial3: true,
      ),
      home: MyHomePage(shader: shader),
    );
  }
}

class MyHomePage extends StatelessWidget {
  const MyHomePage({
    super.key,
    required this.shader,
  });

  final FragmentShader shader;

  @override
  Widget build(BuildContext context) {
    return Scaffold(
```

```dart
      appBar: AppBar(
        title: const Text('Simple Shader Demo'),
      ),
      // 4
      body: CustomPaint(
        size: MediaQuery.sizeOf(context),
        // 5
        painter: MyShaderPainter(shader: shader),
      ),
    );
  }
}

// 5
class MyShaderPainter extends CustomPainter {
  MyShaderPainter({required this.shader});
  // 6
  final FragmentShader shader;

  @override
  void paint(Canvas canvas, Size size) {
    // 7
    shader.setFloat(0, size.width);
    shader.setFloat(1, size.height);

    // 8
    final paint = Paint()..shader = shader;

    // 9
    canvas.drawRect(
      Rect.fromLTWH(0, 0, size.width, size.height),
      paint,
    );
  }

  @override
    bool shouldRepaint(
    covariant CustomPainter oldDelegate,
  ) =>
      false;
}
```

Let's break down what each numbered section in the code is doing:

1. **Shader Initialization**:
   - Loads the fragment shader from the asset `'shaders/simple.frag'`.
   - `FragmentProgram.fromAsset` asynchronously loads the shader program.

- `fragmentProgram.fragmentShader()` creates a `FragmentShader` instance from the loaded program.

2. **Application Startup**:
   - `runApp` initializes and runs the Flutter application.
   - `MyApp` widget is created with the `shader` passed as a parameter.

3. **Shader Propagation in MyApp**:
   - The `MyApp` class takes a `FragmentShader` instance as a parameter.
   - This shader is then passed down to `MyHomePage`.

4. **CustomPaint Widget in MyHomePage**:
   - The `CustomPaint` widget is used to provide a canvas on which to draw.
   - `MediaQuery.sizeOf(context)` gets the current media (screen) size for the painting area.

5. **Painter for CustomPaint**:
   - `ShaderPainter` is set as the painter for `CustomPaint`.
   - This custom painter uses the provided shader for drawing.

6. **Shader in ShaderPainter**:
   - `ShaderPainter` takes a `FragmentShader` instance.
   - This shader will be used for painting.

7. **Setting Shader Uniforms**:
   - The shader's uniforms are set, which in this case are the width and height of the canvas.
   - These values are provided to the shader to control its behavior based on the canvas size.

8. **Creating Paint with Shader**:
   - A `Paint` object is created, and its shader is set to the provided `FragmentShader`.
   - This paint will be used to draw with the effects of the shader.

9. **Drawing on Canvas**:
   - A rectangle covering the entire canvas is drawn.
   - The `Paint` with the shader applied is used, so the shader effect is rendered across this rectangle.

This process can be way more simplified by using `flutter_shaders`. Let's refactor using this package.

```
void main() {
  runApp(const MyApp());
}

class MyApp extends StatelessWidget {
```

```
  const MyApp({super.key});

  @override
  Widget build(BuildContext context) {
    return const MaterialApp(
      home: MyHomePage(),
    );
  }
}

class MyHomePage extends StatelessWidget {
  const MyHomePage({super.key});

  @override
  Widget build(BuildContext context) {
    return Scaffold(
      // 1
      body: ShaderBuilder( //<---
        assetKey: 'shaders/simple.frag', //<---
        (context, shader, child) {
          return CustomPaint( //<---
            size: MediaQuery.sizeOf(context),
            // 2
            painter: ShaderPainter(shader: shader),
          );
        },
      ),
    );
  }
}
```

We have cut a few steps and are using `ShaderBuilder` widget to load the shader for us. You can use other features from the package, such as the `SetUniforms` extension (look at *flutter_shaders/lib/src/set_uniforms.dart*), where technically, you can set your uniforms much easier and like a charm.

26.3.2   Converting from ShaderToy

Converting ShaderToy shaders to Flutter involves several steps to adapt the code to the Flutter environment. For example, let's consider converting a simple laser effect shader from ShaderToy, which can be found at this ShaderToy link[3].

```
//convert HSV to RGB
vec3 hsv2rgb(vec3 c)
```

---

[3]https://www.shadertoy.com/view/4f2GRR

```
{
    vec4 K = vec4(1.0, 2.0 / 3.0, 1.0 / 3.0, 3.0);
    vec3 p = abs(fract(c.xxx + K.xyz) * 6.0 - K.www);
    return c.z * mix(
      K.xxx, clamp(p - K.xxx, 0.0, 1.0), c.y
    );
}

void mainImage( out vec4 fragColor, in vec2 fragCoord )
{
    vec2 fragPos = fragCoord / iResolution.xy;
    fragPos.y -= 0.5f;

    vec3 color = hsv2rgb(
      vec3(fragPos.x * 0.5 - iTime * 3.0, 1.0, 1.0)
    );
    color *= (0.015 / abs(fragPos.y));

    color += dot(color, vec3(0.299, 0.587, 0.114));

    fragColor = vec4(color, 1.0);
}
```

ShaderToy shaders use a `mainImage` function, which differs from the standard `main` function used in Flutter's shaders. Additionally, ShaderToy automatically provides certain uniforms like `iResolution` and `iTime`, which you must manually declare in Flutter.

Key Differences and Adjustments

1. **Entry Point**:
   - ShaderToy uses `mainImage` function, while Flutter uses the standard `main` function.

2. **Fragment Coordinates**:
   - ShaderToy shaders use `fragCoord`, but in Flutter, you should use `FlutterFragCoord()`.

3. **Uniforms**:
   - ShaderToy provides `iResolution` and `iTime` uniforms automatically. In Flutter, these must be explicitly declared and passed from the Dart code.

4. **Shader Inclusion**:
   - The `#include <flutter/runtime_effect.glsl>` directive is specific to Flutter and necessary for using certain Flutter-specific features.

5. **Output Variable**:
   - The output color is stored in `fragColor` in both ShaderToy and Flutter.

```
#include <flutter/runtime_effect.glsl>

uniform vec2 iResolution;
uniform float iTime;
out vec4 fragColor;

vec3 hsv2rgb(vec3 c) {
    // ...
}

void main() {
    vec2 fragPos = FlutterFragCoord().xy / iResolution.xy;
    // ...
}
```

26.3.3   Setting Uniforms in Flutter

In your Flutter application, set the uniforms for the shader using shader.setFloat:

```
// In your custom painter class
void paint(Canvas canvas, Size size) {
  shader.setFloat(0, size.width);
  shader.setFloat(1, size.height);
  shader.setFloat(2, time);

  final paint = Paint()..shader = shader;

  canvas.drawRect(
    Rect.fromLTWH(0, 0, size.width, size.height),
    paint,
  );
}
```

Here, the size.width and size.height corresponds to iResolution, and time corresponds to iTime. These values must be passed to the shader to mimic the behavior of ShaderToy's built-in uniforms.

This example illustrates a straightforward shader conversion. However, there are more complex scenarios where additional steps are required. For instance, when dealing with 2D texture samplers, you should use an AnimatedSampler from the flutter_shaders package in Flutter and call setImageSampler() on the shader object.

```
// In Flutter
shader.setImageSample(0, image); // pass dart:ui Image to the shader
// in GLSL
uniform sampler2D uTexture;
```

Custom Painters and Shaders

For those eager to delve deeper into shaders and the GLSL language, a great resource is The Book of Shaders[4]. This online book offers an extensive and interactive learning experience, perfect for anyone seeking to expand their knowledge.

26.4 Conclusion

Exploring custom paintings and shaders in Flutter opens up a fascinating domain where creativity meets technology. These powerful APIs enhance your applications' visual appeal and offer an engaging and addictive playground for developers. The ability to transform code into captivating visuals is not just a technical skill but an artistic expression, making the development process with Flutter an exciting and rewarding journey.

I encourage you to embrace this opportunity to experiment and innovate. Each raid into custom painting and shaders is a step towards mastering these tools, pushing the limits of what's possible in app design. So, dive in, play around, and let your creativity flourish. The more you explore and create, the more you learn, leading to applications that are not only functional but visually attractive masterpieces.

---

[4]http://thebookofshaders.com/

Closing Words

So, you have come to the end of this book. As you turn the final page, it's not just the conclusion of a chapter in your learning journey but a gateway to new possibilities. Throughout this book, we've navigated through complex concepts, topics, detailed code, and solutions. These pages have enriched your understanding and ignited a spark of curiosity and enthusiasm for the ever-evolving world of Flutter.

Flutter is a continuous journey of learning and discovery. The concepts and techniques you've encountered here are tools that can empower you to build, create, and innovate. Whether you're a student, a professional developer, or a hobbyist, the knowledge you've gained is a solid foundation upon which you can build amazing things.

As you step beyond this book, remember that every line of code you write reflects your creativity and problem-solving skills. The challenges you'll face in the real world might be complex, but the skills you've honed here will be your allies. Keep experimenting, keep learning, and most importantly, keep coding. Practicing makes perfect.

I hope this book will serve as both a guide and a step toward your success with Flutter. May your future code be efficient and elegant and reflect your potential.

Thank you for choosing this book as your companion in your Flutter journey. Here's to many more lines of code, breakthroughs, and innovations in your future endeavors.

Feel free to contact me through social media, email, and my flutterengineering.io newsletter. I am in a mission to write and release more content. I would appreciate your thoughts, feedback, and successes in your career and projects.

Remember: FLUTTER DEVELOPMENT IS FUN.

With best wishes for your continued success.

Majid Hajian

Printed in Great Britain
by Amazon

45971453R00302